'Julieann Campbell works with her interviews like a woman knitting an Aran jumper – the complexity of the pattern in the end is simply beautiful. This is a vital book by someone who knows the significance of Bloody Sunday in her heart, her mind and her soul.'
Susan McKay, journalist and author

'Bloody Sunday was a pivotal moment in Irish history. Julieann Campbell places it perfectly in its time and place. The dominant notes are of anger and grief, and admiration for the indomitable spirit of the families and other campaigners who strove against daunting odds to vindicate the memory of the murdered.'
Eamonn McCann, journalist, author and Irish civil rights leader

'A momentous chronicle, timely and vital, which highlights that the burden of change rests, as always, upon the shoulders of those who suffered and yet, have nurtured the desire that lessons be learned.'
Michael Mansfield QC, who represented a number of families during the Bloody Sunday Inquiry

'The technique used – multiple voices speaking directly to us – is very simple but it has a profound effect. It puts us into the middle of the chaos of Bloody Sunday and keeps us there throughout the grief and anger that follow. A wonderful, wonderful book.'
Jimmy McGovern, BAFTA-winning screenwriter

'So many people – judges, politicians, generals, journalists – have had their say on Bloody Sunday. his book allows the voices of the people of Derry to be heard. Their accounts are exciting, tragic, infuriating, but, above all, authentic. The fear, anger and grief leap off the pages.'
Anne Cadwallader, journalist and author

'Heartbreaking, poignant, powerful.'
Joe Duffy, broadcaster and author

'This was a day like no other in my lifetime... a day that affected the lives of countless thousands on this Island.'
Christy Moore, Irish folk songwriter and musician

ON BLOODY SUNDAY

A New History Of The Day And Its Aftermath

By Those Who Were There

JULIEANN CAMPBELL

monoray

First published in Great Britain in 2022 by Monoray, an imprint of
Octopus Publishing Group Ltd
Carmelite House
50 Victoria Embankment
London EC4Y 0DZ
www.octopusbooks.co.uk

An Hachette UK Company
www.hachette.co.uk

Distributed in the US by Hachette Book Group
1290 Avenue of the Americas
4th and 5th Floors
New York, NY 10104

Distributed in Canada by Canadian Manda Group
664 Annette St., Toronto, Ontario, Canada M6S 2C8

ISBN (Hardback) 978 1 80096 040 4
ISBN (Paperback) 978 1 80096 048 0

A CIP catalogue record for this book is available from the British Library.

Printed and bound in UK

1 3 5 7 9 10 8 6 4 2

This FSC® label means that materials used for the product have been
responsibly sourced

This monoray book was crafted and published by Jake Lingwood,
Sybella Stephens, Nick Fawcett, Juliette Norsworthy, Two Associates,
Edward Pickford and Lisa Pinnell.

For the people of Derry, who have never given up in their
pursuit of truth, justice and civil rights.

**For my uncle, Jackie Duddy, and all those lost or affected
by the events of 1972 and across the wider conflict.**

For my daddy, Pat 'Soup' Campbell, who never did tell
me his own story of Bloody Sunday.

Author's note

This book weaves a narrative of personal reflection and testimony from more than a hundred and ten speakers affected by the events of Ireland's Bloody Sunday in January 1972. Twenty of these interviews have never been published before.

For clarity, and to help readers keep track of each voice, a List of Speakers is included in Appendix 1 at the end of the book (see page 404). Appendix 2 contains the names of all those killed and wounded on the day (see page 418).

Contents

Foreword

We were there. We saw what happened, but nobody wanted to know – or ever asked.

My mother warned me to look after our John – he was only 17 and too young to go on marches. I said he'd be fine with his friends. He took shelter at the rubble barricade. They shot him in the face.

I'd been arrested by the British army and taken away while trying to get someone else to hospital. The boy we were helping died. The next day, back at Strand Road police barracks, a big detective came into the room asking if I was 'Young'. I said I was. Staring at me, he asked how many brothers I had. 'Two', I replied. 'You've only one now,' he said. That's how I found out John was dead.

When I saw the crowds outside our house, I knew he was telling the truth.

Leo Young, brother of John Young
September, 2021

Introduction

Ireland's Bloody Sunday in 1972 was a pivotal moment in its recent Troubles, extinguishing as it did the peaceful civil rights movement and paving the way for decades of violent, deadly conflict.

The civil rights march in question took place on 30 January 1972, in Derry, Northern Ireland's second largest city, built around the River Foyle. The march ended in bloodshed when troops from Britain's 1st Battalion Parachute Regiment opened fire on unarmed marchers, leaving 13 dead and a further 18 wounded. The Bloody Sunday Inquiry later confirmed that all those targeted had not been armed and posed no threat when shot. One man died later, in June 1972, becoming the fourteenth victim. Seven of those shot dead were teenage boys; two were excited about their first civil rights march.

Many buried these experiences and the trauma of Bloody Sunday. Others felt compelled to tell their story in the hope of catharsis or education. As a relative myself, I felt the need to keep asking and keep recording these accounts, knowing just how precious they were. I also gathered other interesting personal material I found relating to Bloody Sunday and the quest for justice, aware that accounts by various bereaved relatives or those wounded, and eyewitnesses, activists and politicians, was a tale worth telling. For decades, these voices were silenced or marginalized in favour of the British version of events. Now it is time to see the whole story of those affected by events in 1972 – a narrative laid out before us in the voices of those past and present. A rare glimpse into history and the profound effect of tragedy on one small, Irish community that imprinted on the wider world.

As children we were made aware of Bloody Sunday in a general, visceral sense. We were told stories about my uncle, Jackie Duddy – a teenage boxing champion – who went on a civil rights march and was shot by British soldiers. We were forbidden from ever attending marches or big crowded events 'just in case' of trouble, and any talk of religion or politics was actively discouraged at home.

We knew Jackie's face from family photographs, book covers and from the Bogside mural. Worse still, we knew him from the oft-used BBC news footage, aired every time the subject of Bloody Sunday made the evening news. I remember how we squirmed as children and teenagers, unsure of what to say, seeing Mum subjected to her brother's dying moments again and again. Nowadays, we have the foresight to tell her to turn away. Jackie's other sister, my auntie, Kay, who lives next door, became the family campaigner in the 1990s, alongside their brother, Gerry, who was on the march that day like Jackie and another brother, Patrick. Through Kay, Gerry and my mother Susie's influence, I write this book today. I like to think Uncle Jackie has a hand in it, too.

*

An occupied settlement since the sixth century, Derry is known by several names. Derived from Doire in Irish, meaning oak-grove, the town was renamed 'Derrie' in 1604 by a charter of James I, and then renamed Londonderry by a second charter in 1613 to coincide with the arrival of representatives of the London Guilds to invest in and oversee the new city, including the construction of its city walls.

Today, the city is generally referred to as Derry by its nationalist/Catholic population, and as Londonderry by some of its unionist/Protestant population. Since the peace process, many also comfortably use the more inclusive Derry/Londonderry.

The road to Bloody Sunday began in the 1960s with a growing awareness of the discrimination and inequality faced by Northern Ireland's Catholic population. Seeds of discontent grew across all six counties, and a generation of newly educated young people left university determined to improve the situation they and others faced. When families bought their first televisions, many recall seeing civil rights protests sweep across the USA, demanding an end to discrimination and racial segregation. They glimpsed possibility. Across the north, pockets of citizens began to mobilize, intent on reform and an end to bigotry. People wanted equal voting rights, access to jobs, opportunity and adequate housing. Civil rights. With the introduction of imprisonment without trial in summer 1971, campaigners added one more demand: an end to the practice of internment, which exclusively targeted nationalist Catholic menfolk regardless of any genuine links to underground republican activity.

When British troops were deployed to Northern Ireland in 1969 under Operation Banner, it was initially as a temporary measure to alleviate the overwhelmed – and notably sectarian – police force of the time, the Royal Ulster Constabulary (RUC). However, the army's presence served to escalate tensions as, within a few months, they were seen to align with the often heavy-handed unionist government and RUC. The British army also brought with it tough approaches and techniques learned in other colonial contexts, such as Kenya, Cyprus and Aden, and applied these extreme counter-insurgency techniques to Northern Ireland and its civilian population.

By the time the Troubles ended, over three thousand six hundred people would lose their lives, with republican and loyalist paramilitaries responsible for the majority of the killings; the British army were themselves responsible for over three hundred deaths, and the RUC for around fifty.[1] A terrible human cost to a political problem. Operation Banner became the longest single deployment in British military history, with troops remaining on the streets until the 1990s and the military's official operation in Northern Ireland ending in 2007. This book focuses on one key event in this recent timeline.

There have been four Bloody Sundays in twentieth-century Irish history – in 1913, 1920, 1921 and 1972. Of these, the 1920 massacre of spectators at a Gaelic football match at Croke Park by a mixed force of British military, Royal Irish Constabulary

(RIC) and Auxiliary police was the most deadly – killing as many as on Derry's Bloody Sunday six decades later, and injuring an estimated sixty to a hundred more.

Derry's Bloody Sunday in 1972 became a watershed event in Irish and British history. In concluding the 2010 *Report of the Bloody Sunday Inquiry* (BSI), Lord Saville described its devastating impact:

> *What happened on Bloody Sunday strengthened the Provisional IRA, increased nationalist resentment and hostility towards the Army and exacerbated the violent conflict of the years that followed. Bloody Sunday was a tragedy for the bereaved and the wounded, and a catastrophe for the people of Northern Ireland.*[2]

Bloody Sunday stood apart from other British army shootings as, unlike the Ballymurphy massacre six months earlier, it occurred in broad daylight with countless eyewitnesses and in the full glare of the press. A great sorrow enveloped Ireland. Within hours the British military informed embassies across the world that they had won an 'IRA gun battle', branding the dead as gunmen and bombers, terrorists. By morning, it made the front page of the *New York Times*. This falsehood of guilt became the official narrative of what happened on Bloody Sunday – compounded by a hasty 'whitewash' report by Lord Chief Justice Widgery in 1972. It remained so for decades until a family-led campaign and international pressure instigated one of the most complex inquiries in history.

Almost four decades after their deaths, victims were fully exonerated when Lord Saville published the *Report of the Bloody Sunday Inquiry*. He found, crucially, that the British army fired first, and at unarmed civilians; and that the majority of victims were either shot in the back as they ran away, or gunned down while helping someone else in need. The report made headline news all over the world.

This book spans the wider civil rights struggle that led to the anti-internment march in Derry on Bloody Sunday. This includes the Battle of the Bogside and deployment of British troops in

1969, and the introduction of imprisonment without trial in 1971, which encompasses the hugely relevant Parachute Regiment killings in Ballymurphy, West Belfast, six months before the paras were sent into Bloody Sunday. It culminates in the search for truth, the £200 million inquiry, and reflections on the epoch-making achievements of a group of strangers thrust together by circumstance. All told from the perspective of the people themselves.

When approached to write this book, I felt it important to consider its relevance among the rich canon of Bloody Sunday literature produced since 1972. Researching this further, it became clear that this book would be the first complete oral history of Bloody Sunday. It was therefore unique, and I feel a real responsibility to present this story in its fullest, most genuine form and do justice to all those who allowed me to share their experiences.

The Irish massacre and its cover-up by the British establishment has fascinated authors and academics for decades. Invariably, they have delved into specific aspects of the Bloody Sunday case, like Eamonn McCann's superbly insightful books documenting specifics of the day, the inquiries and the cover-up, or Greg McLaughlin and Stephen Baker's book exploring the British media's relationship with Bloody Sunday. My own work with the families in 2012, *Setting the Truth Free: The Inside Story of the Bloody Sunday Justice Campaign* (Liberties Press, Dublin), was the first to focus on their remarkable 1990s campaign. This later won a literary prize in Ireland.

By far the most impactful book written on the case is Don Mullan's 1997 bestseller, *Eyewitness Bloody Sunday* (Wolfhound Press, Dublin). Mullan offered fresh analysis and theories based on newly discovered eyewitness statements – unseen since 1972. The book became an international bestseller and was instrumental in changing public perception of the events of Bloody Sunday, adding weight to calls for a new inquiry and the full exoneration of victims. *On Bloody Sunday* – published half a century after Bloody Sunday – moves on from previous work in that it conveys in vivid personal detail the tragedy, conspiracy and dogged perseverance that changed the course of British and Irish history.

Among the 110 first-hand accounts presented in the book are 20 never-before-seen interviews by those impacted 50 years ago. These include relatives, witnesses, civil rights activists, and the last ever interview given by Bishop Edward Daly, a hero of Bloody Sunday, which I conducted just months before his death during my work with the Bloody Sunday Trust. This new testimony is presented alongside extracts of primary material gathered over the past decade or more, including source material for my 2012 campaign book, archive and self-generated press penned on behalf of the families over the years.

Naturally, many of those present on Bloody Sunday have since died – making their testimony even more precious. It's both a privilege and a necessity to include some of these deceased voices from my own work, BSI witness statements and archive press material. On occasion and where necessary, quotes that merit inclusion are sourced from existing publications or archive footage. Bringing together these rich, disparate sources after 50 years ensures the broadest, most genuine narrative and a greater emotional impact.

Alongside the voices of those most affected are extracts from police and army statements, highly relevant memos, intelligence reports and minutes of official meetings between the police in Northern Ireland and British military. Extracts from a memo between British prime minister Edward Heath and Lord Chief Justice Widgery in 1972 are also included. For the most part, these originate from campaign research, or from the Bloody Sunday Inquiry and its subsequent Report, now publicly available via National Archives, UK. With legal issues ongoing at the time of writing, I have opted not to include testimony of individual British soldiers or their identifying ciphers. I'm confident of this story's shocking impact without identifying who fired where and when. These deeply personal accounts instead recall thoughts, feelings and sensory memories that build a fuller picture. A more detailed, factual analysis of Bloody Sunday is available in the ten-volume *Report of the Bloody Sunday Inquiry*, published in 2010 and available online.

In telling this story and illustrating the Derry of 50 years ago, I have opted to include incidents, events and deaths that occurred within the immediate vicinity of Bloody Sunday from 1968 to 1972, or incidents directly related to events in the Bogside. For this, I use with gratitude some research material from the Museum of Free Derry and Bloody Sunday Trust, with which I was involved for over a decade. This factual information includes civilian, combatant, RUC and British military deaths that occurred in the Free Derry area within the time period of the book's core.

As a former reporter and oral historian bound to listen and document, I aim to be as impartial as possible. For this reason, I avoid over-editorializing within the narrative, allowing the people themselves to tell the story as it unfolds. Having worked closely with many involved this past decade or more, I am acutely aware of the sensitivities involved in producing this book and remain mindful of these issues from a moral and legal perspective.

Where possible and to contextualize, I include voices from across the spectrum of the Troubles, including both nationalist and unionist testimony as well as top chiefs within the British military and Royal Ulster Constabulary who gave evidence. While every effort is made to provide balance, it is difficult not to be influenced by cumulative evidence that shows the great injustice dealt to the native Irish during the twentieth century, particularly in relation to Bloody Sunday and other atrocities.

In terms of prosecutions for conflict-related events, it is estimated that over thirty thousand paramilitaries served time for their actions during the conflict, an estimated two-thirds of whom were republican prisoners, and a third, loyalist paramilitaries.[3] In terms of more recent prosecutions, Northern Ireland's Public Prosecution Service (PPS) say that of the 26 prosecution cases brought since 2011 on legacy issues, 21 involved republican and loyalist paramilitaries, with several cases ongoing.[4]

To date, just six former British military personnel have been charged with offences relating to the conflict in Northern Ireland, none of whom served a full sentence, and all of whom were welcomed back into the British army.

No publication could fully tell the story of Bloody Sunday and its effect on a nation, but this book, collated with experience, purpose and passion, is the first fully to immerse readers in events as they transpired and through the eyes of those present. Collectively, these accounts show the true human cost of conflict and a case that is still very much present, debated and unresolved.

Fifty years on, the Bloody Sunday case is of growing historical importance. The efforts of the people of Derry set a benchmark for justice campaigns everywhere. With civilian massacres like Bloody Sunday still occurring around the world today, the city's story is a necessary reminder that states, and their military, are duty-bound to protect and serve all citizens equally and without prejudice.

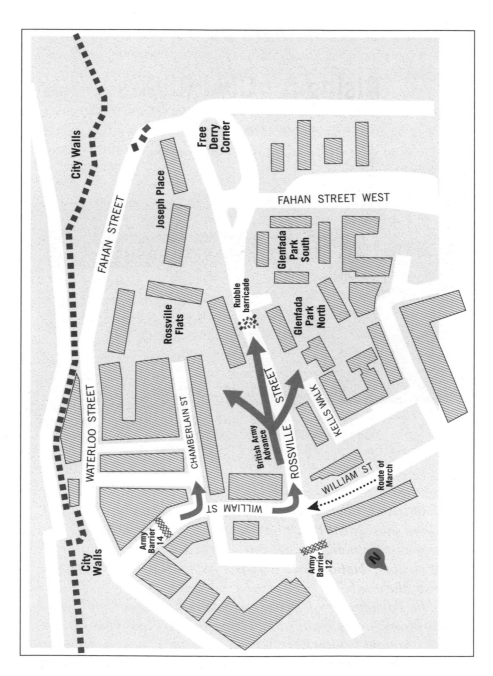

Map of the Bogside area.

CHAPTER 1

Rising for Civil Rights

Springtown Camp pictured in January 1964.

Centuries of poverty, hardship and discrimination had taken their toll on Irish Catholics. The Government of Ireland Act in 1920, and the subsequent Partition of Ireland in 1921, devastated its nationalist Catholic population. As its civil rights museum now tells visitors, 'Nationalist Derry felt abandoned, a very reluctant part of the north.'[1]

The Parliament of Northern Ireland – known simply as 'Stormont' – was established after partition and based in the vast Stormont Estate, East Belfast, from where it governed until 1972 (when Stormont collapsed after Bloody Sunday, bringing in direct rule).

In creating his 'Protestant Parliament and a Protestant State' (1934),[2] Northern Ireland's unionist prime minister Sir James Craig isolated many who identified as Irish Catholic, particularly across its north-west.

Four more decades of neglect since partition had exacerbated matters. Few reading this book today can imagine the cramped squalor in which many of the Irish nationalist/Catholic population were trapped with little means of changing their situation. The city of Derry was – and remains – a majority nationalist/ Catholic city and yet this populace was contained within areas like the overcrowded Bogside, an area once marshland outside the Walls, and later, in a newer housing estate called Creggan, built on a rolling hill adjacent to the Bogside. Thousands of families were crammed into these areas – conveniently contained within one electoral ward in the city, thus maintaining its dominant unionist authority. This is known as gerrymandering. Basically, at that time in Northern Ireland, only those who paid local taxes or rates for properties were given a vote in local elections. As the Catholic community were more often in poverty, had fewer jobs and so had fewer rate-payers, most were denied voting rights. Hence NICRA's (Northern Ireland Civil Rights Association) first civil rights demand: one man, one vote.

Dr Raymond McClean, GP and, later, a Mayor of Derry: The houses were old, damp, dark and dilapidated to the degree that nothing short of demolition and rehousing would really solve the problem. The people themselves were enveloped in the insidious depression and hopelessness of the area and could not see any way forward short of getting a house from the Londonderry Corporation, which they all knew was impossible. The Corporation sat with a dignified silence in the Guildhall.[3]

*

In 1946, this desperation led a large group of Catholic families to take over a disused military base on the city's outskirts that had been built and used by US forces in the build-up to D-Day.

2

Cutting through tall wire fences, local families began taking possession of the camp's 302 corrugated-iron Nissen huts as squatters – despite there being no water, heating, toilets or electricity on the site. Faced with the prospect of mass evictions, the unionist-dominated Londonderry Corporation of the time conceded, granting the squatters temporary residency and charging rent for the huts.[4] Though it was far from ideal and uninhabitable on a long-term basis, many families welcomed the army base as a temporary housing solution. Awaiting adequate houses of their own, they made the best of their situation.

Kay Duddy, sister of 17-year-old Jackie Duddy: My daddy was among the first to squat in Springtown Camp to get somewhere for us to live. We had been living in my grandparents' house, so badly needed our own house. He used to tell us how he carried the base of a spring bed all the way down there – so he had something with him to take possession of one of the huts – and so we got Hut 216 to live in. There was a stove up through the middle of the Nissen huts, but little else. We used to say, 'Yes, there is running water, but mostly down the walls!' But I have to say, every hut in the camp was immaculate, the mothers had them so spotless and well-kept, you could eat your dinner off the floor. They made homes of these huts, and I have very fond memories of living there.[5]

Maura Young, sister of 17-year-old John Young: My parents had nowhere to live, so they had to move into the Nissen huts that the army had left. My mother said it was Christmas Eve night when her and my father walked out there from Rosemount to Springtown Camp and left a chair in a hut. That was their claim on that hut. There was six of us. Eilish and Patrick and Helen were the three eldest and they lived in Rosemount, and then the three youngest, me and Leo and John, lived in Springtown Camp. Me and John were born in the camp. My mammy had John when she was forty-four years old.[6]

The following year, construction began on the Creggan housing estate, built on a hilly expanse adjacent to the Bogside. It was land quite unsuitable for social housing – but ideal in that it strategically increased the size of the South Ward, thus maintaining the Londonderry Corporation's overall control of the city.

Eamon Melaugh, Derry civil rights activist and photographer: Creggan was the first estate built, but Creggan was not planned as an estate. They bought a field and put two hundred houses in it, then they bought another field. I lived there for over thirty years. The only chance the community had to come together was outside mass on a Sunday; there were no social facilities at all. I remember one eight-months pregnant lady badly needed a house. I told her to go and see her doctor the next day and tell him that she wanted him to arrange for the baby to be delivered in the foyer of the Derry Guildhall, and I'd have the press of the world there, and she would get a house. Within two weeks she was in a house. They could bend the rules when they needed to. To get a house from the Corporation you had to go on your knees and talk to the mayor, who was never a Catholic. That was the situation. It was time for people to say enough was enough.[7]

Kay Duddy: When we were finally allocated a house in the new Creggan Heights around 1955, it was like a moving into a mansion. Then we had three bedrooms for our family of seventeen – and we felt so lucky. We were delighted that the water ran from taps instead of running down our walls.

When Springtown Camp's temporary tin huts deteriorated beyond repair, a group of remaining residents were among the first to confront those in power. In November 1959, 19 mothers marched all the way from the camp to the Guildhall to demand urgent housing. Among early demonstrators was a great-aunt of the author, Susie Crumlish from Hut 103, and theirs was one of the first civil rights demonstrations held in Derry. At first refused an audience with city councillors, the mothers were eventually allowed to address the Chamber.

From the *Derry Journal*, 'Springtown Camp mothers in the Guildhall Chambers', November 1959:

> We have lost some of our children due to the terrible conditions we have to live in. We appeal to the mothers of Derry to support us in our fight, and we ask this Corporation to remove this disgrace from our city.[8]

In January 1964, with the camp still in use, hundreds of its residents marched from the camp to the Guildhall in another show of collective strength to demand housing. This bigger demonstration was productive, to an extent, as more – but not all – camp families were housed elsewhere afterwards.

Fionnbarra Ó Dochartaigh, a co-founder of the Northern Ireland Civil Rights Association (NICRA): I remember it had to be a silent march. I can remember people running out of the shops, pubs, bookies, etc., clapping at the march passing once they realized what it was all about. There were placards referring to Little Rock, for those who know of American politics, and the segregation of America. In other words, we compared ourselves with the people in South Africa under apartheid and the black community in America, so there was an international feeling about that. You also had the Vietnam War at the time.[9]

Springtown Camp closed for good in 1967, with many of its families now relocated to the Bogside or Creggan area of the city and expanding the already heavily overcrowded South Ward.

Bishop Edward Daly, a parish priest of the Bogside from 1962 to 1973: The town I arrived in was quiet, peaceful, and my time spent there was the best of my life. The women, I always remember, were particularly striking to me because they nearly all worked in the shirt factories. They were the breadwinners in many houses. They made all the decisions and were very strong.[10]

Eamon Melaugh: Poverty was endemic in Derry. Unemployment was rampant. In Creggan estate it would have been over fifty per cent of the male population in the early 1960s. All credit to the women of this town: they kept the town off its knees in the shirt factories; men were out walking dogs. I came home from living in England ruthlessly determined to change things and began canvassing for support.

Bishop Edward Daly: The conditions in which some people lived in these streets were awful. Houses were terribly overcrowded, with rooms full of beds. People cooked, ate, slept, made love, brought up children all in the one room. How they did it, I don't know, but often generations lived in the same house. There were no indoor toilets, and some houses didn't have running water. Very often the parents lived in the house, and when their daughter got married, they couldn't get their own house anywhere and so the newly married couple would be given the front room to live in. Then they would start having children, and so on. There was no privacy whatsoever, none. But they were very happy. They were hugely welcoming. They didn't stand on ceremony either. When they welcomed you in, you were one of them. There was no putting me on a pedestal, which I loved.

Mary Nelis, a community activist, former Mayor of Derry and former MLA: I was born in 35 Wellington Street. It was a great street, we lived in a two-up two-down house in that old part of the Bogside now demolished. There were poor housing conditions and unsanitary houses, but great community spirit among the people.[11]

John Hume, later a co-recipient of the 1998 Nobel Peace Prize, recalled the 'very widespread and serious discrimination' in his hometown. As for others of his generation, this realization of the status quo spurred him to action in the 1960s.

John Hume, Derry politician: When Northern Ireland was first set up, the border was drawn in a particular manner to ensure there would be two Protestants to every Catholic in Northern Ireland, assuming that all Protestants were unionists, and all Catholics were nationalists. It wasn't a natural area, and from the beginning the unionist mindset was to hold all power in their own hands as the only means of protecting themselves. Of course, that led to very widespread discrimination in houses, in jobs and in voting rights. The worst example of that discrimination was the city of Derry where, although they [unionists] were only thirty per cent of the population, they governed from 1920 right through to the 1970s.[12]

Bishop Edward Daly: Politically, they wanted all the nationalists in one particular area so they wouldn't upset the voting pattern for the council. It was all a power game really, to maintain the power of a minority over a majority, and it worked out a dream. But the cost of it to people on the receiving end was terrible.

Eamon Melaugh: If you were a sub-tenant in a house, you didn't have a vote at local government elections, but there were business-men with sixteen or seventeen votes, dependent on the rateable value of their property. This was outrageous and scandalous. I think it was the only place in Europe where this happened. This was done out of malice and contempt towards the Catholic popu-lation, I can't say anything less condemning than that because that's exactly the case. The area of Bogside, for its size, was the most densely populated area in the whole of Europe.

Eileen Fox, sister of 17-year-old Jackie Duddy: We were a big family: there were fifteen of us in a three-bedroom house with our mammy and daddy. All the girls were in one room, all the boys in another, and for a while, the baby was kept in a drawer, which was made into a carrycot. Dinnertime was like a military opera-tion: we needed five loaves and twelve pints of milk every day, and dinner was always made in these huge pots. We took turns at the table at dinnertime.[13]

Billy McVeigh, local resident and teenage rioter: I was born in the Wells in the Bogside, and I slept in a drawer. We were in a three-bedroom house but there was three families, so each family had a bedroom and we had one toilet outside and one kitchen between

7

all three families. That's just the way it was. When we got a house in Creggan a few years later it was like being in the countryside, playing football and having a green area; it was unbelievable to us. My mother always seemed to be pregnant. I remember going to school in the morning and my mother would be washing nappies by hand, and when I came back later on, she was still there, still washing nappies. But we were happy. I left school at fourteen and my father had me working at the docks by fifteen.[14]

Eamon Melaugh: I wanted to do something dramatic to put an end to what was happening to the Catholic population in particular, but also within large elements of the working-class Protestants, too. I went around canvassing people to join the Housing Action Committee and take part in a protest. I wrote out an advertisement that said: 'Wanted – men of concrete action to do something about housing and unemployment (and maybe adult suffrage)' – this ad appeared in the *Belfast Telegraph*.

In 1965, the University for Derry Action Committee campaign lobbied to bring the north's second university to its second largest city by expanding historic Magee College. The new university was instead mooted for predominantly unionist Coleraine, causing outrage across the north-west of Ireland. In protest, a motorcade to Belfast took place, but efforts were in vain. It was a huge blow to those in Derry and further afield who sought to improve the city's opportunities, and particularly to its generation of forward-thinking young idealists who remained steadfast in their pursuit of change.

Dermie McClenaghan, local resident and civil rights activist: The University for Derry campaign in 1965 left a very deep footprint in the consciousness of people in Derry, about the discrimination and the cheek of unionism. When you think about it, is there any wonder that there was trouble in Derry? That was the Bogside in the 1960s – total, complete and deliberate neglect. As I was getting older, I was getting more annoyed.[15]

Around 1966, the Rossville Flats were built in the Bogside as an attempt to alleviate the critical housing situation. Rather than build out towards the surrounding countryside, city planners opted to again increase the urban squeeze.

Bishop Edward Daly: During redevelopment, the flats went up and they were huge. They weren't built out of any concern for the people, really. They were built for the sole purpose of building up and keeping people in that particular electoral ward. Certainly, they were better conditions than people had been living in, but if there was no privacy in the old housing, there definitely wasn't any in the flats! The walls were thin, and people could hear exactly what was going on in the next flat. So, while the living conditions were better, I don't think Derry people really took to living eight floors up.

On 29 January 1967, the Northern Ireland Civil Rights Association (NICRA) was formed at a public meeting in Belfast, bringing disparate protestors together in one cohesive group.

Spurred on by the impact of the American civil rights movement, NICRA's demands included changes in voting; fairer housing and jobs allocation; an end to discrimination; government reforms; and the disbandment of the blatantly sectarian auxiliary police force, the B Specials. By 1971, another demand became necessary: calls for an end to internment without trial.

Chief among the opposition to the civil rights struggle of the late 1960s was the Revd Ian Paisley from the north's Democratic Unionist Party (DUP). Notoriously outspoken and a huge figure in Northern Ireland politics throughout the conflict, Paisley and his followers, often dubbed 'Paisleyites', frequently held counter-protests at civil rights rallies, with many violent confrontations.

Paisley was renowned for his anti-Catholicism. 'Through Popery the Devil has shut up the way to our inheritance. Priestcraft, superstition and papalism with all their attendance voices of murder, theft, immorality, lust and incest blocked the way to the land of gospel liberty.'[16] As a younger preacher, he had also accused Britain's Queen Mother of 'fornication and adultery with the Anti-Christ'[17] after she met Pope John XXIII. In 1966, Paisley founded his own newspaper, the Protestant Telegraph.

After widespread attacks on Catholic homes in 1968, Paisley told a loyalist rally, 'Catholic homes caught fire because they were loaded with petrol bombs; Catholic churches were attacked and burned because they were arsenals and priests handed out sub-machine-guns to parishioners.'[18] His anti-Catholic stance attempted to legitimize the discriminatory practices of state and government, as indicated below in this except from an interview with author Padraig O'Malley.

Revd Ian Paisley, unionist politician who later led the Democratic Unionist Party from 1971 to 2008: Behind all the rhetoric and window dressing, we know exactly what our enemies want to do. They want to put us out of our own country. And we're not prepared to accept that. As far as Catholicism is concerned in Northern Ireland, Catholics don't want a share in the government of Northern Ireland. They want Northern Ireland to be destroyed and to have a united Ireland. Even if they were to join a government, it's only until such a time as they can destroy the government and the state. The ordinary Ulsterman is not going to surrender to the IRA … We have not only the right but the duty to kill them before they kill me, my family and others.[19]

Fionnbarra Ó Dochartaigh: In January 1967, I was the only Derry-born person who was also a founding member of the civil rights movement [NICRA], and at twenty-two or so, I was the youngest person there. From a small lobby group, NICRA became a mass movement. There was only forty of us who first met in Belfast in 1967. Like the old saying, from small acorns a mighty oak will grow. For years, I and others spoke at street-corner meetings with small crowds of just twenty or thirty people until it became the mass movement it did. We'd had an earlier march in from Coalisland to Dungannon, which passed off peacefully, but we weren't allowed into the square in Dungannon to speak. The police and the Paisleyites blocked us. They sectarianized things, but civil rights was for everybody – that was our whole policy. We had a lot of strong-minded Protestants involved in the movement, like Ivan Cooper and Claude Wilton the solicitor, and Austin Campbell, who was somehow a distant relative of the royal family.

Eamon Melaugh: I went to the first civil rights march in Ireland, which was Coalisland to Dungannon. Bridget Bond and I organized a bus from Derry. What amazed me at that march, and I very nearly got arrested, was the militancy of the women. I was flabbergasted; I got on the bus and made an announcement that the next civil rights march will be in Derry. We decided to have the march on 5 October.

CHAPTER 2

Police Attack at Duke Street, 1968

Rare photo of marchers hemmed in by police during the
5 October 1968 civil rights march in Derry.

A civil rights march was announced, this time to be held in Derry on 5 October 1968 in defiance of the unionist government's ban on marching. As around four hundred marchers congregated at Duke Street, police moved in to surround the crowd, batons drawn. Marchers young and old were then beaten by police as they tried to stand their ground.

A single television cameraman, the late Gay O'Brien from Irish national broadcaster RTÉ, managed to capture police actions on film. His news footage, broadcast around the world, at last showed people outside the north the brutal reality of unionist rule. Today, many regard Duke Street as the starting point of the Troubles.

Ivan Cooper, one of few civil rights leaders from a unionist background, and later an MP: One thing I remember about the 5 October march itself was that my neighbour was a head constable and I remember he said to me during the march, 'What are you doing with this pack of Fenians, Ivan?'[1]

Eamon Melaugh: On the day of the parade, I emptied my pockets. I had a new suit on. I was the only one from Derry to speak at the Diamond that day, and I spoke that day on a chair at the top of Duke Street, calling on the assembled protestors *not* to fight with the RUC for the length of a Derry street – ours was a struggle for the emancipation of the working class.

I put a new suit on me and bought six white hankies; God's honest truth, I put one in each of six pockets, to act as bandages. And that's what happened, all six were used by people who were beaten and brutalized by the savage paramilitary wing of the unionist party, the RUC. There was nothing accidental about 5 October, it was all planned and provided for.

Fionnbarra Ó Dochartaigh: They issued banning orders to Eamonn McCann, Eamon Melaugh, myself and John Gallagher, a great Irish speaker and a great Irish teacher. All four of us were on the list of the banning order. RUC [Police] District Inspector Ross McGimpsey also said to me personally, 'Well, I look forward to meeting you on 5th October,' and I knew that he wasn't planning to shake my hand or clap me on the back.

My sister Deirdre was on the march, as was my mother and father, and of course being one of the organizers, I was too. Deirdre was up the front of the march and people started to make speeches. Ivan Cooper, God rest him, appealed to the police and the people for a peaceful march. Attempts to break through police lines proved impossible. Marchers began to chant '*Seig Heil*' and for a half an hour the situation remained static.

The crowd became more tightly packed between the lines of black uniforms.[2]

Deirdre O'Doherty, a civil rights activist and former radiographer at Altnagelvin Hospital: Someone yelled, 'Run, Deirdre, run!' It was my twin brother, Fionnbarra. We ran down Duke Street with an RUC man chasing us. People who knew us pushed us into a café, and luckily at the back there was an empty table. We sat down immediately, grabbing two big menu cards. Within seconds the same RUC man burst into the café and started looking around. The rest of the people in the café had no idea what was going on outside. I made a point of looking straight at the policeman's face. He was quite young, early twenties, holding his bloodstained truncheon as if about to use it again. To this day, I've never seen a face that showed so much viciousness and hatred. To our relief, he didn't recognize us and left the café.[3]

Fionnbarra Ó Dochartaigh: It was really brutal. I know we were considered second-class citizens, but this was totally indiscriminate. No mercy for women, man or child.

Deirdre O'Doherty: There were so many people injured. Then I heard the siren of the first ambulance arriving, and I told Fionnbarra that I would be more useful helping at the hospital than staying there on Duke Street. I ran alongside the ambulance and shouted to the co-driver that I was a radiographer and would be needed at the hospital. He opened the door, grabbed me and pulled me in beside him, remarking, 'Get in, love – it looks like it's going to be a long bloody night for you!'

From the *Derry Journal* on 8 October 1968:

> The police water cannon were then brought into action, and it drove through the crowd with both jets spraying at full pressure. It was followed into the crowd by a large number of steel-helmeted police with batons swinging. Hundreds

of afternoon shoppers, many of them women and some accompanied by young children, were caught in the deluge.[4]

Deirdre O'Doherty: The waiting room was practically filled with injured people with bleeding head wounds. There were only two to three doctors on and a few nurses. Relatives started to arrive. Another ambulance arrived. By now there were people lying on the floor, with friends and relatives taking off coats and jumpers and rolling them up to make cushions for their heads. I'd never seen anything like this. It was like a war zone. It was well after 1am that I was able to leave. I was curious how many patients we had, so decided to count only the number of skull x-rays. We had each x-rayed about forty-four skulls. I arrived home totally exhausted and went straight to bed.

Eamonn McCann, a journalist and civil rights activist: 'Things are never going to be the same again.' I remember it vividly. They were saying the same sentence, the actual same clichéd sentence. People realized that something new had happened.[5]

Gerard 'Jed' McClelland, a schoolboy in 1968: I was fifteen when it started after 5 October 1968. I was around the corner, on top of a roof with my da, who was a handyman builder. We were on this roof in Spencer Road looking at Duke Street down below. We could hear all the roaring and shouting but we knew nothing about any civil rights march that day, and only found out what it was all about when they aired the footage on the news that night.[6]

Jon McCourt, a student in 1968: I was a young student when the first civil rights march took place in Derry, and when I got home that evening my mother's first question was, 'What were you doing there?' and secondly, 'What happened?' We spent the next couple of years on marches and protests and all the rest, and as far as I was aware, my mother just stayed home and let us get on with it.[7]

Deirdre O'Doherty: I was awakened the next morning before 8am with a loud banging on the front door. It was the RUC, to arrest my twin brother. My mother dressed immediately but refused to let them take him straight away. 'He is not leaving this house without a full breakfast!' she told them. Also arrested at their respective dwellings were the two Eamonns.

Fionnbarra Ó Dochartaigh: The next morning, Eamonn McCann and Eamon Melaugh, who I always referred to as the two Eamonns, and myself, were arrested and taken to the RUC barracks. We were charged with organizing an illegal march and so forth, but it was they, in fact, who made it illegal. We had applied to hold a march and filled in all the necessary forms. A couple of days after, RUC District Inspector Ross McGimpsey was standing at the door to the barracks and I went over to him and said, 'You did us a great favour; the whole world saw you in action.'

Bishop Edward Daly: When Monday came, it was obvious that the events and the pictures of the events in Duke Street had generated concern in Dublin and Westminster, as well as Stormont. William Craig [N.I. Minister for Home Affairs] denounced the civil rights march, suggesting that it was an IRA ploy. He praised the actions of the RUC and denied that they had been brutal.

British prime minister, Harold Wilson, summoned the Stormont prime minister, Terence O'Neill, to London to discuss the situation. Derry people in the nationalist areas of the city were quietly satisfied that their problems were, at last, being noticed and acknowledged by people in high places. Their problems were now on the front pages, like those of the American black community or the people in Czechoslovakia.[8]

Eamonn McCann: In their wildest dreams, nobody imagined the years of violence that would follow. The poison that erupted in Northern Ireland subsequently was not caused by October '68. We were paying for history.

*

The attack at Duke Street misfired for the authorities. Instead of scuppering activism, the numbers calling for civil rights continued to grow, as did international interest in the Northern Ireland situation. Another, much bigger march was planned for 16 November, this time attracting many thousands of citizens from all backgrounds onto the streets.

On the day, hundreds of members of the RUC mobilized opposite marchers. Alongside the RUC were members of their auxiliary police force known as the B Specials, who by now had a fearsome reputation for sectarian violence within Irish Catholic communities. Loyalist protestors who watched from afar jeered as the march set off across the bridge. According to Fionnbarra Ó Dochartaigh, a symbolic breach of police lines was organized.

Fionnbarra Ó Dochartaigh: If the police attacked, the instructions to the stewards were that they were to tell the rest of the people to sit down on the bridge, and that would have caused a major disruption. I remember James Doherty, Johnny White, Michael Canavan and Dermie McClenaghan, they're the ones I remember going over the barricade. The crowd then pushed forward, and we were on the other side.[9]

Jed McClelland: I joined that march and we marched across the bridge. The B-men [members of the B Specials] were all standing at the Carlisle Road end of the bridge with two-foot batons, and they wouldn't let us up the road. We just charged the B-men and one swung at my head and missed that but hit me. But when you're young you don't feel any pain, so we did get up Carlisle Road. That was the first engagement in civil rights for me.

Fionnbarra Ó Dochartaigh: There's no doubt about it, it was a very important march. It was significant in terms of the numbers that turned out, and the fact that the reforms came soon afterwards. In those days we didn't even believe we could get rid of the Londonderry Corporation, but looking back I think the establishment of the Housing Executive was the most important achievement of all.

Dermie McClenaghan: The most significant thing was the numbers. I think it was the biggest march that had ever happened in Derry, and it showed the strength of the civil rights movement. The numbers gave it an authenticity, and I do think it empowered people. It influenced all sorts of movements – the women's movement, the gay rights movement – because it gave people a sense of what they could achieve if they got together.

*

Known today simply as 'Burntollet', the next assault on civil rights came as a student-led People's Democracy march left Belfast on New Year's Day 1969 for a four-day march to Derry. Demonstrators were attacked by civilian loyalist mobs throughout their journey, with the worst attack occurring at rural Burntollet just a few miles from Derry on 4 January 1969. More than seventy marchers needed hospital treatment. Despite extreme provocation, marchers adhered to their non-violent principles of the civil rights movement and didn't retaliate when attacked.

Many of the attackers at Burntollet were recognized as members of the notoriously hostile and sectarian auxiliary police force of the time, the B Specials, by white armbands they wore. Many marchers reported afterwards that police stood by and let the attack happen, including 116 idle constables in riot gear.

Michael Farrell, a leader of People's Democracy march in 1969: There was a police jeep in front of us, and a group of five or six RUC men who stopped the jeep and took out shields and helmets and put them on, and that's when I realized something more serious was happening. I saw clubs, but other people saw clubs with nails through them, and iron bars.[10]

Vinny McCormack, eyewitness and co-author of *Burntollet*: The police moved back from the side of the road leaving the march open to attack. It was almost like a military operation, and that's what startled us. The rocks came first of all, and then the attackers actually mingled with the marchers and the marchers were being beaten almost on a hand-to-hand basis.[11]

Michael Farrell: I was hit by a big chunk of stone and knocked unconscious. I was taken to hospital, and I remember one of the nurses saying to me, 'You people deserve this, bringing trouble into our town.'

As they finally arrived in Derry, the marchers were ambushed again by civilian loyalist mobs before reaching the city centre. Local schoolboy Paul O'Connor was just 13 years old when he met with friends to walk over the bridge to meet the marchers as they arrived. He remembers still wearing his school uniform.

Paul O'Connor, a 13-year-old schoolboy in 1969: A lot of people were bleeding, a lot of people were injured, and they'd clearly just gone through something pretty awful. We'd walked out past a large group of loyalists who were building up a large mountain of stones at Irish Street, and there were flags and lots of RUC. My vivid memory is of us all bolting down that road, everybody shouting, 'Run, run!'[12]

Despite all they had endured and another confrontation with loyalists within the city walls, the People's Democracy march-ers eventually reached their destination at the city's Guildhall Square, where crowds of thousands waited to welcome them.

Paul O'Connor: It was a big moral victory. The people of Derry were waiting to welcome them in, and it was very emotional. They were pulled onto a platform – among them, Bernadette Devlin.

Michael Farrell: This was the moment the British should have said, bring in one man one vote. The march had shown the extraordi-nary situation here, where you could have a demonstration by completely unarmed, completely non-violent protestors who were just physically attacked very badly, and the police – giving them the best of the benefit of the doubt – stood by and let it happen.

Clearly, in a situation like that, there had to be drastic change, and that was the time it should have happened.

Rioting erupted in areas across Derry as word spread of the loyalist attacks on 4 January 1969. That evening the RUC ran amok in the Bogside, beating and berating those who stood in their way and destroying property. Despite marchers remaining peaceful when ambushed by loyalist civilians and off-duty B Specials, they were still publicly blamed for the disorder.

Captain Terence O'Neill, Northern Ireland prime minister, speaking on Sunday 5 January 1969: Some of the marchers and those who supported them in Londonderry itself have shown themselves to be mere hooligans, ready to attack the police and others ... At times one in six of the entire force of the Royal Ulster Constabulary [RUC] was engaged in protecting the march to Londonderry ... Clearly Ulster has now had enough. We are all sick of marchers and counter-marchers. Unless these warring minorities rapidly return to their senses, we will have to consider greater use of the Special Constabulary [B Specials] for normal police duties. I think we must also have an urgent look at the Public Order Act itself to see whether we ought to ask parliament for further power to control those elements that are seeking to hold the entire community to ransom. Enough is enough.[13]

Vinny McCormack: Prime Minister O'Neill made no distinction between peaceful citizens marching in pursuit of fair treatment ('hooligans') and a mob that attacked them with stones, cudgels and petrol bombs. His statement came only hours after hundreds of police had rampaged through the Bogside/Lecky Road area of Derry. Was this what Captain O'Neill considered 'normal police duties'?

The most surprising aspect of the prime minister's astonishing remarks was that the only policies he proposed in response to demands for fair treatment were to seek more repressive powers, and to make greater use of the B Specials, an exclusively Protestant force that had discredited itself only hours before O'Neill's statement, as many of the organizers of and participants in the attacks on the march came from its ranks.[14]

Paul O'Connor: I certainly think that Burntollet was one of the absolute symbolic turning points. Not because the march had been attacked, because in some ways that was to be expected, but because the forces of law and order colluded entirely in that attack from beginning to end, and there were no consequences, no accountability.

*

As demonstrations and counter-demonstrations swept the north in 1969, prominent unionist leader Revd Ian Paisley and his 'Paisleyites' stepped up efforts to quell nationalist dissent. At one public rally, Paisley famously said of his Catholic counterparts, 'They breed like rabbits and multiply like vermin.'[15]

Widespread anti-Catholic discrimination and bigotry was ingrained in the fabric of Northern Ireland. This bias also affected those leaving school, hopeful of job prospects but disadvantaged by their Roman Catholic education.

Eileen Fox: We were still getting over my mammy dying, and my daddy was left with fifteen of us, so we all had to help. My first experience of discrimination was that very first job interview. It was with a local bridal and haberdashery shop, and I was fifteen at the time. The man in the shop was lovely and he gave me the job, and everything seemed to be brilliant. Then, on the way out, he said, 'Sorry, miss, I forgot to ask what school you were at before this?' I told him I went to St Mary's in Creggan, and that was it – suddenly he said the job was taken.

It took me hours to realize what had happened. I tortured myself about it all the way home, wondering what I had said or done wrong to ruin it. When I told our boys and my daddy, my daddy didn't spell it out as such, but he did say, 'Do you know what's wrong, love? It's because you're from Creggan – that's all.' He was always very careful not to label things in any way, he would never say Catholic or Protestant, just that we were from Creggan. Still, nobody was as surprised as I was. I just couldn't believe it. That was the first time I had ever seen or experienced discrimination, the first time it directly affected me. We soon learned we had to fight for what we wanted.

Hugh McMonagle, Shantallow Civil Rights Association: Part of the start of my marriage was spent in the Bogside when the riots were going on and the RUC and the B Specials were trespassing into the Bog and people feared they were going to attack. Up until August, when the Troubles really started, our time was spent there defending the people of Derry. As a nationalist you believed that the unionists, and the police at that time, were, in our opinion, a one-sided military force and they were backed up by the B Specials. Then at times, like in Sackville Street, they had the loyalists behind them, too. You'd say to yourself, 'They're *not* attacking our people. We have a right to defend ourselves. We're human beings and we're entitled to our human rights.'[16]

Geraldine McBride, a teenage Derry schoolgirl in 1969: We lived in Creggan Heights, and I loved it. Neighbours helped other neighbours out when they needed it and there was a lot of sharing, but people did it in a way that always kept other people's dignity. People took such a pride in their houses and had lovely gardens; they would have always grown vegetables in their back gardens back then too, like potatoes, and it was a lovely place to live. My dad was a union man and politics wasn't really talked about in our house. I was quite unaware of politics of any kind. He always told us to treat people as we would want to be treated ourselves, and those who don't – they have the problem.[17]

Diane Greer, an 11-year-old Londonderry schoolgirl in 1969: I remember hearing about the civil rights marches when I was younger. I would have been told that 'Catholics are on the march. Catholics are looking for … Catholics want …' I wasn't hearing the other side of that. I didn't even know at that stage what they didn't have, or even what they wanted. I remember hearing about

Burntollet. People that I knew were there and were maybe there as oppressors. They told the story, and it sounded like a grand battle. It was told like a folk story. I have a very different view of all that today.[18]

Maura Young: My sister Helen was very active when civil rights began because she was living in a two-bedroom house with an outside toilet beside Rosemount Factory. Living there were her and her husband, four girls, and an aunt and an uncle – in two bedrooms. At that time, they were giving three- and four-bedroom houses to newly married policemen, members of the RUC, while she and so many others were living in those conditions. So, she had cause to go out marching. I was never politically minded. Neither was John; as long as we got our pay on a Friday night, we were happy.

In stark contrast to the peaceful ethos of the civil rights movement, paramilitary violence also increased on both sides of the community. Since the partition of Ireland in 1921, the Irish Republican Army (IRA) has existed in phases, their campaign aimed at Irish freedom and an end to unionist/British rule. The unrest of the late 1960s saw a resurgence in their activity. Alongside the IRA and other republican paramilitary groups existed extreme loyalist paramilitary groups, including the Ulster Volunteer Force (UVF) and the Ulster Defence Association (UDA), who were determined to preserve the union of Northern Ireland and the United Kingdom and did so through a campaign of sectarian violence.

For a short time, the civil rights movement co-existed alongside a republican armed campaign in Northern Ireland – both movements intent on bringing about change for its Irish citizens but by entirely opposite means.

Jed McClelland: Civil rights were important because of what we had put up with until then. My mother told us that when we lived out on the Trench Road in a tin hut for two years and how the B-men marched at night to keep the IRA at bay, but when she saw them coming down the road, she would grab me and hide us both

23

in a ditch to let them pass, because we were all terrified of them – and for good reason too.

Raymond Rogan, local resident and early chairman of Bogside Residents' Association: It wasn't actually until the civil rights people in Queens University began agitating that I began then, too, because of the position I was in myself as a so-called community leader. I began taking an interest in the wider community and the society that led to the kind of problems we had. It was then I took an interest and I followed closely the activities of people like Eamonn McCann, Bernadette Devlin and others.[19]

Ivan Cooper: All we did at that time was marching – we marched everywhere. We marched on the bridge, across the bridge. I was a leader of the civil rights movement in Derry, and I was a Prod [Protestant].

Raymond Rogan: Every time there was a demonstration, there would be a counter-demonstration from Paisley or someone. Naturally enough, they say Ian Paisley was an enemy of everybody, but, in actual fact, it was the other side of the coin. It was actually Paisley's response to the actions of the students and activists that fired up the people in the Bogside. The kind of things he was saying and doing and getting away with it. That's when the opposition began to grow to the kind of society we had. His anger backfired.

Billy McVeigh: Because I was from the Bog, I knew people like Ivan Cooper and John Hume from an early age, through my parents. You got to know them, and they got to know you. There would often be meetings held in Dermie McClenaghan's house in Wellington Street and some days, when I was walking past, they'd ask me to keep an eye out outside. There was always the fear of B-men being about and catching people. Everyone knew each another in one way or another. We kept our ears to the ground, and our eyes out for each other.

Geraldine McBride: I knew when I was a teenager that you only had to say where you were from to lose a job. I had Catholic and Protestant friends, and it shouldn't matter what religion you were, but once you named the school you were at, people knew.

We heard about other things going on in the world, like the students in Paris holding civil rights marches and the same in America, and you could see that ordinary people could change their destiny, and it was a great feeling. It was a great time to be alive. It wasn't just for the rich – it was for everyone to help make governments change their policies and for all people to be treated fairly. I loved the style, I loved the dancing and the music; we had The Beatles, we had freedom and choice that even our parents before us didn't have.

CHAPTER 3

'You Are Now Entering Free Derry'

Original Free Derry Corner, early 1969.

As people gathered that night in the Bogside, prepared for more police attacks, local man Liam Hillen took a paintbrush and wrote on the gable end of number 33 Lecky Road. None knew that this graffiti, painted in haste in the early hours of 5 January 1969, would last decades and become a local and international landmark.

The slogan 'You Are Now Entering Free Derry' was suggested by journalist and activist Eamonn McCann, inspired by a similar one at the sit-in protests at the University of California, Berkeley. Chris Armstrong was one of few present when Derry's most famous graffiti first appeared. He even held the paint tin as Hillen, hoisted up by another local, Danny Begley, got busy with some leftover paint.

Chris Armstrong, 18 years old in 1969: It was very cold, and we were sat around a fire opposite the wall – all very bored. Liam wanted to do something, and he suggested writing something on the wall, so people came up with ideas. I remember Eamonn McCann saying it shouldn't be anything sectarian, and he told us about the writing at Berkeley, California, that said: 'You Are Now Entering Free Berkeley'. Liam was never big, so big Begs [Danny Begley] was a lot bigger than us at six foot three inches and held Liam up on his shoulders to reach the wall. I had to hold the tin of paint up high enough so he could reach into it, and it was done.[1]

Liam Hillen, the original painter of Free Derry Corner's slogan in 1969: Big Danny Begley was about six-foot tall, so he leaned up against the wall with his hands interlocked and gave me a lift up. Chris Armstrong held the paint and I dipped into it. We ended up painting it with green paint on a dirty white background.[2]

Danny Begley: I used to joke that Liam owed me a new coat. He destroyed me with paint, I was covered – and it was my brother's coat!

Chris Armstrong: I'm very proud that I was there. That wall is recognized everywhere, and we helped start all of that. It was just a wall, but Free Derry Corner has become a symbol of Derry and its people.

Danny Begley: It was just one of those things, part of our growing up. There was so much more going on than us writing on a wall.

Relations between the north's unionist and nationalist communities steadily deteriorated in 1969, made worse by the disconnect between its nationalist population, security forces and the unionist government of the day. This led to an unending cycle of protests, counter-protests and increasing police crackdowns. When another proposed civil rights march from Burntollet to Derry on 19 April was banned, around two hundred loyalists still gathered there, just in case. A few miles away in Derry, a number of protests ended in clashes between civil rights activists and loyalists, and later with the police, too. By Saturday evening, over a hundred and sixty people were in hospital, and police fired the city's first shots of the conflict when an officer opened fire with live rounds. The violence was captured in the local newspaper.

From the *Derry Journal*, dated 22 April 1969:

> The violence which erupted on Saturday afternoon following a clash between civil rights sympathisers and Paisleyites who had earlier gathered at Burntollet Bridge, the announced assembly point for the banned civil rights march, swept through the city centre, with a strong force of riot police fighting running battles with civil rights supporters.
>
> The trail of violence ran through the Diamond, Waterloo Place and Strand Road as police, supported by an armoured water cannon, drove the crowd back into the Bogside area of the city. There, a massive and bitter confrontation went on into the early hours of Sunday morning, with casualties mounting steadily.[3]

On the evening of Saturday 19 April, father-of-nine Sammy Devenny had been talking to friends at his front door when RUC officers burst into his home, savagely beating not only Sammy but also some of his children and two neighbours, Freddie Budd and Paddy Harkin, who were present as police arrived en masse. Horror at the incident led to riots all over the city for days and weeks afterwards.

Bishop Edward Daly: Sammy Devenny was a family man who worked for a funeral undertaker, well known to myself and all the priests of the city because we met at many funerals. He was not involved in any kind of political activity. His primary interests were his work and his wife and his young children.[4]

Colette O'Connor, daughter of Sammy Devenny and 10 years old in 1969: I remember all this commotion and my daddy shouting, 'Watch the wains!' and all of a sudden, everything was pushed into the living room. I was thrown onto a chair between my two brothers, who were eleven and six at the time. I was stuck in the middle. I couldn't see what was happening, but I could hear all sorts of roaring and a lot of bad language, them calling us everything. Freddie, one of the neighbours who'd been talking to Daddy, lay across us on the armchair and was on top of us, screaming, 'Watch the wains, watch the wains!' When you are young, and you see a man that afraid, of course you're going to be terrified, too. I felt the weight of him heavy on me, and the next thing I felt was the blood coming down on me, literally pouring. They had busted his head open, and when he stood up, he was drenched in blood and so was I.[5]

Christine Robson, daughter of Sammy Devenny and nine years old in 1969: My father was very strong. He fought the first policeman off, then two came at him, then more kept coming, and our Harry said there were eight policemen on him in the end, all battering him. We had a fireplace, and I remember the hearth was filled with my daddy's blood. Everyone was horrified about it. I remember people trying to mop that up, and they couldn't. It was a river of blood. There was blood on the walls, too, and I think that's why all the people were trying to clean it up, because we were so young. My daddy was lying on the living-room floor with blood everywhere. They had beaten his false teeth down his throat, and he choked on them. The police had hit him so hard that the bottom of his glasses were actually embedded into his cheekbones. He needed a line of stitches below each eye.

Bishop Edward Daly: I visited the house shortly after Sammy had been removed to hospital and there was blood visible everywhere. There were shots fired by the police at one stage and the rioting continued well into the Saturday night. None of us had previously witnessed anything like the intensity and the ferocity of that rioting and police action. At times, members of the police seemed to be completely out of control. Their behaviour was despicable. While I and other priests were on the streets endeavouring to calm the rioters, I have to admit that I was as angry as the rioters at what had happened. There were times when one was severely tempted to join the rioters rather than attempt to quell them.

On 17 July 1969, Sammy Devenny died of a heart attack brought on by trauma and injury, one of the first victims of the Troubles. His funeral was among the biggest Derry had ever seen, attended by journalists from all over the world.

Fionnbarra Ó Dochartaigh: It was a massive funeral and people just couldn't believe that this was happening. We were all learning the hard way. We never thought of what could happen, but Sammy Devenny was a major issue. The police were out on the streets, everywhere.[6]

Bishop Edward Daly: He had never fully recovered from his multiple injuries. He was only forty-two years old. His funeral took place in the City Cemetery on Sunday 20 July. The *Derry Journal* estimated the attendance at over twenty thousand. His wife, Phyllis, made a moving appeal for calm. That same weekend, the world was enthralled as Neil Armstrong became the first man to walk on the moon. This event was hardly noticed in Derry. We were too preoccupied with events on this planet.

Geraldine McBride: I was scared stiff of the B Specials, to be honest with you. I was so terrified of them. You just knew if they got you, it wasn't going to be good. They were intimidating because there was so many of them. Maybe it's just me being dramatic, but they all seemed to have one aim: to beat down the Catholics. Then the police attacked Sammy Devenny, who I knew, and his daughter Ann Devenny. I couldn't believe that it would happen in Derry. Things got more serious then. For him to get beaten up like that and to then die months after, it was so sad. He was never the same. He was such a family-orientated man. It made you more terrified of the police and the B Specials.[7]

Raymond Rogan: Because this situation had gone on for so many years people weren't really inclined to attend meetings. It wasn't until there were serious incidents of student marches being attacked by Orangemen and B Specials, and then Sammy Devenny – then people began to take a real exception to what was happening in and against their community. Then they began attending rallies and meetings. I was still of a view that together in that situation we left ourselves exposed. I was a pacifist, if you like, and very aware that any public gathering would be attacked at any time by the RUC.

In summer 1969, over two years into NICRA's campaign for civil rights, the organization published a renewed list of demands[8] – none of which had been achieved yet.

ONE MAN ONE VOTE

We demand the British franchise. That means votes at 18 for all in both Stormont and local government elections.

FAIR BOUNDARIES

We demand an end to gerrymandering by the Unionist Government. We want an Impartial Commission set up by Westminster to draw the electoral boundaries of the proposed new local authorities.

HOUSES ON NEED

We demand a compulsory points scheme for the allocation of houses. A credible scheme has been published, but many local authorities refuse to operate it. There should also be provision for appeal in the scheme to control abuses by local authorities.

ANTI-DISCRIMINATION LAWS

We demand that the law control religious discrimination

which is rife in all areas of life in Northern Ireland. Such a law should also outlaw the incitement of religious hatred, and include control of public authorities, local and central alike.

CIVIL LIBERTIES

We demand an end to the repressive laws of the Stormont Government. That means the repeal of the Special Powers Act, the withdrawal of the Public Order Bill, the repeal or amendment of the Public Order Act, 1951.

CHAPTER 4

The Battle of the Bogside

Police and loyalist protestors chase nationalist protestors during the
Battle of the Bogside in August 1969.

*Every year on the Saturday closest to 12 August, the unionist
Apprentice Boys of Derry hold their main parade commemorating
the end of the 1689 Siege of Derry. The Apprentice Boys are
a Protestant fraternal order with their headquarters in Derry,
and international lodges. They form part of the Loyal Orange
Institution, or Orange Order, which was founded in 1795 to
maintain Protestant ascendancy in the north.*

*Members of the Orange Order are commonly known as
'Orangemen' by the wider population, and their parades often
provoked negative reaction when march routes included nationalist
areas and led to claims of intimidation and provocation by such*

communities. On 12 August 1969, simmering tensions erupted as thousands of Apprentice Boys prepared to march through Derry.

As the march passed the Bogside, locals reacted with the usual shouting and stone throwing. The police, backed by loyalists, tried to force the protestors back. The intense rioting that followed spanned three days and became known as the Battle of the Bogside. Protests and conflict spread to other nationalist areas of the north, too, with Belfast worst affected.

On the third day, 14 August, exhausted RUC officers retreated from the Bogside to defiant cheers. Within the hour, word spread that the British army was to be deployed to Northern Ireland.

Bishop Edward Daly: The sound of drums and flutes provided background music during the early morning. It could be clearly heard all over the Bogside and around St Eugene's. Women rushed to get their shopping done early. After the ten o'clock mass, people, who had already been in the city centre, remarked that the place was 'hiving' with police. In the Bogside, where I attended and visited a few sick and elderly people that morning, things were calm but tense. There were not many people around, and the usual ubiquitous children were notably absent, many families having prudently moved out.[1]

Fionnbarra Ó Dochartaigh: Orangemen wanted to march down past the bottom of William Street as if they just needed to show their control, and the ordinary people took great exception to that. We had gone to meet the two top people in the RUC at their headquarters in Lisburn. We put it in very clear language: we didn't want this Orange march to happen, and if it did happen, there would be an eruption in Derry, especially considering what the RUC had done to many households here, including the Devennys. But the word came back that the Orange march was going ahead – it was a sectarian exercise to more or less assert their right to walk anywhere in the city.

Hugh McMonagle: Things really kicked off on 12 August that year, when the Apprentice Boys went through Waterloo Place, and yes, a few things were thrown at them, but then the RUC started to chase the young fellas up William Street – baton-charging them. I only speak for me personally, but when I got as far as Rossville Street, I thought to myself, 'What the hell am I running for?' I started to shout, 'Stand your ground,' and lifted stones and started to belt them boys. Everyone began to catch on and do the same, and we started to beat them back down William Street.

The sight of young men agitating in smart dress jackets, or their Sunday-best, was commonplace. Sent to cover the Bogside for London's Daily Sketch, *British press photographer Clive Limpkin described those he saw through his lens as 'the best-dressed rioters I'd ever seen'.*[2]

Clive Limpkin, British press photographer: I rounded the corner of Waterloo Place, where a line of local policemen, the Royal Ulster Constabulary [RUC], faced a hail of rocks from the rioters thirty yards up William Street, who screamed the hatred you had read about but hadn't quite believed. Yet it was the hatred of the police that hit you hardest, their bile of religious taunting echoing that of the Bogsiders – and all this coming from a peacekeeping force within the United Kingdom.[3]

Raymond Rogan: When the Battle of the Bogside arrived, even I – the gentle pacifist – was outside throwing stones with the rest of them. One rumour that got me incensed was that the cathedral was about to be attacked by B Specials – a lot of people gathered in Francis Street waiting for these people, but nobody appeared.

That was the start of it; any incursions by the RUC or B Specials, I was there to defend the Bog. It was exciting, obviously, because everybody was there and there were no dissenters. There was a feeling of 'they'll beat us if we don't beat them'. We were all one, and people like Hume and Cooper were very prominent in talking and representing the best interests of the community to the outside world. That was important.

Mary Nelis: Don't forget, in those days we had no phones. The Tenant's Association would have been in touch with what was going on, but I was home with the children and my new-born, packed and ready in case we had to get up and go. That's how scary it was. None of us went to bed.

Jimmy Toye, who had just turned 16 in August 1969: The whole community was on the streets and everybody had a role to play in defending the area.[4]

Jed McClelland: I saw some fierce sights down at the Battle of the Bogside. You're talking thousands of us all taking turns, defending and letting rip – and we did beat them back down William Street. We hated them, they hated us. But we did win, we beat them out of the Bog, right down into William Street and back over to Waterloo Place.

Eileen Fox: When we ran up the town from riots, neighbours used to put big buckets of vinegar out for people to dip rags into – it helped when our eyes and nose were stinging from the tear gas fired by the RUC in the Bogside, and you'd run from street to street to soak it again quick.

Bishop's Field was right in front of our house on Central Drive, and we enjoyed watching all the people gathering there, too. I think they were getting ready for the Battle of the Bogside, but it was all fun and games to us. It felt exciting – more for the good-looking men than anything else – and we'd be standing around all smiles and giggles. It was always our Susie and I and friends who went to watch the riots – it was great craic to us. We would pull ourselves up onto the windowsills of the old houses on William Street and from there we could watch everything. I fancied Charlie, my husband-to-be, back then.

Jed McClelland: I spent three days during the Battle of the Bogside up on the top of the flats throwing petrol bombs and stones. Then I was sixteen, seventeen that October. When you're that age you think this is all great, fantastic – rioting is fun. But it's also getting gassed and rubber bullets. I got hit twice by rubber bullets and I have the two rubber bullets. I stayed and lifted them and then ran. You're young and full of adrenaline so you don't feel anything at the time, until the following morning and then you wake up aching, and think, 'What the hell?'

Mary Nelis: I knew my husband was somewhere in the Bogside, he was very active during the Battle. My memories are of someone going around in a car in the middle of the night in Creggan, telling us the cathedral was being attacked. The Tenant's Association, including myself, we went around the doors asking for – wait for it – ammunition that they needed in the Bogside, which meant petrol bombs. We went around collecting flour, sugar and whatever ingredients were needed for Molotov cocktails and sending it down to the Bogside where the battle was raging.

Fionnbarra Ó Dochartaigh: Communications was very important so we could communicate with the people. Radio Free Derry was set up, first in a house in Wellington Street and then it moved into the multi-storey flats. My job was to get silk-screen posters, leaflets and bulletins out to the people keeping everyone informed of what was going on.

Geraldine McBride: In 1969, the rioting got worse and worse. Things were getting worse everywhere; people who had never rioted were rioting. That August, I remember my granny and two aunts coming to our house, and there must have been about twenty-six people in our house that night because the B Specials were up the back of Creggan and surrounding the whole place. It was the Battle of the Bogside and they were threatening to come in. I remember my granny had us all saying the Rosary. We slept on the floor that night. Those times were hard. We took them as normal, but you knew the Battle of the Bogside wasn't normal. Then I knew after it, this wasn't going to stop in a day or two.

Jed McClelland: My father and mother hated the whole community-resistance idea, but one night there was word sent out that the B-men were going to burn down the cathedral, so everybody was out. My father never took part in a riot in his life, and my next-door neighbour, who was about eighty by then, also came out to help. My father got a wheelbarrow out of the back yard and took it up to Laburnum Terrace, and we used sledgehammers to smash the pathways to make the bricks and stones needed to throw, and there was eighty-year-old Mr Arthur, a very middle-class Catholic, up helping my father do this. We were told they were going to attack the cathedral, so as the B-men approached our direction, we attacked them first with stones. They pulled out their guns and started shooting over our heads. Times like that it was scary when you realized that all we had was a stone.

Eamon Melaugh: There was always going to be something like that happen, it was consequential. There was not a millimetre of ground conceded by unionists, not a millimetre, and this could not go on. It was only a matter of time before the RUC couldn't handle the situation. I was afraid that a number of people would die unnecessarily.

Having narrowly escaped attack by a gang of loyalist-unionists in Derry's city centre, visiting British press photographer Clive Limpkin retreated to safety.

Clive Limpkin: I didn't look back until I was at the City Hotel ordering a treble anything from the porter, who stared transfixed at my trembling. 'If this gets really nasty,' I eventually asked him, 'where's the best place to cover the street fighting?' 'London,' he replied, and poured me another on the house.

*

On the second day of the stand-off – 13 August – Irish Taoiseach (prime minister) Jack Lynch responded to demands for an intervention with a TV broadcast to the nation.

In his address, Lynch criticized the Stormont government and the RUC, which, he said, was no longer an impartial police force.

Hopes were raised after he called for the UN to intervene and proclaimed that the Irish army would set up field hospitals along the border to help. This help never materialized.

From Irish Taoiseach Jack Lynch's televised address on 13 August 1969: It is with deep sadness that you, Irishmen and women of goodwill, and I have learned of the tragic events which have been taking place in Derry and elsewhere in the north in recent days. Irishmen in every part of this island have made known their concern at these events. This concern is heightened by the realization that the spirit of reform and intercommunal cooperation has given way to the forces of sectarianism and prejudice. All people of goodwill must feel saddened and disappointed at this backward turn in events and must be apprehensive for the future.

It is clear now that the present situation cannot be allowed to continue. It is evident, also, that the Stormont government is no longer in control of the situation. Indeed, the present situation is the inevitable outcome of the policies pursued for decades by successive Stormont governments. It is clear, also, that the Irish government can no longer stand by and see innocent people injured and perhaps worse. It is obvious that the RUC is no longer accepted as an impartial police force. Neither would the employment of British troops be acceptable, nor would they be likely to restore peaceful conditions – certainly not in the long term ... We have also asked the British government to see to it that police attacks on the people of Derry should cease immediately ...[5]

The Taoiseach's condemnation did little to change matters. On the third day of rioting between police and Derry protestors, the then-prime minister of Northern Ireland, James Chichester-Clark, requested the support of the British army.

*

In the early evening of that day, 14 August 1969, British soldiers were deployed in Derry and across the north. The army's arrival was met with caution by many within the north's Catholic population, most of whom welcomed the respite but were unsure of the army's role in solving the current impasse.

That night, police shot nine-year-old Patrick Rooney in West Belfast – the first child victim of the Troubles. Patrick was shot dead through the walls of his Divis Flats home as RUC sprayed heavy-calibre machine-gun fire across a built-up housing estate. In other Catholic areas of Belfast, whole streets were set alight and burned by mobs, leaving thousands homeless. An altar boy, Patrick had been serving at 8pm mass all that week.

Sheltering their six children in one room, both Alice and her husband Neely were grazed by the police machine-gun bullets penetrating the walls from outside.

Con Rooney, brother of nine-year-old Patrick Rooney, Belfast:
You could see the flames and hear the crackling and the sky was lit up orange, and you think it's the end of the world. I thought we were all going to be killed.[6]

Alice Rooney, mother of nine-year-old Patrick Rooney, Belfast:
Then Patrick slid down the wall. I thought he'd fainted but when I lifted him up there was blood coming from the back of his head. We laid him on the bed. Neely said, 'Get down and pray.'

Patrick's father campaigned for the rest of his life to have the policeman responsible brought to justice. In July 2020 – 51 years after Patrick's killing – the Public Prosecution Service in Northern Ireland informed the Rooney family of their decision not to prosecute the former RUC officer involved.

Neely Rooney, father of nine-year-old Patrick Rooney, Belfast:
They can't say to me he was in the wrong place at the wrong time. He was in his home when he was shot dead.[7]

*

In Derry that same evening, citizens of the city saw the first presence of British troops on the streets – a sight they would soon become accustomed to. The army deployment was initially said to be a short-term peace-keeping measure, and some troops had already been on standby in Derry since the weekend of 12 July that year, a full month before the recognized start of the Troubles that August.

As one government spokesperson put it, 'The troops ... would be back in barracks by the weekend.' The British army were to remain in the north for a further 37 years until 2007, making Operation Banner the longest continuous deployment in the British army's history.

Mary Nelis: I do recall hearing on the radio that [Irish Taoiseach] Jack Lynch wasn't going to stand idly by. The neighbours across the street had gone. My neighbour told me that the army was coming, and I said, 'Which army?' thinking she meant the army from Dublin, and I couldn't believe the British army were coming.

Jimmy Toye: On that last day, the police seemed to suddenly pull back over Little James Street. Nobody knew what was happening. We followed the RUC down William Street and that's when we saw the rolls of barbed-wire barricades appearing where Doherty's Bakery is now – blocking our way. This was the first day and the first place that the British army arrived in the north. Nobody really knew what to do.

Jed McClelland: When the army landed and put up their wire blockades, we were arguing with them, with the stewards separating us bad boys from the soldiers. The army were trying to be polite and keep control. Then me and Tommy Walsh went up around the Walls to see what was happening up there. We watched the B-men lined up, pointing their rifles at the Bogside, and then we saw the army coming along and grabbing the B-men and just shoving them off the Walls, and we were all shouting, 'Yes!' We thought, at that time, that the army were on our side. There were women coming out at first, making the soldiers tea and sandwiches and all that when they first arrived. It was a bit of relief for us, too. Then it all fell apart.

Jon McCourt: I think that was the first time I heard my mother swear when she realized the army were here. I think from that point my mother started going on marches; particularly after internment she started attending anti-internment marches. For me that was the start of the politicization of my mother – I didn't realize she already had a generation [of experience] on the history of protest and conflict in this country.

From the Derry Labour Party's 'Barricade Bulletin', dated 14 August 1969:

> We were pleased to see the troops. They have behaved well. For this reason, some people seem to think that the troops are here to protect us. They are not, any more than the RUC and the Specials. They are here to protect the interests of the British government in this part of the United Kingdom.[8]

Eamon Melaugh: After the Battle of the Bogside there was great tiredness, great tension. Then British troops were coming on the streets, but that was always inevitable. That had to come, and it was the final admission of the British establishment that they had a failed state on their hands. I was delighted to see them. I have no love for the British army, I'm a conscientious objector and against violence and wars, but I was glad to see it. It was the nail in the coffin of the unionist administration. The police weren't capable of controlling it and had lost all support.

Mary Nelis: I took my children down to chapel to confession and when I got there, Father McLaughlin was standing outside and a military lorry was coming around the roundabout with all these fellas with dirty, blackened faces, and everyone cheering them. I didn't understand what on earth this was about. I remember Father McLaughlin said to me, 'Mary, they think this is all over, but it's only beginning,' and he was right. It was only beginning, as we realized in the months and years that followed.

*

Unrest spiralled from 1969 onwards in communities across the north, fuelled by worsening loyalist and republican paramilitary violence, British intervention and inadequate political leadership. In December 1969, the IRA split into two distinct organizations, the Provisional IRA and the Official IRA, but were still collectively referred to as 'the IRA'. For the first few years after the Battle of the Bogside and the troops' arrival under Operation Banner, NICRA and the peaceful civil rights movement co-existed alongside violent paramilitary action from both republican and loyalist groups.

Within the relatively small city of Derry, many lives were lost in the few years before Bloody Sunday. In 1970, five people would die in the city and a further twenty-eight across the north.

*

On 27 June 1970, a young family in the area was devastated. Eight-year-old Bernadette McCool and her younger sister Carole (aged just three) were asleep upstairs in their Derry home when an explosion engulfed the house, killing them, their father Tommy and two other men. Veteran IRA volunteers Tommy McCool, Thomas Carlin and Joseph Coyle had been preparing a bomb in the McCools' kitchen when it exploded prematurely, causing a fireball. The girls' four-year-old sister Sinead had slept on the sofa and escaped outside with her mother and brother John.

*

With jobs scarce across the north, numerous men opted for service in the British army as a means of income. Creggan teenager William Best had joined the army for this reason and was serving abroad. His sister Rosemary remembers him as a 'gentle giant' who always looked out for them.

Rosemary Best, sister of Ranger William Best: My brother William was the eldest, my mother's first-born. William had joined the [British] army when he came of age and realized there were no jobs in Derry whatsoever. After training, he then went out to Limassol in Cyprus with the UN Peacekeeping Force. My mother and father supported him wholeheartedly. There was no mention or tension about it back then, there were many from the Bogside and Creggan and everywhere else joining the army at that time. He wasn't the only one. People had to earn.

William was stationed abroad and didn't come back to Derry. When on leave, he'd stay with an uncle in England rather than come home because things had started here, and it was just safer that way. My parents would leave us with my granny to go and see him in England instead. At the time, nobody realized just how long things would last, and how many lives would be lost. I'm sure most people thought it would be all over in a couple of months.

In 1971, 17 more people would lose their lives in and around the Free Derry area on the city's west bank. The first British soldier to die in Derry was killed on 1 March 1971. Eighteen-year-old Lance Corporal William Jolliffe from the Royal Military Police died after inhaling a fire extinguisher's chemicals following a petrol bomb attack on his jeep in Westland Street in the Bogside.

Derry woman Ruby McNaught remembers that her mother, Kathleen McLaughlin, risked her own safety to help the young dying soldier in 1971. Afterwards, the Derry Journal *described Kathleen as 'the saintly widow'.*

Ruby McNaught, daughter of Kathleen McLaughlin: He was unconscious by the time my mother and my brother-in-law Jim and others got him out of the jeep. He was lying on the ground, so my mother said, 'Please help me get him into my house, he's some mother's son. He's not going to die like a dog in the street.' The inquest said that he died of inhaling fumes from the fire extinguisher his jeep colleagues had used to put out the fire, so his death was indirectly related to the petrol bomb attack. That night my mother cared for that young man. She knew nothing about him, except that he was some mother's son, yet still she prayed with him and tried to give him comfort as he lay there dying.

This story of helping someone in distress took a cruel twist when my mother and family then suffered a vicious hate campaign, which lasted several months. She would wake every morning to find the front door painted with slogans. She bought a tin of paint and painted it over. The windows were broken regularly, but she just replaced them. She got death threats, and people shouted insults at her in the street and intimidated her. The hate campaign was vile. The Housing Trust offered to rehouse her, but no – she had such strength of character and refused to leave the area where she had been born and bred. After four months, the hate campaign stopped as quickly as it had started.[9]

*

In March 1971, the Stormont prime minister James Chichester-Clark was also replaced by the more robust authoritarian Brian Faulkner, heralding a change in politics ultimately viewed as detrimental to the north. Within and between communities and security forces, the situation continued to worsen.

On 8 July 1971, 28-year-old Seamus Cusack was shot dead in Derry following rioting – the first civilian to be killed by troops in Derry. Although shot in the thigh, Cusack bled out and died of his injuries en route to Letterkenny Hospital. Later the same night, 18-year-old Desmond Beattie from Rosemount in the city was shot dead during local reactions to Cusack's death. In justifying Beattie's shooting, the army accused the teenager of being in the process of throwing a nail bomb at soldiers when shot – despite civilian eyewitnesses insisting otherwise.

On 24 July 1971, eight-year-old Damien Harkin from the Bogside was killed by an army vehicle as he walked home from the Saturday matinee at the cinema with friends. The British army 'three-tonner' transport lorry mounted the pavement – crushing him against a wall.[10] His death is officially recorded as a traffic accident. Arriving at the scene, Damien's mother Lily recognized her son beneath a blanket when she glimpsed his little First Communion shoes.[11]

CHAPTER 5

Ordinary Lives

Gerard McKinney ran the Ritz Roller Skating Rink on
Derry's Strand Road.

*For communities across the north of Ireland, life went on amid
street protests, shootings, bombings, violent clashes and an ever-
increasing British military and police presence. For citizens and
families torn apart by the events of 30 January, the months and
years preceding 1972 would soon be a treasured memory. None
could have conceived of the events to come. The following voices
recall what life was like before Bloody Sunday.*

John Kelly, brother of 17-year-old Michael Kelly: Michael
was my younger brother, and we come from a large family of

nine girls and three boys. I was the oldest brother. Growing up together, Michael was a good guy, a quiet fellow and very respectful. We used to lie in the same bed together, Martin too, and all the girls in another room. When we were young, I used to wake up in the middle of the night with a warm back, because he'd have peed up my back![1]

Bridie McGuigan, widow of 41-year-old Bernard 'Barney' McGuigan: Barney was a family man and a great Derry man. He had a smile that could light up a room and had friends from all over – both Catholic and Protestant. He was always kind to everyone. He believed in education and never wanted his children to lift anything heavier than a pen. He was also a great provider. Every year without fail we had a holiday in Lisfannon. I don't know how we managed but the eight of us would pile into the Morris Minor and off to Lisfannon for our holidays. He also was a great friend to everyone. He used to make headstones for people who couldn't afford them for their graves, and wheel them down to the cemetery and fit them himself. Not for any money – just to help people.[2]

Liam Wray, brother of 22-year-old Jim Wray: We had a family of five brothers and four sisters. Jim was quite a tall, thin fella and, at six foot one, he was taller than the average Derry man at the time. While at St Joseph's Boys School, Jim became head prefect and also a school basketball player because of his height. Our parents were back and forth from England for work, which wasn't uncommon in those days. Jim was close to my mother and, when my father was in England, he became the father figure and authority in the house – a role he was quite happy with.[3]

Leo Young, brother of 17-year-old John Young: I was married and spent half the week driving lorries in England, so I saw very little of him around then. But he was a happy-go-lucky, inoffensive fella who made the best of what he had – he was full of ideas of what he was going to do.[4]

Frances Gillespie, wife of 32-year-old Daniel Gillespie: Daniel was hardworking, he was a milkman. He went to England to work for us to get married.[5]

Maura Young: John was three years younger than me, and we were very close. We had the same interests. He was funny too. Then he got his first job in Burton's Menswear, and he loved it. He was only fifteen when he started. He was always well dressed, until you looked at his shoes. My daddy used to tell him off about the state of his shoes, and he'd say, 'Don't you worry about it, Tommy. They're not looking at the shoes, they're looking at the face!' Ha-ha. He had everything going for him. He had such a life ahead of him.

He loved his hair. His hair was longish and had a natural curl in it, and would curl up, so I used to Sellotape it to help it sit down flat [before he went out]. It worked! But this one day, I'd sellotaped his hair and sideburns down, but in between times, a girl came to the front door, and he answered it, and the girl went away screaming with laughter. He came back in to me and said, 'What is her problem?' I just said, 'John – HAIR!' and he was mortified! Sellotape all over him. He chased me around the back garden.

Olive Bonner, sister of 17-year-old Hugh Gilmour: There was no badness in our Hugh. He left school and got a job straight away in the tyre factory in William Street and was an apprentice motor mechanic when he died. He went to the pictures every Friday night and always bought my mother home a quarter of dolly mixtures every Friday. Hugh never missed his work, but when the Troubles really began, he would come home from work, have his dinner, get a wash and head straight out to Rossville Street for a bit of rioting. Of course, there was nothing unusual in a wee bit of rioting back then, all the young ones were at it. It was just a bit of a laugh I suppose. A sign of the times.[6]

John Kelly: Our Michael picked up a virus when he was three years old, and he went into a coma for three weeks and he nearly died. Father McLaughlin even asked my mother to offer him up to God, but my mother refused to do so. I remember the morning very vividly when he became ill, and my mother had us in the bedroom all lined around the bed and she had us saying a decade of the rosary, praying for him. That sticks in my head.

Geraldine Doherty, niece of 17-year-old Gerald Donaghey: My uncle Gerald was only three weeks old when he was adopted by my grandparents. I remember my mum telling me that when they brought Gerald home to Wellington Street, they brought him round all the relations to show him off; they were so proud of him. He was brought up in a very loving home. My grandmother told him that if he ever wanted to find his birth parents then she would help. But Gerald said that he didn't, that he was happy that my granny and granddad were his real parents and always would be. My granddad was an ex-soldier, who had been a prisoner-of-war of the Japanese army in the Second World War, and my granny was a loving mother, who stayed at home practising her baking for her children, who all loved her cakes. My grandparents were very protective of my uncle Gerald and my mum. When they were younger, they were hardly let out to play with the other children but played mainly in their own back yard.[7]

Paul Doherty, son of 31-year-old Patrick Doherty: I can still call my father to mind. I still remember him coming home from work in DuPont. I remember him playing with us; it was always fun when he was there, and we enjoyed being with him. I feel sad that I only got to know him for a couple of years. Looking back, of course there's bitterness, but there's more regret and sadness that I never really got to know my father. It doesn't feel any easier, even with all the years that have passed.[8]

Kevin McDaid, brother of 20-year-old Michael McDaid: I was seventeen when Michael died. We went to school together and at a young age, we would sell vegetables together. As we got older, we didn't grow apart but we did our own thing and got on great. He eventually ended up getting a car and would take me and my mother and father to Buncrana or Galway; they were the first holidays we ever took.[9]

Liam Wray: Jim was very happy person and full of love and most of the money he earned was put back into the house apart from the odd Saturday night spent in the Castle Bar. He was a big brother you could depend on. He would have been socialist in his view. Non-sectarian, he had two girlfriends I know of – both were Protestant – and after that he fell in love with a Jewish girl, Miriam, and they became engaged. He brought her home the Christmas before he was murdered to meet the family and they both had to seek special dispensation to marry.

Maura Young: John was always working, but we used to go down and watch the riots. It was awful when the CS gas was in the air. Doctor McClean always said that we would see the effects of CS gas by the third or fourth generation, because nobody knew what was in that gas. He always said that: that we would see the effects eventually.

The riots could be funny sometimes, but it could also be scary. Once, the bin-lids were all banging to say the army was coming into Creggan, so everybody was out. Me and John went over to see, when two men passed us with rifles. I said, 'Let's go,' and we ran back to the house. We wanted a bit of fun, but we didn't want anything like that, we weren't going down that road.

Jimmy Duddy, nephew of 59-year-old John Johnston: Johnny was my uncle. My mother was in and out of hospital a lot for all our young lives and died young at forty-nine, so we would have spent a lot of time down at Johnny's house in the Bogside in their big house. We spent weeks, sometimes months there, when my mother was in hospital. Johnny and Margaret had no children themselves, so we were like a family to them. He was very good to us. We were the closest thing he had to children. Johnny was a jolly man, he always reminded me of Tommy Cooper the comedian. He was much more than an uncle. I have a tape where we can hear him and my mother and father talking and joking. I remember him always singing to our aunt, songs like 'You Are My Sunshine'.[10]

John Kelly: Michael reared pigeons and my mother helped him build a pigeon loft out the back. He'd release them at work and my mother would have to sit and wait for them coming back! She was into it with him. He had a girlfriend and was going steady at the time also. This was more or less his life – he wasn't political in any way whatsoever. He wasn't interested in that. I remember rioting down at Essex factory, and me and him went down to get a look. Of course, they fired the CS gas, and it was the first time I'd ever experienced CS gas and I remember us running back up to the house choking. He had absolutely no experience of riots or anything like that.

Liam Wray: I don't have that many memories of Jim in my childhood, but I remember I was playing cricket with a few mates on the Derry Walls and three Teddy boys came along and took our ball. Our Jim intervened, and there was a scuffle. Once the fight was over, they went on their way. I was so proud of him for defending us at that time.

Andy Nolan, a childhood friend of Jackie Duddy: Me and Jackie grew up together. I can't remember NOT having a friend called Jackie Duddy. We were both born in the same year, 1954. Jackie was born in July and me in August, so I suppose he was like a big brother to me as my own was three years older. I was a bit of a wimp. If anyone picked on me, Jackie would always stand up for me and had done for as long as I can remember. I couldn't fight my way out a paper bag, and if anyone picked on me in the street, then Jackie would sort them. I remember once someone hit me for no reason at all. A few weeks later Jackie stopped him and warned him not to pick on me again. He never picked on me again.[11]

Susie Campbell, sister of 17-year-old Jackie Duddy: Our Jackie was going steady with a girl from the Waterside. He wasn't allowed to call to her door for her because she wasn't allowed to go out with boys, so I would call in for her instead like she was my friend. Then Jackie would be waiting for us around the corner.[12]

Geraldine Doherty: My uncle Gerald had ten wonderful happy years with his family until December 1965 when my grand-dad died, and then my granny just four weeks later in January 1966. Gerald was only ten then, and my mum only nineteen, when they lost both their parents in the space of a few weeks. Some members of the wider family thought Gerald should be put back into care, but my mum was determined that she would raise Gerald herself, and she did. Even though she was only nine years older than him, she took on a mother's role and brought him up herself.

Maura Young: Because he was always working, John would be there if there were ever riots on a Sunday. To some of those young fellas rioting, it was a game, throwing stones at a big Saracen truck [armoured personnel carrier]. It was never a continuous thing. You could have timed the riots on a Saturday evening like clockwork, and they stopped for the factory girls passing. They stopped for their tea too! You didn't go down to the riots between six and seven because there would be nobody there – they'd all be away home for their tea, and they'd start up again at 7.30pm!

Billy McVeigh: My friends and I were often down in Rossville Street rioting. I was only about fifteen or sixteen then. We were up so close to the army during the riots we were getting hit by the stones being thrown behind us! You'd hear people at the front shouting, 'No throwing from the back!' because it was us getting hit on the back of the head instead. It could be so funny some-times. People often ask me what it was like in those days, and I'd say, well, if you weren't shot, and you weren't arrested or caught, then the craic was ninety, which in Derry means great fun!

Geraldine McBride: You're still living the teenage life, going to the dances and doing this and that – but it was always in the background. Believe it or not, when we worked in the factory the riots didn't start until we went into work past them. Then, when we went out at lunchtime, they stopped and started again! And that was both the police and the rioters – they worked around our factory bell! I suppose they knew it was their sisters and their mothers and the women who kept things going.

Eileen Fox: My daddy warned us to stay well away, but we paid no heed. We still went down because everybody else was going, too. My daddy would grill us when we came in. 'You weren't down that town, were you?' And we would deny everything, but he knew by our faces that we were lying. He warned us, 'It might be a joke to you now, but it's going to get really bad. It's going to turn to guns.' He always said that to us, you know: 'It's going to turn to guns.' I suppose he was trying to make us understand the seriousness of the situation. And he was right.

CHAPTER 6

Imprisonment Without Trial, 1971

Protestor Billy McVeigh faces an armoured vehicle
during internment in 1971.

*Operation Demetrius – or internment – was launched by
the British army in the early hours of 9 August 1971, aimed
at quelling dissent in nationalist, predominantly Catholic
communities. The crackdown order was officially given by
Northern Ireland's Stormont government and was backed
by the British government, giving the green light for civilian
internees to be jailed indefinitely without evidence, charge or
a trial. The subsequent raids caused widespread riots.*

*Historically, internment has been used as a means of confining
people, often in large groups, with its dictionary definition*

elaborating: 'especially of enemy citizens in wartime or of terrorism suspects'.[1] First used as far back as the mid-1800s, internment has been utilized in its most severe form by Nazis, by Pinochet's regime in Chile and in the Soviet Gulag system. The British have used internment at various points in history, including in South Africa during the Second Boer War (1899–1902) and during Kenya's Mau Mau uprising (1952–60) before instigating it in Northern Ireland in 1971.

Prisoners are held either in prisons or specific internment camps (known also as concentration camps), the defining characteristics of which were that they generally operated outside the rule of law, often with harsh treatment of prisoners. The fact that the British government considered internment appropriate in a Northern Ireland context is indicative of how the state regarded and viewed citizens in the north's nationalist communities – as though they were enemies.

In this 1971 purge, the army arrested 342 men in towns and cities across the north, the majority of whom had no links with activism. Spurious claims of republican activity or IRA membership were justification enough. At the time, authorities insisted there was no sectarian bias to the internment operation. However, a Ministry of Defence document since unearthed by Pat Finucane Centre researchers shows that it wasn't until late 1972 that a specific 'arrest policy for Protestants' appeared in British government discussions.[2]

With no evidence against them, two-thirds of those arrested were released within days, and although some internees remained, the first wave of internment was regarded as somewhat of a failure in military terms. The remaining internees were held indefinitely at either the Long Kesh camp in Co. Down, later known as 'The Maze', or at Magilligan army camp in Co. Derry. As news of the prisoners' ill-treatment in army custody became widely known, so too did public indignation. NICRA refocused attention on demands for an end to internment, planning peaceful demos and calling for urgent action from authorities. In Derry, barricades were built, and Free Derry was reinstated – this time the no-go area would last 11 months and experience much more violence.

Hugh McMonagle: Internment came in and we took to the streets along with the main branch [NICRA] protesting. They started raiding houses, army raids and police raids, so we got ourselves organized and met with the local police commander, Inspector Lagan. We also started having meetings with the army and told them it was a disgrace the way they were going into homes early in the morning for no reason, coming away with nothing. Inciting the young people into full-scale riots.

We then learned that the British army allowed a member of NICRA to accompany them during raids, so people's homes weren't getting destroyed and any misbehaviour of the troops could be reported. If someone was lifted at 3am, you would go to the raid. You would then accompany them if you could. If they were underage, you'd insist on getting a responsible adult in there for any questioning in case they were harassed for information. Everywhere we went, we were all classed as suspicious. You were in a nationalist area, so at that time, no matter who or where you were, you were a potential IRA man – full-stop. You were a Provo-in-disguise. That's the feeling we got and that feeling never changed.

Maura Young: My cousin married a soldier, and when they got married in Pennyburn Chapel, of course, there were soldiers at the wedding. They'd heard about the rioting in Derry. They'd been stationed in Belfast so were curious what it was like here, so I took them over to William Street to watch the rioting and from there on up the town. We turned on our heel, crossed the Guildhall Square and up Shipquay Street, and there was everyone out shopping – totally normal. The soldiers said, 'I don't believe this.' Everyone going about their daily business with riots going on around the corner. It was normal to us.

Ivan Cooper: My [Protestant] family were persecuted because of what I was doing, because of what I felt and what I believed in. I remember my mother going to vote for me in the election of 1969 and people wanted to spit on her. They were ready to spit on her – in the tiny village of Killaloo, of all places! They also refused my money in the church collections. That went on for years. What can I do about it? Nothing. My family thought I was going to be shot, my daddy had died, and the centre of my constituency is Dungiven, and Dungiven had a reputation for being very nationalist. My family were persecuted, very much so. My mother thought I was going to be shot. But they never tried to dissuade me, they were great supporters of me. They had faith in me and took the stick.

Hugh McMonagle: We stopped the young lads from rioting in the estate. People's tyres were getting punctured driving out to work in the morning because of bottles smashed on the roads, so we decided they weren't rioting in the estate any more. We explained that if the army comes in – rather than stoning them, they should do a peaceful protest and walk silently alongside the army instead, and that we would walk beside them if they did.

It worked, too, because once, when I was visiting my brother in Rosemount beside the army barracks – when I was there, a soldier asked me who I was. Now, I think this was brilliant and it proves my point: the soldier said, 'Shantallow, eh' and said, 'People of Shantallow are evil.' I said, 'How dare you.' He claimed that when he went down through the Bog or Creggan, 'They are either shooting at us or throwing stones or hitting us with bottles.' 'You Shantallow ones don't even look at us or speak to us,' he said, 'You just walk around without speaking to us, you just stare at us, you's are evil.'

I took a fit of laughing and told him that he had just proved my point that silent protest was just as mentally damaging as a full-scale riot. It was dignified and it showed the responsibility of the young people in the area at the time.

Bishop Edward Daly: There were days you went back home, and you were soaked in sweat and reeking of CS gas, and you thought to yourself, am I wasting my time here? But I felt it was my duty to be there and serve the needs of people in the community.

Andy Nolan: When the Troubles started, my mother always warned us not to go down the town in case we got into bother or hurt. Of course, we didn't listen and went down to see the riots. We never took part and were spectators like most people.

After the introduction of internment, there would nearly always be a riot every Saturday. Me and Jackie used to go downtown, and we would go to the pictures after looking around the record shops, if there was anything good on. We were great fans of spaghetti westerns and anything to do with Clint Eastwood or Charles Bronson. We also liked horror movies. I remember one Saturday we spotted a spaghetti western was on in the Palace that we'd never heard of before. It was directed by Sergio Leone and the music was by Ennio Morricone – what more could you ask for! We sat through two showings of that and then went on to the Rialto to see a Dracula movie that night.

Billy McVeigh: My granny lived in Glenfada and I had to pass her house on the way to the riots. We were always down there annoying the army. I knew my granny always sat at her window and would have seen me, so I'd pull my coat up, hiding my face passing hers so she wouldn't see me! There I am, fighting a war – and I'm afraid of my granny!

*

An IRA sniper shot dead 22-year-old Royal Horse Artillery Bombardier Paul Challenor from Leicester, England, on 10 August as he was on duty at Bligh's Lane army post. A few days later, on 13 August 1971, a 31-year-old Derry father-of-two, Hugh Herron, was shot dead by a British soldier stationed at an observation post just outside the city walls.[3]

Meanwhile, news of the torture of some internees fuelled existing resentment and resistance. Several men from the north had been singled out for serious interrogation and would later become known as the 'Hooded Men', subjected to the 'Five Techniques' of torture while in army custody in contravention of Human Rights laws. An Amnesty International report later examined the internment processes used in Northern Ireland, and in particular, the case of the Hooded Men, concluding:

'Many prisoners felt they were on the brink of insanity – one alleges he prayed for death, another that he tried to kill himself by banging his head against some metal piping in the room.'[4]

*

That same summer, Derry teenager Gerald Donaghey would be arrested and jailed for riotous behaviour. At the time, even throwing a stone carried an automatic six months' sentence.

Geraldine Doherty: The trouble started up in Derry when Gerald was just in his early teens, and like many boys his age he got caught up in it. He was arrested in 1971 and charged with being involved in the rioting that was going on all around him at the time. Gerald was sentenced to six months in prison, just like anyone who faced a rioting charge at that time. He dodged the police and army for a short time, but he wanted to come back home and so gave himself up so he could just do his time and get back home to his family.

In West Belfast, the August 1971 internment raids resulted in the death of 11 unarmed civilians in an incident since known as the Ballymurphy massacre. The case bears striking similarities to what happened on Bloody Sunday just months later.

CHAPTER 7

Murder in Ballymurphy

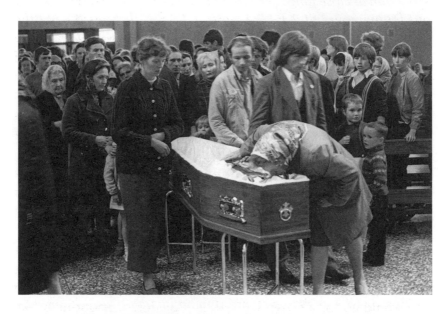

Mourners pay respect during the Requiem Mass of
Father Hugh Mullan in Ballymurphy, August 1971.

*The Ballymurphy massacre occurred six months before Bloody
Sunday and is crucial in understanding the mindset of the British
military and a culture of violence against Irish nationalists that
was seemingly tolerated and condoned at that time.*

*As Operation Demetrius internment raids took place across
the north, over six hundred British soldiers – including elite-
trained battalions of the Parachute Regiment – were deployed
onto the streets of the nationalist Ballymurphy area of West
Belfast to raid homes and round up men they suspected of being
republican or IRA-linked. Between 9 and 11 August, scores of
innocent civilians were targeted and beaten as they were dragged
from their homes without reason.*

Over this three-day period, British paratroopers shot dead 10 unarmed civilians in the Ballymurphy area, including a parish priest, Fr Hugh Mullan, and mother-of-eight, Joan Connolly, who was shot in the face and left to die without medical aid. An 11th man dropped dead of a heart attack when soldiers pretended to shoot him at close range. The first two days' shootings were carried out by members of 2 PARA, with 1 PARA responsible for the third day, 11 August. The British army immediately and publicly labelled Ballymurphy as an IRA gun battle, its victims and injured named as terrorists within hours. No investigations were carried out and no member of the British army was held to account.

The parallels to Bloody Sunday are many and disturbing – yet few outside the north know of this tragedy. It's widely believed that some of the soldiers involved in Ballymurphy went on to Derry. It's also believed that, had action been taken to discipline them and withdraw the entire Parachute Regiment after Ballymurphy in August 1971, Bloody Sunday might never have happened.

Kevin Phillips, brother of 19-year-old Noel Phillips, shot dead in 1971 in Ballymurphy: Noel was doing what kids do, he was doing what anyone would have done at that age: if you heard trouble you would go for a nosy; that's all he was doing. Shooting broke out and everybody ran for their lives. Noel ran down into the field in front of the Henry Taggart army base; he was shot and dropped to the ground. He was in the wrong place at the wrong time.[1]

Briege Voyle, daughter of 44-year-old Joan Connolly, shot dead in 1971 in Ballymurphy: The being afraid started that night when my mother never came home. My daddy was very scared, and my sister Denise was petrified. She didn't feel safe in the house because Mammy wasn't there. Daddy put mattresses on the floor, and we all slept on the floor that night.[2]

Kevin Phillips: The next day my sister went over to the Henry Taggart army base to see if our Noel was there, and they started shouting abuse at her and told her to check the morgue. My brother Robert and brother-in-law went to Lagan Bank Morgue, where we found out about Noel and identified his body. They came back in a terrible state; nothing was ever the same from that point. Nobody came to tell us Noel was dead; we had to find out for ourselves.

Alice Harper, daughter of Danny Teggart, shot dead in 1971 in Ballymurphy: I then went to the Henry Taggart army post for the first time, around 11am. I asked, 'Did you arrest my father?' I was just asking different questions and they just said, no we hadn't time for arrests, we only had time for killing, and that was their words. I was shocked and started to walk away. That's when the soldiers started singing that song chorus at me: 'Where's your papa gone, where's your papa gone?' I returned to Mummy's house, but there still wasn't any word. I went to the army posts two more times that day; we started hearing stories of local people being shot.[3]

John Teggart, son of Danny Teggart, shot dead in 1971 in Ballymurphy: My daddy was a good, loving, family man. He was labelled a terrorist and a gunman. That was a stigma that the family had to endure. This was a massacre on the same scale as Bloody Sunday, although it was forgotten. The paras just went berserk. Father Mullan had telephoned the army base to tell them he was going out to help those wounded in Ballymurphy. He came out waving a piece of cloth, walking towards a field where one of the men shot by the paras lay dying. Father Mullan was shot after anointing Bobby Clarke. He was returning to his house, waving a white hankie, when they shot him.[4]

Briege Voyle: When my daddy came back, he was literally carried in; he was a broken man because it was my mammy in the morgue. We were all screaming and crying, and everybody was yelling, and neighbours started coming in. We sent for the doctor. He gave the older ones something to calm them down.

John Teggart: If the authorities had carried out a proper inquiry of what happened in Ballymurphy six months earlier, instead of calling in the military police to investigate, the paras would never have been deployed in Derry and all those people up there would not have lost their lives.

During the 2019 inquests into the 1971 Ballymurphy massacre in West Belfast, it emerged that Captain Michael Jackson – a rising star in the army – had also been the army's press officer six months earlier in Ballymurphy. Jackson himself described his role within the British army in 1972 as 'a hybrid of community relations and press officer'.

When questioned by barrister Michael Mansfield QC at the 2019 Ballymurphy Inquests about any potential military cover-up, Jackson – now General Sir – reiterated the claim that Ballymurphy had been an IRA gun battle involving up to twenty gunmen attacking troops.

In May 2021, over half a century since the shootings took place, the Coroner found that the ten victims of the Ballymurphy massacre were 'all entirely innocent of any wrongdoing'.

Nine out of the ten were shot by the British army, with no evidence to conclude on the tenth person. As happened following the publication of the Saville Report, *their loved ones spoke afterwards of their joy and relief that their loved ones' names were cleared. They also criticized authorities for not telling the truth years ago, and complained that they should never have had to campaign to prove their innocence.*

'We always knew the truth, now someone's actually acknowledged it,' John Laverty's sister Carmel Quinn told the Irish Times.

Mary Kate Quinn, niece of John Laverty, shot dead in 1971 in Ballymurphy: It's one thing our families giving our side and insisting that these people were not gunmen – but whenever the official record is saying it, it's vindication.[5]

*

The British army attempted to break Free Derry's barricaded no-go area on 18 August 1971, sending in over one thousand three hundred soldiers, flanked by helicopters and armoured vehicles. The army retreated within hours. Among the many shooting incidents occurring that day, 19-year-old local man Eamonn Lafferty was shot dead during a gun battle with troops – the first active Provisional IRA volunteer killed in the city. Riots and unrest continued all over the region. On 2 September 1971, Major Robin Nigel Alers-Hankey of the British army's Royal Green Jackets was shot and wounded in the Bogside, dying months later of his injuries.[6]

A Derry schoolgirl would be the conflict's next victim. On 6 September 1971, 14-year-old Annette McGavigan was caught in crossfire and shot dead by British soldiers near her home in the Bogside. Shot in the head, Annette died instantly. She was still wearing her school uniform. The army claimed they had targeted a gunman. Today, a Bogside street mural entitled 'The Death of Innocence' commemorates the schoolgirl's death – the one hundredth civilian to die in the troubles.

Martin McGavigan, brother of 14-year-old Annette McGavigan, shot dead by the army: The army opened fire into the crowd, and she was shot in the back of the head. I remember running over the street crying. It was like a dream, a nightmare – it wasn't happening. I was only eleven, but that will stay with me the rest of my life. It shattered us as a family. It destroyed my mother.[7]

*

Just days later, a speeding armoured army personnel carrier knocked down and killed three-year-old Gary Gormley in the city. The toddler wasn't officially recognized as a victim of the Troubles, but was classified as a road traffic accident – one of several such cases disregarded by authorities.

On 14 September, Sergeant Martin Carroll was killed by an IRA sniper as he prepared to fire CS gas into a crowd of rioters at the Bligh's Lane army post in Derry. The Royal Artillery sergeant was married with a pregnant wife at the time of his death. Just hours later, in the early hours of 15 September, 41-year-old local man William McGreanery was shot dead by a British soldier as he walked near the same army post. The British army claimed he was a gunman – a claim that dogged the family for decades until 2011, when the Chief of the General Staff of the Ministry of Defence wrote to the McGreanery family officially acknowledging William's innocence.

On 27 September that year, father-of-five Private Roger Wilkins of the 1st Battalion Royal Anglican Regiment was shot dead by a sniper in Derry. Less than a week later, on 3 October, a five-year-old girl was shot and seriously wounded in Derry as the car she and her mother were in was fired upon by the British army, who claimed that a bomb had been thrown from the vehicle.[8]

*

Aside from the growing conflict, families got on with life as normal. In the autumn of 1971, Derry teenager Kevin McElhinney travelled to England to visit his elder brother living there. It was to be their last meeting.

Cahil McElhinney, brother of 17-year-old Kevin McElhinney: The last time I saw Kev, in the September before his death, he was sitting on a bus to Derry after spending a week or so with Avril and I in our Erdington flat in Birmingham. He'd arrived on the ferry before dawn, and he'd sat on our doorstep in pouring rain because he didn't want to disturb us. He didn't smoke or drink, but spent his time going to the Birmingham cinemas. As his bus revved-up to leave Digbeth, I told him to stay safe. He gave me the thumbs-up and said, 'Stones are one thing, but I'll never try to outrun bullets.' I took that to mean he wouldn't get involved in anything dangerous.[9]

Andy Nolan: Jackie and I used to babysit on Saturday nights for his sister, Bernie, if she and Liam wanted to go out. So that was our normal routine most weekends. In the weeks leading up to the march, everything was normal. Jackie was working and I was still at school, supposedly studying for my A Levels, though

I could always be talked out of studying if Jackie called round and mentioned that there was a good picture on somewhere.

In Derry, Free Derry's no-go area remained beyond the reach of the British army, who largely stayed on its periphery with the exception of continuing house raids. According to an October 1971 report by the army's Chief of the General Staff, General Sir Michael Carver, entitled 'Northern Ireland – An Appreciation of the Security Situation', the army had considered three options on the situation.[10]

From 'Northern Ireland – An Appreciation of the Security Situation', by General Sir Michael Carver, Chief of General Staff, dated 4 October 1971:

Course 1. Continuing as we are, controlling the rest of Derry and raiding the [Creggan and Bogside] area for gunmen as our intelligence allows us. We would hope, though without great confidence, that progress in the political field would produce a gradual return to normality.

Course 2. Show our ability to go into the area when we want by establishing regular patrol patterns. This will achieve little except to please the Protestants. It is a practical course, but it will not achieve the removal of the obstructions and certainly will not re-establish law and order throughout the areas. But it could be done with our present force levels.

Course 3. To occupy and dominate the areas, take down the barricades, and, we hope, eventually persuade the RUC to play their full part. This is a practical military operation

although it will involve casualties and, most
important, stir up Catholic opposition as
much as it will satisfy the Protestants. It is
difficult to estimate how great the political
reaction would be. This must be a political
and not a military decision. However, there is
one significant military factor. We could only
occupy and dominate these areas by an increase
in our force levels by three battalions.

As well as considering these courses of action, this army report
also clearly shows the British military's recognition that any
action to quell nationalist no-go areas would appease and 'satisfy'
many within the Protestant populace of the time. However, the
British army decided to remain with 'Course 1', with Derry's
no-go areas of Creggan and the Bogside described elsewhere in
Carver's 1971 report as an area where '200 extremists and a
number of hardcore hooligans operated unchecked'.

*

On 16 October, an IRA sniper shot dead a 24-year-old British
soldier, Rifleman Joseph Hill of the Royal Green Jackets, as his
unit battled civilian rioters near the Bogside. On 27 October,
two more British soldiers – Lance Bombardier David Tilbury
and Gunner Angus Stevens – were killed when the IRA threw a
bomb from nearby Brooke Park into the Rosemount Barracks
army observation post.[11] Such incidents and shootings became a
regular occurrence throughout the north also, with many losing
their lives elsewhere as 1971 progressed.

A Derry mother-of-six was shot dead by British soldiers on
the evening of 6 November 1971 during army house raids in
Derry's Creggan estate. Kathleen Thompson, then 47 years old,
was killed while in her own back garden in Kildrum Gardens,
Creggan. Neighbours at the time claimed Mrs Thompson had
been banging a metal bin-lid on the ground to alert neighbours
of a nearby army raid when she was shot dead. Her body was

discovered by her husband and their 12-year-old daughter, Minty.

Minty Thompson, daughter of 47-year-old Kathleen Thompson: I did hear the bin-lids going, but I wasn't too sure as a child whether she was doing it, or she had told someone else to, but I think she automatically went out to rattle a bin-lid because that's what people did in those times in order for neighbours to come out and help each other.

A while went by and then my father asked if I'd seen my mother and I said no. My grandmother lived with us, and the gas was thick in the air and she had a bad chest and couldn't breathe, so obviously he was going into panic. I went to ask the neighbours who were raided, but they hadn't seen her.

At that stage, we got on the wall outside, and my father looked over the fence, and she was lying in the back garden. After that, it was pandemonium. We were taken inside, out of the way. I remember people brought her body into the kitchen and my father was trying to gather us up, to get us out of the house, and I remember a man saying, 'She's dead.'

I remember the loudspeaker going around all night, telling people that a woman had been shot. But I was still thinking it wasn't true. The next morning, they had to tell us that she had been shot and she was dead. I asked why, but nobody had any answers for us.[12]

*

Violence soared across the city following the death of Kathleen Thompson, including several gun attacks against the army. On Tuesday 9 November 1971, the IRA shot dead a 23-year-old Lance Corporal, Ian Curtis, of the British army's Royal Anglican Regiment, as he patrolled near the River Foyle.

A group calling themselves the Bogside Vigilante Association issued a call in the Derry Journal *of 12 November 1971 for more people to volunteer to help in Derry, 'to protect their families and homes in the event of an influx of British troops into the area'. On 17 November, a 14-year-old schoolboy was shot and wounded by the British army as locals dismantled a barricade in the city.*

As the IRA's campaign continued, almost twenty bombs were detonated in Derry's city centre between November and December 1971, injuring 14 people from both sides of the community. Throughout early December 1971, the British army decided that a more robust approach was needed, and scores of army raids took place throughout Creggan and Bogside housing estates, with 500-strong troops involved in each raid and arrest operation. Riots, attacks and counter-attacks continued.

According to the book Free Derry: Protest and Resistance, *the Official IRA in Derry carried out an unusual operation on 27 December 1971 when they raided local Housing Executive offices and destroyed hundreds of files. Other files said to contain details of families owing rent in the area were symbolically set alight later that night in Creggan in front of assembled press in support of an ongoing rent and rates strike of the time.*

Two days later, on 29 December, Gunner Richard Ham, Royal Artillery, was shot dead by the IRA while on patrol in Derry.[13]

*

As New Year approached, Mary Donaghey was looking forward to welcoming her teenage brother Gerald home from prison after he had served his six months for riotous assembly. Gerald was released on 31 December 1971. When leaving prison, he went straight to his girlfriend's house before heading home to his sister, Mary.

Mary Donaghey, sister and legal guardian of 17-year-old Gerald Donaghey: He wrote to me when he was coming out and told me not to go meet him, that he was going on to see his girl and just to send up his clothes. So, I went and bought him a new outfit of jeans and jacket and things, and he came on home later that night and brought the girl with him. We were really glad to see him out.[14]

69

Geraldine Doherty: My mum always kept the last letter he sent from prison, at the beginning of December 1971. In it he asks my mum about her thoughts on having a new baby to keep my brother company, so he was asking about me before I was even born! He talks about his girlfriend Hester and how he wants to go straight to see her when he gets out. And he asks my mum to go and get him a Wrangler jacket and a pair of Wrangler jeans for when he gets out – he was very specific about the brand. My mum got him the jeans and jacket he asked for, and he was wearing them on Bloody Sunday.[15]

Mary Donaghey: Gerald would have stayed in with the youngster if we wanted to go out. The last night that happened was whenever I went out that New Year's Eve. After that, I would never go out on a New Year's Eve since.

That New Year's Eve in 1971 was marked by two bombs and widespread unrest in Derry. Few realized the year to come would be the bloodiest yet.

CHAPTER 8

'Measures to Control Marches'[1]

A 1971 anti-internment protest in Brandywell, Derry.

By January 1972, support for the peaceful civil rights movement
continued to grow as more and more joined its numbers demanding
an end to inequality. This campaign for peaceful, meaningful
reform co-existed alongside the north's worsening violence.

The insurrection of no-go areas in Derry and elsewhere continued
to infuriate both the British and Stormont governments.

In the first weeks of 1972, the Provisional IRA (PIRA)
detonated two bombs in Derry, and two British soldiers were
shot and injured in separate incidents in the city. Civil rights
activists were undeterred, and plans were underway to defy the

government's ban on marching with another demonstration arranged for Saturday 22 January. This time, demonstrators would march across Magilligan beach a few miles from Derry, where an internment camp was located.

*

Extract from minutes of meeting of the Official Committee on Northern Ireland on 5 January 1972:

> In Londonderry, the situation was more serious than in Belfast. The Defence Secretary had agreed that the Bogside and Creggan areas should only be entered by troops on specific information and for a minimum of routine patrolling … If continued attrition achieved a lull in terrorist activity, the need for a political initiative would become more urgent. At that point, the assessment of the risk of a Protestant backlash – whose potential we could not measure accurately at present – would be crucial. The security forces would be in serious difficulty in fighting two fronts.[2]

These Committee minutes again indicate an awareness by the British state and military of a potential Protestant 'backlash' with regards to their operations in Northern Ireland – with the British military realizing the logistical difficulty of fighting 'two fronts' at once.

On the same day, 5 January 1972, the British army produced a paper entitled, 'Measures to Control Marches',[3] for submission to the Joint Security Council. Later explored during the Bloody Sunday Inquiry, the identity of its author is not known.

'MEASURES TO CONTROL MARCHES' (for consideration by JSC)

Extension of the Ban

1. The current ban on marching expires on 8 Feb 72 and an early decision is required on whether it should be lifted, modified or extended.

2. Although the continuance of the ban has undoubted drawbacks, including problems of enforcement, the consequences of lifting or modifying it are far more serious. Such a move, resulting in a plethora of marches, would place an intolerable burden on the security forces, involving endless security commitments, probable escalation of violence, and a diversion of effort from the main task of defeating the IRA. Enforcement problems are not eliminated by lifting the ban since some types of march would in any case need to be ruled out.

3. It is proposed therefore that the ban should be extended for a period of one year until 8 Feb 73. An early announcement should be made to this effect, thus giving the maximum notice to march organisers and the general public and at the same time demonstrating the Government's firmness on this issue. The subsequent lifting of the ban could of course be considered should the situation improve.

Modification of Existing Procedures

4. On the assumption that the extension of the ban is authorised, some of the existing enforcement procedures require strengthening and this involves departure from previous

73

practice. Certain consequences which follow must also be recognised. These are set out below:

a. The security forces will normally exercise the option of closing a march route entirely and will not normally permit marchers to continue on the pavements as has been done recently.

b. On-the-spot arrests of ringleaders, including perhaps well-known citizens, and other marchers may be made; this would normally be done by the RUC under the Public Order Act, but the Army would participate if any violence were offered.

c. The route-closing policy described above may result, particularly in the case of multiple converging marches, in the closing of all routes leading to the place of assembly, thus in effect cordoning it off and preventing the assembly from taking place at all.

5. Although a certain degree of discretion must be retained by the Commander on the spot, particularly where women and children are to the fore, these measures indicate a generally firmer line to be adopted by the security forces. As a consequence, violence may be precipitated in an otherwise non-violent situation. For example, the complete closure of a route or on-the-spot arrests may cause rioting, in which case the normal anti-riot measures would be required.

6. A public announcement should be made to the effect that all those marching in defiance of the ban are liable to immediate arrest and subsequent prosecution. Steps should also be taken to ensure swift prosecution

of offenders, without automatic reference to the Attorney General which is the current practice.

7. It is proposed that the current RUC Force Order on this subject should be amended to include the change of emphasis in control measures and define the military powers of arrest. It should be reissued as a joint RUC/Army instruction.

Recommendations

8. The Committee is invited to agree:
   a. That the ban on marches should continue until 8 Feb 73 with the understanding that it might be lifted earlier if conditions greatly improve.
   b. To accept the firmer measures proposed in this paper and acknowledge the possible consequences.
   c. To make an early announcement of the continuance of the ban and the intention to adopt firmer measures including the liability of all those defying the ban to arrest and prosecution

When the Joint Security Council (JSC) then met on 6 January 1972 following reports of other illegal marches, a decision was taken to prosecute those involved as a matter of urgency.[4] These prosecutions could potentially include two Westminster MPs, Bernadette Devlin – at the time the youngest female ever elected to parliament – and Frank McManus. According to Lord Saville's 2010 report, this decision was taken subject to the directions of the Attorney-General, and in the full knowledge that such a charge would lead to a mandatory six months' prison sentence – even for the two MPs.

From British prime minister Edward Heath's private secretary, Peter Gregson, to Graham Angel in the Home Office, dated 7 January 1972:

> The Prime Minister has noted … that steps are to be taken to ensure that prosecutions are brought against the identified ring leaders of the recent anti-internment marches. The Prime Minister considers it very important that this should be done and be seen to be done as speedily as possible. He would be grateful for a report on progress.[5]

GENERAL FORD'S MEMO

Following a visit to Derry, General Robert Ford produced a controversial memorandum in January 1972, in which he detailed the army's view of the situation and how best to tackle those deemed 'Derry Young Hooligans'. He noted, 'I am coming to the conclusion that the minimum force necessary to achieve a restoration of law and order is to shoot selected ring leaders amongst the DYH, after clear warnings have been issued.'[6]

The memo was headed 'Personal and Confidential' for the attention of General Tuzo, the army's General Commanding Officer (GOC) in the north. It was discussed at length at the Bloody Sunday Inquiry.

From General Ford's memo to General Officer Commanding Harry Tuzo, dated 10 January 1972:

> THE SITUATION IN LONDONDERRY AS AT 7TH JANUARY 1972
>
> …
>
> **4.** The situation in Londonderry is one of armed gunmen dominating the Creggan and Bogside backed and protected by the vast majority

of the population in these two areas, and of bombers and gunmen making occasional sorties out of these hard-core areas to cause incidents, mainly in the shopping areas of the Strand, William Street (only two shops now operating) and Great James Street. This situation is difficult enough but is not beyond our capacity to deal with using normal IS [Internal Security] methods and equipment, although I feel it probably needs the establishment of a further military base at the West end of William Street (This is now being examined as a matter of urgency, the Stardust Club being the likely choice.)…

6. The weapons at our disposal – CS gas and baton rounds – are ineffective. This is because the DYH operate mainly in open areas where they can avoid the gas (and some have respirators, many other make-shift wet rag masks) and in open order beyond the accurate range of baton rounds. Alternatively, they operate in built-up areas where, because of their tactics and the personal protection they have, CS gas has to be used in vast quantities and to such an extent that it seeps into nearby buildings and affects innocent people, often women and children. Attempts to close with the DYH bring the troops into the killing zones of the snipers. As I understand it, the commander of a body of troops called out to restore law and order has a duty to use minimum force but he also has a duty to restore law and order. We have fulfilled the first duty but are failing in the second. I am coming to the conclusion that the minimum force necessary to achieve a restoration of law and order is to shoot

selected ring leaders amongst the DYH, after clear warnings have been issued. I believe we would be justified in using 7.62mm but in view of the devastating effects of this weapon and the danger of rounds killing more than the person aimed at, I believe we must consider issuing rifles adapted to fire HV .22 inch ammunition to sufficient members of the unit dealing with this problem, to enable ring leaders to be engaged with this less lethal ammunition. Thirty of these weapons have already been sent to 8 Infantry Brigade this weekend for zeroing and familiarization training. They, of course, will not be used operationally without authorisation.

7. If this course is implemented, as I believe it may have to be, we would have to accept the possibility that .22 rounds may be lethal. In other words, we would be reverting to the methods of IS found successful on many occasions overseas but would merely be trying to minimize the lethal effects by using the .22 round. I am convinced that our duty to restore law and order requires us to consider this step.

The first GEN 47 Cabinet Committee meeting of the New Year was held on 11 January 1972. Among items on the agenda was a report from the British army's Chief of General Staff on Northern Ireland's security situation. Numerous other meetings and correspondence followed, as authorities debated how best to handle the north.

From the minutes of GEN 47 Cabinet Committee meeting, noting the British prime minister Edward Heath's summary of security discussions, dated 11 January 1972:

The relative quietness of the security situation in Belfast underlined the importance of the search for a political initiative which the Meeting would discuss as the next item on its agenda. A military operation to reimpose law and order in Londonderry might in time become inevitable but should not be undertaken while there still remained some prospect of a successful political initiative. Meanwhile the Home Secretary should endeavour to secure that the Northern Ireland authorities hastened the initiation of prosecutions in respect of the NICRA march on 2 January.[7]

From the British army Headquarters Northern Ireland (HQNI) Intelligence Summary, dated 13 January 1972:

The anti-internment campaign is gathering momentum and the marches planned, particularly that in Londonderry, will present serious security problems.[8]

From a 'List of Forthcoming Events' attached to a Special Branch assessment for the period ending 19 January 1972:

Sunday, 30th January … Londonderry. NICRA sponsored anti-internment march from Creggan to Guildhall Square at 2.30 p.m. No trouble anticipated.[9]

From the British army HQNI Intelligence Summary, dated 19 January 1972:

Terrorist activity has remained at a low level and there has been a further decrease in the number of explosive attacks. NICRA and

other republican organisations have been busy
planning anti-internment rallies and marches,
and the Government's extension of the ban
on marches for a further year has brought
about angry protests by some Protestant
organisations.

In Londonderry, the traditional hooliganism
and rioting have continued, and nail and blast
bombs have been used by the rioters. Shooting
incidents have occurred daily: there have been
no military casualties, but five gunmen are
believed to have been hit. Four bomb attacks
have been made, on a transformer and three
commercial premises, but there have been no
notable terrorist successes.[10]

From the British army 8th Infantry Brigade's Intelligence Summary, distributed on 19 January 1972:

Civil Protest.

The projected NICRA march from the Creggan
to the Guildhall Square, Derry, planned for
16 Jan, has now been re-scheduled for Sunday
30 Jan. The JCRC has also announced that it
intends to hold a protest meeting in Bishop's
Field, Creggan on 22 Jan. In addition to this,
the opening of Magilligan Camp as a second
internment centre has produced a threat
of marches and demonstrations there. The
predictable outcry about Magilligan was led by
Ivan COOPER MP, who has declared that, 'There
is no change in the initial mood of angry
determination to cause the greatest possible
trouble for the British Army at Magilligan. I
can tell you that the Civil Rights Association
in North Derry, with my full backing, have

plans to cause them plenty of trouble and make
them sorry they ever opened a second camp.'

Comment.

The meeting in Creggan on 22 Jan is not likely
to be the direct cause of any trouble nor
is it likely that the ban on marches will
be defied on this occasion. However, the
normal rioting and hooliganism of a Saturday
afternoon will probably be exacerbated as a
result of the meeting. The march on 30 Jan
from the Creggan to the Guildhall has, on the
other hand, been planned in direct defiance of
the ban on marches.[11]

As can be seen from the same day's HQNI Intelligence Summary
below, the British military of the time made little distinction
between armed republican paramilitarism and non-violent civil
rights activism.

**From the British army's HQNI Intelligence Summary under the
heading 'Outlook', dated 19 January 1972:**

As security force search and arrest activity
continues to affect the IRA's freedom to act
in pursuit of objectives, the assassination of
off-duty security force personnel and selected
civilians is likely to become a terrorist
tactic. The anti-internment campaign has
been given new momentum by the opening of
Magilligan Internment Camp. The planned march
in Londonderry on 30 January 1972 will present
a serious security problem.[12]

*

As RUC Chief Superintendent of the RUC in Derry in 1972, Frank Lagan worked hard to gain and keep the trust of its Catholic community – an effort which drew some scepticism from peers and senior British army officers of the time. The community recall him as a moderate, fair man, who advised against blocking the march route on 30 January 1972. Ahead of the march, Lagan proposed that the marchers be allowed to proceed to the Guildhall but was overruled. In a statement to the Bloody Sunday Inquiry, he again reaffirmed his belief that events could have been 'relatively contained' if the march hadn't been stopped by the army.

Royal Ulster Constabulary (RUC) Chief Superintendent Frank Lagan: I probably felt that Londonderry was a place distinct from other areas in Northern Ireland. In 1972, the city of Londonderry was predominantly Catholic. In this sense and at that time, there were no other comparable areas in Northern Ireland. Some of the people from the city were not as cooperative with the security forces as they might have been in other areas.[13]

From testimony of General Robert Ford to the Widgery Tribunal after Bloody Sunday in April 1972: It was the view of the senior Commanders on the spot, and I supported this view, that it was inevitable that at an early stage the IRA and the hooligans would take over control of this illegal march, no matter what the NICRA organisers wished.[14]

The Stormont Cabinet met that week to approve the renewal of the ban on marches. William Stout, the Government Security Adviser, prepared notes on the meeting for Northern Ireland's prime minister Brian Faulkner. In these notes, he refers to 'what could well be the beginning of a series of processions organized by Civil Rights and other "front" organisations of the IRA'.[15]

Later the same day, Brian Faulkner publicly announced the extension of the ban on marches for another 12 months.[16] The decision was met with strong protests from both communities. Nationalists and civil rights campaigners saw the ban as an attack on civil liberties and their own fledgling campaign, while many within the unionist and loyalist community were angered at the challenge to their own historic right to hold traditional Loyal Order processions. The ban would be the first time since the Second World War that the traditional July 12 Orange Day parade would be barred.

Revd Ian Paisley, unionist MP, to NI prime minister Brian Faulkner in parliament on 18 January 1972: The Government has capitulated to the policy of terror. Today, the IRA has won.[17]

According to a report in the New York Times *of 19 January 1972, Faulkner 'strongly defended his move amid jeers and angry shouts from Protestant politicians in the provincial Parliament'.*

From NI prime minister Brian Faulkner addressing parliament on 18 January 1972: We're doing this to protect the public, the police and the army. Those who take part in parades not only put themselves at risk but expose members of the security forces in situations where they are open to attack.

From a statement by the Northern Ireland Civil Rights Association on the continuation of the ban on marching, published in the *New York Times* on 19 January 1972: It is an indication that the Government is really afraid of the constant expression of opposition to the Faulkner regime. We will of course continue to hold parades despite the ban.

The ban had little effect on civil rights campaigners, who pressed on with their next demonstration, a collective show of civil disobedience on a beach near Derry.

CHAPTER 9

Scenes at Magilligan Strand, 1972

Civil rights marchers, including John Hume, face paratroopers on the shore of Magilligan Strand in January 1972.

Thousands travelled to Magilligan Strand, not far from an internment camp, the weekend before Bloody Sunday for a protest march across its beach. As the march set off on Saturday 22 January, it was met by soldiers of the Royal Green Jackets and the Parachute Regiment, who blocked their path with barbed wire to close off the beach.

As marchers tried to cross, soldiers fired rubber bullets and CS gas at close range into the crowd, incapacitating many. Scores of eyewitnesses and injured spoke of the brutality of the paratroopers, who then beat protestors. Derry MP John Hume later accused the soldiers present on the beach of 'beating, brutalizing and terrorizing the demonstrators'.

Dr Raymond McClean: It was at Magilligan that I first encountered the Parachute Regiment in Northern Ireland, although I had come across them during my time in the Royal Air Force. I was well used to the confrontation every Saturday afternoon in Derry between the army and civilians, it was almost a ritual – almost a tourist attraction. It was clear when we arrived at Magilligan that the attitude of the paras was very different and that they would brook no argument.[1]

Ivan Cooper: I was on the march at Magilligan. I distinctly recall wire barriers on the beach and the presence of the paras. Magilligan was the first time that I had become conscious of the role of the paras, who seemed to me to be a different breed of soldier, a different species, to that which I was used to seeing in Northern Ireland. The paras at Magilligan were very belligerent, and the impression I had was that this regiment had been brought in to 'clean up' the civil unrest in Northern Ireland and that the paras saw themselves in this role. At Magilligan, they engaged in confrontations with the marchers, readily using batons to thrash the marchers with impunity.[2]

Dr Raymond McClean: When protestors started to move barricades, they were battered by members of the Parachute Regiment using batons. Their treatment was very brutal. They cracked a number of heads with batons, causing quite a few head injuries. There was no way of treating the injured. When we returned to Derry on the buses, it was necessary for a number of the injured to go to hospital.

Eamon Melaugh: The British army were acting under political instructions. There were no stones on Magilligan beach, but they beat us up. And they crossed a wire fence to get at us, round the back. John Hume was there of course that day and one of the fellas taking photos that day worked for the *Derry Journal*.

He asked me what I thought (it was the first battalion of paratroopers). I said, 'God help us if we come up against them in Derry.' It was William McKinney, who was then shot on Bloody Sunday.

Not long after events at Magilligan, General Ford selected 1 PARA to operate as an arrest force for the planned civil rights march in Derry on 30 January.

On 24 January 1972, the British army's Chief of the Defence Staff, Admiral Sir Peter Hill-Norton, visited the north, where he met General Officer Commanding (GOC), General Sir Harry Tuzo, General Ford and the Director of Intelligence of the time. Minutes note the army's plans to intensify operations.

From minutes taken during the visit of Chief of the Defence Staff (CDS), Admiral Sir Peter Hill-Norton, notes of view contributed by General Officer Commanding (GOC), General Sir Harry Tuzo:

a. The attrition operation is going well. It is designed to make the IRA desist and the policy is working but at the price of implacable and growing Roman Catholic hostility, not only to the Protestants but to the Army. This hostility is tending to spread upwards through the middle class, encouraged particularly by some Roman Catholic priests and behind it all stands NICRA, the active ally of the IRA.

...

e. The ban on marches is the major current problem. Mr Faulkner deserves credit for his handling of the ban. He did not consult the Orange Order but went ahead and persuaded his Cabinet to do what he thought right. The problem is the difficulty of enforcing the law. The Security Forces regard a march as prevented (by stopping it on the ground

and at a time of their own choice) if its
aim is frustrated. The trouble as usual is
the local news media, particularly BBC TV,
who did not fairly report the march and
the Security Force measures of prevention
on Sun 23 Jan 72. Too much was made of the
attempts to defy the law. If this problem
escalates, as it well may, some blame will
attach to the BBC. (The COS subsequently
gave it as his opinion, and D Int agreed,
that the Protestants have got used to the
Roman Catholic bomber/gunman (whom they
don't see) and are more likely to react
increasingly aggressively to the sight of
NICRA supporters defying the law).

f. As for the future, there is a continuing
need to:
(1) Sustain the attrition operation.
(2) Seek reconciliation with the Catholic
community at every opportunity.
(3) Seek to defeat IRA hostile propaganda
and preserve the good name of the
Army, which is being assailed with evil
intent.[3]

*

**From the same minutes of the CDS visit, in which General Ford
describes the problems faced by the army's 8th Infantry Brigade:**

Hooliganism in Londonderry is the running
sore but is being contained. Fifteen IRA
gunmen have been seen to fall in Londonderry
since 1 January 1972. The interesting thing
is that there is always an instant reaction
to our patrolling but none to the casualties
we inflict by our own sniper fire. The
Creggan and the Bogside are regretfully IRA

strongholds. To go into the Creggan to pick up, say, three wanted men in a bad area, is virtually a four or five company operation.

In the Bogside it is possible to patrol on a one company basis. So, we can go in to either area if we so wish, but only in this sort of strength. The reason is that the Roman Catholic population will respond to a man and has not only an efficient alarm system but permanent roadblocks and vigilantes.

(This situation will undoubtedly be exploited in the march planned for 30 January 1972, when up to 12,000 Roman Catholics are expected to march, come what may, from assembly points in the Creggan and Bogside to the Guildhall Square. They can only be effectively halted on the line of William Street.)

Also on 24 January 1972 was a meeting between Brigadier MacLellan and Chief Superintendent Lagan to discuss the proposed anti-internment march in Derry. Lagan's deputy, Superintendent McCullagh, was also present. The three debated how best to deal with the march, with Lagan believing marchers should be permitted to proceed to the Guildhall. Brigadier MacLellan then reported these views to General Ford, but Lagan's suggestion was overruled.

From the written statement of Chief Superintendent Frank Lagan to the Widgery Tribunal, 1972: I had had several discussions of an informal character with Brigadier MacLellan. He and I are jointly responsible for security in the city of Londonderry. In particular I discussed the action to be taken in relation to the proposed march with him when I expressed the view that the best course was to let the procession to go on unhindered and to limit the activity of the security forces to identifying participants.

The discussion which I had with the Brigadier was a long one. We both did the Devil's Advocate about what should take place.

88

At the end of the meeting the consensus of opinion was that in the interests of the city the parade should be allowed to go through to its meeting in the Guildhall where, I admit, this was in breach of the spirit of the ban, but the law could still be enforced, as it had been previously, by prosecuting in Londonderry the people who had breached the ban. I understood him to be fully in agreement with this view.[4]

From the written statement of Brigadier MacLellan to the Bloody Sunday Inquiry: Personally, I was concerned that if the march had been allowed to go to the Guildhall, the hooligans would have had a heyday, busting the place up and looting. This would have been followed by a sectarian flare up and I was therefore in no doubt that the march had to be contained. I think that any suggestion that you could allow the marchers to go through to the Guildhall to make their protest, to photograph them and then arrest and prosecute them later, was pie in the sky. You needed a large Army presence to arrest one person in the Creggan. Even if you managed that, there would be a problem with witnesses and the whole idea was impracticable. I did not agree with [Chief Superintendent] Lagan that the march should be allowed to proceed to the Guildhall.[5]

CHAPTER 10

Army Plans and IRA Assurances

A British army armoured vehicle patrols near Free Derry Corner
in the Bogside area.

In the week preceding Bloody Sunday, the British army discussed how best to control the situation. Among the evidence within the Bloody Sunday Inquiry are statements from military and police sources giving insight into decisions to send in 1 PARA to police the anti-internment march on 30 January.

From General Ford's oral evidence to the Bloody Sunday Inquiry:
It is a definite change of approach. But of course, the size of this march, and the indications of the extent of the rioting that was

likely to take place, dictated the fact that the army would have to be in control from the start.[1]

From 8th Infantry Brigade Intelligence Summary of 25 January 1972:

Future Events.

A NICRA sponsored march followed by a meeting at the Guildhall, Londonderry is planned for 30 January. It is believed that all civil rights groups will combine together in an attempt to cause maximum embarrassment to the Security Forces.

The main march is expected to form up in Bishops Field, Creggan at 1400 hours and move into the City via Eastway - Westland St - Lecky Rd - Rossville St - William St - Waterloo Place - Shipquay Place. The Shantallow Branch of NICRA is also expected to march from Drumleck Drive via Racecourse Rd - Buncrana Rd - Pennyburn Pass - Duncreggan Rd - Strand Rd and then to William St to join the main march. Estimates of numbers expected vary from 3,000 by the RUC (including up to 200 from Shantallow), to 10,000 by the London 'Times'.

It is possible that a further group may move eastwards from Brandywell up Foyle Rd in order to stretch the Security Forces. The organisers may well alter their plans to take account of Security Forces dispositions and possibly even march after rather than before the meeting ...[2]

*

Ahead of the weekend march, the Northern Ireland Civil Rights Association issued a statement to the press on 25 January 1972,

*entitled 'Reasons for Derry march'. In the statement, NICRA
cited the reasons for returning to the streets in defiance of the
parades ban, made inevitable 'by the continuing and escalating
repression of the British Army' and by the rejection of its 'peace
plan' demands for reform.*

**From a Northern Ireland Civil Rights Association press conference
on 25 January 1972:** So far, there have been six anti-Internment
marches held throughout the north involving thousands defying
the parades ban. Last weekend alone four marches were held
successfully despite the might of the British army and RUC. The
brutality of soldiers at Magilligan and Castlewellan over the
weekend showed clearly how completely this erstwhile peace-
keeping force has been converted into the military arm of the
Unionist Administration.[3]

*It was General Ford's decision to use 1 PARA as the arrest force
for the march on 30 January. In his written statement to the
Bloody Sunday Inquiry, General Ford set out his reasons for
selecting 1 PARA.*[4]

(i) The units in 8[th Infantry] Brigade were
already committed in areas which they knew
around the perimeter of the City.

(ii) The City battalion (that is the one
covering the William Street area etc) was
22 Light Air Defence Regiment Royal Artillery.
This was not an infantry battalion but an
artillery regiment temporarily being used
in an infantry role and was not suited for
a major arrest operation.

(iii) The Province Reserve (1 KOB) were my
reserve. They only became operational on 13
January 1972 and had no experience of arrest
operations, major or minor. A major arrest
operation would certainly have been beyond

their capabilities until at least the middle of February or so.

(iv) As the reserve battalion of 39 Brigade in Belfast, 1 PARA were not committed to permanently holding any particular area.

(v) The third Brigade in Northern Ireland had no reserve battalion.

(vi) 1 PARA had been in the province for well over a year. They had much experience, more than any other battalion in Northern Ireland, both in carrying out arrest operations and in coming under and countering terrorist fire.

(vii) They could be spared for three or four days by Commander 39 Brigade.

From General Robert Ford's oral evidence to the Widgery Tribunal, 1972: It was the view of the senior Commanders on the spot, and I supported this view, that it was inevitable that at an early stage the IRA and the hooligans would take over control of this illegal march, no matter what the NICRA organisers wished.

I viewed 1 PARA as highly professional; whilst it is true in normal circumstances that they were trained to be aggressive, the aggression that I had personally seen them display was a controlled aggression. They were highly disciplined in all I had seen, despite what others had said, and I was satisfied that they would conduct themselves appropriately. The practical arrangements for the transfer of 1 PARA to 8 Brigade would have been made by my staff.[5]

*

From the minutes of a Ministry of Defence meeting on 26 January 1972, attended by senior MoD officials and representatives of both the Home Office and the Foreign and Commonwealth Office:

The proposed Creggan march at the weekend
posed difficult problems. It would be important
to consider carefully both the PR aspects of
not attempting to break up the march in 'no
go' areas, and also the possibility of adopting
some summary procedure for dealing with those
involved in the illegal march rather than the
long drawn-out procedure which had been used
in connection with the Christmas and recent
NICRA marches.[6]

*

From a Current Situation Report compiled by Anthony Stephens, head of Defence Secretariat 10 and circulated to ministers and officials in the MoD, the Cabinet Office and other departments:

A further anti-internment march - which is
likely to be the largest since they were
commenced at Christmas - is planned for
Londonderry next Sunday. The intention
obviously is for the marchers to form up first
within the Bogside and Creggan estates and to
march for some distance within those areas,
before emerging at a point where it will be
feasible for the security forces to prevent
them from continuing. It seems certain that
television crews will be invited to record the
early stages - and that Protestant reaction
to the spectacle of a march apparently taking
place unhindered will be strong. Preparatory
thought is therefore being given to the public
relations aspect of this event.

The choice of tactics for actually dealing
with the march is essentially a matter for the
Joint Security Committee - which is due to
meet as usual on Thursday morning, 27 January.

The Ministry of Defence and the Home Office
are in touch respectively with the GOC and UK
Rep about the line which they will be taking
at that meeting.[7]

From Brigadier MacLellan's oral testimony to the Bloody Sunday Inquiry: I was given a direct order by General Ford to launch an arrest operation if the soldiers were attacked by the hooligans and he specifically allotted 1 PARA for the task. This was not a matter for debate and there was no discretion as far as I was concerned.[8]

*

Key to the British army's defence after Bloody Sunday were claims of an IRA battle. However, in the days before the big march, representatives of NICRA and other concerned local individuals sought assurance from both factions of the IRA in Derry that they would stay away from the march to ensure public safety. The Bloody Sunday Inquiry later concluded this to be accurate.

Dr Raymond McClean: After the introduction of internment, we wanted to demonstrate. I was concerned about going onto the streets as I thought someone would be seriously injured. With others, I met with political representatives of the IRA to put the position to them – we wanted to march but wanted a guarantee that the IRA would not become involved. After a few days, word came back that if we marched the IRA would give an absolute promise that it would stay away. I knew that the march would be large as the assurance received from the IRA would encourage people to attend. I expect NICRA also approached the IRA to obtain the same assurance we had sought.

Ivan Cooper MP: A few days prior to the march, I approached an intermediary and asked him to arrange, on my behalf, to meet a representative of the IRA. I received confirmation within forty-eight hours of my meeting that the IRA would confine itself to the Creggan estate while the march proceeded. I was therefore fairly satisfied. I also had meetings with people in Derry and informal discussions with the police which made me feel reasonably confident that the march could go ahead without a serious outbreak of violence. I had no discussions with the military prior to the march.

Derry businessman Brendan Duddy also sought assurances from the IRA ahead of the march and passed these assurances to the RUC's Chief Superintendent Lagan.

Brendan Duddy, a local businessman: About ten days before the march Frank Lagan came to my house. He told me he was very worried about the possibility of armed paramilitaries being involved in the march. My immediate reaction was that it wasn't necessary. At the time, it was accepted that neither limb of the IRA used weapons on marches. He accepted this but nevertheless asked me to seek these assurances.[9]

Having met with representatives from both the Official and Provisional IRA, the local businessman recalled, 'The guarantee as to arms being taken out of the area was immediately and unequivocally given.'

Police Chief Superintendent Frank Lagan: I expected IRA members to participate in the march. My expectation was that people whom I expected or knew to be involved in IRA activity would take part in the march. I believed that they would do this as individual members of the general community and not as part of organized IRA activity.[10]

Testifying before the Bloody Sunday Inquiry, the former IRA leader Martin McGuinness, who was by then Northern Ireland's Education Minister (1999–2002), provided insight into these decisions.

Martin McGuinness, Second-in-Command/Adjutant of the IRA in Derry in 1972, who would later become Deputy First Minister of Northern Ireland: An approach had been made to the OC [Officer Commanding] on Thursday 27 January 1972 by people representing the civil rights movement. I confirm I was asked by the OC the following day for my opinion on the suggestion from the civil rights people that Sunday should be quiet. What I can say is that the view among Republicans that day was that the march should be allowed to proceed peacefully and without interruptions and an attack by the British army was in no way expected. I have been asked what I would expect the British authorities to know of the assurances which had been given. Because of the position of [Chief Superintendent] Frank Lagan and his connections to the Catholic community, my view was that the civil rights people would be in touch with Frank Lagan, and it was likely that he would have told the British army about it.[11]

Dr Raymond McClean: In the week between the protest at Magilligan and the anti-internment march on 30 January, I became concerned at what was likely to happen. I knew there was a bar at the top of Waterloo Street, which was a source of local civil rights information. I went with my brothers-in-law, Mickey McGuinness and Danny McGuinness, to find out what the word was on the march. A few fellows in the bar confirmed what I had previously been told that the IRA would stand down. I left the bar feeling quite happy, as I was aware that if I had received news of the IRA's intentions, army intelligence must have done the same and therefore the army would be aware of our peaceful intentions.

Martin McGuinness: As far as the paras were concerned there was a lot of publicity at the time about the events at Magilligan the week before, which was a bad situation and very nasty. When I heard that the paras were going to be deployed in the city, I felt at worst that they would repeat the actions they took at Magilligan, particularly at the barriers.

*

The Brigade Operation Order for the 30 January 1972 march was presented to the 8th Infantry Brigade staff officers at 0830 hours on 27 January by Colonel Steele, then approved by Brigadier

MacLellan, and was sent to General Ford at HQNI. It was code-named Operation Forecast, extracts of which are reproduced below and detail the army's Operation Order behind the events of Bloody Sunday.[12]

From 8th Infantry Brigade Operation Order for civil rights march, dated 27 January 1972:

1. <u>Background</u>

   a. The present declared intention of NICRA is that on 30 January at 1400 hrs a march will proceed from Bishops Field, Creggan, and from Drumleck Drive Shantallow, both to converge on Shipquay Place, where a public meeting will be held in front of the Guildhall.

   ...

   f. We expect a hooligan element to accompany the marches and anticipate an intensification of the normal level of hooliganism and rioting during and after the march. Almost certainly snipers, petrol bombers and nail bombers will support the rioters.

   g. Bombers may intensify their efforts to destroy Business and Shopping premises in the City Centre during the event, while the attention of the Security Forces is directed towards the containment of the march.

2. <u>The Threat.</u> These are currently assessed as:

   a. A deliberate attempt to defy the marching ban, resulting in a direct confrontation being made between the marching contingents and the Security Forces.

   b. IRA terrorist activity, to take advantage of the event, to conduct shooting attacks

against the Security Forces, and bombing
attacks against Business, Shopping and
Commercial premises in the City Centre.

c. Hooligan reaction to the general
excitement of the event, in the form of
stone, bottle and nail bombing of troops,
arson of private premises and vehicles,
and a high degree of violence throughout
the City. Although this violence is
expected to continue throughout the
event, it will intensify during the
closing stage of the event, especially
in the William St/Rossville St area; it
is possible that hooligan violence may
continue thereafter for several days.

...

MISSION

5. 8 Inf Bde is, on 30 January, to prevent
any illegal march taking place from the
CREGGAN, and to contain it, together with
any accompanying rioting, within the Bogside
and Creggan areas of the City. It is also to
disperse illegal marchers from other parts
of the City, and is to prevent damage by
rioters and bombers to Business, Shopping
and Protestant areas of Londonderry.

EXECUTION

...

9. Tasks.

...

f. 1 PARA.

(1) Maintain a Brigade Arrest Force, to
conduct a 'scoop-up' operation of as many
hooligans and rioters as possible.

(a) This operation will only be
launched, either in whole or in
part, on the orders of the Bde Comd.

(b) The Force will be deployed initially to Foyle College Car Park GR 434176, where it will be held at immediate notice throughout the event.

(c) The Scoop-Up operation is likely to be launched on two axes, one directed towards hooligan activity in the area of William St/Little Diamond, and one towards the area of William St/Little James St.

(d) It is expected that the arrest operation will be conducted on foot.

...

p. Coordinating Instructions.

...

(4) Use of Force.

(a) CS Gas. Is NOT to be used throughout this event, except as a last resort only if troops are about to be over-run and the rioters can no longer be held off with baton rounds and water cannon.

(b) Baton Round. These are to be fired in salvos to disperse illegal marchers and rioters. There should be no less than eight riot guns deployed at each barrier in order that effective salvo fire can be sustained ...

...

(6) PR.

(a) All press statements concerning this event will be made through Bde HQ, to whom all press enquiries should be made.

(b) Unit PROs [Public Relations Officers] should make every effort to collect and conduct press and TV men around deployment areas, in order that the

newsmen will subsequently give a
balanced report to their readers and
viewers on the proceedings.

*

*For distribution, 35 copies of this Order for Operation Forecast
were made, and a copy was sent that day to everyone on the distribution list, including HQNI and the MoD in London. Brigadier
MacLellan is recorded as having said that, 'The plans went back to
London. So, the whole thing was approved before it ever started.'*[13]

*In addition, a Photographic Coverage Order was also issued
by the army on 27 January 1972, which requested ten 'still'
photographers present for the operation that Sunday. Seven
photographers from battalions in Derry, and one from each of the
reinforcing battalions 1 KOB, 3RFF and 1 PARA. Army headquarters in the north (HQNI) were to deploy a cine-camera team
in a helicopter too, and all photographers were to be in position
by 1300 hours on 30 January, fulfilling the order to 'provide max
photo coverage of the NICRA march and all associated incidents
on 30 Jan 72'.*[14] *Unfortunately, very little of this material was
located when the new inquiry was established in 1998.*

*At a meeting of the Joint Security Committee at Stormont
on 27 January 1972, chaired by John Taylor MP, the Minister
of State at the Ministry of Home Affairs, discussions included
the events at Magilligan on 22 January, and also events to
come. Minutes of the meeting show that the army had originally
planned for two separate marches in Derry that were to meet
up. The proposed march of the Shantallow branch of the Civil
Rights Association, on the outskirts of the city, instead merged
with the main branch leaving from Bishop's Field in Creggan.*

**From the minutes of the Joint Security Committee at Stormont
on 27 January 1972:**

Proposed Marches on Saturday (Dungannon to
Coalisland) and Sunday (in Londonderry) posed
considerable problems. Tactics will be as for

last weekend. The Marches will be stopped at
points selected on tactical grounds.

It was agreed that Special Powers Act
Regulation 38 should be used to prevent
assembly in Dungannon Square. The Londonderry
Marches presented more serious difficulties
and security action will be primarily an
Army operation. It is planned to stifle the
Shantallow March at source, but it would be
pointless to attempt the same tactics in the
Creggan area. The basic plan here will be to
block all routes into William Street and stop
the March there. The operation might well
develop into rioting and even a shooting war.
Depending on the amount of road transport into
Londonderry for the occasion roadblocks may be
set up and vehicles searched. This would have
useful delaying effect.

Prosecution for breaches of the ban on
processions was disappointingly slow. The
Minister of State at the Ministry of Home
Affairs undertook to look into this.[15]

*At 10 Downing Street on Thursday 27 January, Britain's prime
minister Edward Heath, and his home secretary, met with the
Northern Ireland prime minister, Brian Faulkner. They discussed
ongoing security operations and IRA activity, and the policing of
the march that Sunday.*

**From a 'Note for the Record' of meeting between British PM
Heath and Northern Ireland PM Faulkner, dated 27 January
1972, at 5.45pm:**

Mr. Faulkner recognised that the civil
disobedience parades in the coming weekend
in Derry would be difficult; but there had
been no alternative to refusing permission for
them. If Orange parades were to be banned,

it would be impossible in political terms to
let civil rights or other parades go ahead. He
assumed (and it was confirmed) that the British
Government remained of the view that parades
and marches should be banned for as long
as internment lasted. It would be important
to make clear that those parading were not
genuine 'civil righters' but were 'civil
disobedients'. It would also be important to
ensure that television cameras saw the parades
being stopped. The Prime Minister thanked
Mr. Faulkner for coming and said that he would
look forward to a general discussion with him
later about possible political moves.[16]

*

*Also on Thursday 27 January 1972, a car containing five RUC
officers was ambushed by the Provisional IRA on the Creggan
Road in Derry. Sergeant Peter Gilgunn and Constable David
Montgomery were killed, and Constable Charles George
Maloney was injured by gunfire. They were the first police
officers to be killed in the city since the start of the Troubles.*

From a Northern Ireland Civil Rights Association press statement in the *Derry Journal* of 28 January 1972:

A meeting of stewards for Sunday's planned
civil rights demonstration and rally at
Guildhall Square, Derry, will be held at the
Creggan Centre at 8pm tonight. Stewards will
receive final instructions from members of
the NICRA executive and be fully briefed on
plans and tactics. Special emphasis will be
placed on the absolute necessity for a peaceful
incident-free day on Sunday. Civil rights
organiser, Mr Kevin McCorry, has pointed out

that Mr Brian Faulkner and Mr John Taylor are
counting on an outbreak of violence to justify
any British army violence used on Sunday.

'Sunday will be a "make or break day" with
the cause of civil rights and the release of
internees. Any riot, any trouble, any incident,
must be confined to members of the British
Army. They disgraced themselves at Magilligan on
Saturday last with their unprovoked savagery. Do
not let them disgrace you, the city of Derry and
the whole democratic cause,' Mr McCorry said.[17]

*

*With the orders for Operation Forecast already distributed in
writing, a 'coordinating conference' was called for all commanding
officers at 1430 hours in Brigade Headquarters, situated in
Ebrington Barracks on the east bank of the River Foyle.*

From the written statement of Chief Superintendent Frank Lagan to the Bloody Sunday Inquiry:

During the meeting Brigadier MacLellan gave a
description of the area and spoke about what was
expected and what needed to be done. He discussed
the different regiments' assignments and the
different barriers. The discussion was fairly
general. The arrest operation was to be carried
out by the Paras. Nothing was discussed in my
hearing about 1 Paras [sic] role or the potential
for IRA involvement on the day. I do not think
that the issue of risk (i.e. of injury or loss of
life) was discussed either. I assume that matters
relating both to the arrest operation and to arms
were dealt with by Brigadier MacLellan directly
with the Paras and that it was not necessary for
him to address these matters with everyone who
had attended the meeting.[18]

From the Confirmatory Notes of Orders Group for 3 Platoon A Company 2 RGJ [Royal Green Jackets], taken on Friday 28 January 1972:

```
Position of S.F. [Security Forces]:

a. General Harry [Tuzo] has said that this
   march could be the most crucial event in
   the Ulster crisis. If the Civil Rights
   people start the aggro their cause will
   lose credibility. If we start it we'll
   probably cause a major flareup all over N.
   Ireland.
b. S.F. must be strictly controlled. The Right
   behaviour is very important. NO repeat of
   Magilligan.
c. T.V. will be out in force looking for
   brutality.
d. IRA must not be allowed to make propaganda
   out of this.
e. Emphasis is low key.
f. A Coy 2 RGJ has the most important job
   in the Bde, we have been selected by Bde
   as the most reliable coy. The march will
   converge on us. We are representing the
   whole bloody army at this point.[19]
```

*

From the memo sent by NI prime minister Brian Faulkner to General Tuzo, dated 28 January 1972:

```
This weekend will undoubtedly be a further
test of our resolve and the march in
Londonderry will certainly be a most difficult
one to handle. I know that detailed plans have
been made and I hope everything goes well.[20]
```

CHAPTER 11

The Day Before

The army stop and search in Westland Street.

On Saturday 29 January 1972, a joint British army/police state-ment was issued publicly, warning that any violence that occurred the next day should be blamed on march organizers.

A Joint British army and RUC statement issued on the morning of Saturday 29 January 1972:

> In Northern Ireland there is now a Government
> ban on all marches and the Security Forces
> have a duty to take action against those who
> set out to break the law. The Police have
> brought prosecutions against persons identified

as organisers or taking part in such marches. Since Christmas fourteen summonses have been issued and a further seventy prosecutions are under consideration.

In carrying out their duty the Security Forces are concerned to avoid or reduce to an absolute minimum the consequences of any violence that may erupt from the confrontation between sections of the community or between the Security Forces and those taking part, in illegal march. The Security Forces choose the time and the place at which to intervene and its policy, which is clearly in the public interest, allows the possibility that marches may in some cases proceed for some distance before being stopped. This does not, however, mean that participants will be allowed to break the law with impunity.

Experience this year has already shown that attempted marches often end in violence that must have been foreseen by the organisers, and clearly the responsibility for this violence and the consequences of it must rest fairly and squarely on the shoulders of those who encourage people to break the law.[1]

That day, as part of publicity for the march, the Irish News *carried an advertisement with details of its assembly point in Bishop's Field that Sunday at 2pm. Unaware of army plans to close off the city centre, NICRA also advertised the march destination as Derry's Guildhall Square – as did the* Derry Journal *the same day. Alongside its poster, NICRA also issued a statement on Saturday 29 January 1972, which was widely reported in local newspapers.*

From a NICRA statement published in the *Derry Journal* of Saturday 29 January 1972:

A call for a massive turnout at the Civil Rights Demonstration planned for Derry tomorrow has been made by the Executive of the Civil Rights Association. Making the call the Executive pointed out that the British Government are now full-tilt on repression and coercion and that a massive peaceful demonstration was vital if world opinion was to be impressed by the justice of the democratic cause in Northern Ireland.

The twin major aims for Derry are a demonstration that is both huge in numbers and perfectly peaceful and incident free. It is pointed out that any violence can only set back the civil rights cause and play straight into the hands of the Tory-Unionists by providing a justification not only for any violence they might contemplate against the demonstration itself but also for the daily violence of the security forces.[2]

In the days before the march, the various battalions each held their own Orders Groups on the weekend's Operation Forecast. Notes of some of the battalion meetings survive and were highlighted at the Bloody Sunday Inquiry.

The Orders Group for 1 PARA took place on the Saturday morning before and ran long, from 1030 hours until 1215 hours. Notes of 1 PARA's meeting, recorded by their Commanding Officer, Lieutenant Colonel Derek Wilford, also survived and are reproduced in the 2010 report.[3]

From manuscript notes taken by Colonel Derek Wilford following the Orders Group of 1 PARA, held at 1030 hours on Saturday 29 January 1972:

['Aslt pnrs' is an abbreviation for 'assault pioneers', 'Coy' is an abbreviation for 'Company', 'RMP' is an abbreviation for 'Royal Military Police']

1. <u>Situation</u>
   a. Bde Op O.
   b. Appreciation.
   c. Bde Plan.

2. <u>Mission.</u> The Bn is to arrest max no of rioters.

3. <u>Execution</u>

a. <u>Gen Outline.</u> The bn is to move to Londonderry via Drumahoe, taking up its posn in Foyle College Car Park by 1300. D Coy is under comd 22 Lt AD Regt. If the march takes place and confrontation becomes hostile the Bn will deploy fwd to break up the rioters and make the max no of arrests. At this stage I cannot give a detailed tactical plan. I [Wilford] will give the coy deployment in our FUP and then give my concept of how I think the battle can go.

...

g. <u>Concept of the battle.</u>

(1) The parade will come into contact with SF Barricades at William Street. There are two approaches.

<u>First.</u> From Rossville. This will cause the crowd to attempt a bypass through to Waterloo Street. In this event I would want to put a coy down the Strand into Waterloo Street and two coys in William Street from Lower Road and the Presbyterian Church.

<u>Second.</u> From William Street. We can take this the same way except this time putting two coys in from the Church.

You will appreciate that much will depend on the view I can get of the crowd and once you get the order to move you will have to move fast. I shall probably bring you forward in anticipation.

<u>Minor Tactics.</u> Speak of Derry Rioters. Background Gas & bullets.

   h. <u>Coord Instrs</u>

     (1) Timings

         (a) In posn by 1300.

         (b) Mov plan to Derry.

         (c) Length of Op. Plan on 48 hrs.

     (2) <u>Arrest Procedure.</u>

     The arrest team of RMP with RSM and
     Paddy Wagon and escort with move fwd
     to a loc in Great James Street. Normal
     arrest procedure then take prisoners and
     documentation to Fort George or Craigavon
     Br (sit).

4. <u>Logistics.</u>

   a. B'fast.

   b. Main meal at Ech Drumahoe. QM and team
      in posn.

   c. During action. Combat rats.

   d. Meal fwd in evening on demand.

5. <u>Comd & Sig</u>

   a. HQ Tac

     (1) Foyle Car Park.

     (2) B9 mobile.

   b. Sig instrs, as issued (RSO) MOVE,
      MOVE, MOVE!

*

General Sir (then Captain) Michael Jackson recalled being told at the Orders Group briefing of 1 PARA that, 'some sort of violent reaction was possible, perhaps probable on the IRA's part'.[4]

Extract of written statement of General Sir Michael Jackson (Captain of 1 PARA in 1972) to the Bloody Sunday Inquiry: There was concern about the containment line following the lines of the barricades. We believed there would be a reaction out of the IRA because we would be 'invading their turf' when going in for the arrest operation. We therefore had an expectation of IRA activity. There was a large 'no go' area and I can recall seeing maps with the so-called containment line marked on them. Beyond those lines the security forces simply did not go. It was known that firefights were common in Londonderry as they were in Belfast. If I remember rightly a policeman had been shot on the Thursday before we went in.

We could never rule out the fact that we might be shot at – any time, any place. The IRA were good at ambushes. These could take place anywhere at any time and it would be foolhardy in the extreme to assume that you would not be shot at. It would have been foolish militarily to accept any IRA assurances that they would not be on the march, if any such assurances were given. They would say anything for their cause. It would have been foolish to have been lulled into a false sense of security. It was a fundamental principle that we had to be prepared to be attacked at any time.[5]

Extract of Major Loden's statement to the Widgery Tribunal in 1972: It was clearly understood that the peaceful element of the march was to be left undisturbed. We were quite clear that on no account were peaceful marchers to be interfered with.[6]

Geraldine McBride: I was eighteen and Hugo was twenty. I was due to get married that April, and Hugo had to actually ask my daddy for permission to take me on the march. They were so protective, and it was my first march. My daddy said yes but warned him to bring me home at the first sight of any trouble. I remember my mammy chirped in and said, 'If we had done this fifty years ago, they would have a better life. They're fighting for the life we should have fought for!'

Andy Nolan: The day before the march we did our usual thing. We went down the town and around the usual places, and since there was nothing on in the Rialto or the Palace, we headed towards the Odeon to see if anything good was on there. Unlike most

Saturdays there was no riot in William Street, so we cut across to Sackville Street. At the corner there was a Saracen, but we kept on going because we had nothing to worry about. Of course, as soon as we got around the corner, the soldiers stopped us and asked us the usual questions. They were paras and their reputation had preceded them. I didn't know if they were going to stir trouble, but they frisked Jackie as normal and let him go on. Then they lifted me off the ground with my arms and legs stretched out while another one searched me and emptied all my pockets. I must have been held like this for quite a few minutes. I remember Jackie laughing his head off. Anyway, they finally let me go and we walked on towards the Strand Road where, as soon as we turned the corner, we were stopped and searched by another para patrol. After they let us go, Jackie said to me, 'I think they've got something against us – let's go home,' so we headed to Guildhall Square to get a bus home. We met a guy that worked with Jackie and told him what happened. We really took it as a joke.

Larry Doherty, press photographer with the *Derry Journal* in 1972: [There was a] press briefing which took place at the City Hotel the night before. It was the place where most visiting press used to stay. When I reached the hotel, it was packed. There was an air of expectation about the march. Then there was a briefing from an army press officer called [*redacted by the inquiry*] who was quite well known. We were all standing around at the bottom of the stairs. I remember him saying that we should all go in behind the army rather than take pictures 'from the other side' because 'the army is going in hard'. At the time, I did not attach any significance to this and interpreted it as meaning that the snatch squads would be going in and arresting people and that there might be some baton rounds. I felt it was just a warning to the visiting press who might not have been experienced in the ways of Derry to stay out of the way. It was only afterwards that I attached significance to those words and came to the view that there must have been some element of planning to what happened that day.[7]

Mary Donaghey: I lived with my husband, Jackie, my baby son, Dennis, and my brother, Gerald Donaghey. My parents had died about six years previously, when Gerald was about ten years old, and, since then, I had brought Gerald up, more or less as my own son. We lived in a maisonette to the west of the Bogside Inn.

Mary Donaghey recalled a concerning incident that occurred on 29 January, the evening before Bloody Sunday, in which her home was targeted by gunfire. Her younger brother Gerald was at home, with Mary's two-year-old son, Dennis, having offered to babysit while she visited an elderly friend.

Mary Donaghey: When I got home sometime near 8pm, Gerald was very upset. He told me that a shot had been fired through the upstairs bathroom window. The bullet was lodged in the wall at the top of the stairs. I went upstairs to look and tried to remove it, but it was embedded too deeply. Then I saw the bathroom window was shattered. There was glass everywhere. I was horrified as I realized that if anyone had been walking up the stairs they could have been killed. Gerald and I were both very shaken by this. From the angle of the bullet hole and the shattered window I could see that the bullet must have travelled downwards, I assume from the army sangar on Bligh's Lane. The bathroom window faced towards Bligh's Lane sangar. I didn't report the incident to the police, as I didn't think anything would come of it. I was just glad that Dennis and Gerald weren't hurt.[8]

Sophia Downey, sister of 17-year-old Michael Kelly: I was living with my husband, George Downey, in Shantallow. I remember that a car with a loudspeaker fixed on the top had been travelling around in the days leading up to the march, advertising it. The march was against internment and was in support of one man, one vote, and organizers wanted as much support as possible, so George and I decided to go on it with some members of my family.[9]

Andy Nolan: That night we went babysitting in Bernie's and told her what had happened, and we joked about going on the march the next day to get the guys who searched us. Apart from that, it was a normal Saturday, but I do remember Jackie's last words to Bernie. As we were leaving Bernie's, she told us to watch ourselves on the march and Jackie joked about finding the soldiers who searched me, and then joked, 'I'll see you in a few months' time because we'll probably get lifted tomorrow.' The worst we expected the next day was that there would be a riot and they'd use rubber bullets; everyone had seen what the paras were capable of the previous Saturday at Magilligan.

*

This account of the night before from a 19-year-old soldier – a radio operator with Support Company of 1 PARA in 1972 – merits inclusion as it indicates the mindset of the regiment chosen to police a peaceful civil rights march in Derry.

Submitted as part of the soldier's witness testimony to both the Widgery Tribunal in 1972 and the latter Bloody Sunday Inquiry, its (vastly inaccurate) description of the mainly Catholic housing estate in Creggan – home to hundreds of ordinary families – is also a good example of the anti-Irish propaganda and bigotry prevalent at the time.

From a Radio Operator with Support Company of 1 PARA of the British army: I was sitting with the rest of my 'muckers' of the Anti-Tank Platoon in the barracks when our Lieutenant came in and informed us that we were due for an operation in Londonderry the following day. He said that the heart of Derry had been bombed out. Several hundred soldiers had been hospitalized and that not one arrest had been made. We knew that the Creggan Estate was an IRA fortress with towers, machine-guns and barbed wire as well as land-mines guarding its approaches. The people of the Creggan had not paid rent and had hijacked all their food for several years. This was the symbol which led to the name 'no go area'.

As I looked at my friends, I could see that after all the abuse and nights without sleep, frustrations, and tensions, this is what they had been waiting for. We were all in high spirits and when our Lieutenant said, 'Let's teach these buggers a lesson – we want some kills tomorrow,' to the mentality of the blokes to whom he was speaking, this was tantamount to an order.[10]

*

Dr Raymond McClean: I was a little concerned when I went to bed that night. There was a story all around town that the paras would be in Derry for the march. I was aware that their whole psychology was fast aggression and a policy of getting the job done. They had no training to equip them for handling a peaceful march.

THE PORTER TAPES

The Porter Tapes were hours of recordings of British soldiers talking in code in the lead-up to Bloody Sunday and afterwards – and contained a number of disturbing conversations and orders.

The military radio messages had been recorded in 1972 by local amateur radio 'ham' Jimmy Porter from his TV repair shop in William Street, on the edge of the Bogside. In the 1990s, they would come to light after 25 years. The tapes had been buried for safekeeping in the garden of a friend of Porter's across the border in County Donegal. They captured much radio chatter, and also confirmed that troops disobeyed orders by stopping a dying victim – 17-year-old Gerald Donaghey – from being transported to hospital. Porter's tapes were rejected by the first inquiry into Bloody Sunday, Lord Widgery dismissing them on the grounds that they were illegally obtained and submitted too late.

James Porter, amateur radio ham and the owner of a TV repair shop on the edge of Derry's Bogside: I have been a radio amateur since 1936. I qualified as an Electrical Engineer in 1939 and have worked in this field throughout my working life. In 1972 one of my shop premises was located at 38 William Street. This shop was on the periphery of the Bogside. It was in this shop that the radio recordings were made of the events that took place during the parade on Bloody Sunday. I began recording RUC and army radio transmissions in Derry in 1969. I recorded RUC and army radio transmissions on 30 January 1972 (Bloody Sunday) and army radio transmissions on or about 28 January, on 29 January and 2 February 1972. I also witnessed various events from within and around my shop at 38 William Street at various times including Bloody Sunday.[11]

Transcript of Porter's non-secure British army radio transmission recorded on 29 January 1972 between a British army officer [Codename 1.9] and a soldier [Codename 6.1]:

1.9: 6.1, this is 1.9. Did you see that last nail bomb, where it came from?

6.1: No, but we presume it was thrown from my right, from the alleyway along the Grandstand Bar, over.

1.9: Say again, over.

6.1: The nail bomber came from my right, in the alleyway to my right.

1.9: Roger. Is there anything you can do to improve your fire position?

6.1: No, it is a very good one actually.

1.9: 6.1, this is 1.9. I want you to move, move back so that you can see down the alleyway by the maroon lorry, over.

6.1: I can see the whole of the alleyway, over.

1.9: I understand you to say you are already covering this alleyway, is that correct?

6.1: This is correct. The last nail bomb that was just thrown came from the alleyway alongside the Grandstand Bar. Thrown by a youth in dark clothing, over.

1.9: Roger. Why didn't you shoot him? Over.

6.1: My sights were not on him, and he was only in view for a second, over.

1.9: Roger, have the place covered, out.

6.1: I can see the nail bomber. Do you want me to shoot him? He has nothing in his hands at the moment, over.

1.9: Say again, over.

6.1: This is … I can see the nail bomber, but he doesn't appear to have anything in his hands, over.

1.9: Roger, out.

1.9: 6.1, this is 1.9. Are you absolutely certain that the person you can see is the real bomber? Over.

6.1: Positive. Over.

1.9: Shoot him dead. Over.

6.1: 1.9, this is 6.1. Missed him by about two inches, over.

1.9: Bad shooting, out.[12]

Dated just one day before Bloody Sunday, this transcript is a chilling precursor to the events of the next day in that it clearly conveys a British army officer giving a shoot-to-kill order against an unarmed person.

James Porter: I gave my original recordings of the army and RUC radio transmissions made on Bloody Sunday to my friend across the border a couple of days after Bloody Sunday. I did this after having listened to them. I also made copies. The box that I put them in had another seventeen or so tapes in it (including tapes of the Battle of the Bogside). The box was sealed with adhesive brown tape. I did this to essentially preserve the contents. I consider my friend to be most reliable. I told him what the box contained.

Transcriptions of the army radio recordings, as well as the tapes themselves, were submitted to the subsequent Bloody Sunday Inquiry when it was established in 1998. Porter also revealed that he had photographic evidence of a message that 1 PARA had left on the shutters of a shop window in William Street.

'Paras were here and they fucking hammered fuck out of you.' The graffiti was signed below by a later-identified member of 1 PARA.[13] According to the Derry Journal, *Porter said the shutter itself 'had a crude drawing of six coffins and six crosses, and was later confiscated by the soldiers, but not before he had photographed it in the presence of two witnesses'.*

CHAPTER 12

Sunday Morning

An early morning walk up Fahan Street from the Bogside.

As morning broke over Derry on Sunday 30 January 1972, many local people noticed an increased British military and police presence throughout the city. With the anti-internment march just hours away, the heightened security measures worried many.

1 PARA arrived in Derry that morning with their Commanding Officer, Lieutenant Colonel Derek Wilford. Soldiers already stationed in the city had begun erecting barricades across every street leading to Guildhall Square, with each barrier given a number. Barrier 12 was in Little James Street, Barrier 13 in Sackville Street and Barrier 14 in William Street, leading to the city centre.

Martin Cowley, a Derry man and *Irish Times* reporter in 1972: In January 1972 I was a reporter on the *Irish Times* covering Northern Ireland affairs. Generally, there were some concerns about the parade given the events at Magilligan Strand the previous weekend. I had reported on that march and the violence when soldiers had blocked the protestors. I had a driving lesson on the morning of 30 January. As I drove out of Derry along the Limavady Road I saw a long convoy of army vehicles heading towards the city. I assumed they were coming from Ballykelly army camp. The length of the convoy increased my apprehensions about the afternoon's march.[1]

Bridie Gallagher, sister of 20-year-old Michael McDaid: I was twenty-eight at the time of Bloody Sunday. Our Mickey was such a jolly fella and a lovely brother, it's still hard for me to talk about him. He would come over after mass on a Sunday to play with the boys, Seamus, Hugo and Damien, and they doted on him. That Sunday morning, he had called in, as usual, to have a bit of craic with them and build Lego that they'd got at Christmas.[2]

Maura Young: I was twenty, twenty-one that April. Our John said he was going on the march because everybody was going. A lot of us ended up going really. John got up that morning and my ma said, 'You're not going on that march.' He said, 'Now, Lily … They're interning people, and they could come here and take me out my bed,' and he was right. But he was going for the craic too.

Lord Fenner-Brockway, British socialist politician and one of the speakers organized for the public rally on Bloody Sunday: I was invited by the Northern Ireland Civil Rights Association to Londonderry to address a meeting on civil rights on 30 January. I had introduced a Bill dealing with this subject in the House of Lords in the previous session and agreed to do so on the condition that I should not participate in the illegal march which was planned. Mr Kevin McCorry, an officer of the Northern Ireland Civil Rights Association, accepted this condition.[3]

Ivan Cooper: On the morning of the march, I decided to take a walk around Derry. As the then Member of Parliament for Mid-Derry, there was a constant flow of people approaching me to speak to me. It was a nice morning. I recall that I was wearing a cardigan. I saw paras in the vicinity of St Eugene's Cathedral who were calling to people on the way to mass. The tenor of the comments being made by the paras was that they would deal with the people that afternoon and that they were looking forward to seeing the people later. They seemed to me to be very belligerent. I thought to myself that they were bracing themselves for action and that their presence in Derry was meant to intimidate people, and to deter them from going on the march.

Denis Bradley, formerly Father Bradley and curate at Long Tower Parish in 1972: My memory begins early on the morning of Sunday with the build-up of troops. There was a concentration of troops and a number of soldiers appeared on the ground and began to seal the area off by erecting barriers across the road. They used barbed wire to cut off roads. I had been in the area for about one year and was reasonably used to the army, but I was very surprised at the level of activity and the number of troops on the ground. I remember thinking about the march that afternoon and wondering how many might turn up.[4]

Eamonn Deane, a primary school teacher in 1972: I was twenty-eight years old, a schoolteacher at Long Tower Boys' Primary School in Derry. In the morning of the civil rights march, I was travelling to the Waterside with several of my colleagues to take part in a football match. At the junction of Bishop Street and Abercorn Road we encountered a group of paratroopers. It was immediately clear to us that these paratroopers had a much more aggressive attitude towards us than any soldiers we had previously encountered. Their attitude was one of intimidation and scorn. We were all aware of what had happened the previous week at Magilligan and aware that there had been a change in atmosphere and a change for the worse in the relationship between civilians and soldiers.[5]

Ivan Cooper: I walked from Francis Street east down William Street. There were paras and soldiers everywhere in the streets off William Street. I heard more shouting by soldiers at people, and I realized then that the afternoon would be difficult. The paras were all carrying SLR rifles. I must have seen around a hundred soldiers with red berets in the area and side streets. There were also Saracens positioned around William Street.

Eamonn Deane: It seemed to me that the message that the paratroopers were trying to give us was that we should stay away from the march that afternoon. In fact, this encounter with the paratroopers had the opposite effect. I decided that I wanted to go to show solidarity with the other members of the local community in their protest against internment.

Sophia Downey: On the day of the march, we travelled to my mother's house in Derry by bus. As we passed Magee College on the bus, I saw about ten or fifteen army Land Rovers parked in a row, facing the road. I remember George saying, 'There's going to be bother today.'

Mary Donaghey: I made Sunday lunch for the family about 12pm, earlier than usual, so that we could all take part in the civil rights march that afternoon. After lunch, I remember asking Gerald if he wanted his dessert, but he said that he would be back later at about 6pm and that he would eat it then.[6]

Dermie McClenaghan: Pauline was with her mother in Nelson Drive, and I was to meet her off the bus at the Guildhall. Just as I was walking past the gate at the bottom of Magazine Street, a big soldier came down and grabbed me and pulled me through the gate. He stands me up against a wall and does the usual things, and then said, 'Dermie, don't be going on the march. I know you'll be going, there's no good telling you – but you see those two ladies you're with. Send them home again.' This was a few hours before the march started. I told him the whole town was going on the march, and he said again, 'I'm telling you now – tell the girls to go home.' But I ignored it. It just shows that they *knew*, or they had a good idea what was going to happen.

Bernard Gilmour, brother of 17-year-old Hugh Gilmour: At that time, I was twenty-three years old and lived at the Rossville Flats. After mass that day, I went up to Creggan through the flashpoint at Brandywell at about twelve noon. At the cemetery wall there were about twenty jeeps along the moor. A group of paratroopers were standing there. I was in the army myself so I'm well aware of what a para looks like. One particular para stands out in my mind; he was ordering people onto the path. As he was doing so, he was singing a song to the tune of 'You're Gonna Lose That Girl'. Only he was singing the words, 'You're gonna lose that boy', as if he was singing it to the girls that walked past, concerning their boyfriends. The other paras were in the background behind this one and were generally shouting abuse like, 'Get out of the fucking way, Paddy!' It was only this one particular para who was singing. I walked past with my wife and son. We were taking him to my mother-in-law's so she could babysit while we went on the march.[7]

Eamonn Baker, a Queen's University student in 1972: I was an English Literature student at Queen's University in Belfast, and I was home that weekend to see my family and to take part in the civil rights march. There was a sense of community outrage in Derry at the time at this policy. Tensions were also running high after what had happened the previous week at Magilligan, and, particularly, the brutality that had been shown by the paratroopers there. I knew that the Stormont government had declared the civil rights march to be illegal and this increased the community sense of injustice. The Catholic population of Derry was determined to turn out for the march and make it a success.[8]

James Porter: I was at my shop at 38 William Street just before 1pm. I set my tape recorder to start recording the army radio transmissions at about 3.30pm, which is about the time that they started transmitting. The parade route would take the marchers past my premises. I learned that the parade was going to be stopped by the army at a point close to my premises. From past experience, I knew that any action by the army to stop the parade would result in serious rioting. I decided to set up two recording channels. One channel would be on the police radio net and the other channel would be on the army radio net. I also had facilities to scan and monitor the frequencies of all other channels used by the security forces.

Eamonn MacDermott, local resident and a 14-year-old schoolboy in 1972: We weren't long back from mass, because everyone had to go to mass in those days and were playing football in the street. The next thing a pile of Saracens arrived. They drove up around the corner and it was the paras with the red berets that jumped out. We had obviously stopped our football to watch, and the first thing they said was, 'Are you's Catholic or Protestant?' So, we gave them the good Catholic answer – none of your business! I was fourteen at the time, but my younger brothers and their friends were there too. One of the soldiers booted the ball over the wall of the old Foyle College, and they were very aggressive and hyped up.

My parents were at a later mass than us and the paras stopped them. My father was a doctor and so a very respectful man, and they said, 'Where are you going?' They said they were going into their house, and the solders said they had to search him, and they stuck a gun to my mother's stomach.[9]

Dr Domhnall MacDermott, a local GP and Chief Medical Officer of the Knights of Malta volunteer first-aid organization in 1972: There were about twenty Pigs parked along both sides of the street. There were about fifty soldiers there, all of whom I recognized as being paratroopers. They had blackened faces and were wearing helmets and holding guns. They had the attitude of being all set and raring to go. When I entered my house, I could see that my sons were all in the house. I asked them what they were doing inside. They told me that the soldiers had kicked their ball into the wasteland area nearby and chased them inside calling them 'Fenian fuckers'.[10]

Eamonn MacDermott: Everyone who came to our house that morning was searched, except for one funny story. A friend of my mother's was going out with an Englishman. He drove a very fancy Jaguar or whatever and parked an inch off the army Ferret outside our front door. The paras in the Ferret screamed at him to 'get that fucking car moved', and this fella got out, and spoke back to them in an upper-class English accent, 'I will NOT move my car – how dare you speak to me like that.' You could almost see the paras jumping to attention – this was the voice of authority as far as they were concerned, I think because he spoke to them in the voice of their officer class. Well, that man was the only person who wasn't searched that morning.

Maura Young: John left the house before me. Once I'd got him out of the house, I borrowed a T-shirt he had from a girl in England, so I was feared of running into him on the march.

Bridie Gallagher: Me and my husband Hugo were going on the march. Walking over the lane, we met our Mickey on his way to meet his friends. We were chatting and looking forward to the march, because we knew it was going to be a big day out. All of Derry and people from far and wide were coming. We were delighted. That was the last time we saw him.

Mary Donaghey: Between about 1pm and 1.30pm, Gerald left the house to meet his friends to go on the march. He was wearing a blue shirt, blue jumper, tight Wrangler jeans and a Wrangler jeans jacket. His jeans were always so tight that he couldn't get his cigarettes into the pockets and he would have to carry them in his hands. In fact, he could barely get any small change into his pockets. I remember that he was carrying Park Drive cigarettes. As Gerald left the house, I was upstairs with Dennis, and remember that I looked out the window and saw him on the path below. I called out and waved goodbye to him. I remember that Gerald turned around and waved goodbye. That was the last time I saw my brother alive.

Dr Domhnall MacDermott: I understood there would be no IRA guns during the march. Although I have never been connected to the IRA, as Chief Medical Officer of the Knights of Malta, I knew what was going on. I understood that the Provos [Provisional IRA] thought that the British army proposed to use the march as a ruse to get them out of their Creggan stronghold. For that reason, the Provos were all told to stay in Creggan and not go into the Bogside that day. I was told that the IRA would not be present with guns in the Bogside during the march. For that reason, I felt it was safe.

Denis Bradley: I had gone on the march aware that the Provisionals [IRA], were not going to be there. I knew this because I was aware of who they were. I knew how they reacted. I lived among them. My parish was densely populated with the Provisionals.

Sophia Downey: At my mother's house, which was in the Creggan district, my brother Michael Kelly was upstairs in bed. He had his lunch there. He came downstairs for his dessert but didn't eat it because five or six of his mates came to the door to collect him and they set off for the march. George, my husband, went with them. Michael was wearing a blue suit and a yellow round-neck jumper. The march that day was Michael's first march. He wasn't interested in politics; he had never been in trouble before. He wouldn't have taken part in the rioting because my mother went down to the Bogside regularly and she would have found out. In addition to Michael, my brother John went on the march too, and I went with my other sister, Marion.

Eamonn MacDermott: We were getting into the car for the march, and the paras were shouting things like, 'We'll see you over there.' We thought today might end up like Magilligan. My father told me to stay with him and go in the car while the others went on the march. My father was with the Knights of Malta and had set up the first-aid posts in the Bogside and Creggan since the Battle of the Bogside, but he was also a great believer in that if a march was illegal – you marched. Even if it was just a hundred yards just to break the law, on the principle of being banned. You marched.

CHAPTER 13

Setting Off from Bishop's Field

The civil rights march makes its way up Westland Street.

In the afternoon of 30 January 1972, tens of thousands of people from Derry and further afield congregated around a patch of land called Bishop's Field in Creggan, adjacent to St Mary's Church. From here, the march would set off around 3pm. Many recall the jovial, hopeful atmosphere of the day.

Ita McKinney, widow of 35-year-old Gerard McKinney and over eight-months pregnant at the time: Gerry was not a political man at all. He got up that morning to go to work at McLaughlin's iron mill on the Strand Road where he was a manager. I made him his sandwiches and a cup of tea before he left and said we'd have dinner for six. So, Gerry lifted me up and gave me a kiss and a hug and said, 'I'll see you at six, doll.'[1]

Geraldine McBride: We went down to Bishop's Field and met up with John Young and all of them. I was actually proud to be on the march, because it was important, and the IRA had made it known they wouldn't be there, so it felt safe and that helped persuade my father to let me go.

Dr Domhnall MacDermott: A large group of us left the house to go on the march. All of us got into the car and I drove to Creggan, near to where the march was starting at Bishop's Field. I didn't go on the march as I knew it was illegal and I was conscious of my professional standing in the community. Instead, I intended to be present in the Bogside when the march reached William Street, where I suspected that there may be some trouble because of the army barricades in the area. When I attended the marches in the Bogside, I wanted it to be clear that I was there in my capacity as a doctor.

John Kelly: The reason Michael went on the march was 'cause all his friends were going and he wanted to join them. A big day out and all the girls were there.

Gerry Duddy, younger brother of 17-year-old Jackie Duddy: At the time of Bloody Sunday, I was fourteen years of age and my brother Jackie was seventeen. Jackie was killed that day. We lived near the shops in Creggan where the march was to set off from. We had had Sunday dinner but had been told not to go on the march. I could see thousands of people walking past outside our front door. As far as I was concerned, I was going on the march. I had to avoid my da as I sneaked out of the house. Jackie helped me get out by letting me know when my da wasn't looking.[2]

Michael Quinn, a civil rights marcher aged 17 years old: I was seventeen and still at school when I went on the civil rights march in Derry in January 1972. At that time everybody of my age was interested in the political situation and the civil rights movement. I recall that my mother pleaded with me not to go on the march and warned me that I would be shot. She was concerned about the paras. It was common knowledge that they were to be there that day. However, I laughed it off and said that they had no reason to shoot us.[3]

John Campbell, son of Patrick Campbell: My daddy went to 12pm mass in St Mary's and came up to get his dinner. He went to the march with his docker friends. I went on the march with mates, and we knew there were going to be riots, so the last person I wanted to be beside was my da! [Laughs] I'd be getting pulled by the cuff up home.[4]

Eileen Doherty, widow of 31-year-old Paddy Doherty: Internment was a big issue in Paddy's life. He felt very strongly about it. Any marches, Paddy would be on them. He was on the Magilligan march the week before he died. I was on the Bloody Sunday march with him. Paddy was a steward. We walked up through the cemetery together and I met all my friends, and that was the last time I saw him.[5]

John Kelly: I was on the march too and the last time I saw Michael alive, as far as I know, was just beforehand. It was his first march, he had never been on one before, and my mother hadn't allowed him to go until we persuaded her. He was seventeen years old and asked my mother permission; that just shows you how respectful he was towards her. I remember talking to him just before he joined the march up in Bishop's Field, just outside St Mary's Chapel, and I said to him, 'Just be careful, Michael. If anything happens, get off-sides.'

Maureen Gallagher, a Knight of Malta volunteer first-aider in 1972: In January 1972, I was a volunteer in the Order of Malta. I was twenty-one years old. The Knights of Malta were generally asked to attend all public events, whatever they were, and that is why we were asked to attend the march on Bloody Sunday. One of the rules for a Knight of Malta was that it did not matter what race or religion an injured person was – we treated them.[6]

Eamonn Baker: My family home was in a street facing the Bishop's Field and I could walk out my front door and join the people who were gathering there for the start of the march. My first reaction to the sheer size of the crowd was that the march was going to be a real success.

Philomena McLaughlin, a 13-year-old schoolgirl in 1972: I thought I was going on the march on Bloody Sunday, even though I was only thirteen. My friends and I gathered up at the Creggan shops and the place was buzzing, and all of a sudden, I felt this hand on the back of my neck – it was our Jimmy. He ordered us home, so we went, and we sat in the street listening to the radio instead.[7]

Leo Young: I wanted to go on the march because there was thirty thousand people expected and I wanted to be a part of it. Besides that, I was the older brother and my mother specifically asked me to keep an eye out for our John, who was only seventeen and the baby of the family. Before the march, we had heard rumours that this particular band of soldiers were also coming to Derry, but at that time nobody had any idea how ruthless the paras could really be.

Billy McVeigh: When I met all my friends in Bishop's Field, we had this attitude of wow, look at the crowds of people here. If the Brits start harassing us today, this will show them.

Ivan Cooper: As I was waiting for the march to start, I spoke to William McKinney. I think he had two cameras around his neck. It was through his work with the *Derry Journal* that I had come to know him. It was always the joke that even if violence flared up on a march and CS gas was in the air, William McKinney would still be in the thick of the action taking photos with his camera. You would immediately be struck by William's thick glasses and tight curly hair.

Damian 'Bubbles' Donaghy, a civil rights marcher aged 15 years old: It was a cold day, but everyone was happy and positive as we set off from the Creggan shops. People were saying that the paratroopers were in town, but we were too young to realize what that meant although we knew about events the weeks before on Magilligan Beach.[8]

Paddy Walsh, a local civil rights supporter: At that time, I was about thirty-eight, and I assembled with the crowd at Creggan to join up with the march. I was aware that it was to go to the Guildhall.[9]

Andy Nolan: I called for Jackie after my dinner, and we waited around with everyone else to go on the march. We met Adrian O'Brien and other friends there and were to meet others in the Bogside.

Sophia Downey: Marion and I joined the march at Bishop's Field. It was a frosty day, but not cold. Everyone was singing on the way down to the Bogside.

Maureen Gallagher: The march started from Bishop's Field. The atmosphere there was good, and everyone was talking about the meeting that was due to take place at Free Derry Corner, which was where the march was heading. Everyone was looking forward to hearing the speeches.

Hugh McMonagle: The atmosphere was fantastic, it was like a carnival, the whole attitude. The march took off and, to me, the crowd was getting bigger as it went on as people joined in along the route.

Michael Quinn: It was a cold sunny day; it was freezing. Nonetheless I met up with friends in Creggan and there was a huge crowd. I had never seen so many people. We set off about 3pm and there was a reasonably happy atmosphere, but a certain sense of foreboding because the march has been banned.

Larry Doherty: Everyone knew everyone at that time and people were just milling around, having good craic. I remember speaking to Willie McKinney, who worked with me at the *Derry Journal* office. He was carrying a second-hand camera that I had got for him, and a cine-camera. I shot a few frames, both of the crowd on the field and also of the people as they formed into a march.

Martin McGuinness: The mood of the march was cheerful. However, everybody had known about the bad experience at Magilligan the previous week, when British troops had attacked civil rights marchers, but on this occasion there was great confidence because this was Derry, and with 20,000 on the streets, everybody was together and feeling strong.

Denis Bradley: I was on 12pm mass that day. In the afternoon I left my house. I didn't actually join the march but walked along the footpath beside it. I was quite surprised by the number of people involved.

Conal McFeely, community leader and former Chair of the Bloody Sunday Trust: Events that took place at Magilligan the previous week had been the subject of much discussion in the house. Although I came from a conservative Catholic family where politics was not a high priority, I was politically aware at the time and considered myself in the vanguard for social change through the civil rights campaign. I was particularly influenced by the student protests in France and the campaign for civil rights and equality by the black community in America. I believed that I had a right to challenge the status quo in Northern Ireland by street protests if necessary.[10]

Danny Gillespie, a civil rights marcher aged 32: I had been on about three or four previous marches and there was nothing different about this march. I was quite near the front, and I could see the lorry at the front and knew quite a few people on it.[11]

Dr Raymond McClean: I went on the march with Mickey and Danny McGuinness. We were cracking jokes and telling yarns. The atmosphere was so relaxed and cheerful that I decided to leave my emergency medical equipment in the car at Creggan, as it didn't seem as if there would be any casualties to treat.

Hugh McMonagle: We had a new banner for the Shantallow Civil Rights Association, and we marched behind our banner as part of the main march. The greatest feeling was when you got down as far as Termonbacca and looked back up the hill [Southway], you could see the size of the march snaking downwards. You got this euphoria of feeling, you felt so proud that the people of Derry had turned out like this to protest; we thought this was great and that they would have to listen to us now.

Jed McClelland: We joined the march from Creggan, through the Brandywell and around the Bog. I was about nineteen by then and a student at Jordanstown Polytechnic in Belfast.

Conal McFeely: My brother Donncha and I accompanied Gerald [Donaghey] on the march. Gerald was only seventeen years old and we were all idealistic, impressionable teenagers. Like many of our age in our community we were fired up by the campaign for civil rights. It was a commitment that was to cost Gerald his life. I was only eighteen years old at the time and so Bloody Sunday had a profound effect on me and my family.

Lord Fenner-Brockway: It appeared that the whole population of the area was participating except older women, who I was informed were looking after the children. It was not a march as I have so frequently seen in London, in other towns of Britain, and in Europe. The people might have been engaged in a Sunday stroll – except that their faces were serious. I saw only one child among them, about thirteen years of age. I did not see a stick carried or a weapon of any kind. There was not even shouting of slogans or singing of resistance songs. I have never seen anything more peaceful or less aggressive.

Patrick 'Patsy' O'Donnell, a civil rights marcher aged 41: I wanted to go because of the issue of civil rights – that's what it was all about. I left with two or three friends, including Jimmy Bradley, and we met others we knew on the way. My wife stayed at home looking after the six children. I was looking forward to the march and the meeting afterwards. We were a bit behind the lorry, but people were joining the march along the way and we got pushed further and further back as the march went along.[12]

Hugh McMonagle: The whole way, we kept looking back, amazed at how many were protesting. Anyone with any bit of sense in government or Stormont could see the support for civil rights – people came from all over, from Belfast, Dungannon, Donegal. The people were laughing and joking and then shouting abuse at the army sitting at the Gasyard sangar, though no stones were thrown or anything.

Mickey McKinney, brother of 27-year-old Willie McKinney: I was only twenty years old at the time and I remember being on the march with my mates as it made its way down Southway. The last time I saw our Willie, he was up a tree in Southway with his camera, getting a good angle of the march. I said to the mates, 'There's our Willie up there!' and that was the last time I ever saw him alive.[13]

Mary Donaghey: It was the biggest march I had ever seen. After most of the marchers had gone past me, I joined the tail-end of the march and followed it up Iniscarn Road and east down Westland Street, until I reached the Bogside Inn. At that point, I decided to turn for home. It must have been about 4pm.[14]

Jimmy Toye: I can't remember joining the march. I probably joined in Westland Street as I couldn't be bothered to go up to Creggan. I was eighteen at the time and I worked at our local family grocery shop in Blucher Street. I decided to join the marchers to show my support. I had heard that the IRA were not going to do anything. However, I did expect there to be rioting as this was routine at the time. I often had a go at the rioting myself; most young ones did.

Eamonn MacDermott: At Bishop's Field, my mother and sister went off with others, and me and my father walked to Southway, then we got the car, and we followed the march down. It was quite funny, because I remember there was a car full of Provos in front of us, behind the march. I remember we said to each other, 'There's the Boys,' and they looked at us as if to say, 'There's the doctor.' They were in front of us, tailing the march until it reached the top of Westland Street. Then the march went on towards the town and the car of Provos drove back up the New Road to stay out of the way in Creggan. They kept their word.

Geraldine McBride: The craic was ninety [great fun] and we were marching and singing and chatting away. But when we got to Laburnum Terrace, I could see the army in the distance and I said, 'That's a lot of army,' and then someone said it was the Paratroop Regiment. I thought to myself, Oh Jesus, Mary and Joseph. I said to Hugo, 'That's the soldiers who beat them up at Magilligan!' He promised we'd leave if there was any bother.

Don Mullan, child eyewitness and author of *Eyewitness Bloody Sunday*: It was my first civil rights march. I was fifteen years old and a schoolboy from St Joseph's Boy's School. I had gone on the march with a neighbour, Paddy McLaughlin, who remains a good friend of mine. At some point we got separated.[15]

Patsy McDaid, a civil rights marcher aged 25: I went to the march with my brother-in-law, Joseph Allen. As we walked along on the march, people all around were talking to us. Some of the people you knew, but some of them you didn't; it didn't really matter, you just talked to people as you walked along. People were saying that by the time the march finished, they would need to re-do the roads as so many feet had marched along them.[16]

Alexander Nash, a civil rights marcher aged 51: I joined the anti-internment march at the Bishop's Field. I walked with it to William Street. I went down as far as Porter's TV shop and nothing was happening, then I walked on the footpath as far as the corner of Chamberlain Street. While I was there my son came over to tell me that my other son, Alan, was home from England and was up at the High Flats to see me. I left and went over.[17]

John Kelly: The intention was for the march to get to the Guildhall, but the road was blocked. The army had blocked/barricaded William Street with barbed wire and army vehicles to stop the march getting there. Little James Street was also barricaded off. If we had got to the Guildhall, there wouldn't have been any murders.

Bernard Gilmour: The march was already starting by the time we arrived. We went along with it. I remember seeing the bishop outside the cathedral, blessing the march. He was telling us to watch ourselves.

CHAPTER 14

Snipers in William Street

Local photographer Larry Doherty captures the march as it
reaches William Street.

*The sea of thousands had now reached St Eugene's Cathedral,
turning down William Street towards the city centre by 3.30–
3.45pm. Marchers were in jubilant form, singing civil rights
anthems and cheering. Troops manned every road in and out of
the city, sealing off entrances with army barbed-wire barricades.
Many observed British army snipers on rooftops of the surrounding buildings.*

Andy Nolan: I was still with Jackie when we met our friend, Robert
McMonagle, and his girlfriend, Margaret, near the Bogside Inn.
Instead of carrying on with the march, we all set off for William

Street from there, using the direct route, to wait and watch the march coming down the street. When we got to William Street, we could see that the paras were positioned outside McCool's shop. Just up from the junction there was a small barricade. There wasn't much to it, but it was in the path of the march, and so we cleared it all away and waited for the march to come to us.

Larry Doherty: I think they were singing 'We Shall Overcome', but the atmosphere was still very good natured. There did not appear to be any antagonism in the crowd. I took some shots, trying to capture the immense size of the march from my vantage point. I then saw that stewards were telling the marchers to turn right towards Free Derry Corner. The main body of the march went that way. Some youths were unhappy about this and broke away and carried on straight past me and towards Barrier 14. I followed them.

Paddy Walsh: I must have been fairly near the front. I remember at the junction of William Street and Rossville Street the main part of the march headed southwards along Rossville Street towards Free Derry Corner, where there was to be a platform.

Alana Burke, civil rights marcher aged 18: I joined the end of the march quite late at the top of William Street where the City Baths would be now. There was the usual bit of stone throwing at Aggro Corner, but nothing unusual. The only difference was that there were thousands upon thousands of people on the march. I was eighteen at the time. My daddy had just died six months earlier. My mother was a proud nationalist woman and passionate about civil rights, believing that nationalist people were entitled to the same rights as everyone else in the north. She had told us earlier that day about the march, so I just went for the craic. I remember I was wearing my new brown corduroy 'maxi-coat' and I thought I was the bees' knees.[1]

Martin Cowley: As the crowds proceeded down William Street, I caught sight of a shadowy figure of a soldier lurking in a derelict

SNIPERS IN WILLIAM STREET

building there, either Stevenson's bakery or a former shirt factory. It struck me as particularly sinister since troops were usually visible on the streets during such demonstrations, not peering from the ruins of a burned-out building.

Andy Nolan: The march finally arrived. It was amazing to see so many people. As they came to where we were, I spotted a few friends from school and chatted to them, and, in doing so, I lost contact with Jackie, Robert and Margaret. I ended up waiting around with one of my school friends, Frank Monaghan. Some of the crowd had carried on down towards the Guildhall while the rest carried on towards Free Derry Corner.

Dr Raymond McClean: I was with several friends somewhere in the middle of the march, and as I walked down William Street, I noticed several soldiers in the waste ground to my left. I noted with some concern that they were not wearing the usual riot gear, and were lying in a prone position, pointing rifles at the crowd. I thought that their attitude was menacing but felt this was probably just to intimidate the crowd.

Bernard Gilmour: They all had blackened faces. One or two of them had sights on their rifles, which were pointing towards the crowd on William Street and towards Free Derry Corner. I assumed that the paras were there perhaps to stop the breakaways. I didn't really fear them at that time; they were just like ordinary soldiers. I later came to know that they were like the B Specials and were brought in to quell a big crowd. At about the same time as I saw the paras, I became aware of gas in the area.

Martin McGuinness: As we came down into William Street past the cathedral, I was not concerned that the march would be attacked save for the possibility of trouble at the barrier if the marchers were prevented from going to the Guildhall. I always worked on the basis that the British soldiers were out there some-where even though I could not see them, because I knew that snipers and British army units were always there. I wasn't looking for any. I was part of the march. There was a huge crowd. That was where the focus was.

Dermie McClenaghan: I marched that day with friends I knew from Magee, and it was buoyant and happy, and we were shooting the breeze with each other [chatting]. On a march you separate sometimes, so I later joined Pauline as we were coming down William Street. Being nosy as usual, we didn't turn right over to Rossville Street but went on down to William Street where the riot was.

Jimmy Toye: When I got to Rossville Street, there were a hundred or so people milling about. Most people from the march were going south towards Free Derry Corner. People were milling around in Rossville Street. It was a routine that there would be a skirmish or a riot in William Street and people would go and observe it. I saw clouds of gas and could hear shouting and roaring. I also heard the noise of rubber bullet guns.

Hugh McMonagle: We got as far as Rossville Street where the young fellas were starting to riot, and we tried to get people over to Free Derry Corner and away from the town to avoid confrontation.

Martin Cowley: Arrangements surrounding marches and rallies never went like clockwork, and people just stood around Rossville Street in the shadow of the flats while the troubles continued further down William Street. I did not continue down William Street because I was more interested in staying with the main body of the parade and waiting for the proposed speakers' rally rather than watching low-key trouble involving youths and troops.

Paddy Walsh: I proceeded towards Barrier 14. There were some soldiers lined across the barrier and behind the barrier with shields. They were blocking our entry along William Street towards Waterloo Place and onto the Guildhall. Everyone became very angry at this point. I was angry too, because we were not being allowed access to go through to the Guildhall, and to walk in our own town. I recall maybe even trying to get at the wooden barrier to remove it.

Martin McGuinness: I had no sense that something massive was about to happen. Every day there was a riot, usually at the junction of Rossville Street and William Street, so by the time I had walked across the car park in front of the flats, I was not in the least worried or scared. There would be speeches at Free Derry Corner because of the meeting taking place there, and afterwards people would leave and go back home to their houses. You could have written the script.

Denis Bradley: I remember being aware that the army had blocked off the bottom of William Street as the march approached at that point. I was annoyed because there was a disorganization about the march. I recall there was a public address announcement but frankly most people did not hear it.

Martin Cowley: I was still waiting to hear Fenner-Brockway, and with the stone throwing or rioting at William Street apparently of low intensity, I wasn't very interested. All the signs were that it was nothing out of the ordinary. I certainly do not recall hearing any explosions or seeing anyone with nail bombs.

Eamonn Deane: Sally and I had heard announcements over a megaphone that the crowd was to gather at Free Derry Corner to hear speeches. We made our way down to Free Derry Corner without incident and when we arrived, Lord Brockway had just finished speaking. Bernadette Devlin was about to start her speech. She was waiting for the crowd to build up. Sally and I were perhaps five or six rows back from the front of the platform that was on the back of the lorry. Our backs were to Rossville Street. Many people had gathered behind us; I got the impression it was a very large crowd.

Eamonn Baker: I knew that the march would be prevented from reaching the city centre, and I felt a strong sense of injustice about this. Derry was our city, and it was not acceptable for the police and the army to tell us where we could and could not go.

Denis Bradley: There was obviously no plan by the organizers of the march about what would happen when the march met the army. No one had thought that one out. My memory at that stage is, however, that most people just stood around chatting. This is what Derry people do. There were some young people throwing stones at the barrier. The army were fending them off and were occasionally firing CS gas. Slightly later, water cannons were used. Neither CS gas nor use of the water cannon was particularly new to me.

CHAPTER 15

The Breakaway Riot

Young protestors confront the army at Barrier 14. Jim Wray can be
seen in a seated protest (see lower left of the photograph).

*With most marchers now headed towards the speaker's platform
at Free Derry Corner, some instead chose to continue down
William Street to confront soldiers at what was known as Barrier
14. It was the usual breakaway riot, with youths throwing stones
and antagonizing troops.*

*The army retaliated with rubber bullets, water cannon and
CS gas, incapacitating many in its path and scattering demonstrators in all directions.*

Denis Bradley: I had the strong impression that apart from the
speakers down at Free Derry Corner, Bernadette Devlin and Lord

Brockway, the afternoon was breaking down into a normal street riot. There had been hundreds if not thousands of similar such riots; I had initially spent three months in the cathedral parish having been appointed in 1970 and there were almost nightly riots. You knew the routine. Also, the army got to know you.

Jed McClelland: At William Street, there was a big line of stewards all linked together with arms, stopping anyone from going forward towards the Guildhall. The army had blocked us, and the stewards wouldn't let anyone down. Then about three hundred of us decided 'Fuck this', and we broke through the stewards and marched towards the army's barricades where the riot started, and we were all throwing stones. It wasn't paras then, it was Green Jackets, who were all 'frightfully nice' and asking us to 'Please, stop rioting.' It was the usual craic, really. Because it *was* good craic to us in a way.

Danny Gillespie: Some of the people behind me were throwing stones over my head towards the soldiers manning the barrier. Rather than risk being hit by a stone, I decided to turn round and retrace my steps back up William Street. It was at this time that soldiers began to fire rubber bullets and CS gas. I then met with a friend called Paddy Crawley and we could see down towards Barrier 14 and that stones were being thrown and the soldiers were retaliating. Paddy had a chest complaint made worse by the CS gas drifting towards us.

Eamonn Baker: People in the crowd were trying to direct the march south down Rossville Street to hear political speeches at Free Derry Corner. I was not interested in hearing political speeches as this all seemed rather boring to me at the time. A small part of the crowd carried straight on east towards the army barrier that had been erected there, in order to confront the soldiers. Out of either curiosity or bravado I moved along with these people up towards the barrier that I now understand was known as Barrier 14. If I was arrested and convicted of riotous behaviour, I would be facing a six-month term of imprisonment and this would ruin my university career. I had not been involved in rioting before, and perhaps it was curiosity as much as anything else that made me get involved.

Maureen Gallagher: As I approached the junction of William Street, Rossville Street and Little James Street, a man called out to me and Rosemary. He asked us to go to a house in Chamberlain Street, saying that someone had been hit by two rubber bullets and needed help there.

Eamonn Deane: I was near the back of the march, and as the march went down William Street, I was aware that a small riot was taking place at a barrier that had been erected across William Street to prevent the march from proceeding towards Guildhall. There was another riot taking place at a barricade across Little James Street. Neither of these riots were anything out of the ordinary in Derry at the time and were no more violent than anything I had seen before.

From British army's 8th Brigade Log,[1] **dated 30 January 1972:**

```
1550hrs - Crowd cfm 2000. Area Eden Place/
Pilot's Row. Hooligans area 12, 13, 14, 15.

CS used by the crowd at 14.

1551hrs - Serial 15 clear. Serial 14 under
bombardment from hooligans.
```

Maureen Gallagher: I walked towards the army Barrier 14 made of barbed wire. There were soldiers standing behind it (to the north), and some Saracens. There was a lot of noise coming from that direction. I saw a very small crowd of people, mainly teenagers, throwing stones towards Barrier 14 around McCool's paper shop. A couple of rubber bullets were fired by the soldiers and there was CS gas in the air, but at that point the gas was not too bad, and it did not really affect us. I cannot say exactly how many people were involved in the commotion, but it was a very small crowd. I did not see anything else thrown except stones. I heard no bangs or shooting except for a couple of rubber bullets.

Eamonn Deane: I decided to move away from the area to avoid being affected by CS gas. I remember feeling angry with the rioters at the time because in a way they were proving the army's point. I felt that if the march remained peaceful, it would have been a much better demonstration against internment and a much better display of solidarity. I was able to see a water cannon being used on the crowd.

Paddy Walsh: We ran into some abuse at the barrier. The army were shouting names at us, calling us 'Irish pigs'. There were some young boys throwing stones, and myself, and about fifty others, were trying to pull them away. The boys were giving us abuse, too. The stewards could do nothing about it. It was then that the dye started to come from the water cannon. I was wringing wet. I sensed that it was time to get out.

Billy McVeigh: I must be honest, we were usually front-line rioters, both before and after Bloody Sunday. There was a riot to the left in Great James Street, which we were part of for a while, then we went on down to William Street. I've always thought about that point where they blocked us. It wasn't just a water cannon they sprayed at us – it was different. I was so used to the riots back then that I knew the difference between these things, and I've always been certain it was muddy water or sewage.

Gerry Duddy: I remember talking to Jackie minutes before he was shot. We were worried about being caught on the march by our older brother Billy, who had cornered me earlier and told me to get home because there was going to be trouble. He said if I saw the other two [Patrick and Jackie], then tell them to get home too. Then I went up to where the rioting was going on and the water cannon moved in. I thought, 'Well if I get soaked here, then I'll be caught for being at the march,' so I kept back from William Street and went back to the junction of William Street and Rossville Street.

I bumped into Jackie and I warned him, 'You better watch out, Billy's looking for you.' 'I'm alright,' he said, 'I'm a big boy.' So, I left, and I said, 'Well I'm telling you now, Billy's looking for you, and he's going to send *you* home, too.' So, Jackie went that way, and I went … I don't know what direction. That was the last time I saw him.[2]

Eamonn Baker: Some of the younger lads who were confronting the army at Barrier 14 had got hold of a bit of tin sheeting. I was one of the lads who stood behind this tin. I can distinctly remember the noise and the force of the impact as the army fired rubber bullets into this tin sheeting. The lads who were behind the tin would move back and pick up stones from the ground, before charging towards the barrier and lobbing the stones over the top of the tin. It was very exciting, and I felt caught up in the bravado of it all. I saw my father as I was doing this standing further west down William Street, and a lot of other men who were watching the rioting that was going on.

Denis Bradley: This was no worse or no better than any other riot. I remember distinctly becoming very annoyed and disappointed by the degeneration of the march into a riot, because I thought the march was important.

Michael Quinn: I was standing talking to a friend when this guy came up carrying a civil rights banner, grabbed me and told me to take one end of the banner with him out onto the waste ground north of William Street. I did not want to go because I didn't want to get too close to the soldiers. I did not know the guy, but I subsequently discovered that it was Jim Wray. I reluctantly agreed to hold one end of the banner, which I think said 'Northern Ireland Civil Rights Association'. We didn't go far with the banner and, as they were firing rubber bullets and gas, I probably only held it for a few minutes.

Sophia Downey: The march came to a halt. Soldiers had stopped it at the front and a lot of rubber bullets and gas was being fired into the crowd. People in the crowd were shouting 'Stand your ground', but my sister was a bit of a panicker and felt sick with the effects of the gas, so we ran down towards Free Derry Corner. Others were doing the same and I recall seeing shoes scattered in the street where people had stepped out of them as they ran.

Larry Doherty: There was shouting and roaring. The crowd were throwing stones and the army was firing gas. I could not say which came first. People started to be sick from the gas and I was trying to take photographs of them. I took pictures of the gas exploding in the air. However, the gas started to make me sick, so I went back down William Street and stopped on the waste ground opposite Kells Walk. I was trying to vomit and to fill my lungs with fresh air.

Denis Bradley: I was not surprised by the CS gas or stone throwing. CS gas carries a very strong and spontaneous reaction. It could be all around you without grabbing you. When it did, it grabbed you totally. It really got you. All control left you. The only thing you wanted to do was to get out of it. You did not want to take that second breath. The only thing that came through my mind when the CS gas got to me was, I did not want to take the second breath. I needed to go somewhere else. You were not aware of any other thought, feeling or reaction.

Eamonn Deane: I was a little affected by the CS gas and I remember coughing and spluttering. I made my way over to Kells Walk, crossing over some waste ground; I met my girlfriend, Sally, there.

Denis Bradley: The noise of CS gas canisters was not like rubber bullet fire; it was a delicate 'whoosh' sound. I ran down Chamberlain Street trying to catch my breath and cough the stuff out. I stumbled down the street, half running, bent over. I probably fell off the footpath. I was spluttering and wasn't aware of where I was going. I wasn't directionally focused.

Alana Burke: We were caught up in everything and when the army started spraying the water cannon, I was soaked to the skin with its dye and choked with CS gas fumes. I remember being very sick and disorientated, but not scared. That probably sounds strange, but I just thought the crowd would disperse and the army wouldn't come any further. A man took me into a house in Chamberlain Street. After a glass of water, he advised me to go home.

Joe Friel, a Bogside resident aged 20: I lived in the Rossville Flats. I was well used to seeing trouble, but it would have been foolish for me to get in any bother, as I worked as a tax officer for the Inland Revenue in the Embassy building. The army occupied the top floor. I had to pass the army every day and needed security clearance to get into the building. From the flat I could hear the roar of the crowd. I could hear a lot of shouting coming from the William Street area, but I couldn't see what was happening. I was bored in the flat after dinner and asked my father if I could go to hear the speeches at Free Derry Corner. He said I could and told me to look out for myself.[3]

At the speaker's platform further into the Bogside along Rossville Street, thousands of marchers were congregating around the ad-hoc meeting place of Free Derry Corner to hear speakers including Bernadette Devlin MP and Lord Fenner-Brockway.

British army's 8th Brigade Log:

> **1552hrs** - Bulk now moved down Rossville St towards Flats. Flat topped lorry behind flats may be used for speaker.
>
> **1553hrs** - CS & baton rds used to disperse hooligans at 12, 13. Some hooligans were wearing respirators.

Lord Fenner-Brockway: When we reached Free Derry Corner there was a lorry for the speakers and a crowd around it of about two thousand. It was a quiet and orderly crowd, except that a few girls were singing 'We Shall Overcome', and a rather more militant song in denunciation of British troops. There was no evidence of disorderly indignation, however, and the people were as serious and quiet as they had been at the beginning of the march in the Creggan.

British army 8th Brigade Log:

> **1554hrs** - Gen move to south of Rossville Flats. Flat top truck near Foxes Corner. 15 now clear. 14 stoning continues.
>
> **1554hrs** - 200 at Aggro corner.
>
> **1554hrs** - Crowd now dispersing towards Rossville Flats and way they came. CS being used against hooligan element.
>
> **1555hrs** - Would like to deploy sub-unit through barricade 14 to pick up yobbos, in William St/Little James St.

*

Lord Fenner-Brockway: Evidently CS gas had been liberated; even in our car five hundred yards away, my eyes began to stream and breathing became difficult. There was the noise of other firing from the barrier, which I was informed was of rubber bullets. I was given one of these bullets afterwards and was surprised to find that it was approximately six inches in length and one and a half inches in diameter, and very hard and pointed; at close range it appeared to me to be potentially damaging and possibly fatal.

*

British army 8th Brigade Log:

> **1555hrs** - C/S have been deployed nearer to liaise for easy deployment.

CHAPTER 16

Shots Fired at the Waste Ground

Soldiers armed with rubber bullets face peaceful marchers at
Barrier 14 on William Street.

*With thousands now crammed into the Bogside, the major-
ity were moving towards or at Free Derry Corner or crowding
William and Rossville Street.*

*Rioting continued at Barrier 14, and just after 3.55pm,
Colonel Wilford sent a radio message to Brigade Headquarters at
Ebrington suggesting one of his companies be sent in. However,
Brigadier MacLellan delayed giving the order for the arrest operation for a further 12 minutes. Around the same time as Wilford
sent his message to HQ, soldiers in William Street fired the first
shots of Bloody Sunday.*

John Johnston, a first-time civil rights marcher aged 59: I had never been on a march before, and because I was worried about gas, having a bad chest, I made sure I was towards the end. As we got near the Rossville Street crossing, I could see that there were big clouds of gas around the barrier down William Street, so I thought I would cut across to my right and go and see an old man, about ninety, who lives in Glenfada. He can't get about much and I often go round to make sure his windows are shut tight if there's a lot of CS around.[1]

Dr Raymond McClean: The crowds were then making their way from Lower William Street and across Rossville Street, with tears streaming down their faces, and many with handkerchiefs held to their mouths for protection. There was some minor panic as people walked into pockets of CS gas in the congestion at Rossville Street corner. Suddenly I heard three or four sharp cracks in rapid succession. These sounds were clearly distinguishable from the sound of rubber bullets or CS gas being discharged. I said to Daniel McGuinness, 'That sounds different, doesn't it?' He replied something like, 'I'm afraid it was.' I became really concerned for the first time that day.

James Porter: At about 3.55pm I heard a number of shots fired in upper William Street approximately a hundred yards from my shop. These were the first shots that I heard fired. I was listening to the radio at the time and for quite a period thereafter and I was surprised that these shots were not reported by the army Observation Posts to Brigade Headquarters, particularly when the Observation Posts appeared to be reporting every little thing. I heard the shots fired before Call Sign 90A reported that all was peaceful [over radio]. I was very surprised when I heard this.

Maura Young: When we passed the cathedral, we heard someone say that there was rioting in William Street, so I cut over past the Stardust to go home and met our Patrick. He was the eldest and the boss. I told him I was heading home because of the rioting. He told me to come on, we'd walk home together. We walked up around Little Diamond when we heard the shots. Patrick thought it was CS gas. It was a different type of crack – two big cracks. We went on up towards Rosemount and a soldier stopped Patrick on the hill and searched him; they were quite rough and had him up against a wall.

Jimmy Toye: I think I was in Rossville Street for about ten or fifteen minutes before I heard two high-velocity shots. I knew they were army high-velocity shots because I was used to hearing shooting where we lived. I would often hear, during the day or lying in bed at night, the different shots during a gun battle.

Raymond Rogan: I was on the march. I don't know what it was, but coming down William Street I automatically sensed that there was going to be trouble. I had family and wanted to get back to the house and see where they were, which I did. It was shortly afterwards that we started hearing the shots and we knew right away they were high-velocity bullets, the real McCoy.

The first shots were fired by two soldiers of the machine-gun platoon, who had fired five shots between them from their position at the derelict building on William Street. The first casualty was a 15-year-old boy, Damian 'Bubbles' Donaghy, who was shot in the thigh in the waste ground across the street.

Damian Donaghy: When the march reached William Street, we were gathered near Brewster's Close, and we could see soldiers hiding in the old bakery where the Post Office is now. We could see them lying low and everyone was throwing stones at them. Then a few rubber bullets were fired, and one bounced off the wall and I dived to get it as a souvenir. By the time I dived to get it, the next thing I knew I was lying on my back and was shot.

May O'Neill, a young mother in her thirties in 1972: They just started firing out of the blue. He fell at my feet. I thought he was dead.[2]

Gerry Duddy: I then heard a single shot. I turned to my left and I saw Damian Donaghy, or Bubbles as I called him, yell out, 'I'm shot,' and me and another fella with me laughed, thinking that Bubbles had been hit by a rubber bullet. As people carried him away, there was a single second shot. I still didn't realize that these were live shots that had been fired.

John Johnston: I went onto the open ground and I think I was about two-thirds of the way across, about level with that old, wrecked lorry, when there was a big thump on the back of my right leg. I thought, my God, I've been whacked by a rubber bullet and went to hobble on, though I couldn't move well.

Damian Donaghy: A couple of other people came over to lift me. I knew I was shot, and I shouted to big Gerry Duddy, 'I'm shot,' and he shouted back that it was only a rubber bullet.

John Johnston: Then a man shouted to me, 'Christ, Mr Johnston, you're shot. Your trousers are soaking in blood.' I looked down and so they were; they were light grey, and they were soaked right through. Some men came to give me a hand and, as I was helped away, I could see a young lad lying propped up against a wall to my left.

Damian Donaghy: Both me and John Johnston were taken into Mrs Shiels' house in Columbcille Court. Fr Carlin, the parish priest in Creggan, came into the house and he took us to hospital, John Johnston first and then me.

May O'Neill: We carried the boy into the house. I wanted to go with him to the hospital, but they wouldn't let me in case I was arrested.

Gerry Duddy: I realized that live bullets had been fired when one of the fellas who carried Bubbles told me that he had seen blood on Bubbles' jeans caused by a real bullet. He wasn't doing anything wrong – nothing to justify him being shot.

Jimmy Duddy: Johnny [Johnston] was the second man shot on Bloody Sunday. He was in terrible shock afterwards.

John Johnston: When they got me into Columbcille Court, the Shiels' flat I think, Doctor McClean discovered I had been hit at least three times; once in the shoulder, another in the leg and a graze on my left hand from a ricochet. I'm told now that my big overcoat saved me. What with that, a good jacket and a woolly cardigan, the bullet must have been slowed down.

John Johnston, then the manager of a men's drapery store, was the oldest person shot on Bloody Sunday. He had pieces of metal removed from his wounds and spent ten days in hospital.

John Johnston: I can tell you with all truth, I never heard a shot nor any bomb before I was hit, not a solitary thing did I hear except the rubber bullets and the stones. How could anyone pick me as a gunman? There I am walking away with my back to the troops; they were just shooting at anything, like herrings in a barrel.

John Johnston died in June 1972, just five months after Bloody Sunday, his early death attributed to the injuries and trauma sustained.

Shortly after Damien Donaghy and John Johnson were shot, a member of the Official IRA retaliated by firing one shot back at soldiers from a position across William Street. The shot hit a drainpipe. This man is designated OIRA 1 in the 2010 Report of the Bloody Sunday Inquiry and his colleague, OIRA 2.

*

Elsewhere, marchers and bystanders were being overcome by the fumes of CS gas, and thousands of others were on their way to, or congregating at, Free Derry Corner for speeches.

British army 8th Brigade Log:

> **1558hrs** - Minor stoning at serial 9.
>
> **1559hrs** - Gen mov of crowd from Rossville Flats into Lecky Rd.
>
> **1600hrs** - Press Belfast Telegraph estimate crowd 3000.

From Colonel Welsh to Brigade HQ at 1559 hours: General crowd movement now is down into the Lecky Road from the area of the flats. It seems as though a lot of people feel they've made their protest and are now returning back to their homes.[3]

Denis Bradley: By the time I got to the waste ground around Eden Place, I was in slight shock. I felt sick though did not vomit. I had no consciousness of danger in my stomach. The young people were doing their normal rioting, but most of the people were drifting away. I had no sense of danger or foreboding about what would happen. I was of course conscious of the possibility of snatch squads. That did not perturb me as I had my collar on. Usually snatch squads ran past me. I was still annoyed, however, because you can never stop a riot once it has started, only before it starts. It was too late by now and I had a strong feeling by this stage that I should leave.

Martin Cowley: Suddenly everyone was diving for cover amid the sounds of gunfire. I was momentarily confused as to whether it was live gunfire because it just came out of the blue. The sounds seemed to be coming towards us – that is from further down Rossville Street where the soldiers were. Everyone was stunned. There was nothing that I heard or saw that prompted the firing.

*

From report of 22 Lt AD Regiment to Brigade, around 1603–1604 hours: Hello Zero, this is 90A. There is now a crowd of about 500 on Fox's Corner [Free Derry Corner] being addressed from a loudspeaker van. These appear to be normal civil rights people. There's still a crowd of about 150 hooligans at junction Rossville Street/William Street. Over.[4]

British army 8th Brigade Log:

1602hrs - Hooligans still at barrier 14.

1603hrs - 500 at Foxes Corner being addressed from van.

1604hrs - 150 hooligans at Aggro corner.

1609hrs - Groups advancing on 14, behind corrugated iron shields.

1609hrs - Those dispersing up Creggan Road, women, children and old people.

*

Danny Gillespie: I could see a man about the same age as myself or perhaps a bit older. He was hit in the mouth with a rubber bullet fired from the direction of Barrier 14. I didn't see him being hit or who fired the shot. He didn't fall to the ground but was obviously in some pain from his injuries as the bullet had badly cut his lips and face. I noticed that his lips were cut to shreds and my opinion was that this was caused by broken glass that had been packed into the bullet. The bullet was on the ground so I picked it up and I could see where it had been cut open so that glass could be pushed into the opening, but the glass was now missing. There were photographers and other people from the media standing around. I pointed the rubber bullet out to them. An American photographer took a photo of the bullet in my hand.

Many among those present during riots in the 1970s attest to seeing or hearing about such 'doctored' rubber bullets – that is, made more lethal with shards of glass or razor blades inserted into an incision in the tip of the bullet itself.[5]

Paddy Walsh: I noticed a Pig behind the barrier getting ready. You could tell when this was going to happen. I seem to recall the army were there before the paras. I have a recollection of the regular soldiers moving back to make a pathway for the paras to come through. I decided to get off-sides.

CHAPTER 17

'The paratroops want to go in'

The British army sprays water cannon at protestors near Barrier 14.

Brigadier MacLellan authorized 1 PARA's arrest operation as suggested by Colonel Wilford at 4.07pm. When doing so, he specifically ordered that troops going through Barrier 14 were 'not to conduct a running battle down Rossville Street'. This order went unheeded.

The arrest operation was limited to sending one company of 1 PARA through Barrier 14 in William Street for a scoop-up of rioters. Without authority, another company was sent in, too.

From the *Report of the Bloody Sunday Inquiry*, 2010: Colonel Wilford did not comply with Brigadier MacLellan's order. He deployed one company through Barrier 14 as he was authorised to do, but in addition and without authority he deployed Support

Company in vehicles through Barrier 12 in Little James Street. The vehicles travelled along Rossville Street and into the Bogside, where the soldiers disembarked. The effect was that soldiers of Support Company did chase people down Rossville Street. Some of those people had been rioting but many were peaceful marchers. There was thus no separation between peaceful marchers and those who had been rioting and no means whereby soldiers could identify and arrest only the latter.[1]

British army 8th Brigade Log:

> **1609hrs** – Orders given to 1 PARA at 1607hrs for 1 sub-unit of 1 PARA to do scoop up OP through barrier 14. Not to conduct a running battle down Rossville Street.[2]
>
> **1609hrs** – Serial 14 being lifted now.

Hugh McMonagle: Me and Jim and Mickey Shiels and a brother of mine stood across the street at Aggro Corner, and the next thing I looked over Great James Street and the crowd were starting to throw stones over there too. Then I looked around as the army started to run and the Ferret cars came in and then I saw the three-tonners moving too, and so we all shouted to run.

From Chief Superintendent Lagan's written statement to the Widgery Tribunal, 1972: The Brigadier, who had presumably gone to his Operations Room, came into the office and said 'The paratroops want to go in.' I said, 'For heaven's sake hold them until we are absolutely certain the marchers and the rioters are well separated.' He left me again. After an interval he returned and said, 'I'm sorry, the paras have gone in.' I did not hear the order to the paras to move, over the radio.[3]

British army 1 PARA log:

> **1610 hours** – Move 3 now through K14. Also, C/S 1 No running battles.

Eamonn Baker: I can remember seeing armoured cars at the junction of Rossville Street and William Street, heading south down Rossville Street. I could also see soldiers running behind these vehicles and travelling in the same direction. I immediately became very scared. The soldiers had effectively got in behind me in a pincer movement. I was at university and couldn't afford to get arrested, and I turned and ran back up William Street and into Chamberlain Street.

James Porter: When the soldiers entered William Street through Barrier 14, I watched from my front window and saw about a hundred soldiers come from lower William Street from the direction of the barrier. I also saw a man who I understood was General Ford at the back of the men waving a stick in the air and shouting something that I couldn't hear … within minutes of the soldiers having moved through Barrier 14, I saw from the rear window of my shop many soldiers running via Eden Place towards the waste ground from the direction of Chamberlain Street. The army radio transmission [I recorded] conflicts with what I saw.

Jimmy Toye: There seemed to be a surge of people coming south towards me. I thought that there might be a snatch squad coming towards the junction of William Street and Rossville Street. In those days, the snatch squads did not normally venture past this junction and rarely came as far as the Rossville Flats.[4]

Hugh McMonagle: We ran through the gap into the waste ground. We had only stayed around to try and get the young fellas to stop. When I looked to my right, I saw the Ferret car turn in towards us, and I'll tell you, I was running but my knees were hitting my chin, we ran so fast. While I was running, I saw someone down and I thought they had tripped. I ran on and jumped in behind a wee wall beside the flats. While we were running, the gunfire had started. I knew the difference between that and rubber bullets.

Eamonn MacDermott: My father parked literally in the middle of Rossville Street and I waited by the car while he headed off to see if he could find the injured. The next thing the paras moved in. I remember that at that exact moment I could hear Bernadette Devlin over the loudspeaker saying, 'Come to the meeting, they can't arrest us all', and no sooner had she said, it, the army moved in. Then the first shots started. I could see my daddy walking slowly back towards me, and I was calling, 'Daddy, they're shooting, they're shooting!' and he thought I was exaggerating. Then he heard the whizz of a bullet passing him, too, and realized they really were shooting. We jumped in the car, us in the middle of Rossville Street, and we tried to turn the car but there was a paving slab under the front wheel, and we couldn't move. People were running past us and ducking, and as people ducked down, we could see the soldiers coming behind them and right towards us. Then someone grabbed the paving stone and pulled it away from under the wheel, so we could drive away quick.

Michael Quinn: I went to the back wall of McLaughlin's hardware store to shelter from the gas, and a large number of people did likewise. While we were sheltering there, a man warned us that the army was coming in. As he was speaking, some Saracen armoured cars passed us by and travelled over Rossville Street. I began to run across the waste ground, towards the front of the Rossville High Flats.

British army 8th Brigade Log:

> **1610hrs** - 70 hooligans, Chamberlain Street, dispersed from Aggro corner, moving down Rossville Street.
>
> **1612hrs** - Pigs and 4 tons have dispersed crowd temporarily in Chamberlain Street. Reforming by Rossville Flats.

Denis Bradley: It was almost certainly at this stage, although I am not entirely sure when, that I was told by someone, or I heard others saying, that people had been shot by live bullets in the region of William Street. Even though I hadn't heard anything, I thought I had better check it out.

James Porter: I was also surprised to hear the evidence to the Widgery Inquiry that at about 3.00pm the wire-cutting party at the Presbyterian church was fired at, because I knew that this had not been reported over the radio either. I did not hear any shots at this time.

I remember hearing on the army radio transmissions questions about whether the hooligan element was present in William Street. I looked out of my front window to see what the situation was. What I saw then was that the whole of William Street that was within my view was empty.

Maureen Gallagher: A rubber bullet was fired from the first Saracen. I felt it skim past my right cheek. It missed me and I heard Rosemary cry 'I'm hit.' The rubber bullet had hit Rosemary on her left cheek and the left-hand side of her neck.

Jimmy Toye: There were more high-velocity shots. These, again, came from the direction of William Street. The shots were heavy and close to me, but I could not see who was shooting.

Eamonn Deane: I then heard a single shot, which came from the direction of William Street. Immediately after that, I heard the women at the pram ramp shouting out that a young man had been shot in William Street. They also shouted that he had been shot from the Sorting Office. Apart from rubber bullets, which had been fired at rioters from the barricades, this was the first shot of the day that I had heard. It was definitely a high-velocity shot, which is easily distinguishable from a rubber bullet.

British army 8th Brigade Log:

> **1614hrs** – Crowd at Foxes Corner dispersing rapidly.

Martin Cowley: We all fell flat on the ground, some on top of others, lying low and then moving sideways like a giant crab. My abiding memory is that I could smell the gunfire in the air. We moved in fits and starts before seizing the moment and running through an alleyway to seek cover close to the Bogside Inn.

Eamonn Baker: I played a lot of football at the time, and I was pretty fit. However, all I can remember is running like hell south down Chamberlain Street thinking to myself that I was still not running fast enough to get away from the soldiers.

Dermie McClenaghan: Just as we arrived at the flats, two jeeps came in and three or four soldiers came running out towards us and started battering Pauline with rifles. So, I'm trying to get between Pauline and him, and he's saying things like 'fucking Irish pig' and so on. I'm trying to get him out of the road and Pauline's crying a bit, so I pulled her away, and this big soldier was still shouting at us 'fucking Irish'. I found out later that by the time those two jeeps came in, there was already two people shot. I didn't know that.

Eamonn Deane: I recall the first part of Bernadette Devlin's speech when she said something along the lines of 'If the Brits want to stop us having a legal meeting, let them try. There are fifteen of us to each one of them.' Before Bernadette could go any further, we heard screams and shouts of 'They are coming in' and 'The paras are coming' from people further north up Rossville Street. Due to the size of the crowd at Free Derry Corner, I could not get a good view of what was going on, but I heard the noise of a large amount of people panicking. People around us were shouting out things like 'Stand your ground.' 'Let them come – don't panic!'

British army 8th Brigade Log:

```
1615hrs - 2 HV shots heard in area of
Rossville Flats. People lying on ground.
```

Dr Raymond McClean: Within a minute, a man shouted for me to come with him quickly, as two people had been shot at the back of the march. I went with him, and someone showed us to the Shiels' house, where I found a teenager and a middle-aged man, both of whom had been shot. The boy had an entry bullet wound on the upper third of the inner surface of his right thigh, and a jagged exit wound over the middle third of the outer surface of the same thigh. He was pale and shocked but was not losing much blood externally. The boy was Damian Donaghy.

Larry Doherty: People started to shout that two men had been shot in William Street. I didn't really believe them at the time. There was pandemonium, and people were very angry. I was told that the two people who had been shot had been taken to Bridget Shiels' house on Columbcille Court. I headed for the house. I was walking, still taking deep breaths to try and clear my lungs of the gas.

Dr Raymond McClean: I then examined the middle-aged man whose name was John Johnson. He had a gunshot wound over his upper inner-right thigh, and a peculiar, jagged wound over his left shoulder region. I hadn't seen a wound like it before. It was shallow and appeared to be three holes joined together in a line. I thought it had been caused by a ricochet. If it had not been a ricochet the bullet would have gone through the shoulder and caused a lot of damage. He was not losing much blood. He was quite pale, but his pulse was quite good. He was shocked and was not talking.

Maureen Gallagher: As I entered the room, I saw to my right an elderly man being treated by Doctor McClean and a couple of other people. To my left, lying on the settee, was a young boy. Both injured had gunshot wounds. I remember thinking to myself that this was the first time I had ever seen someone who had been shot. The atmosphere was one of shock – no one had been expecting trouble or that anyone would get shot.

Dr Raymond McClean: It was quite quiet in the Shiels' house; there was no shouting. Nobody talked about what had happened. I was aware that the army had carried out the shootings, but I don't know how I knew. Someone must have said something to that effect. While I was in the lounge, I heard several bursts of gunfire outside, each burst consisting of three or four shots.

Larry Doherty: I couldn't quite believe it. I squeezed into a corner of the room. I wanted to get some pictures, because I felt this was big news, but I certainly did not want to interfere with what was going on. I stood well back and took the best pictures I could without a flash. I had no flash as this was a daylight march. At that time, I thought I would have the biggest pictures of that day.

Mary Donaghey: Once home, I settled Dennis in. I then looked out the living-room windows, which overlooked Westland Street and Meenan Square. Every now and again, I could see people running up Westland Street. I also saw some people running down Lecky Road, but I didn't think anything of what I saw.

Larry Doherty: When I was in the house, I could hear banging outside. I thought that the banging I could hear was rubber bullets being fired. The shooting was quite fierce. Suddenly, there was pandemonium outside the house. People had been shot and were dying and dead. They were looking for priests and doctors. At the call that people had been shot, Raymond and I left the house. We headed south, through Columbcille Court towards Abbey Park. As we did so, people were still shouting that people had been shot. I couldn't quite believe it.

Major General Robert Ford: As C Company went forward, I said to the leading platoon, 'Go on 1 PARA, go and get them and good luck.' The words were picked up by one of the media microphones. I consider these were normal words of encouragement being given to soldiers about to go into a dangerous situation.[5]

CHAPTER 18

Advance into Rossville Street

Marchers flee through flats courtyard on Bloody Sunday.

More shots rang out after British troops advanced into Rossville Street at 4.07pm, opening fire with live rounds. Marchers fled from the commotion. Running up Chamberlain Street into the Bogside, teenager Jackie Duddy fell in the courtyard of the Rossville Flats, shot in the back. He had been running alongside a priest when hit. Father Daly later spoke of how the boy had giggled as they passed each other, bemused at the sight of a priest running.

A few yards away, 18-year-old Alana Burke couldn't run fast enough. She was caught up in the army's advance as their colossal army vehicles roared behind her. Another man, 32-year-old Thomas Harkin, was hit by the same vehicle.

Alana Burke: I could see the soldiers coming towards us on foot. Someone shouted to me 'run' and that's when I heard the rev of the army vehicle. I remember seeing it coming and being frozen to the spot, the weight of my soaked coat weighing me down. Someone tried to help me, but we lost each other. At that stage I was petrified and on my own. I glanced behind me and I saw the Saracens coming in one after the other, then I heard the thud and hit the ground and remember crawling along the earth and not feeling my legs at all.

Paddy Walsh: I ran down with a crowd, southwards. The paras were chasing us with batons. I thought that they were going to make a snatch. About forty of us formed a line across Chamberlain Street as a blockade. The paras were facing us having come in from William Street and southwards down Chamberlain Street. We were looking north up along Chamberlain Street.

Danny Gillespie: People in the path of the Saracens had to dive to get out of their way. One of the Saracens then suddenly veered off and, at first, I thought that it had crashed, partly because of the sudden movement and partly because of the 'crashing' noise that it made. I then heard someone shout that a girl had been run over.

Jed McClelland: The Pigs came in and it got very tense because we knew they were going to attack. I was standing at the TV shop in William Street, and we could sense the tensions rising. Then all of a sudden, the red-caps [paras] came in. Once we saw them, we knew we were in bother. They'd been in Ballymurphy six months earlier, so we knew the score – and I took off running along Chamberlain Street, with the paras following us and shooting at us. You could hear the bullets flying 'Whizzzzz' overhead.

Eamonn Deane: Suddenly, a volley of shots rang out. They were all high-velocity shots and appeared to me to be coming from the William Street end and, also, from the city walls to our east. My recollection is of a large number of shots being fired. There appeared to be no order to them, the firing was random.

Alana Burke: I knew it was a Saracen that hit me – I couldn't run fast enough to get out of its way. I was totally disorientated, lying there praying that someone would please help me. Even talking about it still sends me reeling after all these years and I get awful flashbacks. A man carried me, semi-conscious, to a house in Joseph Place. I suppose I thank God that he did, because Jackie Duddy was shot just a minute or two after that.

Jimmy Toye: It was panic – everyone running back, scattering with the roar of army vehicles. I stood my ground thinking they would stop because this was a no-go area, but no, this was different. I couldn't see very well with so many people pushing and running towards me. Then crack-crack, the unmistakable sound of British army high-velocity bullets and very close by.[1]

Bernard Gilmour: The first live round I heard that day was when we were heading over the waste ground to the Rossville Flats' car park. I heard the sound of an SLR [self-loading rifle] being fired, perhaps three or four rifles firing single shots in quick succession. The bullets sounded like the clap of your hands with an echo like a crack. I must have heard around thirty to forty shots in a few seconds. Almost immediately, the people standing at Free Derry Corner hit the ground. People were also lying flat on Rossville Street. There was a lot of squealing. About five seconds after the shooting started, I heard the revving up of the Pigs. I assumed that they were coming to sort out the rioters. I thought to myself, 'Here they come!' I thought there would be a baton charge and I wanted to get home.

Geraldine McBride: Then Hugo and I got separated at the bottom of William Street. A surge of people pushed us both to opposite sides of the street as the army came in and I lost him. He had no choice but to go around the long way to get back to where we were. He would have been arrested otherwise and we were getting married, so we couldn't afford for him to be arrested.

Peggy Deery, a Derry mother of 14 children: I was not really on the march, as I had got caught up in the crowds that were rushing away from the barrier in William Street. My sister and I were only intending to look at the end part of the march. I was standing just out on the waste ground by Eden Street, and I heard a man nearby shout, 'The army's coming in!' I looked over towards Rossville Street and there were big Pigs coming in and one headed over towards where we were.[2]

James Porter: I looked out of the rear window of my shop. From here I could see armoured vehicles and about a hundred troops in the waste ground. At one stage, I saw an army vehicle careering around the waste ground as if the driver was trying to hit people with it. I then saw it hit a man a glancing blow. He was knocked down, but he got up and ran off. I also saw troops entering the waste ground from Chamberlain Street via Pilot's Row. They were heading towards the Rossville Street High Flats.

Dr Domhnall MacDermott: I could see Bernadette Devlin and others standing on the platform. I was in mid-conversation with Vincent Coyle when I heard a 'psss-ss' sound like wasps over my head. I remember thinking, 'How could there be wasps in January?' I continued towards Free Derry Corner and as we got nearer to the civil rights platform, I could hear Bernadette Devlin saying, 'Sit down. If you sit down, they won't shoot you.' I then saw Eamonn near my car jumping up and down shouting 'Daddy! Daddy! They're firing real bullets!' At that point, the penny dropped, and I realized the things buzzing over my head had been bullets and not wasps. I was worried about members of my family who had been out on the march.

Bridie Gallagher: Just as Lord Fenner-Brockway was introduced the army started shooting and there was panic. We all got down low, on our hunkers, and made our way across the street, and a crowd of us got into a derelict house behind Free Derry Corner. The sounds of those guns, I'll never, ever forget it. I can still hear the loudness of the cracks. It was the first time we had ever heard real gunfire, so everybody panicked. Hiding in that derelict house, nobody spoke a word, everybody was just stunned. I don't know how long we were in there.

Gerry Duddy: People were quickly becoming hysterical, and I remember hearing women shouting that it was live bullets the army was firing. As I was running it seemed to be a real scrum, lots of people in front of me. I could hear live bullets coming from behind me, and I remember hearing women and men screaming, 'We're going to get murdered today!' All of the bullets were coming from behind, and the most important thing as far as I was concerned was to get to cover.

Paddy Walsh: I remember a lady opening the front door to her house in Chamberlain Street. She opened her door. All of a sudden, as her door was still open, the first shot of live ammunition rang out. Chamberlain Street is a very narrow street, and I heard a sound like a 'whoosh' and a 'whack', and the bullet hit a brick just above the window. I didn't realize it was a bullet until I saw the brick hit and damaged. I immediately shouted to the lady, 'Get down, get out of the way!' She closed the door and went inside.

Jimmy Toye: I knew it was time to move. I headed along the pavement at the side of the rubble barricade where some people were still standing around and moving about. Crack-crack. The first bit of cover was just around the corner of the flats, so I got in there with my back to the concrete. The crack-cracks were intermittent.

Eamonn Deane: The atmosphere at Free Derry Corner immediately became one of absolute panic and bewilderment. Everyone who was gathered there immediately crouched or lay down and looked for the nearest piece of cover. Sally and I were no exception. I recall feeling that the firing from different directions pinned down the crowd. We were either all crawling or in a running crouch and we all felt vulnerable until we reached the cover between the buildings.

Sophia Downey: We had to stop because Marion was being sick with the gas. We sat on a low garden wall. People were running past and I could hear bangs from the rubber bullets being fired. Then a man I knew ran past and shouted, 'They're coming in! Get the fuck up – they're shooting bullets from the Walls!' It was at that point that I realized that the sounds were different to rubber bullets; they were cracking sounds. It was unbelievable that we were sitting on a wall where there was shooting all around us! It had never occurred to me.

Billy McVeigh: I'm not sure which direction I went when the paras came in, but we just ran like hell. It was all so frantic, and those few seconds were just adrenaline. Where I ended up was at the telephone boxes at the back of the flats. There was heavy shooting by then.

Bernard Gilmour: Once we got into the flat, there were many people in there, some of them strangers. We went straight into the bedroom to look out the window to see what was happening out there. Those soldiers were not only firing at the people heading towards the gap in Blocks 2 and 3 of the flats; they were also firing at the flats themselves and it appeared to me that they were firing at us in the window. They were kneeling down and taking proper aim.

Bishop Edward Daly: He [Jackie] was running alongside me, kind of laughing and excited, and then there was a shot and he gasped right beside me and fell. I went over to him and opened his shirt, and he was covered in blood and he was gasping.[3]

Eamonn Baker: There was a body on the ground, and I could see that it was Jack Duddy. I had been to school with some of Jack Duddy's brothers and I knew who Jack was, although I did not know him well.

Bishop Edward Daly: When I saw him, I knew there was little we could do. He was in big, big trouble, and we worked frantically with him and Charlie Glenn the Knight of Malta worked frantically with him.

I took out my Holy oils and I gave him the Last Rites and I anointed him on the forehead. I prayed with him a little and a few other people crawled out beside me. The paras were still firing, and we decided to make a dash for it to try and get young Jackie away. We were terrified. This seemed like it was in our imagination, like this was a film we were seeing. It was hard to believe it was reality. I was terrified.

Hugh McMonagle: We saw the young boy and he was just white. Then Mickey Bridge got up and walked out shouting, 'You bastards, you shot a wain! Shoot me, ya bastards!' Just at that moment another Saracen came in and swung around and parked facing us sideways. Mickey kept on shouting, 'Shoot me, ya bastards!' and I was calling to him to come on as they would shoot him too. Then another Saracen came in, and Mickey kept on shouting; then he squealed – they shot him.

Bishop Edward Daly: There were two or three other soldiers in the kneeling position firing, down on one knee and firing in that position. They were talking and shouting to one another; they seemed to be very elated and very excited. They were not taking cover, and some of them were quite out in the open.

I am quite satisfied in my own mind that there was no fire on the soldiers from behind me. I can speak quite categorically about this because I was there from the beginning until the end of it. I'm quite satisfied that what happened that day was murder, carried out by men in uniform, of people who were unarmed. It's something that is burned into my mind ever since.

Around this time, Bishop Daly and others saw a lone gunman arrive on the scene and edge himself towards the corner of a wall in the direction of the troops, intent on firing back. Besides OIRA 1, who fired in retaliation after the army first opened fire on Donaghy and Johnston, this figure, known as Bishop Daly's gunman, was the only other civilian gunman to attempt to fire back at soldiers on Bloody Sunday.

Bishop Edward Daly: A young man came out of Chamberlain Street. He had a short firearm with him, and he came to the edge of the wall there, and he fired one or two shots. We screamed at him to go away because we were afraid the soldiers would think that we were firing at them – and he went away.

Army firing continued, with British soldiers then shooting mother-of-fourteen Peggy Deery in the leg.

Peggy Deery: Soldiers jumped out of the Saracens. There was a man standing there. He seemed to be mesmerized. I ran towards this man; I told him that I thought the soldiers looked as if they were going to shoot. I looked. I saw a soldier take aim and fire. He was only about twenty feet away from me. I'll never forget his face. I can't forget his face.

I tried to get up, I didn't realize I was shot then, and I staggered forward and fell again and cut my eye open, a deep cut over the left eye. When I was down the second time, I saw a man suddenly fall and crawl away around the corner into Chamberlain Street. I thought he was shot, but then he came back around again and him and Michael Kelly carried me round into Chamberlain Street.

One of those who helped Peggy into a house – teenager Michael Kelly – would be shot dead a few minutes later at the rubble barricade on Rossville Street. Peggy was adamant that the teenager had no weapon. She knew Michael Kelly – he worked with her son – and he was no gunman.

Jimmy Duddy: Myself and my mate Martin Cook were the last people up Chamberlain Street and the street was empty. We saw the soldiers and heard two bangs and then just after than I saw Jackie Duddy being carried up and I knew he was dead. I was eighteen. Then around the corner I saw Mrs Deery with a chunk taken out of her leg. Then Mickey Bridge was lying down, then Mickey Bradley too.

Jed McClelland: I ran into the back of the flats; there was a whole crowd of us running, terrified for our lives. There was a woman running beside me here and a priest nearby, and she fell, and I almost fell jumping over her to get on and away – the fear just driving you forward.

Gerry Duddy: I saw people sheltering behind a small, red wall about three feet high that ran along the car park of the flats. I dived for cover. Looking to my left I saw people helping someone who was lying on the ground, probably having been shot. I didn't know at the time, but later found out that the body lying on the ground was Jackie.

According to the Report of the Bloody Sunday Inquiry, *the house in Chamberlain Street where Peggy Deery and Mickey Bridge were taken was then invaded by soldiers. Eyewitnesses told Saville of harsh treatment and obscene language as they arrested all 19 males in the house.*

'Let the whore bleed to death,' said one soldier about Peggy Deery. Another is recorded as calling those in the house 'fucking Irish bastards', and of remarking to both gunshot victims, 'Let them bleed to death, they deserve it.'[4]

Peggy Deery: I know Mrs O'Reilly, a neighbour, was there too; she was holding my hand and helping me with the pain. When the ambulance arrived, Mrs O'Reilly said she would come to Altnagelvin with me, and when we got outside, I was on a stretcher by then, I could see that the soldiers had lined a lot of people up against the wall, and they were really beating a small chap, hitting him with rifles and kicking him. Mrs O'Reilly shouted at the soldiers to stop it and they swore at her and threatened to smash her head for her. She got hysterical at the shouting and beating, and had to be helped into the ambulance, and we then left for Altnagelvin.

After an emergency operation on her leg wound that night, Peggy Deery suffered severe complications and was rushed to Belfast City Hospital for specialist care. With her entire thigh muscle destroyed, she received over a hundred stitches in a skin graft operation. She spent seven months in hospital and the next two years in a wheelchair. Afterwards, a metal calliper was fitted as support to her damaged leg.

*

Patsy McDaid: When we reached the car park of the Rossville Flats, I saw a woman being carried; it looked like she had been shot in the leg and so I ran over and helped the men carry her into a house in Chamberlain Street. The house was packed with people and we laid the woman, Peggy Deery, on the sofa where people attended to her. Peggy was the only woman shot on Bloody Sunday. I'm not sure if I was going for help, but when I got outside, I crossed over the street and sought shelter from the shooting behind a high wall, where there were thirty or forty people all hiding.

Patrick [Patsy] McDaid was wounded after helping Peggy Deery to safety. Nearby, 30-year-old Pius McCarron was hit by pieces of flying debris caused by gunfire ricocheting off walls, and 40-year-old Patrick Brolly was injured by gunfire as he took shelter in Rossville Flats.

Patsy McDaid: We couldn't see the soldiers aiming at us and we couldn't escape this corner, so some people decided to run for it across open ground to safety. I made a run for it and at the far side I saw a wall and as soon as I ducked to dive over it, I was hit. Bending down saved my life; if I had been standing a fraction straighter the bullet would have went straight through me. Instead, the bullet cut deep across my back. I didn't know I was hit at the time, but I dived down, and someone had to show me the blood before I believed I was hurt. Then I began to panic. There was so much blood.

Eamon Melaugh: I stood my ground; my salvation was I had a camera with a lens in it.

Patsy McDaid: There was a whole crowd of people in the house taking cover. Someone said I should be taken upstairs into one of the bedrooms. I was laid down on a bedroom floor and someone pulled my coat off and my jumper up. As the people with me pulled my jumper up, I could move my arms. I was lying in the room on my stomach, facing down. All I could see were other people's feet. A woman with a basin of water came in and knelt down beside me. The only thing she had with her was some TCP and she started to bathe the wound. All I could think about was how bad I had been hit and whether I was going to live or die.

Michael Quinn: I had a strong impression that the shooting was quite intense, and it was terrifying. I lost count of the number of shots. At this point, I knew I had to go. The crowd ran into Glenfada Park and someone shouted that the army was coming in.

The sound of gunfire echoing through the Bogside sent the huge crowd of marchers at Free Derry Corner either running in all directions or crouching to hide themselves.

Lord Fenner-Brockway: On the platform, I was about to speak when a stream of men and women, possibly sixty, came running, as though for their lives, from the furthest point of the open space. Those who came running did not stop at the meeting, but ran either side of it, apparently making for their own homes. Miss Devlin appealed to the crowd to keep calm and no one moved. After a pause, I was about to speak again when more men and women came running into the open space from the distance, and almost immediately, there was the sound of the shooting of live bullets, distinct by sharper sound and continuity as from machine-guns. I only caught a glimpse from afar, but momentarily I saw vehicles chasing those who were running.

Andy Nolan: Me and Frank had decided to go to Free Derry Corner to hear all the speeches. Just as Lord Brockway was about to speak, all hell let loose. We heard the sound of gunfire. We could see army and police on the Derry Walls, and I assumed they were shooting at the crowd. I don't know how I did it, but I jumped the barricade opposite the Bogside Inn, and we found ourselves using the wall of the pub for cover. Even then we were still in a jokey mood, and I told Frank to stand to my left so that he would be in the line of fire.

Hugh McMonagle: I dug behind the wee wall with everyone. It was jammed behind there, as people tried to shelter. All I heard was the Bang, Bang, Bang, and I just lay there on my back for a few minutes, and I was afraid to put my head up in case they could see me or there was a sniper. I looked up towards the Walls and I could see the soldiers moving about, and I thought to myself that if I could see them, they could see me. A typical Catholic, I thought if I was shot, nobody would find me, and I'd die without a priest.

Lord Fenner-Brockway: As soon as the firing began, I saw an amazing scene; nearly the whole crowd of two thousand fell to the ground on their faces and in considerable confusion. Before I knew what was happening, I was pulled off the lorry as the noise of firing increased. The firing was disturbingly near.

Martin McGuinness: There were a lot of people around. I could see a lot of them diving for cover and scattering and getting out of the way and lying down on the ground. I could not see what was happening beyond the barricade because of my poor eyesight. I crouched down like many others. I stayed crouched down until I could make sense of what was happening. People were bewildered and trying to make sense of it all.

British army 8th Brigade Log:

> **1617hrs** - 4 shots fired at call sign Q21, 2 shots returned.
>
> **1621hrs** - Ref shots. 1 man seen to fall area of Bogside Inn. 1 further shot fired by OP 0. [Observation Post 0]

Sophia Downey: Marion and I ran towards the building site at Lisfannon Park. Trenches had been prepared for the new houses, and as we were running past, a man pulled both of us down into one of the trenches. We lay in the trench for a while, maybe ten minutes, during which time the shooting continued.

CHAPTER 19

The First Fatality

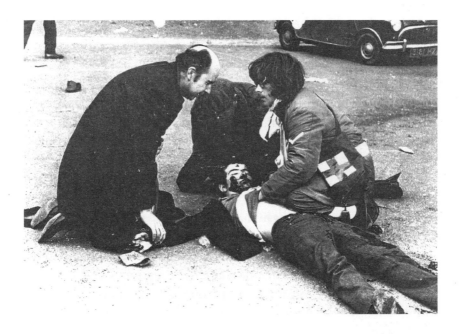

Bishop (then Father) Daly gives Last Rites to Jackie Duddy.
On the right is Knight of Malta Charlie Glenn.

As army gunfire intensified, the group of men tending Jackie Duddy in the Rossville Flats courtyard knew he needed urgent medical attention.

Bishop Edward Daly: He was bleeding badly, and I had tried to stop the blood. We were working on him, and I gave him the Last Rites, and we realized we needed to get him to hospital as quick as we can.[1]

Hugh McMonagle: I'll tell you something, I have seen wars on the TV, but that gun battle on that day on Chamberlain Street scared the hell out of me. We were walking and could hear the bullets whizzing past us. We were bent over carrying him. It meant the young fella was getting heavier, which we knew wasn't right.

Eileen Fox: We tuned the radio in, and we heard the army saying that someone was being carried along Chamberlain Street. Obviously, we didn't know that it was our Jackie they were talking about.

Eamonn Baker: There was a man running in front of me, and I now know this man's name is Michael Bradley. He was perhaps a yard in front of me. He was shot. I did not have a sense of a bullet hitting him and the first I knew of it was when he gasped out, 'I'm hit, I'm hit.' He seemed to fall to the ground in slow motion.

Jackie O'Reilly, stepdaughter of Mickey Bradley: Mickey was shot at the back of the flats. He was maimed for life, because he was shot through the right arm, in one side, through the chest and out the other side of the chest. It was a lifelong injury that affected the whole house, if you want to say, mentally, and physically. He couldn't work after Bloody Sunday. Mickey was never the same person again, never.[2]

Bishop Edward Daly: We got Jackie to the top of High Street where Mrs McHugh had a shop and she came out, very upset. We laid him down and I put the handkerchief into his shirt. I think he might have been already dead at that stage. The ambulance was very quick, a matter of minutes perhaps, and then Hugh told me to go back down there, as there were lots of other people hurt.

Hugh McMonagle: Charlie Glenn was working on him, Bishop Daly was working on him, and whatever way I looked at him – it was the features, the eyebrows, the face, and I thought to myself, 'That's Duddy …' I knew his mother and father, and he was a dead ringer for his mum. I remember saying to Father Daly, 'Father, that's young Duddy from Creggan – that's Maureen Duddy's son.' I shouted at a soldier to do something, and his reaction was to clap his hands. To this day, I still hear that.

Walking back down Harvey Street, I looked to see the army coming up the street with batons and I thought, here we go. I walked towards them and who was standing at one of the door-ways but Badger – Hugh – McDaid, and Hugh pulled me in. The army wanted in, but he wouldn't let them. He sat me in his house, and for the time I was there it was a full-scale battle outside, guns going bang – bang – bang.

When it stopped, we waited a while and then I left his house and thanked him. I went down to the Bogside and there was just silence – a silence that I'd never felt in all my life. I came around Chamberlain Street and walked around towards the flats with everybody there.

CHAPTER 20

Targets on Rossville Street

Hugh Gilmour is shot and fatally wounded while running towards his home at the Rossville Flats.

There were further casualties on Rossville Street as shooting continued, and 17-year-old Hugh Gilmour was shot dead as he ran towards the safety of his home in the Rossville Flats. Shortly afterwards, 17-year-old Kevin McElhinney was shot dead crawling along the ground towards the same flats.

Jed McClelland: I ran on to the far end of the flats. I lay down on the tarmac of the road where there was a path slightly higher. I'm literally trying to get as low as I can, hoping that this pavement edge is going to help me hide. I'm lying there terrified at what's going on around me. I could see through the gap of the flats' staircases into Rossville Street, and I watched two men drop dead there and the blood trickle along the ground. People were screaming.

Billy McVeigh: Someone said the soldiers were coming around the corner and were going to shoot us all. We were all petrified and huddled on top of each other like a pyramid at the phone box, trying to protect ourselves. I remember the wee fella in the middle under everybody was shouting about being let out because he was squashed with the people piled on top of him. I remember shouting back to him that I'd rather have been him, stuck in there, than be me on the outside.

Geraldine McBride: I didn't know where Hugo went, but I saw some fellas and I knew Gilsy [Hugh Gilmour] and he said to me, 'You better run,' as the soldiers had started coming in. I thought they were firing rubber bullets. As we were running, he stumbled but then got back up again and then there was a shot and he said, 'I'm hit! I'm hit!' He was near the doorway of the flats, and it was a loud bang, but I just thought he was hit by a rubber bullet. He sort of stumbled on and I don't know how he was able to run on with the injuries he had.

Eamon Melaugh: I had a camera on me, and they fired a couple of rubber bullets at me, and I actually threw stones back at them, that's how angry I was. After the young fella shouted, 'I'm hit, I'm hit,' he ran on then staggered – he lived in the flats. I went over. It was below his flat window and his parents didn't know for some time. I had thought that kind of thing would have happened under the police's control, but I was wrong. It was the army who attacked the people.

Jimmy Toye: People were moving around, like mice trapped in a cage. More people pushed in around me at that stage, and, at one point, Hugh Gilmour was to the left, lying very close to me. He was staring, eyes wide and glazing over. His wee checked shirt was slightly open, and I could see the pink protrusions of his intestines bulging out beneath his shirt, but not a lot of blood.

Billy McVeigh: Within a few seconds of Hugh being hit, this bubble appeared on the front of his shirt and got bigger and bigger. It took a few seconds to come out. Next thing I remember, Barney McGuigan was lying on the floor behind me too. I was quite close to both of them, and I still have nightmares that I'm shot in the back. It still gives me bad nightmares all these years later.

Geraldine McBride: I had done some first aid for a few years, but I opened his shirt – I knew. I'd never seen gunshot injuries or any injuries like that before and I thought, Oh my God. He was looking for his mother, and I knew his mother lived in the flats, but I told him, 'She can't get down now Gilsy, we have to wait 'til all this stops.' We knew he was dying, and we said a prayer with him, and then his head just went forward, and he died. I should have moved back towards the wall, but I couldn't move. There was bullets going this way and that way and bouncing along the ground. I was sat out in the open, and his head was on my knee.

Kevin McElhinney had been on the march with his friends. He was shot dead while crawling away from the gunfire on his stomach. As he edged along the pavement in front of Rossville Flats, Kevin was shot in the buttock and the bullet lacerated organs on its way through his body. The teenager was later found to have another injury to his leg where another bullet had grazed him as he crawled.

Jimmy Toye: The firing was nerve-racking. Some people were standing up with their hands in the air shouting, 'Arrest us, arrest us.' Others beside me were praying and I could hear, 'Hail Mary, full of grace …'

Michael Quinn: I reached a rubble barricade, which was positioned near the Joseph Place end of the flats. As I was climbing over the barricade, I heard what I took to be shots fired by the army. To my right, I noticed a small crowd of people standing at the gable wall of Glenfada Park. I joined this crowd and then went around into the small car park at the rear of Glenfada Park. While I was there, I saw a young man who appeared to be nineteen or twenty years of age who was shot in the leg. I am quite sure this man had nothing in his hands when I saw him. At this stage, the shooting had ceased for a short while.

Eamonn MacDermott: On Bloody Sunday there were no petrol bombs or blast bombs – by then, rioters didn't throw petrol bombs any more – they were non-existent to ordinary rioters. In 1970, the British army had announced they were going to shoot-to-kill petrol bombers and did shoot one in Belfast. That basically stopped all use of petrol bombs in the north, and if you watch any footage of rioting in 1971 and 1972, there were no petrol bombs. The IRA would occasionally throw blast bombs, but ordinary rioters would never throw petrol bombs after that. In fact, petrol bombs only reappeared on the scene after the Brixton riots in 1981, because the Brixton rioters were throwing petrol bombs and people here thought, well, if they can throw them, we can throw them, and that's when they reappeared here.

CHAPTER 21

At the Rubble Barricade

Michael Kelly lies shot at the rubble barricade. Michael McDaid can be seen walking into view on top left. He was shot dead seconds later.

Four young men were shot dead at Rossville Street's innocuous rubble barricade – Michael Kelly (17), Michael McDaid (20), John Young (17) and William Nash (19). Upon rushing to help his dying son, 51-year-old Alexander Nash was shot and injured too.

Don Mullan: The most vivid memory I have from Bloody Sunday is actually a sound – the sound of Michael Kelly, who was literally a few feet away from me. It was like he had been hit by a knock-out punch and it had winded him. I remember him just clutching his stomach and collapsing into the foetal position, falling. I remember loads of bullets hitting the barricade and people falling there and a bullet hitting the wall above my head and bits of brick and mortar coming down around us. At that point I began to run and then I remember someone lying behind a little wall at the entrance to Glenfada Park shouting, 'Get down, get down, they're firing live ammunition,' and after that I literally remember nothing.

Michael Quinn: At that stage I was not aware of anyone being shot other than the man I saw being shot, until people shouted that there were people dying on the barricade at Rossville Street. The shooting then resumed and the people who were standing at the gable wall at Glenfada Park/Rossville Street rushed into the car park where I was standing. Just then, a small group of people carrying the body of a man, who was wearing a blue anorak, crossed the car park and went into one of the houses. After some hesitation, I decided to get out of Glenfada Park.

Denis Bradley: Someone shouted to get a priest. He was very young – between fifteen and eighteen years of age. I think I shouted something like, 'I'm here.' I remember that the lad was grey, and his face was pale, and he was looking up at me. I didn't think he was dying; he was conscious and obviously badly injured and there was blood, but not a tremendous amount. I didn't know for certain that he had been shot, but he was breathing.

Sophia Downey: Someone told me that Michael had been running away from soldiers when his sock became caught in the wire on the rubble barricade, and that he was shot as he bent down to try and release it.

Denis Bradley: I remember giving him the Last Rites. It all happened very quickly. I knelt beside him and I whispered in his ear. I remember saying to people that they should get him in some-where. A number lifted him up on their shoulders and began to carry him away down another small alleyway which exited out of Glenfada Park North to Abbey Park. He was very light. I was subsequently told his name was Michael Kelly. As people lifted him up, I started to walk beside him, and I became aware of something behind me, in the direction of Rossville Street. It was pure panic. Chaos. People were shouting, running. There was shooting and the penny was beginning to drop. I began to understand that something terrible was happening out there in Rossville Street. The paras had taken the streets.

Alexander Nash: I saw three men lying on the small stone barricade in Rossville Street. I looked and saw that one of the men was my son William – I knew because I could see his face clearly. I ran across to help him as fast as my legs would carry me. I put my left hand in the air to signal that the shooting should stop. I was shot in that arm and was hit in the ribs also. When I was hit, I was fired at four or five times more. I dropped down beside Willie and the other two men.

Denis Bradley: I was by this stage still vaguely aware of the riot going on in William Street and something was going on at Free Derry Corner. I still had a strong feeling about wanting to go home. I began to walk in the direction of Free Derry Corner. I became aware of shooting in the distance. Something was happening. People were running and there was panic. My instinctive impression was that a snatch squad had appeared. That was part of the normal riot situation.

Alexander Nash: I put my hand on my son's back and said, 'Willie!' His eyes were wide open, but I knew straight away that he was dead and that the other two men were dead too.

Denis Bradley: I looked over towards the barricade from the edge of the wall and saw bodies on the barricade. I remember their contorted positions. I drew the conclusion that they had been shot, because they were not lying behind the barricade as if taking cover. They were in different contorted positions.

There was certainly an older man and two others. The older man called out. He was obviously alive. He may have put up his arms. The others were not making any movement and were more likely dead. They were only fifteen to twenty feet away. I was very close ... I have the strongest memory of wanting to go out to these men. I had just anointed a young boy. I wanted to do the same to these bodies.

Eamonn MacDermott: We were all miniature ballistics experts at that stage; we knew what was what, growing up in it. We knew the SLR had a distinct sound and when the shooting started there was only one sound in the air, the SLR rounds, no others. That always stuck in my head, the fact that it was just one sound of only one type of weapon. We had heard so many gun battles up until then, we recognized the different weapon sounds. You can't mistake blast bombs – it's a totally different sound.

Denis Bradley: I remember being more terrified that I'd ever been in my life before and feeling I should go out to them [at the barricade] and this guy pulling me back saying, 'Don't go out there,' and the feeling of being a coward almost; you know, that there were people dying around me and I didn't want to die. Bullets were flying everywhere. When I looked out, I could actually see the bullets hitting the ground. It's the first time I've actually seen bullets ricochet in that concentrated fashion. You could see a kind of spark of dust rise or something where the bullets hit.

Bishop Edward Daly: When I went back down, I just anointed everyone in sight because there were bodies all over the place and a lot of people wounded. I was afraid to go out to the bodies at the rubble barricade, though, because they were still firing at everything that moved.

Patsy O'Donnell: When I was in Glenfada Park, I heard the shooting and saw the crowd running, so instinctively I ran too. When I got to the end of Glenfada just at the pile of rubble in Rossville Street, I saw the people crouched along this wall. Some were standing. I was going to run across Rossville Street to take shelter behind the flats when I saw a person lying behind the barricade and people were shouting, 'They're shooting, get down!' so I ran up the length of the yard and I saw a man or boy further up Glenfada Park fall to the ground.

CHAPTER 22

In the Square and Abbey Park

Marchers shelter in Glenfada Park with the first casualties from
the rubble barricade.

*In Glenfada Park, two men were shot dead and a further five
injured when the paras opened fire. Joseph Friel (20) was shot
and wounded as he tried to make his way home to the Rossville
Flats. Daniel Gillespie (32) was hit by a bullet in the head and fell
unconscious. Schoolboy Michael Quinn (17) was wounded by a
bullet in the shoulder that exited through his face as he tried to
escape the soldiers' advance. William McKinney (27) was then
shot in the back and killed as he tried to help the wounded, the
same bullet wounding Joe Mahon (16) in the leg. Joe then feigned
death as soldiers approached.*

Nearby, Patsy O'Donnell (41) was wounded as he threw himself across a woman to protect her from firing. At the alley-way entrance to Abbey Park, Jim Wray (22) was on the ground and already wounded by the first burst of fire when he was shot again in the back at close range.

Teresa McGowan, wife of Daniel McGowan: I didn't go to the march on Bloody Sunday because I was pregnant at the time. We lived in Lone Moor Gardens and still do. Danny went, and he was shot on the leg on the shin bone. Danny had been between the flats when the shooting started, and people scattered. Wee Gilmour had been shot coming around the corner to the telephone box, and he said everyone was around him and saying a prayer because he was dying, he said it was desperate. Then the shooting started again, and he went to the other side of the telephone box; they were scattering for shelter.[1]

Joe Friel: The actual shooting stands out in my mind. The crowd was squealing, crying, roaring and shouting. I saw sheer unadulterated terror on people's faces. I froze momentarily, then ran back towards the Rossville Flats to home. There were so many people packed into the doorway I couldn't get in. I could still hear shots being fired, getting louder. There was no pattern to the shots, the lulls between bursts were only a matter of seconds. There was complete chaos on Rossville Street. People were running in every direction bumping into each other. Realizing I'd not be able to take cover in the flats, I crossed Rossville Street to Glenfada Park in sheer fear and have a clear memory of people falling to my right, to the north.

Danny Gillespie: I saw a group of about eight people coming into Glenfada Park North from the entrance by the rubble barricade. Some were carrying a youth I know as Michael Kelly away. He was obviously dead. There were people running about and I heard more shooting. I began to run towards Rossville Street to try to get away. I heard a sharp 'crack' and I knew that I had been hit. I fell forwards with my face down on the tarmac. My hat had been blown off. I could feel a stinging and burning sensation and I thought that I had lost the top of my head. Everything went black.

Denis Bradley: The next memory I have is of soldiers, paratroopers, coming round to the gable-end wall at the corner of Glenfada Park North from a northerly direction. The first soldier round was surprised to see us, or that was my first impression. He raised his gun, pointed it at me and shouted to us to move on into the car park of Glenfada Park North.

I hadn't seen paratroopers before. They were different looking, bigger, tougher and taller, more physical and aggressive. They didn't talk to you like other soldiers. Their blackened faces struck me as odd as it was daytime. I had seen soldiers with blackened faces, but only during night operations. I realized then that I was in the middle of a war for the first time despite being used to the presence of soldiers before. I remember at around this point another soldier starting firing from the hip or waist in a southerly direction from the entrance to the Glenfada Park North car park at the east. I remember being horrified.

Joe Friel: I ran along Glenfada Park. People were running with me to get out. Everyone was panicking. I could see soldiers about five or six feet into Glenfada, coming from the north-eastern corner. The soldier in front was moving forward at no great pace and was firing. He had his gun in front of him just above waist height and was moving it from side to side – not swinging it, just moving it a few inches from left to right. The other soldiers weren't firing their weapons. I heard three shots – bang, bang, bang. I felt a slight blow to my body no harder than a tap by a couple of fingers. My first thought was that I had been hit by a rubber bullet, I couldn't take in that I had been shot. I looked down and could see blood. Within a second or two, a big gush of blood came out of my mouth. I shouted, 'I'm shot, I'm shot!'

Joe Mahon, a civil rights marcher aged 16: As we ran up towards Abbey Park, they just started firing. The only one I saw firing at that time was holding the gun at his hip and just firing into the crowd. Next thing I knew I was lying on the ground. Then I heard a voice behind me, who I later found out was William McKinney, and he just said to me, 'I'm hit, son, I'm hit!' He was lying right behind me and I could see another pair of feet nearby too.[2]

Denis Bradley: The soldier was just shooting, not particularly at anyone. The angle of fire seemed to me slightly over people's heads. I didn't think the soldier had lost his head. I didn't think he was going to shoot me. He didn't say anything to me. One of the other soldiers told me to 'get along'.

Patsy O'Donnell: I saw soldiers and, just at the corner, there was a woman crouching behind the fence. I saw a soldier take aim in my direction and I threw myself on top of her and behind the fence as low as possible. I heard the crack on the wall behind me and looking round I saw a hole in the wall, and I saw the top of my coat torn and I realized there was something wrong with me. I said to the woman, 'I'm hit.' We rolled around the corner to the yard and sat there with Father Bradley and others, and I realized then I had been shot in the shoulder.

Danny Gillespie: I regained my senses. Two young boys were asking me if I was alright and were helping me to my feet. The ground was lifting around me from the shots. The tall boy on my left was shot and I heard him groan. He fell on top of me and pushed me back onto the ground. He was lying over my legs and was still. I rolled to my left, so he fell off me, and pulled my feet out from underneath him and got up. I ran west towards the alleyway leading to Abbey Park. There was jelly-like blood running across my face and into my eyes. I stumbled up the shallow steps and fell twice running up them. My legs were like jelly and I was shaking.

Joe Mahon: I was just lying there and saw one paratrooper come across when I heard a woman's voice saying, 'Lie still – pretend you're dead.' That woman saved my life. Just as the paratrooper approached me, God rest Jim Wray, he went to move, and the paratrooper stopped and fired twice more right into his back.

I saw his coat rising twice. Then he moved on. After a while, he came back and actually stood over Jim Wray. He took his mask and helmet off and I saw his face clearly. I will never forget his face. Just as he was walking off, he saw me moving and knelt down, put the rifle on his shoulder and aimed. I turned away, waiting for the bullet, when a young Knight of Malta came running out and saved me by distracting him, and he just walked away laughing.

Joe Friel: I staggered but I don't think I hit the ground. Three fellows grabbed me and took me to the Murrays' house in Lisfannon Park. The three men who helped me were Leo Young [John Young's brother], Eugene McGillan and Jackie Chambers. I was carried into the house feet first and was laid on the floor in the front room. I was continuing to throw up blood and I remember apologizing for throwing up on the carpet. There were two medics there, and a girl called Eibhlin Lafferty pulled open my shirt and cleaned up the blood. There was a crowd in the house, mostly old women, who all knelt around me and started saying the rosary. Mrs Murray, whose house it was, ran upstairs as she couldn't take it.

Caroline O'Donnell, daughter of Patsy O'Donnell: The soldier knelt and took aim and my father jumped on top of a lady, and as he jumped the bullet went through his shoulder. Then there was mayhem in Glenfada Park – there's footage of civilians all lined up against a wall and he was there.[3]

Patsy O'Donnell: The soldiers arrived immediately and with guns pointed at us, ordered us up and marched us down Glenfada Park. They ordered hands up and I couldn't put my right hand up because my right shoulder was shot, and they butted me with their rifles in the back and wrist and eventually I got my arm up. I told some of the people I was with that I'd been shot, and they told the soldiers, who took no notice.

Michael Quinn: I ran across towards the alleyway leading to Abbey Park, and as I was nearing this entrance, I felt myself being struck upon the right cheek by a bullet. No one was with me. I felt a very hard thump in the face. It was like slow motion. I could see the flesh and blood coming out of me. I stumbled but got up and ran on through the alleyway. As I was passing through, I noticed the man who I had seen being shot earlier lying in the shadows of a nook in the alleyway.

Denis Bradley: I think it was about now I became aware of the bodies in Glenfada Park North. I wanted to go to them. I think there were three, but I couldn't swear to it. I tried to go towards them but was grabbed by the soldiers and was pushed on through Glenfada Park North. I was kicked at this time, not very badly, and I think I was hit by a rifle on the elbow. It was obvious that I was a priest if you cared to look, but the soldiers didn't care. I was panicking in the sense that everyone was panicking.

Michael Quinn: I thought, 'I've been hit.' I had been running bent over and did not look back at all. If I had not been doubled over, I would not be here now. I subsequently discovered that the bullet had struck me on the shoulder; the bullet had then passed into the right-hand side of my face exiting through the left-hand side of my nose. I stumbled but made it to the gap.

Frances Gillespie: Daniel was injured in the head. He was brought to the front door and I was standing there with Cath in my arms and saw him coming into the street with another man. His face was covered with blood – I thought half of his face was blown off him. But I still didn't recognize him with all the blood. They were taking him into the Andersons' in Number 91, and they brought him over. He cried and cried, saying they'd killed 'wains … bits of wains'. He was in his thirties then.

Danny Gillespie: My wife Frances was at the door. Mr Moran and Mr Canavan asked her for a cloth so that they could help clean me up. I sat down and cried. I was very shaken and very angry. Later, I went to Vinny Coyle's house for treatment. There was a doctor and a Knight of Malta there. They shaved my head so that the wound could be cleaned. The bullet had grazed my scalp and I still have a groove where the bullet passed. I didn't go to hospital as I was worried that I'd be arrested if I did.

Eamonn Deane: Sally and I moved up Westland Street. At this point, we met a group of men whom we knew to be republicans. There were around five or six men in this group, one of whom was Martin McGuinness. We were perhaps one of the first groups of people who had come away from the area where the shooting was taking place. We could still hear the shooting at this time and Martin McGuinness asked me what was going on. I told him that the Brits had come into the Bogside and were shooting people. I recall Martin McGuinness's reaction was one of shock and disbelief.

Joe Mahon: I have a guilt – I never shouted to Jim Wray to lie still and that's what really has been in the back of my mind all these years. I saw the para approaching, and I didn't warn Jim Wray, and they murdered him. I felt like a coward. I should have told him to keep still. They can't say Jim Wray was throwing stones or armed; he was on his stomach.

ABBEY PARK

Around the corner, crowds sheltered from the gunfire as Gerald Donaghey (17) and Gerard McKinney (35) were shot dead in Abbey Park. According to a brother-in-law of McKinney's, John O'Kane, who saw him being shot, 'He shouted, "No, no, don't shoot" before he fell on his back, then he blessed himself and he said, "Jesus, Jesus" before he died.' The same bullet killed both men.

John Kelly: The next time I saw Michael he was being carried out of a house in Abbey Park. I'd been taking cover because of the shooting and was lying just behind where the monument is now. I hadn't seen anybody being shot or where it was coming from, but I just knew it was army fire. Then we looked across the street and saw a group of people surrounding something. We were standing among the crowd when I heard someone calling me from behind – it was my other brother-in-law, George Downey. He had been along with Michael not long after he was shot and had helped carry him out of Carr's house.

Larry Doherty: I saw in front of me a first-aid man kneeling above a man lying on the ground. There were other people standing around, and the first-aid man seemed to be trying to revive the man on the ground. The man was lying across the steps [Abbey Park]. There was a wooden cross at the side of the group. I could hear a lot of shouting around me – people were very angry and saying that people had been shot during a peaceful march. I did not see any soldiers. It was like a dream. I assumed that the man on the ground was one of the men who the group were saying had been shot. I was scared at that point and went over to the group. I started to take photographs. I was not really looking for a story at that time. I just thought that I should photograph what was happening in front of me without intruding. I felt that I was in a new ball game.

Regina McLaughlin, daughter of Gerard McKinney: My daddy went out to Gerald Donaghey, to reach out to another to help another life; that's how he would want us to live too. He went out with his hands in the air.[4]

Patsy O'Donnell: The soldiers marched us down towards Rossville Street, and I, being at the front of the line and unable to look round (the soldiers kept telling us not to look round), turned up William Street, as far as City Taxis. There were two taxi drivers and at least three women there, and they took me in to sit me down. A few moments later a soldier burst in the door and I jumped up and ran to the other side of the room. He grabbed me and pushed me back out onto William Street, and just one step outside the door another soldier batoned me on the head and I needed seven or eight stitches in this wound.

Caroline O'Donnell. Realizing my father had been shot, the paras came after him and kicked his head and used the butt of their rifles to batter his head in. They kicked him with steel toecaps and ran away, leaving him for dead. He could have died of those head injuries, but some taxi men came out and dragged my father in and got him help. They thought he was going to die from his head injuries, not from the bullet wound.

Patsy O'Donnell: I saw Father Bradley, who was pleading with the soldier to leave me alone. Somebody in charge came along and said to the soldier, 'Leave that man alone, he is shot, he's alright.' The two taxi drivers who were there put me in a car and took me to the first-aid centre in Creggan. A woman took me from there to her house, and then she rang my doctor, Doctor Fallon, who came and took me to Altnagelvin.

Michael Quinn: When I reached Abbey Park, someone grabbed me by the arm, and we kept on running through Abbey Park and across the old Bogside. I was met there by friends and the three of us ran to Blucher Street where I received first aid from members of the Knights of Malta. I was then taken by car to the first-aid post at St Mary's School, Creggan, from where I was taken by ambulance to Altnagelvin Hospital. I could see by my friends' faces that my injury was serious. They looked horrified. I did not realize the extent of my injuries at the time. I did not know whether part of my face had been blown off. All I could see was the skin blown apart and the blood.

Dr Raymond McClean: I went outside and started to walk across Glenfada Park. I found a man lying on the steps of the square being tended by two young boys. This man was Gerard McKinney, and on examination I found a significant amount of blood around his upper chest region. On further examination I found that he was already dead. I told the boys to continue their efforts at resuscitation. Someone told me that several other people had been shot and were in houses across the square. In the first house I found Michael Kelly, who had an entry bullet wound just to the left of his umbilicus. I could not find any exit wound. Michael was already dead when I examined him.

Lying beside Michael was Jim Wray. He had two entry gunshot wounds on the right side of his back. He had an exit wound on the left side of his back, and another larger exit wound at his left shoulder. Jim was also dead when I examined him. Again, I told the young first-aiders to continue their efforts at resuscitation. I did this mainly to keep them occupied, and in the hope that if they were kept busy, they would be less likely to panic in what was an extremely horrific situation.

Larry Doherty: The next thing I remember is going into a house in Abbey Park. I cannot remember what made me go into the house. It's possible that the shooting started again, or that there was antici-pation of shooting – I was out in the open at that point. The house was packed with people; we had to squeeze up the stairs to find a place to stand. We stood looking out of a window overlooking the path between Abbey Park and Glenfada Park, and the steps where the body of Gerard McKinney lay. I remember seeing people hiding behind the walls around the gardens of Glenfada Park South.

Raymond Rogan: My wife and I were watching through the window the crowds running for their lives. Just below that, we saw young Donaghey and Gerry McKinney, who was a good friend of mine. They were shot just at the steps below our house. People were carrying the wee lad up out of the way, and I went out and told them to bring him in.

Martin McGuinness: There was still shooting going on at that stage. It was heavy shooting. It was as heavy as I had heard in Derry for some time. I was bewildered. It was an incredible development. What was happening? My sense while in Abbey Park was that it was all very close. The shots were being fired in a valley and I could not be sure what was happening. I then moved back through Lisfannon Park to the Westland Street area near the Bogside Inn ... It seemed to me that every person in the area of Rossville Street and William Street was at grave risk.

Larry Doherty: I paused for a moment at the gable end of the eastern block of Glenfada Park North. Father Irwin was there. He was a curate in the cathedral. I could see bodies on the other side of Rossville Street, to the south of the flats. Father Irwin said that he had to get across Rossville Street to those men. He held up a hankie and went across Rossville Street. I went with him, also holding a hankie. I thought I would be safe with a priest.

Raymond Rogan: We brought the Donaghey lad in and left him in front of the fire. There was a Doctor Swords, I believe his name was, a few doors away and someone went to get him. We looked at the boy. At that point I had already seen the wound and it was just oozing, and I was surprised because he just looked like a young child. Doctor Swords said if we could get to hospital right away then there was a chance. We had searched [the lad] at that point because my wife wanted to find out who he was to notify his people – but all she could find on him was a holy medal around his neck.

Dr Raymond McClean: I went next door where I found William McKinney lying on the floor. He had an entry bullet wound over his right chest, and a jagged exit wound in his left chest. There was not much external bleeding. He was quite conscious when I examined him. He was pale and shocked, but extremely calm. He said to me very calmly, 'I'm going to die, Doctor, am I?' I lied a bit and said, 'You have been hit badly, but if we can get an ambulance and get you to hospital quickly, I hope you will be alright.' I saw Father Mulvey in the hall and asked him to see William, which he did. I stayed with William until he gradually lost consciousness and died.

Larry Doherty: As I crossed Rossville Street, I looked to my left. I remember seeing a Saracen near the northern gable end of Block 1 of the Rossville Flats. The back doors were open, facing me, and there were bodies in the back of it, I think two or three. I remember seeing Father Mulvey remonstrating with some soldiers in the area. I thought that these were injured people who were being put into the Saracen so that they could be taken to hospital and saved. Later, I realized that they must have been dead.

Dr Raymond McClean: Father Mulvey told me that he had seen the bodies of three young men, thrown roughly into the back of an army Saracen, at the Rossville Street barricade. He had remonstrated with the soldiers, but they completely ignored his protests. Father Mulvey was extremely angry. Later, I learned that the three young men thrown into the Saracen were William Nash, John Young and Michael McDaid. I wondered why the bodies of these three young men were taken away in an army Saracen, while other bodies and wounded people were left lying on the road. I wondered about it and was vaguely disturbed but didn't really know why. We continued our efforts at resuscitation until the ambulances eventually arrived from Altnagelvin Hospital. During this period of attending to the wounded and dying, I had lost all concept of the passage of time.

Larry Doherty: I remember that when I got to the other side of Rossville Street, my legs were shaking – I realized what I had done, walking out into the line of fire.

THE SUSAN NORTH TAPES

Susan North was a freelance journalist who, in 1972, accompanied photographer Fulvio Grimaldi when events in the Bogside spiralled. While sheltering in the Rossville Flats, Susan switched on her tape recorder and left it running, documenting a community in anguish. Here is one such excerpt from the audio.[5]

    F: Mummy

    F: [Shrieking] Tell the world

    F: Mummy

    F: [Shrieking] Tell the world of 'em

    M: I know they'll go round the world you know

F: [Shrieking] And pass around the word

M: This is the beginning of the end for them ... they can't hide that

F: [Shrieking] Tell them about ... bastards just killing all my people

F: It's gone up to eleven total, right

F: [Shrieking] And tell them what the Dublin government is doing

[overlap of speech]

M: Mummy, you're doing none no good talking like that

F: I think it was about eight you know

[Female shrieking]

M: Mummy ... mummy don't

F: [Screeching] Mr, tell the Dublin government that they're no good or

M: Mummy

F: [Shrieking] Tell the Dublin government who stand there and they're watching their people get slaughtered

F: Mummy ... you're crying them out like

F: [Shrieking] They're watching their own Irish people getting slaughtered

[Female screeching]

CHAPTER 23

The Final Shots

Paddy Walsh crawls out to help Paddy Doherty.

Two more men were shot and injured, 51-year-old Patrick Campbell as he ran towards the Rossville Flats, and 38-year-old Danny McGowan, who was shot and injured as he helped carry Patrick to safety. Behind the Rossville Flats, 41-year-old Barney McGuigan ignored warnings for his own safety, waved a white handkerchief and tried to get to 31-year-old Patrick Doherty, who had been shot nearby and was dying. Barney was shot in the head and died instantly. These were the final shots that day.

In all this time – 20 minutes of concentrated British fire – the Official IRA fired three ineffectual shots in response, despite the army claiming they had met a 'fusillade of fire'.[1] No soldier was hurt or vehicle damaged.

Dermie McClenaghan: The bravery I saw that day – I never saw anything like it in my life. They walked out there in the middle of that gunfire. People were talking about the shooting from the Walls, and I *knew* that day they were shooting from the Walls. I was running about with Red Mickey at the time, and we went out, but the shooting started again, and panic arose. Father Mulvey came up to us and said, 'Get in, the shooting's started again' – he'd seen two people already. So, I took Pauline into a house, because she got upset again, God love her. Red Mickey was hurt and got to Letterkenny Hospital.

Jimmy Toye: I made myself as small as possible against the wall. I remember thinking that as long as I had a few people crouched in front of me, they might get hit first. Yes, that's what I was thinking. We didn't know what was happening. Was it one soldier firing? A group of soldiers? I knew every sound of the British army vehicles, helicopters, gunshots, etc., from experience, and I could hear the Saracens feet away and the clank of their doors. I knew they were just feet away.

John Campbell: My da [Patrick] was shot just at the front of the Rossville Flats, running up towards the steps to Fahan Street – the same area where Danny McGowan and Barney McGuigan were shot. My daddy was making for the back alley at Joseph's Place, and he was shot between running and the alley. Danny McGowan lifted him into the alleyway, and he ran out again, and he then got shot in the leg on the steps. God have mercy on Danny – if he had stayed where he was.

Bernard Gilmour: I saw Paddy Doherty hit as he was crawling along in front of the wall. The bullet lifted him up into the air.

Ivan Cooper: I heard a shout. Shots were still being fired at this time which seemed to me to be flying over my head and bullets were skipping all around. I looked up and saw Barney McGuigan facing me and standing near to the telephone box.

Teresa McGowan: Danny could hear a man asking for help because he was shot, and it was Paddy Campbell. He was from over Joseph Place, and Danny took him over there and people pulled them in. Danny went to turn, and he was shot then. The bone was splintered.

Geraldine McBride: Mr McGuigan, who seemed so old to me at that time but was only forty-one, came out with another fella. I knew Mr McGuigan: he was a nice man, a community-minded man who would often have tried to stop boys rioting in Creggan. Him and the other man called to me to come in; that I couldn't sit out there. He pulled me in by the hand; there was a group of people there. We were stuck against the side of this wall, and you could hear the soldiers coming up. You could hear noise all around you, magnified where we were, all this roaring and squealing and crying. They got me in there to the side of the wall. Then we could hear this man shouting, 'I don't want to die on my own – Oh Jesus, Mary and Joseph, help me!' – and that was Paddy Doherty. He wasn't far away, and I couldn't see him, but we could hear him.

Ivan Cooper: Barney McGuigan was in a state of panic, clearly concerned for the person who he knew had been shot and who he could see was lying close to him. I was conscious of Barney's shouts as I was edging my way towards him in my crawling position. There was still shooting all around and people crawling in all directions. I still couldn't see the person who Barney had shouted to me about.

Geraldine McBride: Mr McGuigan said, 'If I take a white hankie and go out, they won't shoot me,' and he took out something white, and stepped out. I remember it so well: there was actually two shots and he turned around and then he was shot in the head. I remember his head exploding and his eye coming out, and I went hysterical then. My mind went. Apparently, I was squealing and squealing.

Hugh McMonagle: I was walking in a trance. I was there, but there was nothing coming to me. When I walked over, people were just standing around. 'They're all dead,' someone said to me.

'They shot them all.' I looked around and saw the blood, and he pointed and told me that part of someone's head was over there. I was just walking around, and everyone was just stood around, and then I went to sit on the pad [kerb]. I kept looking around, thinking, 'What's happened?' I couldn't fathom it.

Ivan Cooper: As I continued to crawl towards Barney, he started to move in a standing but crouched posture. He was about thirty feet away from me. I think that Barney had a cloth in his hand to signal that he was on an errand of mercy and was unarmed. He waved the cloth in the general direction of the north end of Rossville Street, but I can't remember if I saw soldiers at that stage. My eyes were totally fixed on Barney. He had only taken a few steps and, as he came out into the open, I think that I then heard the same cracking noise as I had heard earlier of a shot being fired. The scene which I saw seemed to be in slow motion, and the few seconds which this scene lasted were telescoped. Barney just folded up. He crumpled and fell down on his side, like a bag rolling off a lorry. I still couldn't accept that he had been shot. Barney had never had any connection with any subversive organization and would never have been throwing nail bombs.

Bridie McGuigan: I was upset that day because my mother died on 29 January 1971 – so it was her first anniversary. Barney kissed me before he left, and I never saw him again. Later, I was in the cemetery putting flowers on the grave when I heard the shooting coming up from the march and I knew something was wrong.

Teresa McGowan: Danny couldn't even talk about it. The only thing that he remembered about it was sitting there and the bullets flying around him. He had been near where the monument is now, at the steps behind the monument. He remembered his friend Paddy Doherty crawling along the ground, and he said you couldn't lift your head with the shooting.

Anne Grant, daughter of Paddy Walsh: You can see the different stages in the photographs: my father crawling out behind Paddy

Doherty, him leaning over Paddy Doherty and then carrying Paddy Doherty – and you just realize, my God, he put himself out there to help somebody.[2]

Ivan Cooper: I will never forget the scene. I then heard a woman who was really screaming in a high-pitched tone that would not stop. I could also hear wild sobbing. There was a melee. I continued to crawl towards Barney's body. I still couldn't see and never did see the other person who he had been trying to reach.

Paddy Walsh: I only had one intention: to reach cover. All of a sudden, I remember hearing a thud. It was like the sound of someone falling. I didn't know whether someone had fainted. I didn't hear a shot. I stopped and turned around to go and help the man. Fellows were passing me, shouting, 'They're shooting at us, they're shooting at us, get out!' I went to the body to try to do something for him; I didn't care what was going on around me. I have no idea where I was, but I remember creeping out towards the body. As I was crawling out, a lady shouted at me, probably from the Rossville Flats, 'Paddy, get down!' The lady must have known me. I stopped and put my head down a moment, then continued. I remember seeing his feet. He was lying on his back, face up. I think he was wearing a donkey jacket. I reached the body and began to search him to find out who he was. There wasn't anything.

Jimmy Toye: The shooting was intense. I also recall people around me reciting 'Hail Mary'. Then, after hearing the clank of the hinged flap below the doors at the back of the Saracens, I heard English voices shouting and other shouts and roars. The people who had been standing around me moved west into Rossville Street with their hands above their heads, shouting, 'Arrest us.' I do not know why they did that; I think they thought they would be caught and killed if they did not give themselves up. I did not see what happened to them. I think that this time was the most frightening part. I thought that the army had gone berserk and would come around the corner and kill us. I had seen no guns or anything else on Hugh Gilmour and there had been no fighting or anything – I could not understand why this was happening.

Geraldine McBride: I didn't remember what happened after that until twenty years afterwards, when I met a man called Barney McFadden, who asked if I had ever forgiven him. I asked for what, and he said, 'I knocked you out.' I don't remember. He said I was screaming so hard they thought I was going to get them all killed, so he knocked me out cold – to save lives. I had a black eye and a sore face afterwards, and I could never work that out until I found out why twenty years later. I felt so bad because I could have got people killed.

I also found out I was taken into a house and my blood pressure went down so low they thought I was going to die of shock. The young boy Gilmour had nothing in his hands. Neither had Mr McGuigan; he only went to help somebody else.

Ivan Cooper: As soon as I reached Barney, I knew that he had been fatally wounded. I was absolutely appalled. He was lying in a pool of blood, which sticks strongly in my memory. Then there was something put over Barney's body by a middle-aged woman. Sat by Barney's body, I was not conscious of the presence of the army, as I was completely enveloped by what had happened to Barney and the shouting, sobbing and screeching around me. I was now aware that, for the first time in all the demonstrations in which I had taken part, a person had lost his life.

Paddy Walsh: I could not tell whether he was dead when I lifted him, but he didn't move. He didn't speak to me. I couldn't see if his eyes were open. I thought he was dying. I remember thinking, if he moves maybe he isn't dead, but he didn't move. I would say he was dead by the time I reached him. I also searched him for weapons because I thought that he must be armed – or why else would they have shot him? I did not find any. Indeed, I do not remember finding anything on him, but later his sister-in-law or wife told me that he had his wage packet in his pocket. I also looked for a rosary on him, but there was nothing. I couldn't see a wound, or any blood. I searched every pocket. I was thinking to myself, why was he shot? It could have been me.

Dr Domhnall MacDermott: I drove north past Free Derry Corner and when I looked north up Rossville Street, I could see three bodies lying piled on top of each other at the rubble barricade. I was within twenty yards of the bodies and it was clear to me that they were dead. Shots were still ringing out round the rubble barricade and so I did not attempt to go up Rossville Street and attend the bodies there. In any event, there was nothing I could do for them now. I saw people crouched around everywhere, trying to find cover.

Jimmy Toye: At the same time that people were attending to Hugh Gilmour, I noticed a man, whom I did not know at the time but subsequently learned was Barney McGuigan, lying approximately two yards to the south of where I was. He was lying on his back with his feet pointing towards me. I saw that there was a pool of blood around his head, which was steaming in the cold air of the day.

Paddy Walsh: I didn't have a rosary on me that day, it was my work clothes, and I remember being angry about that. I said a prayer over his body. As I was lying there with him, I heard the shoosh of bullets going over my head, but I didn't realize they were bullets at the time. I was just concentrating on the one man, and I was oblivious to all else. After a while, people started coming out and I remember someone saying that the body I was with was Paddy Doherty. That man was taken away crying. That's when I knew who it was.

Jimmy Toye: Then the shooting subsided and people were starting to move again. As I stood up, a man – Barney McGuigan – was lying feet away. There were other men around me as we stood by him and they were crying. I remember one man saying that there was nothing that we could have done. It was absolutely horrific. I will never forget this scene.

Jed McClelland: I'm still flat on the ground, trying to get as low as I can. At the last house of this second block of the flats, the door opens and there is a man and woman on their knees, and they're calling to me, 'Come on son, come on son,' and I crawled into their house on my belly – that's how I got into their house – and they slammed the door shut. Then it began to settle down and we heard no more shots.

Sophia Downey: After a while, it stopped. There was complete silence for some time and then people started moving out from shelter. We climbed out of the trench, as did the man who had pulled us in, and started to walk home.

Captain (now General Sir) Michael Jackson: The mood among the soldiers there was quite tense. People are when they think that they might get shot. I cannot describe in detail what took place next. However, I do have a clear memory of seeing a Pig with three bodies in the back and thinking to myself, 'This is serious.' I did not see any soldiers firing their weapons. Everything then seemed to calm down and become quiet. Derek Wilford was working out what to do. I have an impression of him saying something like, 'What do I do now?' I also have a recollection of not much (in the sense of orders) coming from above.[3]

British army 8th Brigade Log:

> **1626hrs** - 2 sub-units got involved in fire fight - shots from Rossville Flats. 2 civs lying dead and wounded. Sub-units secure in area.

Martin McGuinness: In my view the shooting lasted for between fifteen and twenty minutes. There were times when it stopped and then began again, but it was an intense period of fire. I think hundreds of shots were fired by the paras. I was only twenty-one years old at the time. It is difficult to estimate how many shots were fired. I was in a state of confusion, but it would seem to me that there were a lot more than the hundred or so the British army admit to having fired; it is nonsense to say that only a hundred shots or so were fired.

Andy Nolan: We stayed at the Bogside Inn for quite a while until the shooting had died down. We were totally unaware of what had happened, but decided it was best we went home. On the way up Westland Street, we met another friend from school, who was in a bit of state. He told us another friend from school – Mickey Quinn – had been shot. We carried on up to Creggan. I went home and told the rest of my family what had happened.

British army 8th Brigade Log:

> **1627hrs** - sub-units of B3 have arrested 30+, in addition to 2 hits.
>
> **1627hrs** - 100 hooligans at 20.

Paddy Walsh: I walked home that day with a friend of mine, and he said he had to hit a girl to calm her down after Barney McGuigan was murdered.

Martin McGuinness: Nobody knew what was happening. A lot of people were taking cover in and around the houses in Joseph Place, but I thought that was too open … When I arrived at Abbey Park, I met people coming from the Glenfada Park area and it became clear that the situation was serious because they were saying that people had been shot by the paras.

Raymond Rogan: We carried Donaghey out to my car and sat him across the back seat. I knew Leo Young at that time, and Leo sat in the back with Donaghey laid across his knees, and we went on. We were arrested on the way to hospital and dragged out. I remember protesting to the soldiers, telling them that there was a young lad dying in the back of the car, and he put the gun at me, and I remember he said to me, 'One stiff's not enough for us.' It was some time before the car was taken away [by paras]. By that time, the young fella was obviously dead.

Larry Doherty: On the other side of the Rossville Flats, behind the flats, I saw a body covered by a blanket surrounded by an enormous pool of blood. I didn't know who it was at the time and no one pulled back the blanket to see. I took some photographs. My attention was then drawn to a group of men who were walking towards me along the length of Block 2 of the Rossville Flats, carrying a man on their shoulders. I saw the man's face, but I did not know him. I now know that he was Patrick Doherty. By this time, I had started to realize that the situation was much worse than the Damian Donaghy/John Johnston story, which I thought would be the biggest story of the day.

Ivan Cooper: As I stood near Barney's body, I became aware of something going on on the other side, the west side, of Rossville Street. People were being carried from the area around the rubble barricade into Glenfada. I felt at this time completely powerless and useless despite my status as MP for Mid-Derry. The army was, in any case, clearly not interested in talking to anyone.

British army 8th Brigade Log:

> **1630hrs** – Car at 20 with 1 man dead, 1 wounded. Latter sent to hr.

Jed McClelland: The next thing we know all the paras are battering at the door and screaming at us to come out – so everyone living in the lower level of the flats had to come out with our hands above our head and we were all made to line up against a wall spread-eagled. The para looking after me, as it were, kept roaring at me, 'You Fenian bastard,' and all this stuff, so I turned around and answered him. 'You don't talk back,' he said, and he hit me with the rifle-butt and busted my tooth on my lip. We were still spread-eagled. We were there for about fifteen minutes and we were going to get arrested and put in Saracens, like they did with everyone else, but there was so many of us they pulled back and let us free and away. There was no more rioting with these boys – they were going to shoot you dead.

Police Chief Superintendent Frank Lagan: Very few radio communications came through on the army radio communications system from 3.55pm to 5pm. There was a lull in radio traffic, and everyone was anxious to know what the outcome of the arrest operation was.[4]

CHAPTER 24

Aftermath

Marchers shelter near the body of
Barney McGuigan.

*In the immediate aftermath of the shootings there was a sense
of shock and disbelief. Those still present in the Bogside stood
around in hushed groups, trying to make sense of what had just
happened. Ambulances for the wounded had been held back
by security forces before being finally let through. Some of the
wounded were tended on the scene, and others taken to hospital.*

*According to local eyewitnesses, the British army then
attended to some of the dead from Rossville Street. Soldiers*

were seen manhandling some of the bodies, dragging them into awaiting army vehicles.

Ivan Cooper: People were walking around with blood on their clothes. There were terrified people crammed like pigs behind the wooden fencing in Glenfada Park North. As I was running, I noticed three people lying dead or injured, then two others lying on the ground, and people moving around everywhere, some were bloody and injured, others were crying.

Eileen Doherty: I remember someone telling me that my son Patrick was down the street where the shooting had been. He was only ten. I went frantic and started to make my way down Rossville Street looking everywhere, when I heard my name called out. It was Paddy's cousin, Paddy McCallion. He said, 'Do you know Paddy was shot?' I said, 'No, is he alright?' He said he thought it was bad, but I think he knew he was dead.

Bernard Gilmour: Some time after I had seen Paddy Doherty shot, I heard that something had happened to my brother Hugh. I think I may have seen what I now know to be my brother's feet below our window, somewhere near the telephone box. I could only see someone's feet from the window. I didn't know they were my brother's.

Dr Raymond McClean: There was silence, as if a cloud was hanging over everybody.

Eamonn MacDermott: There was a common fear that if Creggan emptied for the march, the Brits would move into Creggan, so the IRA were all in Creggan and stayed there, just in case. When it all kicked off in the Bogside, they rushed down, but it was too late as, by the time they got there, everything was over.

Jimmy Toye: An ambulance arrived, and I felt it was safe to move out, but I was conscious of the army on the city walls and knew that they could shoot down at us. I was very careful, and I had to traverse Old Bogside Street into Lisfannon Park and then home. I never spoke. Nothing. I sat in our house. Nothing. I was on my own, and in my own thoughts.

Eamon Melaugh: Twice I called for ambulances, both on 5 October and Bloody Sunday, asking 'Could you send ambulances?' I don't ever want to do that again.

Bishop Edward Daly: When the ambulance came it took some people away and others were manhandled into Saracens and taken to the hospital. I stayed around for a while, but wanted to get out of the area and home to the cathedral.

British army 8th Brigade Log:

> **1631hrs** – Checking a further ambulance.
>
> **1633hrs** – We are mov out of area. 2 people shot in Chamberlain St are dead, bodies being recovered. We have 1 cas.

Larry Doherty: I assumed that Patrick Doherty was injured and was being taken to an ambulance so that he could be treated. I now know that he was dead. In fact, I never really realized that some of the people who I had seen earlier on were dead or dying. I had truly believed that they were just injured and that they would be taken away in ambulances and saved. It was just unbelievable to me.

Dr Raymond McClean: I told the ambulancemen that as far as I knew there were four dead men, including Gerard McKinney. I don't remember into which ambulance each individual was put. I do not remember whether the bodies were carried straight to the ambulance, or whether they were put down on the way.

Meanwhile, a car transporting injured 20-year-old Joe Friel to hospital was stopped by the army en route and Joe Friel was apprehended. The soldier who stopped the car later claimed that

Friel had possessed a gun on the day, and that Joe had admitted as much to him in the hours afterwards.

'I totally reject the evidence he [the soldier] gives regarding our alleged conversation,' Joe Friel said in his 1999 written statement to Lord Saville.

'The only conversation I had with the soldier was when I asked him to take me to hospital. I didn't even attend the march on Bloody Sunday, and the idea that I was a gunman, out that day without my glasses on, is ludicrous.'

British army 8th Brigade Log:

> **1634hrs** - Body lying south of Rossville Flats with civs around it.
>
> **1635hrs** - 2 bodies to be taken to Altnagelvin.
>
> **1635hrs** - 1 child's body brought out and dumped on street. People accused 14 & 15 of shooting child. Not accurate, may connect with yesterday [rioting].

Dr Raymond McClean: After the bodies had been taken away, small groups of people stood around on the steps between Abbey Park and Glenfada Park. I started looking for the people I had been with on the march. I was told that people had been taken to Fort George. Someone talked of Father Daly carrying an injured boy out of the area. Two or three dead were mentioned at the shops – people I now know to be Hugh Gilmour, Bernard McGuigan and Patrick Doherty. When we arrived home, my wife Sheila, whose pregnancy had prevented her attendance on the march, was hysterical. Danny and I couldn't speak. Eventually Sheila quietened down and all three of us sat in the house in silence.

Geraldine McBride: The first thing I remember is waking up in the ambulance being taken to the hospital. I woke up in the ambulance, under the bridge, and the soldiers in it were fighting with one another, squealing at each other. Then they were shouting at me, 'What's your name?' The way my mind was working, I was thinking, 'They're going to shoot me now.' One was shouting, 'Search her, search her!' and another said he wasn't touching me because I was distressed enough. I must have been like someone going crazy. They took me to the hospital, and I'll never forget the hospital. They opened the ambulance door, but they were just pulling people out of the ambulances. With some there was no respect shown, just pulling them out. Such little respect.

British army 8th Brigade Log:

> **1635hrs** – 2 shots fired at Q21, 1 shot returned, details to follow.
>
> **1636hrs** – 60 people around body at GR 43141684.
>
> **1636hrs** – Confirm B4 u/comd 1 PARA.
>
> **1637hrs** – My HAWKEYE no longer required, return them to base.

Raymond Rogan: We were arrested and transferred to Bridge Camp underneath Craigavon Bridge. I was still outraged and naming all these high-ranking officers that I knew in the RUC, and fair enough, within a short period of time, about two or three hours in Bridge Camp, two CID men came in, and I was released. I had heard this bang too, and this CID man said, 'That's your car.' I said, 'What!?' And he said, 'Aye, your car had to be blown up, there were bombs in it.' That was the first I'd heard of any bombs.

Maura Young: I got home, and Patrick then left to go home because he was living down in Shantallow then. Then our Helen came in and she was hysterical; she said she was nearly shot. She'd been at Free Derry Corner seeing Bernadette Devlin and all, and she said Eamonn McCann threw her under the lorry when the shooting was going on. My father told her not to be silly, what would they be shooting at? She was telling him, 'Da, they're shooting people!'

Alexander Nash: The Saracen tank came up, two big soldiers came out of the tank, one of them said, 'Three more dead bodies.' They dragged the three bodies one by one, pulled them into the Saracen, put them on top of each other and locked the door. I was lying alone, wounded but still conscious. I was sure I was going to be shot again, but the Saracen pulled away. I got up and walked across, and a priest heard my confession and gave me an absolution.

Alana Burke: The worst part of it all was the ambulance. I was semi-conscious on the floor and there were bodies on either side of me. It's hazy but I just remember thinking: are these people dead? Am I dead? I thought, maybe I was dead and looking down on the bodies in the ambulance.

John Kelly: They were carrying Michael out when I saw him, and I helped get him into the ambulance. As a matter of fact, I remember the ambulance. Michael was lying on the right-hand side, and then Willie McKinney, and Joe Mahon was lying on the floor. Myself, Georgie Downey and Georgie Cooley were in it too, and I think we counted about thirteen people in the ambulance, with two dead and one badly injured. It was parked outside Glenfada Park where the museum is now, and that's where we loaded Michael into it. We went to turn down Rossville Street and the paras stopped the ambulance. I put the window down and told them to fuck off, that we were trying to get to the hospital.

Bernard Gilmour: By the time I got down there, Hugh had been put in an ambulance. I have a feeling that Hugh and Barney McGuigan were put into the same ambulance. Someone told me that Hugh had only wounded his hand.

Teresa McGowan: I saw this man lying there, and I didn't realize it was Danny. He seemed to have aged so much since the morning. At first, he was unconscious, but then the pain brought him round and I saw that his leg was shattered. It looked like a bundle of broken sticks. I didn't know whether to bandage it or not, so I just held it stiff to try and minimize the pain until the ambulance arrived. Danny's brother and a neighbour went with him to hospital.

British army 8th Brigade Log:

```
1639hrs - 2 ambulances Rossville Flats, 1
stretcher into Flats, 1 x body GR 431 41684.

1639hrs - Amb move through Castle Gate, 1
man and 1 woman with GSW [gun shot wounds]
not stopped. 2 shots at wall - Q21 returned
three shots.
```

Alexander Nash: I went into the house beside an ambulance and a man gave me first aid. They then put me into the ambulance – there was a dead body on the floor and a woman was being given a tourniquet. There was another man beside me sitting up and I have heard since that he died. My son Willie had £3 on him and was wearing a distinctive signet ring when he left the house on Sunday. When his clothes were returned to us, the money and the ring were missing.

Bishop Edward Daly: On the way I was stopped by the army again at Little Diamond and I showed them my cuffs that were soaked in blood and told them, 'Look what you've done!' They said nothing and sent me on my way. I remember when I got home, I went to wash the blood off my hands, and I clearly remember the disbelief I felt. Sheer disbelief.

Martin Cowley: Later, I returned to my mother's home and, from a neighbour's house, telephoned my news desk in Dublin to brief my duty news editor and begin filing the first section of my report to a copy-typist. News reports tended to be phoned through in stages. At that stage I did not know the full extent of what had happened.

Bishop Edward Daly: The parochial house was filling with people who didn't know where to go. Some of the priests went over to the hospital, but I stayed put. I don't know how many people I gave the Last Rites to.

Martin McGuinness: In the Westland Street area, I met up with some other [IRA] volunteers. It was quite clear that there was a very serious situation and that we needed to gather ourselves. We were very angry and emotional. I realized that other volunteers would be looking for instructions how to handle themselves. After all, this was a civil rights march. Having weighed it up, it was my personal view that we should not react. It was better to let the world see what the British army had done. If we brought weapons into the area, we would give the British army an excuse to go further. Therefore, the decision was taken not to engage the British forces. Having taken the decision, it was relayed to the volunteers. I am confident that no one disobeyed the decision.

James Porter: I left the shop and went to the corner of William Street/Chamberlain Street to see whether I could see the bodies that had just been reported. A number of residents had come out of their homes and had gathered there in groups. I noticed that one group was with someone who appeared to be a journalist and a soldier. The soldier was telling him and the people that the army hadn't shot a boy dead, but that others had done it and had dumped the body to discredit the army. I looked down Chamberlain Street, but I couldn't see any bodies there.

Larry Doherty: I stood for a while, talking to people. Most people had left the area, but there were still soldiers on the William Street side of Rossville Street. I went up Beechwood, towards Creggan. I think Pat Cashman was with me. I remember bumping into Charlie Hazlett, the journalist, on Frederick Street. I said, 'Charlie, how do you see it?', which was press speak. He said, 'Lorcan, there could be as many as twelve dead.' Until then, I had thought that there was perhaps four dead. When at Beechwood, I telephoned my wife because I knew she would have seen the news flashes about the day. She said she had heard of two fatalities. I said, 'Grace, there could be as many as twelve.' She broke down crying.

Martin McGuinness: I assumed that there were enough journalists and independent people in the Bogside area that the British army would not attack the Free Derry area itself, but we still did not know how many people had been shot or killed. It could have been two or three or thirty. What we did know was that if people had been shot, they were innocent marchers. I thought that the British army would be exposed before the world through the activities of the journalists and the like who were on the ground in the Bogside.

Damian Donaghy: We passed [General] Ford, who was speaking to the press, then they tried to stop us on the bridge, but Father Carlin wouldn't stop and drove on through the checkpoint. We were taken to Altnagelvin and it was pandemonium. I remember seeing John Hume and then seeing Alana Burke coming in, but I never imagined that so many people were shot. I didn't know the full extent of what had happened until the next day. I was only fifteen and I was scared at the time and I admitted throwing stones. I lived with my granny because my mother and father had died when I was young.

Hugh McMonagle: Then I thought to myself I couldn't go over to William Street as I'd seen the army over there, but I met a fella and we went up Westland Street and across Laburnum [Terrace] and I was going to go out the Northland but then said to myself, 'What are you walking out for – face the bastards,' and instead I walked down Great James Street. On the left-hand side there were two Saracens sitting and all I heard from inside them was 'Woo-hoo! Way-hey!' [cheering] and I just stared and went on. I remember going past Fort George and up the Culmore Road, but I couldn't tell you anything after that.

Billy McVeigh: I was one of the last to go home; we stayed around not knowing what to do. I was nineteen. I was just numb. Like a sense of air, but there was no air. Like the Thunderclap Newman song, 'Something in the Air'. But it was an eerie, sinister feeling around us. Even before Bloody Sunday, we felt there was something in the air – but we never expected this.

Jed McClelland: I got back to the house eventually, and my mother was screaming her head off as she thought I had been shot. A fella up the street had told her I was shot in the arm down the town, and she went crazy.

British army 8th Brigade Log:

> **1641hrs** – 1 LV shot at sldr of Q23 from
> Charlotte St. Hit flak jacket. No cas.
> 1 shot returned, no hit claimed. Later
> 2 shots fired at gunman, no hits recorded.
>
> **1645hrs** – Both ambulances leaving Rossville
> Flats.
>
> **1647hrs** – 1 burst of fire from MG from GR
> 42531589 at 1645 hrs, 1 rd returned, no hit.

Ivan Cooper: I was horrified. I couldn't begin to say how horrified I was – that I as an organizer had been partially responsible for all this. How I felt was very simple: I felt responsible. All those deaths. I felt very much responsible. I remember going to the chapel in Creggan and looking at all those coffins.

British army 8th Brigade Log:

> **1640hrs** – Matron of Hosp says three bodies
> and child's body to be examined for GSW.
> Plus two people with GSW.

1640hrs – Veh Reg [vehicle registration] for prisoners.

1640hrs – Ref body of child. Local evidence says that the child was brought from the area of the Bogside.

After the soldiers went in shooting and as Derry counted its dead, Major General Robert Ford gave a television interview to a waiting BBC reporter. In it, he insisted that his troops had returned fire and had discharged three rounds altogether, after having 'between ten and twenty' IRA rounds fired at them. This was demonstrably untrue. This early interview no doubt contributed to the public's perception of Bloody Sunday being a battle between the British army and the IRA.

*

The following is a transcript extract of Major General Robert Ford, to the BBC Film Crew in the Bogside on 30 January 1972:[1]

General Ford: The paratroopers did not go in there shooting. In fact, they did not fire until they were fired upon and my information, at the moment, and it is very, almost immediately, after the incident, is that the para battalion fired three rounds all together after they had something between ten and twenty fired at them from the area of the Rossville Flats over there.

BBC Reporter: They fired three rounds only

General Ford: My information at the moment

BBC Reporter: I believe there are more than three dead

General Ford: That they fired three

BBC Reporter: I certainly I have seen three dead myself

General Ford: Well they may well not have been killed by our soldiers.

CHAPTER 25

Word Spreads

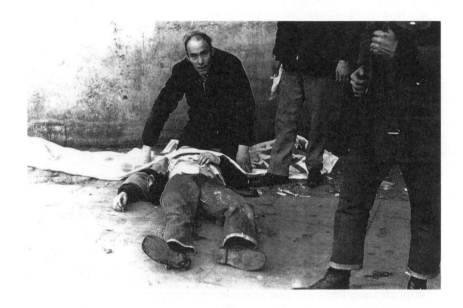

The body of teenager Hugh Gilmour lies covered with the civil rights banner.

As marchers and eyewitnesses made their way home, rumours became fact, and the press began to report what had transpired. It became clear that British soldiers had indeed opened fire on the marchers. All over the city and beyond, people tuned into TV and radio news to find out how many had been hurt.

Ita McKinney: I had this instinctive feeling after seeing those pictures of the trouble in town. Eventually, a man came to the house saying he had some news. 'Tell me! Tell me!' I screamed at him, tearing at his shirt. He said that there was a man called McKinney in the hospital who had had a heart attack, but he wasn't sure if it was Gerry. I think I scared him off with my screaming. After that, I don't remember much. I just knew inside myself that Gerry was dead. I can't remember anybody ever saying to me; the house just filled up, and when I saw my brother John coming in, he was eating a handkerchief and crying – and I knew for sure then that Gerry was one of them.[1]

That January, Ita McKinney was over eight-months pregnant. She gave birth eight days after her husband's murder, calling the baby Gerard after his father.

British army 8th Brigade Log:

> **1650hrs** - 1 dead person returned to this loc, has N/B in pocket. Felix [explosives officer] requested.
>
> **1651hrs** - HQNI updated.

Gerry Duddy: When I got to Westland Street, I was very frightened and nervous as hell. I thought it was unbelievable – there were bodies lying around who had been shot. People in the area were standing around, saying that three or four people were dead. Then I met friends and there was a full stream of people making their way back up to Creggan. By the time we got to the chapel at the top of the New Road, people were saying there were six or seven people dead. The fellas I was walking with knew that Jackie had been shot – but none of them told me. When I got back to Creggan I made my way home. As soon as I got to the front door, I knew something was wrong.

Eamonn Deane: As soon as we got home, we turned on the television and radios to try and find out what had happened. My father and some of my brothers and sisters had been on the march, and they came back to the house as well. My father told me that he had got trapped inside the Rossville Flats.

British army 8th Brigade Log:

> **1652hrs** - One other amb at Rossville Flats. Crowd of between 50 and 60 in area.
>
> **1653hrs** - 2 or 3 shots fired in area of Little Diamond. No strike seen.
>
> **1653hrs** - 1 shot from area of Rossville Flats into Sackville St. NFR.
>
> **1655hrs** - 2 shots at my C/S 5. Return of 2 rds.
>
> **1655hrs** - 2 or 3 further shots in Little Diamond area by en.

Philomena McLaughlin: I remember a neighbour came out and turned the radio station over, saying that people were being shot dead down the town. The adults were all out in the street, talking. Ethel came home first, and then Susie and her husband, and her husband stood against the wall for a minute, and then slid right down it and put his head in his hands and started sobbing.

British army 8th Brigade Log:

> **1659hrs** - 1 PARA locs. B1 William St/Little Diamond. B5 North and Rossville St. B3 W/ Chamberlain St. B4 Gt James' St.
>
> **1703hrs** - C/S being reorg on line William St/ Little Diamond to William St/Little James' St. 1 reserve C/S at Gt James' St.
>
> **1704hrs** - At 1656 - 1 x 7.62 fired at gunman at Factory Abbey St/William St. Hit claimed.

Hugh McMonagle: I went in and my wife met me, and she said, 'There's thirteen dead.' I couldn't even answer. I just looked at her.

She asked if I was alright, and I sat down, and told her that they murdered them. I remember her coming over to me, and she says I wept like a wain. Why did they do that? There were no guns, it was like a carnival. It was teaching us a lesson: 'Paddy – lie down.' I told her it was wee Duddy out of Creggan. I knew it was one of the Duddys.

Paul Doherty: I was eight at the time. We were playing in the street and reports began to come back about people being shot, but we were really too young to take it in. Then people began arriving at the house, but we didn't really believe that anything had happened until our mother told us that our father was dead.

British army 8th Brigade Log:

> **1706hrs** – <u>Casrep from 1 PARA</u>
>
> 2 minor acid burns. (Treated by MO). 1 injured back. (Returned to base).
>
> 2 en bodies taken to Altnagelvin Hosp.
>
> **1710hrs** – HQNI updated.
>
> **1711hrs** – Photographers at Rossville Flats taking photos of Civil Rights Banner covered in blood.
>
> **1712hrs** – 2 more bodies at Altnagelvin.
>
> **1715hrs** – 2 gunfire flashes at amb from area of Eglinton Place.
>
> **1716hrs** – Task completed in William St. What now?

Eamonn MacDermott: There was no acid bombs. Who the hell would be throwing acid bombs? The thing people don't seem to realize about Bloody Sunday is that the army came in much further than they had ever come in before, so nobody was prepared for them. It was a march. The riot was one thing as there were riots every day and we expected them, but nobody would have prepared acid bombs for the simple fact that the army had never been as far as the Rossville Flats since 1971. It was totally unexpected.

Larry Doherty: Back at the hotel people were trying to work out what had happened. The army press officer wasn't there. Someone called out the name William McKinney. I said it was not William McKinney, it was Gerard McKinney. John Hume was there, and he turned to me and he said, 'William McKinney – out of your office.' The stark reality of everything that had happened left me aghast. Willie was one of the most popular members of the *Derry Journal* staff. He was a lovely chap, not at all aggressive.

Anne Grant: When my daddy did come home that night he obviously couldn't sleep, but then he disappeared for a couple of days. His head was all over the place at what the British army had done that day. It was just so hard for him to take in.

British army 8th Brigade Log:

> **1719hrs** – B3 moving back now. Remainder to mov in ten mins.
>
> **1720hrs** – Another amb opposite Rossville Flats.
>
> **1723hrs** – Pull back and withdraw serials 1, 2, 3 and 5.
>
> **1726hrs** – Sitrep 1725. Fahan St empty. Rossville Flats about 30. Rossville St and William St quiet.
>
> **1729hrs** – Gnnr [name redacted] shot in foot. Negligent discharge.

As detailed in this log entry above, one soldier was injured by gunfire on Bloody Sunday; however this gunshot wound was self-inflicted as he had shot himself in the foot around 5.30pm.

British army 8th Brigade Log:

> **1736hrs** - Amb crossing bridge from Lonemoor Rd.
>
> **1737hrs** - All quiet. Usual Sunday traffic.
>
> **1740hrs** - 2 RGJ Killrea got phone call from Creggan, there is a car in Creggan with 2 dead and 1 not expected to live. Gunmen are expected to retaliate tonight in strength.
>
> **1742hrs** - Ordered to withdraw reserve and take down wire.

Police Chief Superintendent Frank Lagan: Just before 6pm General Ford returned to Brigadier McLellan's offices with a number of military officers including the Brigadier. Someone in the offices had a domestic radio. The news came on and it was announced for the first time that thirteen were dead. Neither General Ford nor Brigadier McLellan made any attempt to approach me, and I decided it was time for me to leave.[2]

Mark Durkan, a former Foyle MP and, later, Deputy First Minister of Northern Ireland: I was eleven when it [Bloody Sunday] happened, playing football. I remember hearing there was shooting up the town and running home, and seeing people drifting past who had been on the march. I remember one man, who just said, 'It was a massacre, a massacre.' Between the radio and scraps of TV news, it grew from one dead, three dead – it mounted. A sense of numbing shock, but a pounding anger that I felt, and I knew everybody else felt as well.[3]

Maura Young: I went over to the shop, and it was so strange. Did you ever get a creepy feeling that everyone is looking at you? Well, I went into the shop like that. It was Nana Rogers who told me it was awful down the town and there was shooting, and people shot. That was around tea-time. I said, 'Jesus, our John isn't home yet.' Usually, he would have phoned a girl in England every Sunday night from that shop, and so I asked in the shop if he'd been in yet. They said no. Then she said I should phone the hospital. I didn't think I needed to, and she said, 'I'll do it for you.' I think she knew.

British army 8th Brigade Log:

1743hrs - <u>Sitrep 1 PARA</u>

1 When launched attacked from three directions. Little James Street, through barrier 14 and from west.

2 Chased hooligans down as far as low building at Rossville Flats.

3 At this stage came under fire. Fire fight occurred - PARA went firm in area. Taken til present to reorg on original line. Full report of shooting incidents to follow.

4 During fight identified 2 snipers, shot them and recovered their bodies from outside Rossville Flats.

5 Injuries to 1 PARA; 1 man bad back injury having fallen over wall plus 2 men suffering from acid burns. Acid thrown from Rossville Flats. No of arrests approx. 50.

Bridie Gallagher: A while after we got back, my brother John came to tell us that Mickey wasn't home. We went to John Hume's house to see what we could find out; lots of other people were there too. We were told that Mickey was arrested. I remember we were worried hearing that because we knew that people arrested could get six months in jail. We didn't know that anyone was dead then.

When we got back to my parents' house, there were lots of people in the hall. My daddy was sat on the sofa, and he said, 'Mickey's dead.' I was a bit sharp with him and told him that he was only arrested. But my mother was in the bathroom being sick, so they had obviously heard something. She was in a bad way. Shortly after that, two priests came in and they confirmed that Mickey was dead. It was so heartbreaking. He was only twenty that September before he died. To hear my poor mother cry like that. A big part of her died that day.

British army 8th Brigade Log:

1746hrs - From Altnagelvin. Total GSW - 17 of which 5 dead. Youngest is 15 years.

1750hrs - Remove all barriers.

1750hrs - Approx. 50 arrested to date.

1751hrs - Military Lines to Bligh's Lane out of order. Civil lines only. No evidence of enemy interference.

1755hrs - RUC require assistance at Altnagelvin. Hume, Cooper and Devlin stirring trouble.

1956hrs - CO 1 PARA at this loc. Padre leaving his loc for your loc.

The Hume, Cooper and Devlin accused in the army log of 'stirring trouble' at the hospital were John Hume, Ivan Cooper and Bernadette Devlin, who were all elected representatives of the House of Commons at the time of Bloody Sunday.

*

Dr Domhnall MacDermott: On arriving home at about 6pm, I rang the Altnagelvin Hospital again. I was told that nine people were dead as a result of the march. Throughout the evening I kept ringing one of the staff I knew at the hospital to find out the latest news on the casualties. Each time I called it seemed like there were more casualties.

Brendan Duddy: I wasn't a marching person, but I'd decided to go down and listen to the speeches. My memory of what happened after that is very vague. I met up with Nell McCafferty who was running in my direction, and we went to take cover, and then to Nell's house. People started to arrive very quickly. Bernadette Devlin was among those who came to the house. I stayed there until about 6pm, and by then, details of the catastrophe had started to emerge. I began to realize the scale of the disaster that we had on our hands.

Maura Young: I went home and said I needed to go to the hospital because they think John's hurt. My father moved to get up, and I told him not to; I'd ask a neighbour, John Ward, who could give me a lift. At John Ward's house, his wife said, 'Aye surely, he'll take you.' I don't know if they already knew or what. As we were coming out of the house to the car, a friend of John's, Terence Donnelly, who was a boxer alongside Jackie Duddy, was coming back from a boxing match he'd been fighting. I told him I was going to the hospital because people thought our John was hurt, and he said, 'I'm coming along with you.' He was just seventeen.

Eamonn MacDermott: We turned on the news. My mother swore by hot sweet tea after traumatic events, and it always seemed to work. We were probably all in shock, but you didn't call it that back then. We turned on the television and watched the English news at 6pm, with news coming in of two people dead. We knew that was wrong as we had seen more ourselves. My uncle had been at evening mass at Pennyburn, and he rang us to tell us that priest had told them seven people were dead. I remember that RTÉ radio basically binned all their programming that night, and it was all about Bloody Sunday and Derry. Listening to the radio, the number of dead just went up and up.

Mary Donaghey: At about 6pm, I started to make the tea, although neither my husband Jackie nor Gerald had returned home. I heard a knock on the door. It was a man I knew, James Shiels. He told me he had been on the march and that he heard Gerald had been shot through the head. As soon as he told me this he just turned and hurried off and I didn't get the chance to ask him any more about it. I was worried, but I was certain that there must have been some mistake. I remember being very angry with him; I thought he did this as some sort of joke.

Gerry Duddy: Inside our house, one of my sisters, Susie, told me that Jackie had been shot. I couldn't believe it. I was only fourteen, but I remember I wanted to get a gun and shoot the bastards who did it. The house was full, and everyone was hysterical. I can't really remember much about what happened afterwards in the house. I was staggered that Jackie had been shot. He wasn't doing anything. Jackie lived for his boxing. I remember going training with him, having to walk for miles from Creggan and back to do this. He was a great fella. What's sad is that I never really got to know him.

Andy Nolan: We were having our tea while we waited for news to come in. I don't know what time it was, but a knock came to the door. It was Gerry Duddy and Adrian. They told me Jackie was shot. Of course, I didn't believe them. They went on out and I said I'd be straight over. Of course, everything was confirmed when we saw the news. I don't remember much after that.

Jed McClelland: We found out on the news and it was a total shock. Initially there was just one person dead, then two, then six, and as the night went on, the whole world was trying to work out what the hell had gone on here. Basically, the BBC news told us that terrorists, the IRA, attacked the paras and that the paras had to fire back. That was their immediate reaction on the 6pm evening news.

British army 8th Brigade Log:

1820hrs - <u>Shotreps.</u>

Timings between 1615 and 1640.

1. Gunman GR 43061657 fired 2 rounds at
   Roaring Meg. C/S 21 in Long Tower St fired
   2 x 7.62 back. Gunman fell and was dragged
   back into Meenan Square.

2. C/S21 (Long Tower St) fired 5 x 7.62 at
   gunman seen GR 42571625. Seen to fall -
   dragged away.

3. 1 x 7.62 at gunman GR 48011629 by C/S 23
   (Barrack St) - stepped into alleyway.

4. 3 LV fired at C/S 23 (Barrack St). 1 shot
   his soldiers flak jacket - no cas. 8 x
   7.62 returned at gunman GR 43021632. Not
   known if hit.

Betty Curran, a child in 1972: Although I was very young, there is a memory – I'll never forget it – and it is of my mother not being able to eat her Sunday dinner. She pushed it away and said, 'I can't eat that after what I saw in this city today,' and pushed her plate away. That to me was such a human story, especially to us as children. I was just a child wondering what was wrong with my mammy and why she wasn't eating her dinner.[4]

Mary Donaghey: Shortly afterwards, a neighbour, Mrs Kathleen Flood, came round to my house. She told me she had heard that Gerald had been shot in the leg and taken to hospital. I knew Mrs Flood very well and knew she would not have told me anything unless she was sure of her facts. I think I was in a state of shock as soon as she told me the news. Later that evening, before I learned that Gerald was dead, I found out that it was my cousin, Damian Donaghy, who had been shot in the leg that day.

British army 8th Brigade Log:

> **1822hrs** - 30 people standing around the Bogside Inn.
>
> **1826hrs** - Bogside Inn - crowd growing now over 40.
>
> **1828hrs** - Bogside Inn - now about 10 - men not yobbos.

Dr Domhnall MacDermott: As I had driven home, I saw that the paratroopers had arrived back outside. They stood around in the street and played very loud jazzy music on their radios. I remember that some unionist neighbours came out with tea and buns for the paratroopers, who stayed there until 10pm.

Mary Donaghey: Some time passed, and there was still no sign of either Gerald or my husband, Jackie. Mrs Flood stayed with me in the house to support me. By this time, I was extremely anxious and generally distracted.

British army 8th Brigade Log:

> **1830hrs** - Ref dead youth with 1 NB [nail bomb] in pocket - there were 4 NBs - Felix has them.

Eileen Fox: Then my aunt Dolly and uncle Dusty arrived and told us again, 'We heard your Jackie was shot today.' How they found out so quickly, I don't know. We still didn't believe it, though, and everyone was praying it was a rumour. My daddy was in bed after night shifts, so Dolly went up to tell him, too. We had all been warned not to go near the march, so we knew he'd go mad that Jackie had disobeyed him. We heard him upstairs, shouting, 'I told them not to go! Do they not listen?'

British army 8th Brigade Log:

> **1835hrs** - 32 pris. Sp Coy 1 PARA have still
> not sent arrestees. Can action be taken to
> encourage those who made arrests or else
> will have to release them.

Mary Donaghey: After a while, my husband Jackie returned home. I told him what James Shiels and Mrs Flood had told me and he went straight back out to look for Gerald. About an hour later, I think around 7pm, Jackie returned. He had been up to Altnagelvin Hospital and he told me that Gerald had not been admitted to the hospital. He had also been taken to the mortuary to see if Gerald was there, but he was not. Jackie told me that he had been shown ten to twelve bodies lying all over the place, some in the corridor. There were police and army present at the morgue. I couldn't believe what he was telling me. For the first time, I realized that something terrible had happened in the Bogside that day. However, as Gerald's body was not at the hospital or mortuary, my hopes were raised that he was alright.

British army 8th Brigade Log:

> **1837hrs** - ATO tasked by 22 Lt AD Regt to
> investigate Ford Cortina 3955F2 with dead
> body in back seat. 4 NBs found in pocket.
> Car clean.

Eamonn Deane: I went to mass at 7.30pm that Sunday and it was only then that I learned that thirteen people had been shot and killed by the paratroopers. There was talk of who had been shot, but some was misinformed.

Bridie McGuigan: I rushed back to the house to make sure the children were OK and then I was told that Barney had been shot in the foot. This was to get me to Altnagelvin. By that stage people knew Barney was dead. When I got there, Father O'Gara sat me down on a bench and I don't really remember much more after that. I do remember seeing a soldier and trying to get at him, but that is about all.

Eileen Fox: My sister Kay went to the nearest shop to phone the hospital – to make sure it was true – and the woman at the hospital just said, 'Jackie Duddy? Yes – dead on admission,' and put the phone down. Our Kay went crazy. We were all praying and crying, but at the same time, there was a silence in the house. We just wouldn't believe it; then Kay came back and was half-carried in the door, and we knew it was true. We just lost it. Our poor wee Jackie, he was the one who helped everybody, that's what hurt us most. He was never a saint, just a normal bubbly teenager, kind and funny. I think our boys hero-worshipped him a bit because of the boxing, and they were so close, thick as thieves, really.

British army 8th Brigade Log:

```
1840hrs - 11 Dead - GSW those identified:
Patrick Doherty, Michael Kelly, Barry [sic]
McGuigan, William McKinney, Jack Duddy,
William Nash + 1 dying.
```

Regina McLaughlin: I remember being at home when the news came on and Mammy began getting very distraught and crying. We weren't sure what was going on, but she kept saying 'Your daddy's dead, your daddy's dead.' Somehow Mammy just knew that he wasn't coming home. She just felt it. A man later came to the house to say there was a man in hospital with a heart attack – I think they were trying to soften the blow instead of just blurting out, 'Gerry's dead.'

Bridie McGuigan: Later, when I came home, I insisted on telling my children myself. We had three boys and three girls – the oldest was sixteen and the youngest was just six. I brought them into a room and told them their father was dead.

Cahil McElhinney: Avril and I had spent that afternoon at the Plaza Cinema. When we got home, we switched on the radio and heard there had been people killed at a Derry march. Within what seems like minutes now, there came a knocking on the front door of the downstairs flat. But I knew it was for me; something told me it was terrible news. I rushed down and there was Auntie Joyce, from Handsworth, on the steps. 'Kevin?' I asked. 'Yes,' she said.

British army 8th Brigade Log:

1855hrs - From Altnagelvin 11 dead 13 GSW.

Mark Durkan: I remember seeing on the news at the time when it was put to an army commander, 'Do you know a Catholic priest has said it was murder,' and the commander said, 'I would say that priest was a liar.' I was always very struck by that.

Eamonn MacDermott: In the meantime, the paras had come back because they were stationed right outside our house in Springham Street. We had thirty-five windows in the house, and the paras came up and banged on the front door and told my father to turn off all his lights and pull the curtains. They had already shot out all our streetlights in the street when they got back from the Bog. My daddy just closed the door on them, and then he turned on every single light in the house – and didn't pull one curtain.

Dr Domhnall MacDermott: I created a lot of light in the street as my house had so many windows. The next day a neighbour told me he had stopped outside our houses and the paratroopers had asked him to turn off his car headlights. He said he refused and put his headlights on full beam. I can only presume that the paratroopers were afraid that the Provos [Provisional IRA] would see them in the light cast.

Ivan Cooper: I felt that I was needed at Altnagelvin Hospital. I considered I should be at the hospital to support people, and in particular, the relatives of the dead and injured. Although I knew that people would not blame me, I had to live with the responsibility for having brought the people of Derry onto the streets for the march that day.

Martin McGuinness: This was the worst day that I had ever experienced in my life; it was devastating. Whenever the full extent of what happened becomes clear it will still seem unbelievable that it could have happened. I was shell shocked at the time and amazed that it could have happened.

Ivan Cooper: As we reached the underdeck of Craigavon Bridge, there were a lot of police officers stopping vehicles on the bridge. I was asked to produce my driving licence, which I was unable to do. Police officers were shouting to us 'ten-nil – ten-nil' and were making other silly jibes, which, at the time, still did not mean much to us. My details were taken and, after ten to fifteen minutes, we were allowed to continue on towards the hospital.

Sophia Downey: Some of Michael's friends came to the door. I could tell that something was wrong. My father went to the door and I followed him, but he pulled the door shut so that I couldn't hear what was being said. My father was told that Michael had been shot in the leg. At the time, we didn't have a car and so we went across the road to ask for a lift to hospital.

Regina McLaughlin: Everything was kind of chaotic after that and we were shifted next door to the Carlins' house. Then I remember the news again, seeing the streets of Derry and people lying around dead. I remember looking at one particular body covered in a sheet with one shoe on and one shoe off and thinking, is that my daddy? I think my uncle then sent me out to play.

Bridie McGuigan: My heart broke that day, and it has never healed. We were madly in love. We got married in 1953 and he was such a handsome man, a great dancer, and he was everyone's friend.

CHAPTER 26

The Morgue

Children say a prayer at the bloodied civil rights banner in
the Bogside.

*At Altnagelvin Hospital in Derry's Waterside, frantic family
members were gathering in their dozens, desperate for information on the whereabouts of loved ones, as other victims continued
to arrive.*

*Even waiting outside the hospital was traumatic for those
present. Relatives waiting in the hospital's car park watched as
British army Saracens arrived carrying some of the Bogside dead
– and witnessed shocking mistreatment of bodies by soldiers.*

John Kelly: We eventually got there, and I remember them carrying Michael into Casualty on a trolley. A doctor and some nurses came to check him, and they said, 'I'm sorry, he's dead.' I remember looking at him and asking them, 'Are you sure? Check again.' And they checked him again and said, 'I'm sorry, he's dead.' The next thing I remember was that we had to get word back to the house and we were stuck in the Waterside. Someone was able to phone a neighbour with a phone, and they went to tell my father.

Frances Gillespie: Daniel was told that his brother had been shot dead and went to the morgue to see, but it wasn't true. He said he would never forget it. When he got to the morgue door, the police were standing in the corner in the darkness singing that Coca-Cola song, 'I'd Like to Teach the World to Sing'. Honest to God.

Maura Young: We went to the hospital. Nightmare, just a nightmare. It was awful. Bedlam, with doctors walking about with blood on their coats, you'd think you were in a butcher's shop. I was standing and a priest came out, Tom O'Gara, and he asked if he could help. I told him about my brother, John Young, and he brought out this list. I thought to myself, 'Oh Jesus Christ, he has a list.' He asked my brother's name again and his age, and he shook his head. I told him John didn't look seventeen: he was a big fella, broad-shouldered – he looked around twenty-one or twenty-two, not a wee seventeen-year-old. Then he said to John Ward and Terence Donnelly, 'Will you two come with me?' They left me standing in Casualty.

John Kelly: I remember wandering down the corridors and going in talking to some of the others. The place was packed with people, and I remember the paras wandering about, laughing. They were having great craic, ye know. Eventually I remember seeing me da and our 'Fia, my sister, walking in. I looked at my da, and said, 'Da, Michael's dead.' He slid down the wall in front of us with shock and started to cry.

Eileen Doherty: A friend of mine took me over to the hospital, and I remember the first thing I noticed was the police, and you could see from the way they were laughing together as they were talking that they were having a grand day.

Father O'Gara took me to a wee waiting room and asked me to describe Paddy. He went up to the ward looking for him. Then, he and a friend of Paddy's went into the morgue, and Paddy was the second person they looked at. He had his eyes open. I heard a woman scream from the top of her voice; it was Mrs McGuigan. Then John Hume was walking towards us, and he saw me. He started shaking his head and said, 'Now, Mrs Doherty', and then he started to cry.

Ivan Cooper: There were relatives arriving at the hospital clearly distressed as they looked for people. There was a general melee. Women were walking around crying. I distinctly recall the sisters of Jackie Duddy following me around the hospital as they looked desperately for their brother. I saw soldiers arriving at the hospital and pushing past people using their rifles. They seemed completely oblivious to the utter anger and hatred which was being directed at them. There were paras there too, distinguishable by their red berets.

Geraldine McBride: They took me in at the hospital, and I remember I had a green PVC coat on, and it was covered in blood and my trousers were covered in blood. They took me into a ward and the doctor put me a drip in because of the shock. The doctor was trying to talk to me, but I couldn't even speak. All I wanted was my mammy. I could hear all this roaring and screaming – that must have been the relatives coming into the hospital. While I was hearing this screaming, what sticks in my mind is that someone brought the two policemen who were stood at my doorway a tray with cups of tea. While all that was going on. I don't know why, but I never forgot seeing that.

Ivan Cooper: There were wild rumours flying around the hospital and the rumour machine was working overtime. People in the hospital were confused, hysterical and angry, and the circumstances were hard for the medical staff. I remember Mickey Bradley being brought in in a very distressed state, shouting.

Maura Young: They were at the morgue, and I was still standing in the corridor when they brought someone through. I think it was Mickey Bradley. He'd been shot through the arm and was squealing with the blood running out of him. The nurse pulled the bed and it slammed against the wall, and he complained because it was sore, and I remember the nurse said to him something like, 'Good enough for you!' She was covered in blood too.

Patsy McDaid: It was mayhem later in Altnagelvin Hospital, with all the wounded crowded together, doctors running round and the dead being brought in too. The doctor examined me, asking me where the bullet went in, and was amazed that it had just cut across me. He said you could see my bone through the wound. A few millimetres had saved my life.

John Kelly: We had to go to the mortuary to identify Michael's body. I could have done it, but naturally, it was up to my father. The scene was awful, bodies everywhere, blood everywhere, an awful sight. There were some on the trolleys, some on freezers, about ten people in total, I think, and we had to go through every one of them individually to find Michael. We recognized the suit he wore. We left, and on the way out of the mortuary we were stopped by two cops standing at the door wanting to ask us a few questions. I told them to get lost, we had enough to deal with.

Joe Mahon: The bullet went through my hip, through the stomach and lodged in the other hipbone. In Casualty, people say I never spoke or moved, but I can remember being half-aware of what was going on. I think I was in shock. Apparently, they thought I was dead until they found a pulse in my neck. Surgeons removed part of my bowel and intestine, and after that, I took lead poisoning from a bullet fragment and needed more surgery.

John Kelly: We were sitting in the car outside Altnagelvin Hospital, waiting on me da who was signing forms. I looked to the left near the Casualty area when an army Saracen pulled up. This was just after 6pm. What we saw was grotesque to see

– total disregard for a human being. All of a sudden, the back doors of the Saracen flew open, and they started dragging bodies out by the feet and the hands, one after the other. It was Young, Nash and McDaid, the three boys they had lifted from the barricade. We watched them do this and take them into Casualty and we watched them then bringing them out again and throwing them back – throwing them back – into the back of the Saracen and taking them away to the mortuary. Then my father came out. We couldn't believe what we had just seen, it was so horrific.

Sophia Downey: They paras showed no respect for the bodies, dragging them into Casualty by their shoulders and feet. As they were doing it, they were laughing and talking. Then they brought the bodies back out again, they were dragging them by their hands. I just can't get the picture of those bodies out of my mind.

Ivan Cooper: A man informed me that a Saracen had arrived outside the hospital carrying dead bodies. I went to the rear of the hospital. Paras were taking bodies out. There was blood everywhere. The soldiers carried each of the bodies by the arms and legs and treated each of the bodies in the same way. No stretcher was used. The bodies were all handled as if they were 'stuck pigs', with the body sagging. I was standing close to the Saracen just watching without saying a word. The soldiers were joking with each other and laughing and talking about the events of the day as the bodies were carried. They were jubilant and gave me the impression that they were thinking that they had busted an IRA unit in the Bogside. The bodies were taken into the hospital and then brought quickly out again and thrown back in the Saracen and it was driven away. I assumed to the hospital mortuary.

Michael Quinn: Casualty was pandemonium. I recall people on benches and people crying out. I was in hospital for eleven days.

Eileen Fox: My daddy and Kay and Susie went to the hospital to identify him, Kay holding my daddy up even though she was in pieces herself. Someone, probably out of respect for the dead, had thrown what we would have called 'an IRA coat' – a parka with fur around the hood – around Jackie to cover him up. Probably just some kind man who had lifted him from the street, but my daddy saw this coat and went crazy. He threw the coat off him, and screamed at them, 'Don't you dare try and stitch him up!' He thought they were trying to make Jackie look bad. We knew he wasn't involved in anything. We had all been taught about the importance of civil rights and things like that, but we were all cowards otherwise – we wouldn't have dreamt of it.

Ivan Cooper: The hospital administrator finally produced lists of two or three names at a time, which, at intervals, were handed to me by him in a completely cold and unsympathetic manner. I stayed at the hospital until it was confirmed that the names of all the dead had been provided. As it turned out, more would be identified later.

Maura Young: I saw the Gilmours coming in. You had to go to a glass window in Casualty, so someone went to the glass window and said, 'We're here to see Hugh Gilmour.' They'd known Hugh was shot and injured. The woman behind the glass just said, 'In the morgue!' and shut the window. There was a policeman behind me, and I think it was Floyd who went for him. That's what she said to them, 'In the morgue!' No tact at all. It was bedlam.

I remember sliding down a wall and I was sitting on the ground. This big soldier came in, he had army dress uniform trousers on him and a white coat over – I don't know if he was a doctor or if he was there to see what was happening, but he looked around. 'Fucking bloody mess,' he said, and walked away up the corridor. Then John was identified in the morgue.

Bernard Gilmour: At the end of the day, I went to the morgue to identify my brother. When I was there, I smelt the stink of oil and saw a man's hands covered in oil. I lifted the sheet because I knew that would be Hugh. It was him.

The clergy later released statements condemning the actions of British soldiers and appealing for calm.

Telegram from Most Revd Dr Farren, Bishop of Derry, to British prime minister Edward Heath:

```
I am shocked and deeply saddened by the
terrible events this afternoon in Derry. I
protest in the strongest possible manner
against the action of the army resulting in
so many deaths and injuries. I demand an
immediate and public inquiry.¹
```

Press statement from Cardinal Conway, Primate of All Ireland and Archbishop of Armagh:

I am deeply shocked at the news of the awful slaughter in Derry this afternoon. I have received a first-hand account from a priest who was present at the scene and what I have heard is really shocking. An impartial and independent public inquiry is immediately called for and I have telegraphed the British prime minister to this effect. Meanwhile I call upon the whole Catholic community to preserve calm and dignity in the face of this terrible news.²

Ivan Cooper: At about 8pm, I remember receiving a message at the hospital that I was to return to John Hume's home, as Jack Lynch, the Irish prime minister, the Taoiseach, wanted to speak to us, and particularly to me, to receive our account of the events of the day. John Hume's house was packed with people when we arrived. I gave the Irish prime minister a garbled account of events over the telephone. After I had put the telephone down, I received a call from the hospital administrator to say that another body had been identified.

Maura Young: I came home, and the place was packed, but still no Leo. There were crowds standing outside the house. My daddy came out of the house and he said to me, 'Are they telling me the truth?' and I had to tell him, yes. Then Father McLaughlin and Father Carlin arrived, too. Father McLaughlin said that Leo was arrested and was being taken to Ballykelly army base. He and Patrick went down to the barracks to see.

Eamonn MacDermott: I remember the paras were stood around our street boasting to each other about what they'd done that day, mimicking the actions of shooting with their guns and things. There was no shame, they were cock-a-hoop at a great job. They stayed in our street outside the house until about 9.30pm that night. It was scary seeing them outside. I was very wary of them being out there, knowing what they'd just done, and I went to my friend's house for a while. It was scary at that stage, but we were kinda defiant too.

Geraldine McBride: By that time, Hugo was over at the hospital looking for me and nobody knew where I was. My mother said she was alright until Hugo and Willie came in after 9pm and they asked her, 'Where's Geraldine?' My mother said she squealed at Hugo, 'What do you mean? Is she not with you?' Then she went ballistic and phoned my father, who was working in the power station, to come home.

John Kelly: We went back home and there was a mass of people outside. The house was packed, and my mother was sitting at the left-hand corner beside the fireplace. We walked in and looked at her, and said, 'Sorry ma, Michael's dead.' Jesus Christ almighty, bedlam – the cries of her, it was awful.

British army 8th Brigade Log:

1945hrs – [Report from] 1 PARA

1. Tac GP estb in Gt James St to obs buildup of the march and the subsequent aggro of 2-300 males.

2. The 1 PARA Boys were called fwd in readiness and launched at 1610 hrs:

C Coy - Block 14
Sp Coy - Block 12.
A Coy - Block 11.
All mounted in Pigs.

3. Sp Coy drove through the rioters in Little
James St and cut off some dozen of them.
C Coy turned down Chamberlain St and into
Eden Place. Both C/S then came under fire
from HV wpns from in the Rossville and
Glenfada Flats.

4. The Coys deployed and returned fire at
seen gunmen. Sp Coy mov fwd to N end
of Rossville Flats and went firm. C Coy
covered the left flank and A Coy right
flank. During this time more rioters were
arrested.

5. 2 dead civs were rec from the W side of
Rossville Flats by Sp Coy, who were still
under fire from the Glenfada Flats.

6. Occasional fire from hidden snipers
continued, and some fire was returned.

7. All C/S regrouped in William St at 1650
hrs and were complete in their original
FUP at 1730.

Statistics

8 - Civilian Terrorists engaged:

6 Nail Bombers.
1 Petrol Bomber.
7 Gunmen.

9. 43 arrests were made.

10. Cas received: 2 with acid burns. 3 with
minor injuries.

11. Claim hits - 5 but could be more.

12. 106 rds expended. 64 Baton Rds.

Mary Donaghey: I asked Jackie to go out again and keep looking for Gerald. When he returned, he told me he'd been back to the hospital and the morgue, but Gerald was not in either place. My hopes were again raised. As soon as Jackie had returned home, I asked him to go out again for the third time looking. All evening, friends had been calling in to find out if we had any news.

At about 9.30pm, after Jackie had left for the third time, Father Rooney, our parish priest, called at the house. He told me he had some very bad news for me – he told me that Gerald was dead. I believed Father Rooney immediately and became distraught. At about 10pm, Jackie returned. He had just discovered Gerald's body at the morgue at Altnagelvin Hospital. Even before the sheet had been lifted off Gerald's body, Jackie said he had recognized Gerald's boots sticking out from under.

British army 8th Brigade Log:

> **23.32hrs** –
>
> 1. Good 1st hand evidence ref on this after-
>   noon's activities. members of 1 PARA and
>   other Regts are required - soldiers may
>   have to speak on television.
>
> 2. Details of dead which may link with the
>   ungodly and their activities.
>
> 3. Full report on all other shooting
>   incidents.

Bridie Gallagher: We were just shocked. Stunned. We couldn't take it in. It was awful seeing my mammy and daddy like that. What we all felt I could never put into words. Our world was totally shattered, numb with grief. That night, Hugo and I hardly slept and cried most of it, realizing Mickey would never be here again. Knowing we had to tell our three boys what had happened. They were so young. My brothers Danny and John had to go to the morgue to identify Mickey's body. That really took its toll on them.

Geraldine McBride: I didn't get home until after 11.30pm. Father McAteer brought me home and took me into my mother and father. Once I saw my mother, I knew I was safe, and I just broke down. When my mammy heard about John Young and Jackie Duddy – she nearly went off her head. I knew John, Jackie used to hang around our house with Andy Nolan, and Peggy Deery lived next door to me.

I remember my mother coming in to nurse me to sleep. She said I woke up the first night at 3am, screaming out of me, 'They're coming, they're coming!' She said I was back up again a few hours later the same. I told Hugo some of what I saw the next day, but I didn't tell him everything I had seen.

British army 8th Brigade Log:

2345hrs - Culmore customs post blown up – demolished. Fire bde called & escorts followed - fire bde returning were told to go away by people there. Suspect ambush. Will not investigate tonight due to liability of ambush but may do so at first light.

2348hrs - 51 arrested & bailed today. Names to follow.

2350hrs - Crowd outside Bogside Inn dispersed peacefully.

CHAPTER 27

A Cover-Up Begins

Ariel view of the Bogside in 1972.

On the ground in the Bogside that evening, Lieutenant Colonel Derek Wilford, Commanding Officer of 1 PARA, gave an interview to reporter Gerald Seymour for ITV News.[1] The following extract is from this transcript, as submitted to the Bloody Sunday Inquiry.

Gerald Seymour (ITN): Colonel, once the paratroopers went into the Bogside there seem to have been a very large number of casualties.

Colonel Wilford: Well I suppose large er five is quite large in these circumstances it's unfortunate but when we got up there past William Street here where we're standing and er, up towards Rossville Flats er we came under fire, er we came under fire from the bottom of the flats we were also petrol bombed and er, some acid in fact was poured on us from the top of the flats.

Gerald Seymour: Local people are saying that you used excessive force when you went in there.

Colonel Wilford: Well, what is force if you're being fired at you return fire and they know that perfectly well.

Gerald Seymour: How many gunmen do you feel you've hit in the Bogside?

Colonel Wilford: Well, I am told from my quick sit-rep, you must understand it's a very quick sit-rep that three gunmen were hit. We have not got the weapons, but this is the usual thing we saw people come forward I am not going to say that I saw weapons taken away because I don't know yet I haven't spoken to the men on the ground although I was forward when the shooting was going on.

Gerald Seymour: You have no worries about this action?

Colonel Wilford: None at all.

Gerald Seymour: Local people have also said that you were disrespectful, or troops were disrespectful and flung around the bodies of dead Bogsiders.

Colonel Wilford: Well I am sure we did not. In fact, I was there when those bodies were recovered, and I ordered, in fact, the vehicle to go forward er to pick them up. We did not know at that stage whether they were dead or whether they were wounded, and a vehicle went forward under the very real threat of fire because we were still being fired at that stage.

Gerald Seymour: How do you feel about today's operation in the Bogside?

Colonel Wilford: Well I think any of these sorts of operations are unfortunate it should er, we shouldn't have to do it but they put us in a position where we, we can do no other when we're fired at we must protect ourselves.

Within hours of the shootings and before Derry families had even fully identified their dead, the cover-up had begun. Captain Michael Jackson, adjutant of 1 PARA at the time, drew up a 'shot list'.[2] It was a record of shots fired by 1 PARA as told to him by Army personnel on the evening of 30 January 1972. This crucial document purported to report each occasion when British soldiers shot at gunmen and bombers.

Captain Jackson at first denied being its author but was recalled to the Bloody Sunday Inquiry decades later in October 2003 after a soldier found the handwritten 'shot list' by chance, left on an office photocopier, at the army's 8th Brigade offices. The list was indeed in Captain (now General Sir) Michael Jackson's handwriting. He was the only witness required to testify a second time to the inquiry.

The list reads as follows:

Following engagements took place during gun battle from approx. 16.17 to 16.35 hours:

1 Nail bomber shot. Hit in thigh (back of Chamberlain Street).
2 Petrol bomber shot. Apparently killed (car park).
3 Bomber (at top floor flats) shot. Apparently killed.
4 Gunman with pistol behind barricade shot. Hit.
5 Nail bomber (lighted fuse at car park) shot.
6 Nail bomber at car park shot.
7 Gunman with pistol fired two rounds at soldier armed only with baton gun at alleyway. Soldier fired one round and withdrew swiftly.

  8 Nail bomber (William Street) shot. Hit.
  9 Three nail bombers (at Glenfada Park) shot. All hit.
10 Gunmen, pistols (at G Park) shot at. One hit, one unhurt.
11 Sniper in toilet window. Fired upon. None hit.
12 Gunman, rifle (at 3rd floor Rossville flats) shot at. Poss hurt.
13 Gunman with rifle (at ground floor R flats) shot. Hit.
14 Gunman, rifle (at barricade), shot. Killed. Body recovered.
15 Gunman, rifle (at barricade), shot. Killed. Body recovered.

Using these erroneous details, the British military informed embassies across the world that, having come under fire, they had won an 'IRA gun battle' in Derry, Northern Ireland. The dead and wounded were thereby denigrated as gunmen and bombers, terrorists. A slur that would last decades.

The army also prepared a statement for the press, in which it was likewise claimed that troops came under sustained attack before they opened fire.

From a statement issued by British army's HQ in Lisburn, Northern Ireland, concerning the events on 30 January 1972 in Londonderry:

The troops came under nail-bomb attack and a fusillade of fifty to eighty rounds from the area of Rossville Flats and Glenfada Flats. Fire was returned at seen gunmen and nail-bombers. Subsequently, as troops deployed to get at the gunmen, the latter continued to fire. In all a total of well over 200 rounds was fired indiscriminately in the direction of the soldiers. Fire continued to be returned only at identified targets.[3]

By morning, news of the British army's hard-won IRA battle was on front pages throughout Ireland and Britain, as well as dominating the next day's New York Times.

CHAPTER 28

The Next Morning

Front page of the *Daily Mirror*, Monday 31 January 1972.

A city awoke in shock and disbelief the following morning.
    Derry itself became a ghost-town. Monday's profound shock was conveyed as thus in the Derry Journal: *'A silent, shuttered Derry mourned its dead. Factories, shops, stores, banks and offices all closed down in mute but eloquent protest.'[1] Front pages in Britain led with the killings, too. Under Britain's* Daily Express *headline 'Gun Fury', it reinforced the army's stance that 'Paras face "fusillade" then open fire – 13 shot dead in Bogside' (Daily*

Express, *31 January 1972). On the whole, press outside Ireland reflected an inaccurate version of events.*

From the Republic of Ireland edition of the *Daily Express*, 'Gun Fury – Paras open fire as violence flares – 13 shot dead in Ulster':

> Thirteen men were shot dead and 25 people, including two women, were wounded after British troops charged demonstrators in the crowded Londonderry streets yesterday.
>
> And Major General Robert Ford, OC Northern Ireland Land Forces, insisted, 'There is absolutely no doubt that the troops opened up only after they had been fired on.'
>
> General Ford added that the dead 'might not have been killed by our soldiers'.[2]

Eamonn Deane: The next day the school was closed. Local teachers had arranged to meet at a nearby school.

Don Mullan: My best friend Shaunie McLaughlin and I had returned to the Bogside the day after and retraced our steps. Around the rubble barricade I remember pointing out the bullet on the wall above. I remember crossing the road and finding the blue-and-white civil rights banner on the ground, now heavily bloodstained.

Eamonn MacDermott: On the Monday after, it was a totally surreal atmosphere. We went over the Bogside that morning and there were crowds standing about in Rossville Street. There was a silence, no rioting, no talking, nothing. People spoke in hushed tones because it didn't feel right to be talking. People were sharing different stories of what they had seen. It was like a pilgrimage, almost; people were walking from one spot to another, quietly pointing and talking. We went to the rubble barricade and into Glenfada Park looking at where everything happened.

From the front page of Britain's *Daily Telegraph*, '13 killed in Londonderry – Troops in battle with IRA', dated 31 January 1972:

> Thirteen people died in Londonderry yesterday following a vicious battle between IRA gunmen and troops when a 10,000-strong civil rights march through the city was broken up by security forces. The shooting started after a mob which tried to storm a street barrier was dispersed with rubber bullets and purple-dyed water from a water cannon.[3]

Denis Bradley: Silence is my real memory. It was not a lack of noise as such. People didn't speak normally as they had spoken before. It was monosyllabic. It was reverential.

Eamonn MacDermott: I was only fourteen, but we walked around and talked about it all, seeing the bloodstains still on the ground. It was impossible to get your head around it; it was just trying to cope. Maybe the way we coped was just to be there, where it happened. Nobody was inclined to throw stones even. It might well have been the first day since internment that there was no riot. There was no appetite for anything. Just shock. Bishop Daly told me later that the whole city should have had trauma counselling, because the whole city suffered.

Denis Bradley: When I went down into Rossville Street I was met by a lot of cameras. I remember being very uncomfortable about it. I had just gone down to see the scene. I was confronted by journalists and asked to make statements. I thought it was too quick, too intrusive and it seemed indecent.

From the *Guardian*, '13 killed as paratroops break riot', by Simon Winchester, dated 31 January 1972:

> The tragic and inevitable doomsday situation which has been universally forecast for Northern Ireland arrived in Londonderry yesterday afternoon when soldiers firing into a large crowd of civil rights demonstrators, shot and killed 13 civilians.

Seventeen more people, including a woman, were injured by gunfire and another woman was seriously injured after being knocked down by a speeding armoured car. The army reported two military casualties and said that their soldiers had arrested between 50 and 60 people, who had been allegedly involved in the illegal protest march.

After the shooting, which lasted for about 25 minutes in and around the Rossville Flats area of Bogside, the streets had all the appearance of the aftermath of Sharpeville. Where, only moments before, thousands of men and women had been milling around, drifting slowly towards a protest meeting to be held at Free Derry Corner, there was only a handful of bleeding bodies, some lying still, others still moving with pain, on the white concrete of the square.[4]

Dr Domhnall MacDermott: On the Monday after Bloody Sunday, I closed my surgery for the day. The town was in complete mourning. I remember going over to the Bogside. It was a scene of desolation. I talked to John Hume and a few others who were there and went home. I had not been home long when Kathleen told me that Bishop Farren wanted me to call him back.

At the insistence of Cardinal Conway, the two Derry doctors, Dr Domhnall MacDermott and Dr Raymond McClean, were asked to attend the post-mortems that day.

Dr Raymond McClean: I received a call that Cardinal Conway wanted me to act as a representative of the Church at the post-mortem examinations of the victims. I went straight to the hospital. By the time I arrived, the post-mortems on Gerald Donaghey and Michael McDaid had already been completed.

Dr Domhnall MacDermott: None of the deceased were my patients. However, I knew Barney McGuigan very well. He had worked for me part time as a handyman. He had painted my house and worked in my garden. I also knew William McKinney, who had worked at the local *Derry Journal* [and] as an amateur photographer. I remember he attended a lot of the marches and would take pictures of the people on them.

Dr Raymond McClean: I attended the remaining autopsies, taking my own notes. I arrived home from the post-mortems at around 12 midnight. At the post-mortems, I focused on trying to get accurate information on entry and exit wounds as I expected that the post-mortem evidence would be aligned with eyewitness accounts to give a proper picture of what had happened, although this did not happen. I was surprised at the damage high-velocity bullets can cause. There was a lot of internal damage to the victims. Several of the stomachs were opened and I realized that the victims and I had had the same lunch – roast beef, potatoes and peas. It made me aware that I could have been one of the dead.

From a Public Statement from all teachers across Derry's Catholic schools:

> A firm decision was taken to strike for three days (Monday, Tuesday and Wednesday). This action was taken as a protest against the butchery of peaceful demonstrators by the British army in Rossville Street yesterday. Eyewitness accounts from teachers present refute utterly the blatant lies of the British army.[5]

Geraldine McBride: When I heard John Young, my best friend, was dead, I couldn't believe it. John and Hugo and me would have went to the dances together. John worked in Burton's Menswear and we used to call him the Burton's Dummy, because he was mad about the style and had a three-piece suit and a Crombie coat, he had all the new style that came out, and he was always so funny. My mother loved John Young and he was always in our house. I miss John. The day of the Saville Report I broke my heart about him because I never really grieved him. I don't think I was right in the head after it to even grieve. He wasn't a boyfriend, but I could have told him anything.

Damian Donaghy: The next day, when people were coming to visit the wounded, I was coming around from my operation and I think I was told at first by a nurse how many people were actually shot. It was total shock. I thought it was maybe just me and Mr Johnston who had been shot, and that Alana had been injured too. We were at the top of the ward and at the far end there were a couple of British soldiers who were laughing about what had happened in the Bogside. They weren't paratroopers, but they still gave us abuse, so I grabbed the crutch and went for one of them.

From the *New York Times*, 'British soldiers kill 13 as rioting erupts in Ulster – deaths come as Catholics defy ban on Londonderry march', dated Monday 31 January 1972:

> At least 13 persons were shot dead by British troops in Londonderry [today] when rioting broke out after a civil rights march held in defiance of a government ban. It was the worst day of violence since the disorders first broke out in Ulster three years ago, and it brought the total number of dead to 230. Already this year 25 have died.
>
> The army said that the dead were snipers who had fired at troops trying to break up rock-throwing mobs with nausea gas and rubber bullets. But local people contend that the soldiers had panicked and fired wildly. Three soldiers were reported injured, one with gunshot wounds.[6]

Also from the front page of the *New York Times*, 'IRA vows vengeance', dated Monday 31 January 1972:

> A spokesperson for the militant Provisional wing of the Irish Republican Army said that all guns had been cleared from the route of the march and that no shots had been fired until the troops had opened fire. 'The deaths will be avenged,' he said.[7]

Alana Burke: They said at hospital that one of my vertebrae had been very badly crushed by the Saracen and it was cutting off the supply to my legs. I didn't know if the feeling was ever going to come back, but I still insisted on going home after a couple of days. They put me in a wheelchair because I still couldn't walk, but I just needed to be home around my family. I had to learn to walk again, and it affected my whole life afterwards.

Geraldine McBride: That next day, I heard Father Mailey downstairs in our house talking to my mammy. She asked me to come down because the priest wanted to talk to me. The priest said, 'I know you've been through trauma, but Mrs Gilmour would like to see you.'

My mother said to me, 'Geraldine, if it was me and my son, I would want to know.' I went, and I'll never, ever forget it. I had to pass the doorway where it happened to get up to their flat. When I went in, they were quiet, whimpering maybe. Hugh was the youngest. The mother just grabbed my hands and told me she wanted to know everything.

She asked me, 'Had he a gun in his hand? Had he a petrol bomb in his hand; had he anything in his hand? I said no, and she said that was all she wanted to know. She asked if he suffered, but I don't think he did, it was so quick. Believe it or not, he had a very peaceful death. He just put his head forward and I knew that he was gone. His father just sat and cried and cried. He really didn't ask a lot. His mother asked all the questions.

It was just such a sad time. I don't think I really coped at all. It was like I was on the outside looking in. I wasn't a brave person. I didn't want to see them because I knew there was details that I would have to face myself. I just remember the mother and father were so dignified. Heartbroken. You could feel the sorrow; it was like a silence, that's the only way I can explain it.

In an editorial the next day, Brian Cashinella, a journalist for The Times *in London, reported hearing General Ford calling out at Barrier 14, 'Go on, the paras. Go and get them.'*[8] *He also noted that the paras appeared 'to relish their work, and their eagerness manifested itself, to me, mainly in their shouting, cursing and ribald language. Most of them seemed to regard the*

Bogsiders and people who took part in the parade as legitimate targets' (The Times, *1 February 1972). Another article in the same edition, co-written by both Cashinella and his colleague John Chartres, referred to the Bogside as an 'IRA stronghold'.*

From *The Times*, 'March ends in shooting', by Brian Cashinella and John Chartres, Londonderry, on Sunday 30 January (and published the following day):

More than 200 heavily armed parachutists this afternoon stormed into the IRA stronghold of Bogside, Londonderry, and a hospital official stated tonight that 13 people had been shot dead and 17 others, including two women, wounded in a brief but fierce gun battle.

The Altnagelvin Hospital said that three of the injured were in a serious condition. One of those badly hurt was a young girl who had been run over by an armoured car. A soldier was slightly wounded, and two others were injured by acid bombs thrown from the roof of some flats as the troops moved in.

It was by far the worst day of violence seen in this largely Roman Catholic city since the present crisis began in 1969 and Bogsiders were tonight complaining that troops had fired on unarmed men, 'including one who had his arms up in surrender'. A photographer who was directly behind the parachutists when they jumped down from their armoured cars said: 'I was appalled. They opened up into a crowd of people. As far as I could see, they did not fire over people's heads at all.' An Army spokesperson at Northern Ireland headquarters said: 'It is not true we fired indiscriminately into the crowd – we were fired on first.'

Lieutenant Colonel Derek Wilford, the parachutists' commanding officer, said later that two gunmen who had been firing at his soldiers from a pile of rubble at the base of the flats had been shot dead. He said no weapons had been found on the men, but he was quite certain they were gunmen. The body of another man was found on the back seat of a car which was stopped at a road-block on one of the routes leading from Londonderry into the Irish Republic. He had an unexploded nail bomb in his pocket. Reporters were shown the bomb protruding from his jacket pocket before the car was driven off by soldiers so that the bomb could be defused on open ground.[9]

The last lines of the above news report from The Times *reiterate army propaganda that began to filter out in relation to a deceased bomber found in a car escaping to the republic. Gerald Donaghey's body had been nowhere near the border that evening.*

*

At Strand police barracks in Derry, Leo Young was being questioned by detectives. He and Raymond Rogan had been stopped by the army the day before as they tried to take Gerald Donaghey to hospital.

The army had kept the car with the mortally wounded Gerald still inside.

Leo Young: We were dragged out by the scruff of the neck. I pleaded with the soldiers about the young fella in the back of the car. He was still alive; I had held him and looked into his eyes. He was dying and needed help. But his body did not arrive at Altnagelvin Hospital until over two hours later, around 6.30pm. He died in their hands, not in mine.

Upon Leo's arrest, his clothes were seized for forensic tests. He had been taken to Strand Barracks initially that Sunday evening, then on to the army base at Ballykelly where he was interrogated all night.

Leo Young: The next day I went back to Derry. That's how I found out something happened to John. Back at the Strand barracks, a detective came in and asked if 'Young' was here. He glanced at a folder, as callous as you can imagine, before looking me straight in the face and asking, 'How many brothers do you have?' I said I had two, and he replied, 'You've only one now.' I didn't really grasp what he was implying; it didn't hit me until I was halfway home. I could see our house on Westway, and people gathered, and thought, 'Jesus no – don't let it be true,' but it was. They were waiting at the door. I felt so guilty facing my mother, but she just said, 'You better go up and see him,' as he was already laid out upstairs. It was terrible: I knew John had been murdered; he had been shot near the eye and the bullet travelled down and broke his spine on the way out.

Maura Young: I can still hear our Leo screaming and crying when he saw all the people outside our house. Someone ran into the house to say that he was over the street. I went out the front and saw Leo standing over the street on the corner, squealing, crying.

My mammy and daddy never ever got over it. John was their baby. You just watched the light going out in their eyes. He had got a new suit the Saturday before; he had designed it himself and was all delighted that it had a bigger vent at the back so he could sit down without opening the suit jacket. My mother came home that day and told me, 'I was up the town today and I called in to the shop – and our John looked lovely.' That was on Saturday, the day before. He died that Sunday. I always remember that.

CHAPTER 29

Seven Priests Accuse

Front page of the *Derry Journal*, Tuesday 1 February 1972.

The following afternoon – a Monday – seven priests from across three Derry parishes who witnessed events in the Bogside held a press conference in the City Hotel. Present were Revd Anthony Mulvey, Revd Edward Daly, Revd G. McLaughlin, Revd J. Carolan, Revd Denis Bradley, Revd Michael McIvor and Revd Thomas O'Gara. A prepared statement was read aloud.

From a press conference held by seven Derry priests on 31 January 1972:

> We accuse the Colonel of the Parachute Regiment of wilful murder. We accuse the Commander of Land Forces of being an accessory before the fact. We accuse the soldiers of shooting indiscriminately into a fleeing crowd, of gloating over casualties, of preventing medical and spiritual aid reaching some of the dying. It is untrue that shots were fired at the troops in Rossville Street before they attacked. It is untrue that any of the dead or wounded that we attended were armed.
>
> We make this statement in view of the distorted and indeed conflicting reports put out by army officers. We deplore the action of the army and government in employing a unit such as the paratroopers who were in Derry yesterday. These men are trained criminals. They differ from terrorists only in the veneer of respectability that a uniform gives them.[1]

Bishop Edward Daly: There were seven of us in all. We were appalled and revolted by what we had witnessed. We shared in the heartbreak of the families. We were trying to cope with our own heartbreak and felt a duty to tell the world the truth.[2]

Captain (now General Sir) Michael Jackson: I cannot accept in any way that 1 Para exceeded the orders it was given.[3]

From *The Times* (London), dated Monday 31 January 1972:

> Miss Bernadette Devlin, MP for mid-Ulster at Westminster, said that she was flying to London today in an attempt to raise the incident in the House of Commons. Several Labour MPs are also believed to be tabling questions.

'What happened was mass murder by the army. Let nobody say that they opened fire to retaliate. They shot up a peaceful march. Then they let loose with bloodthirsty gusto at anything that strayed into their sights. This was our Sharpeville and we will never forget it.' Miss Devlin called for a general strike to continue until British troops were withdrawn from Ulster.[4]

Bernadette Devlin left Derry for Westminster. Having literally dived off the speaker's platform under gunfire the day before, she was one of few in the Bogside in a position to speak out. At the time, the 21-year-old MP for Mid-Ulster was the youngest female ever elected to the British parliament.

On Monday 31 January, she travelled to London to address the House of Commons and bear witness to events. As the sole present eyewitness to the mass shootings and an elected MP, Devlin expected a fair hearing among her peers. Instead, she was berated and denied the opportunity to speak.

Before announcing an inquiry into the army's actions in Derry, Reginald Maudling falsely told the House of Commons that soldiers opened fire after being attacked by gunmen and bombers.

From the British home secretary Mr Reginald Maudling's address to the House of Commons, dated Monday 31 January 1972:

The Army returned the fire directed at them with aimed shots and inflicted a number of casualties on those who were attacking them with firearms and with bombs.

As for talk about incursions into the Bogside, let me dispose of this rumour straight away. There was never for a moment a suggestion that the time had come to teach the people of Bogside a lesson. The troops were, of course, moving in to arrest hooligans who were bombarding them with stones and bricks, and it was obviously right and proper for soldiers who had been bombarded for a considerable time with stones and bricks to move in to arrest the people who were bombarding them.[5]

For this insult, Bernadette famously walked across the Chamber and slapped the British home secretary Reginald Maudling. 'The Home Secretary made a statement to the house which defies any description other than a wilful lie,' she said afterwards. Fifty years later, an article on Devlin [now McAliskey] recalled it as 'the slap heard 'round the world'.[6]

The following transcript is from a television interview conducted with Bernadette Devlin-McAliskey after the events in British parliament on Monday 31 January 1972.[7]

[Emerging to applause]

Reporter: Miss Devlin, what exactly provoked you into your actions this afternoon?

Bernadette Devlin MP: The fact that thirteen people were murdered by the paratroopers in Derry yet the British home secretary got up and made what he called a statement. It did not have one substantiated fact in it. It lasted three minutes and at no stage did he even say, 'I regret the fact that thirteen people are dead.'

Reporter: So this was an emotional reaction of your own?

Bernadette Devlin MP: It wasn't an emotional reaction. It was quite coldly and calmly done. I was the only member of parliament in the Chamber today who was in Derry yesterday, I was fired on by the paratroopers, and yet parliamentary democracy was such that I was not allowed to speak.

Reporter: What do you think you'll achieve by this action of yours this afternoon?

Bernadette Devlin MP: What I achieved was simply delivering to the home secretary a simple proletarian protest – the fact that he was responsible for the murder of thirteen people, and as far as I'm concerned, that was simply a token effort.

Reporter: Do you really think this is the proper way in which to make your protest, in what some might say is an unladylike and undemocratic way in the Chamber of the House.

Bernadette Devlin MP: Unladylike? There is a young girl who was carried out of the Bogside, the paratroopers did not ask her if *she* was a lady. Undemocratic? I've already said I was the only person who was there, and I was not even allowed to ask a simple question. Undemocratic is thirteen unarmed civilians being shot in the back by a murdering group of thugs with the tacit support of the home secretary and no doubt, the orders of ministers.

*

From the *Guardian*, 'Furious Miss Devlin swoops on Maudling', dated Tuesday 1 February 1972:

Miss Devlin, looking brave though a bit shaken afterwards, said she had no apologies to make for what had happened. 'The only thing I regret, considering how big he is, is that I didn't catch him by the throat,' she told reporters.[8]

*

That same day, ITN television news interviewed Colonel Wilford, Commanding Officer of the 1 PARA Regiment, on the killings that occurred the day before. The following transcript was submitted to the Bloody Sunday Inquiry and was originally broadcast on ITV on 31 January 1972.[9]

Colonel Wilford: That's absolute nonsense we were fired on by Thompson machine-guns, by M1 carbines and other weapons, pistols were seen particularly.

Reporter: But what exactly was seen by you or your company commander before your men opened up?

Colonel Wilford: A man with a Thompson sub-machine-gun was seen from the area of the Rossville Flats. He came round the corner and fired in indiscriminate bursts of 15 to 25 rounds, hard to say from a burst, but certainly a large number of rounds, which hit the ground in front of the company commander, and that fell about twenty feet in front of them, they then dived for cover and returned fire.

Reporter: But local people have alleged that a number of people who were shot were in fact shot in the back as they were running away.

Colonel Wilford: Well I can't comment on that. If they were shot in the back, I would hope it was not my people. We fired at seen gunmen with pistols with rifles and Thompsons and nail bombs.

Reporter: Do you feel in any way that your tactics were too tough yesterday?

Colonel Wilford: No, we went in there to make arrests, and to make arrests is a relatively easy matter. We fired a few rubber bullets to get the initiative, we were then to rush out and pincer them in, which we did, and as you know we picked up fifty-nine. This is a relatively easy matter, we started doing this and we came under fire, and we only had one course open to us then, that was to take cover and return fire.

*

As a day of national mourning across Ireland was announced for that Wednesday to coincide with the funerals, the Irish Taoiseach Jack Lynch made a televised address to the nation from Dublin.

In it, he accused the British army of 'recklessly' firing on marchers in Derry.[10]

From Irish Taoiseach Jack Lynch's televised broadcast to the nation on Monday 31 January 1972:

The Government met during most of today to discuss the present situation. The Government are satisfied that British soldiers recklessly fired on unarmed civilians in Derry yesterday, and that any denial of this continues and increases the provocation offered by the present British policies both to the minority in Northern Ireland and to us here. In order to show our extreme concern about present British policies, the Ambassador in London has been recalled.

...

The Government have called for the immediate withdrawal of British troops from Derry and from other areas of the north where there is a high concentration of Catholic homes.

They have called, too, for the cessation of the harassment of the minority in the north. We have called for the end of internment without trial, which is recognised by almost every observer to have been a disastrous mistake. We have also asked for a declaration of Britain's intention to achieve a final settlement of the Irish question, and a convocation of a conference for this purpose. The Government are satisfied that these steps are essential to the ending of violence and the obtaining of peace.

Certainly, the non-unionist population in Northern Ireland will never again tolerate a unionist Government whether it is attempted to be imposed upon them by force of arms or otherwise. Equally certain, the people of the rest of Ireland will support the minority in their refusal to re-enter a system of government from which they expect continued discrimination and permanent brutality.

The Government are determined to use every means

available to them to bring this message home to the British Government and the British people. In that regard, distinguish between the two. I have said before, and I repeat now again – that I do not believe the British people wish their Government to act in the way they are acting in Northern Ireland, and would themselves repudiate the kind of local administration that now exists there.

We are a small nation, placed by destiny close to a larger and more powerful neighbour.

For too long throughout our history might has always been the ultimate arbiter in our relationships. In recent years, there have been indications of welcome and fruitful changes in this pattern which were working to the benefit of both peoples.

The present British Government, however, appears to have reverted to the old unprincipled doctrine that might is right. We must, and will, turn to other nations for support.

In this time of grave national danger, Irishmen and women will show to the world their patriotism by their dignity and their discipline. Oiche mhaith [Good night in Irish].

CHAPTER 30

The Wakes

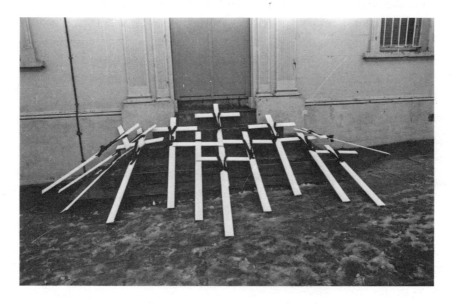

A public street vigil in Dungiven, Co. Derry, in the days after
Bloody Sunday.

*As is Irish custom, wakes for the dead begin as soon as families
receive the bodies of their loved ones back from the morgue. For
two nights after a person dies, Irish Catholic families wake them
at their home so family and friends can see them laid at rest and
say their farewells. At times, the loved one's coffin can rest in
the chapel overnight before the funeral. Doctrine and duty are
paramount. Relatives cover any mirrors in the wake room and
open a window to aid departing souls. Also, one cannot leave a
loved one unattended in their open coffin – ever. Before leaving
a wake room, one must ensure another person is there within its
threshold. On the third day, the deceased person is buried.*

John Kelly: The next thing I remember was that all the bodies were brought home for the wake, and I remember Michael lying out in his wee coffin in his bedroom – he was beautiful in his coffin – not a mark on his face. My mother was heavily sedated. Thousands of people came to the house to give condolences. Even an ex-RUC man came in, devastated, and admitted they were murdered. Michael's death affected my mother very badly. She had been sheltering in a flat in Kells Walk when the shooting took place, oblivious to what was happening to Michael below her.

Bridie Gallagher: The next two days were so surreal, and we were all so sad and shocked. So many people called to our home for the wake, and all my mammy and daddy's family arriving. We wanted his body home, but seeing him being brought back in the door in a coffin was awful. My heart was sore. I can still hear my mother's broken-hearted cry and her deep sighing.

Don Mullan: I remember passing the Duddy home on Central Drive and all the crowds outside. I never went into one of the wake-houses, which was the most natural thing in the world. I was really traumatized by it all.

Bishop Edward Daly: Tuesday was spent visiting the wakes and families of the victims. During the entire day, huge crowds of people made their way from one home and from one family to another offering sympathy and prayer.

Eileen Fox: Our house was a maze of people. There was so many of us and so many people came to pay their respects. Our youngest ones were wandering around, all upset, and everyone was so good to us. I remember we were crying, and my daddy came over and scolded us for being selfish. 'How dare you sit there crying when your mammy only asked for one of you – just one – to keep her company in heaven?' My father might not have said much, but when he spoke, he always said the right thing. That did help us through life, in a way – imagining that she wanted one of us up there with her. I thought that was amazing of my daddy, especially because his heart was broken, too. He was never the same afterwards.

John Kelly: That night a few of us were sitting in the room beside Michael when all of a sudden, my ma came running into the room where Michael was laid out. She ran to the coffin and lifted his body out of it, shouting and crying, 'Michael! Son! Michael! Son!' We had to restrain her and try and place him back in the coffin. My ma was less than five foot, but we had to hold her back.

Geraldine McBride: I didn't go to the funerals. Hugo took me down to John Young's wake and I'll never forget John's house. I'll never forget his mother and father, and Maura was there, and she was going mad, she was just so angry. Maura was never the same after it, I swear to God, they were so close.

Bridie McGuigan: I remember my youngest son Garvin, who was just six, asking me during the wake, 'Is my daddy in that brown box?' When I answered, 'Yes', he said, 'But I thought he was in heaven. How is he in there?'

*

A detailed press statement was drafted by the British government; this account further cemented the British army's 'official' version of what took place on Bloody Sunday. It was prepared for public release on Tuesday 1 February and relayed to the American press via the British Information Services, based in New York's Third Avenue.[1]

British Information Services: Policy and Reference Division

February 1, 1972   Policy Background

NORTHERN IRELAND: LONDONDERRY

On January 31, the Defence Department in London provided a detailed account of the events in Londonderry on the previous day in which army units were involved.

The march in Londonderry on 30 January was held in contravention of the government's ban on all processions and parades. This ban of course applies to both communities in Northern Ireland.

Of the 13 men killed in the shooting that began after the bulk of the 3,000 marchers had been peacefully dispersed, four were on the security force's wanted list. One man had four nail bombs in his pocket. All were between the ages of 16 and 40.

The shooting started with two high-velocity shots aimed at the troops manning the barriers. No one was hit and the fire was not returned. Four minutes later a further high-velocity shot was aimed at a battalion wire-cutting party. This shot also was not answered.

A few minutes later a member of the machine-gun platoon saw a man about to light a nail bomb. As the man prepared to throw an order was given to shoot him. He fell and was dragged away.

Throughout the fighting that ensued, the army fired only at identified targets – at attacking gunmen and bombers. At all times, the soldiers obeyed their standing instructions to fire only in self-defence or in defence of others threatened.

The bulk of the marchers dispersed after reaching the barricades, on instructions from march stewards. A hard core of hooligans remained behind and attacked three of the barriers. When the attacks reached an unacceptable level, the soldiers were ordered to pass through and arrest as many as possible. They were not, however, to conduct a running battle down the street.

As they went through the barriers the soldiers fired rubber bullets to clear the streets in front of them. They made 43 arrests. The troops then came under indiscriminate firing from apartments and a car park. The following is the army's account of the return fire:

1 Nail-bomber hit in the thigh.
2. Petrol-bomber, apparently killed in the car park.
3. A bomber in the flats, apparently killed.
4. Gunman with pistol behind barricade, shot and hit.
5. Nail-bomber shot and hit.
6. Another nail-bomber shot and hit.
7. Rubber bullet fired at gunman handling pistol.
8. Nail-bomber hit.
9. Three nail-bombers, all hit.
10. Two gunmen with pistols, one hit, one unhurt.
11. One sniper in a toilet window fired on and not hit.
12. Gunman with pistol in 3rd floor flat shot and possibly hit.
13. Gunman with rifle on ground floor of flats shot and hit.
14. Gunman with rifle at barricade killed and body recovered.

Other troops besides the paratroops were fired at, the army report stated. Four shots were fired at a foot patrol. One round was returned, and the gunman was hit. Three shots were fired at another foot patrol and one round was returned. No one was hit. Two low-velocity shots, one of which hit a soldier's flak-jacket, were fired at a foot patrol. Two rounds were returned, followed by further rounds at the gunman a minute later. There was no hit. A burst of automatic fire was also met with a single round from the soldiers in return.

In separate incidents, two other gunmen were hit by return fire.

Eileen Fox: It was ages before we realized how many people were shot and that it wasn't just Jackie. We went around the various wakes and heard the stories about what happened. Until then, we had only heard the army version of events really.

Bishop Edward Daly: That evening the thirteen coffins were carried, one by one, in poignant processions from their homes to St Mary's Church in Creggan, where the Requiem Mass was to be celebrated at 12 noon on Wednesday. The huge church in Creggan remained open for the entire night and crowds of people gazed in disbelief as they queued to pass the thirteen identical coffins placed inside the altar rails before the altar. I believe that this was the first occasion when many people realized the true enormity of what had taken place on Sunday afternoon. The sight of those thirteen coffins assembled side by side in one place was almost too much to bear.

*

From the *Derry Journal*, statement by Eddie McAteer, leader of the Nationalist Party, dated Tuesday 1 February 1972:

> It was a simple massacre. There were no petrol bombs, no guns, no snipers, no justification for this well organised slaughter. Derry's Bloody Sunday will be remembered as the British army's greatest day of shame.[2]

From the *Guardian*, 'Bogsiders insist that soldiers shot first', by Simon Hoggart in Londonderry, dated Tuesday 1 February 1972:

> 'That is it: there isn't any solution now,' said the man at Rossville flats. He stared across at the crowds milling around the familiar debris of Londonderry – hundreds of them, scarcely talking to each other as they shuffled their feet in the biting wind.

Some of them say they expected Sunday's events to occur sooner or later: now it has happened. It simply sets the seal on their final withdrawal from the Northern Ireland State.

The Army is presenting its case in Belfast and London: here the people are certain about what happened to them. Every single Bogsider, and every person who took part in Sunday's march, says there were no shots at the Army, no nail bombs, and no petrol bombs. They maintain the absolute innocence of all the dead, and say the soldiers came in firing at anything that moved.

The whole Roman Catholic section of the city was virtually at a standstill yesterday after a three-day strike had been called. All shops west of the River Foyle were closed, except for the occasional kiosk and food shop, and virtually all Roman Catholic workers in the city stayed away from work or returned home soon after going.

In the daylight, police and troops kept clear of the Bogside, and police in the town centre patrolled in small groups after the IRA warning that it would avenge the 13 dead.

...

In a community hall in the Bogside, members of 11 of the families who lost sons, brothers, or fathers on Sunday, described their experiences. Most said they had left the march to go home before the shooting started, and some did not know their relatives were dead until they saw their bodies in the Londonderry morgue.

The Bogsiders now accuse the Army of certain specific atrocities: they say men were shot as they ran with their hands in the air seeking shelter; they say people who were tending wounded men were fired upon; and they say that in some cases men were shot after they had been arrested. They add that they believe soldiers tried to prevent ambulances from getting into the area of the fighting, and that the ambulances were fired on as they arrived.

The meeting of relatives was tense and bitter. Occasionally, one of the people began to weep. They applauded loudly the most militant statements. They made it clear that they would not cooperate with any 'British' inquiry, which they said would be designed to whitewash the Army. They said they would only cooperate with an inquiry set up under the United Nations or another international body from which both British and Irish representatives had been excluded.

Lieutenant Colonel Derek Wilford, the paratroopers' commanding officer, last night gave his own version: 'We moved very quickly when the firing started. Their shots were highly inaccurate. I believe in fact they lost their nerve when they saw us coming in.

'Nail bombs were thrown and one man who was shot was seen to be lighting a bomb as he was shot. This is open to conjecture, but I personally saw a man with an M1 carbine rifle on the balcony of a flat. I don't believe people were shot in the back while they were running away. A lot of us do think that some of the people were shot by their own indiscriminate firing.'[3]

From the *Derry Journal*, 'Reported clash between British soldiers', dated Tuesday 1 February 1972:

It is understood that after the Derry massacre on Sunday there was a difference in opinion among men of the Coldstream Guards and men of the Parachute Regiment. It is also understood several soldiers came to blows in Ebrington barracks and that the disturbance was quelled only when several men of both regiments were put under restraint. The Coldstream Guards, it is understood, objected to the massacre of Derry civilians, and also pointed out that what while the paratroopers, who are not stationed in Derry, would soon be moving out, the Coldstream Guards would be left 'holding the baby'. A spokesperson for the army said last night there was no truth in the story.[4]

CHAPTER 31

Nail Bombs and Hate Mail

```
                                    Loughgall
                                    Co. Armagh
                                    1st February 1972
```

Dear Mr and Mrs Wray (James and Sarah),

As I hold no regrets whatsoever for the death of your son James
there doesn't be so much talk or fuss when some of the poor soldiers or policemen are brutally murdered in cold blood by the so
called "Irish Rats Association". Yes, the "I.R.A." are the cowards,
as your son was not shot by a cowards bullet, and he was not murdered, he was happily killed because he was a terrorist along with
his other twelve Rebel friends.

Also remember that our troops are not serving on foreign grounds,
Northern Ireland is part of the "United Kingdom", so the army is at
home on British Territory. If you don't like living in this country, why don't you then move south or west to the bloody Free
State? There we wouldn't have to pay you out our welfare benefits
and allowances which you are gladly accepting under "Her Majesty
The Queen".

"May sweet Jesus have mercy on his soul", ha! ha! what a laugh,
that's what it says at your son's death in the "Irish News", what
you should have stated is this "May Hell Roast Him" and the rest of
his mates.

Your son was a fucking bastard and a fenian cunt, he was full of
hatred so he can say goodbye to glory. Your Rebel bastards are
doomed.

"The Wray family", get out of your home or be burned out.
Ulster is British, God Save the Queen. No Surrender.

```
            Your enemies
            Loughgall                   Head of "UVF"
```

Hate mail received by the parents of Jim Wray after
Bloody Sunday.

*Critically injured, 17-year-old Gerald Donaghey had died of his
injuries on Bloody Sunday while left alone in Raymond Rogan's
car at police barracks. Over the next few days, claims would
emerge that Gerald had been a nail bomber with bombs.*

Despite overwhelming evidence from civilian, military and police witnesses, who say the teenager was unarmed, photographs soon emerged of Donaghey's lifeless body in the back seat of the car, a nail bomb crammed into the pocket of his tight jeans. By evening, there were claims of four nail bombs in total, one in each of his pockets.

The army and police alleged that Donaghey, as a member of a youth republican movement, had been armed with the bombs throughout the march – thereby justifying his murder.

Mary Donaghey: During the next few days before the funeral, local rumours were circulating that nail bombs had been found by the army in the pockets of Gerald's jeans before they took him to the morgue. I was shocked that my Gerald would have been involved with such things. I couldn't believe it. In any event, I couldn't work out how Gerald could have got nail bombs into his pockets. He could hardly get his cigarettes into them, never mind anything else.

Raymond Rogan: My wife Margaret, being a mother, had searched him for ID and found nothing on him anywhere but the holy medal around his neck.

Leo Young: Gerald Donaghey had definitely nothing in his pockets. I searched his pockets myself when I was looking for ID because nobody knew who he was. He didn't have any ID; he was just a fresh young boy that we had to get to hospital.

Many decades later, this issue would be investigated at length during the Bloody Sunday Inquiry. Evidence from both civilian and military witnesses would attest to Gerald's body being searched and his pulse checked with no mention of nail bombs on these occasions. It was only after his body was taken away that explosives were reported.

The car had been stopped at Barrier 20 in Barrack Street on Bloody Sunday, which was manned by soldiers of the Royal Anglian Regiment (1 Royal Anglian). While there, its uninjured occupants were arrested before the car was driven, first to Company Headquarters at Henrietta Street, and then to a Regimental Aid Post on the south side of the Craigavon Bridge, known as 'Bridge Camp'.

Once at Bridge Camp, the Medical Officer of 1 Royal Anglian examined the boy and found him to be dead. It was at this location that nail bombs were said to be found.[1]

Martin McGuinness: I confirm that not one person shot on Bloody Sunday was in the IRA. I have been asked about Gerald Donaghey. My understanding is that following Bloody Sunday the youth wing, Fianna Éireann, claimed that he was a member. I did not know Gerald Donaghey. I had never met him. He was not a member of the IRA. Membership of the Youth Movement did not signify membership of the IRA.

Raymond Rogan: Soldiers had driven my car from the top of Barrack Street, down to Bridge Camp, and it was examined. Strangely, nobody said anything about any bombs in his pocket until CID – Special Branch, that is – arrived. Then they sent for an expert to come and check these bombs that were seen in his pocket. It was impossible! You couldn't keep your hand in these pockets; it was jeans. I saw a photograph afterwards with the bombs hanging out of his pockets and how they got them into his pockets I just don't know. We could hardly get our hands in to search him, they were so tight. And there were four of these things? Unbelievable.

When I got back to the house after I was released, Margaret was in an awful state. She knew we had been arrested and she heard on the radio that a car had been stopped on the way to the border with an injured man with bombs in his pockets. She'd heard that on the radio. She knew right away that it was our car, so she was relieved to see us back. It wasn't until the next day that we knew young Donaghey was dead. The story about the car at the border was obviously propaganda, as we discovered afterwards.

Mary Donaghey: Before the funeral, I learned that Raymond Rogan, whom I knew, had tried to help Gerald after he had been shot. Both of us were also baffled as to how Gerald came to have nail bombs in his trousers. I have since learned that his body was taken to an army post before being taken to the hospital. I've also been told that an army doctor examined Gerald at the army post and that he too didn't find any nail bombs.

I want to know why it took him so long to reach the hospital and whether he would have lived had he been taken to the hospital sooner. I want to find out who planted those nail bombs on his body and why. Most of all, I want Gerald's name to be cleared and I want those who killed him and planted those nail bombs on him to be brought to justice. I don't think that this is much to ask.

Leo Young: All the evidence proves that he had nothing in his pockets. If there had been any nail bombs, an army lieutenant wouldn't have made one of his own soldiers drive [the car] to the barracks. Donaghey had been shot through his pocket too, the same pocket that supposedly held nail bombs. In fact, the only people who found items in Gerald Donaghey's pockets were the RUC, so you can draw your own conclusions.

HATE MAIL

Some families recall their parents getting abusive letters in the post after Bloody Sunday. The wounded too. These were often from loyalist paramilitary organizations, revelling in the tragedy.

A shocking example of this sectarian vitriol survives and is at the Museum of Free Derry, courtesy of the Wray siblings.[2] *The letter is signed from the Ulster Volunteer Force and dated 1 February 1972, just two days after the shootings.*

Letter to James and Sarah Wray two days after their son Jim was shot dead.

Loughgall
Co. Armagh
1 February 1972

Dear Mr and Mrs Wray (James and Sarah),

As I hold no regrets whatsoever for the death of your son James there doesn't be so much talk or fuss when some of the poor soldiers or policemen are brutally murdered in cold blood by the so called 'Irish Rats Association'. Yes, the IRA are the cowards, as your son was not shot by a coward's bullet, and he was not murdered, he was happily killed because he was a terrorist along with his other twelve Rebel friends.

Also remember that our troops are not serving on foreign grounds, Northern Ireland is part of the United Kingdom, so the Army is at home on British territory. If you don't like living in this country, why don't you move south or west to the bloody Free State? There we wouldn't have to pay you out our welfare benefits and allowances which you are gladly accepting under 'Her Majesty The Queen.'

'May Sweet Jesus have mercy on his soul', ha! ha! What a laugh, that's what it says at your son's death in the Irish News. What you should have stated is this 'May Hell Roast Him' and the rest of his mates.

Your son was a fucking bastard and a Fenian cunt, he was full of hatred so he can say goodbye to glory. Your Rebel bastards are doomed.

'The Wray Family', get out of your home or be burned out. Ulster is British, God Save the Queen. No surrender.

Your enemies
Loughgall
Head of 'UVF'

CHAPTER 32

The Funerals

Front page of the *Derry Journal*, Friday 4 February 1972.

Tens of thousands of mourners lined the Creggan streets outside St Mary's Church in Derry for the funerals of the Bloody Sunday dead on Wednesday 2 February 1972. The main seats, or pews, in the chapel were reserved for the many visiting dignitaries, including clergy and politicians, while families were crammed in

289

where they could.

    All over Ireland, prayer services were held at the same time as the Derry funerals in tribute. In Dublin, tens of thousands of workers stopped work as a mark of respect to those who had died. Thousands then took to Dublin city-centre streets, carrying 13 coffins. The British Embassy in Dublin was later burned to the ground.

    In Derry, they gathered to mourn their dead.

Regina McLaughlin: We were all kept away from the wake and the funeral. Which was a big part for me. I thought to myself, how do I know if he's even dead? He could have left us and went away – we didn't have the closure of seeing him.

Ita McKinney (Regina's mum): Gerry's clothes were brought back to me – or sent back. I can't remember how they came back to me, but there was a jumper, a big Fair Isle jumper that I'd bought him for Christmas, and he had just worn it a few times, and the two holes were in it and the holes were in his jacket, they were in his shirt, they were in his heavy coat, and I just put my fingers, you know, through the holes where the bullets went.[1]

Bridie Gallagher: When it came to taking Mickey's body to Creggan Chapel, it was so hard on us, and on all Mickey's friends who were outside, watching him leave home for the last time. And then seeing the thirteen coffins in front of the altar, Mickey among them somewhere. We broke our hearts. My sister Margaret was overcome with it all and I had to take her into the chapel sacristy during the funeral when she wasn't well. Everything felt so unreal. I can still remember the cemetery, seeing his body put into a grave. I can still see that … I can't ever stop seeing it.

Patsy McDaid: We were in hospital during the funerals, but I'm not sure how long I stayed in there for. In the ward, we had the RUC coming in to get statements and the first time they came in, Father Daly told them to leave, but they came back later. It wasn't until after everything that I found out thirteen people had been killed. We knew people were wounded but it was an unbelievable shock to think that so many died. Every time I pass the Bloody Sunday monument in Rossville Street, I think to myself, 'Your name could have been on it', because it so nearly was.

Eamonn Baker: Although my family lived just by the chapel in Creggan where the funerals took place, I could not bring myself to go. There was some conflict at the time about who was allowed into the chapel for the funerals since space was limited. Many prominent politicians felt they had to be there and there was no room for a lot of people who wanted to go.

Eamonn MacDermott: It was the wettest day ever. The rain just poured from the heavens all day, and we stood for hours with the thousands and thousands outside for around two hours or more. We could hear the funeral service from a big loudspeaker in the chapel. The dignitaries got the main seats, and the ordinary people were outside at the funerals.

Philomena McLaughlin: I remember seeing all the coffins in the chapel, the silence on the day of the funerals – this awful veil over the whole estate – it was a terrible, terrible feeling. A girl in my class had lost her brother, too. None of our house were allowed down the town after that, just in case.

Eileen Fox: We needed tickets for our own brother's funeral – which was a disgrace – and we were warned not to lose them, or we wouldn't get in. The families were sat in the sides of the chapel, too, because the main seats were kept for all the visiting dignitaries.

Bridie McGuigan: My mother died in 1971 and was buried on February 2, which is my daughter Alice's birthday. A year later, Alice's father was buried on her birthday. My son Charles was just sixteen and he carried his father's coffin – no child that age should have to do that. My other son, Bernard, was an altar boy at his father's funeral mass.

From the front page of the *Derry Journal*, 'The skies wept, too, as Derry laid its dead to rest', dated 4 February 1972:

Ireland was united in grief on Wednesday. St Mary's Church in the Creggan Estate was the centre of world attention for a poignant hour as Derry buried its murdered dead.

Church and state, priests and people, joined in a unique ceremony which expressed the emotion of a sorrowing nation.

From north and south, from east and west they came, the mourning thousands, to honour the dead, to comfort the bereaved, to pledge by their living presence a Christian response to horrific tragedy.

There were few dry eyes among the distinguished congregation. Outside, the thronging thousands ignored the bitter cold, and even the driving rain seemed heaven's tears. There were 200 priests from every corner of the land ...

There were hundreds of stricken relatives, sustained however by the overwhelming manifestation of a national sharing in their individual grief. There were thousands of people from all parts of the land, many of whom had made long and arduous journeys to be present.

There were the deeply affected thousands of local people from every area, every street in the city, present in mourning accord to share in yet another tragic yet historic occasion in the serried story of their city, on ground hallowed centuries ago by the blood of martyrs ...

Seven of those [twelve priests conducting the mass] had, seventy-two hours earlier, shared with their people in the Bogside the terror unleashed on the streets and risked injury and death to bring succour and the Last Rites of the Church to dead and dying.

And before the high altar, thirteen coffins reposed, the stark reminders of the purpose of the sombre gathering, containing the remains of thirteen young men, struck down ere they could experience a normal life span.

Many of the relatives, overcome by the immensity of the tragedy, broke down and wept. Doctors and Knights of

Malta moved swiftly and noiselessly to give medical aid and comfort to those whose emotions became uncontrollable as the true significance of the size of the loss struck with stunning clarity.[2]

Eileen Fox: We thought our mammy had a big funeral, but nothing had prepared us for Jackie's. It was the most surreal experience I ever had. There were hordes of people pushing and pulling trying to get into the chapel and we were even afraid that our younger brothers and sisters were going to get lost in the crowd. As if that in itself wasn't scary enough, as we approached our seats, we could see a row of coffins at the altar. Throughout the mass the only sounds that broke the silence were sobs of anguish and heartache as people struggled to catch their breath and remain calm. My heart broke for our Gerry; it was his fifteenth birthday. Some birthday that was.

Dr Domhnall MacDermott: On the Tuesday after Bloody Sunday, I visited a patient of mine, Mrs Peggy Deery, on one of the wards of Altnagelvin Hospital. George Fenton was a bone surgeon at the hospital, and he had asked me to see her as her family doctor. She had been shot at the top of her thigh. Half of her sciatic nerve had been torn away by the bullet. Nerves do not grow back. Fenton wanted to amputate the leg. However, she had a rare blood type, and it was not possible to give her a blood transfusion immediately. She then experienced kidney failure and had to be rushed to the Belfast Kidney Unit. I understand she nearly died and was in intensive care for five or six days. After she had recovered from her kidney failure, it was discovered that she did not require amputation. This was something of a miracle.

Regina McLaughlin: I remember very little about the aftermath. I obviously blanked it out because I have no memory at all. Mammy was badly affected, for years and years and years. She had been heavily pregnant, and my brother Gerald was born the week after Bloody Sunday. The sense of loss was awful. We were all so confused and, as we got older, I think we got angrier. Seeing how Mammy's emotions would change coming up to Christmas, then the anniversary. She became so withdrawn and unhappy, and all the hurt would be relived, but she never talked to us about it.

Jed McClelland: I stayed off school for the three days – the three-day wake. I went to the wakes and funerals, and on the Thursday morning there was this odd feeling around town. I can't explain the feeling, but everyone felt the same, and it was like, 'Jesus Christ, what just happened?' We were lucky none of us were harmed as such, but it created a fear. We were terrified of them. But it backfired on them big-time when so many young fellas went to join the Provos [IRA]. The army said they were crushing the IRA, but the exact opposite happened. They were queuing up in their hundreds to join the IRA after Bloody Sunday. Most were rejected, as they weren't serious about it, but there was still a surge in joining up.

Mary Donaghey: Gerald's death was devastating for me. He was a very gentle and considerate young man, who would always help me out. He was like a son to me, as well as my brother. At the time he was killed, I was pleased for him that he was going out with a girl and that they intended to marry. All this was taken away from him.

Dr Raymond McClean: For the next few days no one went to work. All the shops were closed. The three days after Bloody Sunday were like a wake. There was an awful silence in the place. People went around talking in small groups everywhere. No one could understand. There was a lot of anger and talk that peaceful means of protest were over. The events of Bloody Sunday gave the Provisional IRA a major boost. I believe that people queued in the Bogside to join the IRA. I have been told, although I am not sure if it is true, that the local IRA was not keen on mass recruitment as it did not wish to work with uncommitted members, but the Dublin branch thought that the new recruitment was good publicity.

From the *Derry Journal*, 'Internees' "Utter Revulsion"', dated 4 February 1972:

> The internees in Long Kesh Camp in a statement released last night, expressed their utter revulsion at the brutal massacre of peaceful civil rights demonstrators in Derry.
>
> 'This massacre of peaceful marchers was in the true tradition of the British army who acted in a similar fashion at Amritsar in India in 1919 and on Bloody Sunday at Croke Park in 1921. It was evident that this was a cold-blooded, calculated action for which Stormont and Westminster governments must equally share the blame.'[3]

Jed McClelland: I went back to school in Jordanstown in Belfast that Thursday and the class was mixed, half Catholic and half Protestant, but nobody spoke, it was weird. Even the Catholics didn't talk about it. Nobody did. Nobody mentioned it for decades – until the big anniversaries came up twenty years or so later. I can't remember when the time came when everybody felt that they could start speaking about it again – but it was a long time. It was an unsaid thing; nobody talked about it.

Jimmy Toye: The days after were filled with the shock, the silence, palpable – the memory will never leave me. The horror of 1971, the deaths of the British soldiers that came in later years, these images will never leave me. But Bloody Sunday was different. The ten or fifteen minutes of absolute terror where I thought, 'This is it.' That's what I'll never forget. The killings around me, traumatizing me like a car accident. I was in a car accident years later, so I know what that kind of trauma feels like.

Raymond Rogan: The feeling at the deaths – it wasn't a feeling of anger. More of sadness and resignation that they could do this with impunity and say that they were fired on.

Eamonn MacDermott: We went back to the school that Friday, but we were very unsettled, and it was hard to settle back into any normal routine, it was totally surreal. Everyone was traumatized, and I'm sure today we would have counsellors flying in from all over the world, but in those days, there was nothing. Nobody even asked about people who witnessed things, and so many of us were schoolboys and it affected everything.

Bridie Gallagher: After the funeral, my brother James went to try and talk to people around the town to find out what had really happened to Mickey. A lot of families were doing the same, trying to figure it out. That's when we found out that Mickey was shot at the barricade, and that the soldiers had thrown his body, and those of Nash and Young, into the back of an army Pig by their arms and legs – like pieces of meat! That was hard to take.

CHAPTER 33

The Widgery Tribunal

Lord Chief Justice Widgery arrives in the north ahead of the
1972 tribunal.

On Tuesday 1 February 1972 – two days after the shoot-
ings in Derry – the then-British prime minister Edward Heath
announced an inquiry into events. He appointed Lord Widgery,
Lord Chief Justice at the time – to oversee the tribunal.

Three decades later in August 1995, Jane Winter, then-director
of London's British Irish Rights Watch, would find a document
at the Public Records Office in London that confirmed Widgery

was influenced from the beginning. The Heath–Widgery memo is discussed in more detail later, but one section of the memo records the British prime minister advising Widgery ahead of his new tribunal to remember, 'We are in Northern Ireland fighting not only a military war but a propaganda war.'[1]

Dr Raymond McClean: When the Widgery Tribunal was announced, I was absolutely disgusted. I felt that the examination of the events should be independent, conducted by an American or European judge. The only reason I became involved with the tribunal was that the families were cooperating, in conjunction with the clergy, to take part. The clergy felt that the issues should be heard.

Mickey McKinney: I remember them discussing whether to go to the Widgery Tribunal and my father thought they should go because 'in six months' time it'll be water under the bridge'. So many people were being shot and killed and nothing was ever really being done about it. The army just made the same old excuses, that they must have been in the IRA or that someone had come and taken guns away.

Bishop Edward Daly: For myself and everyone else who witnessed the murders, there was now a very difficult decision to be made. The British government had established a Tribunal of Enquiry under the chairmanship of Lord Widgery, the British Lord Chief Justice, the most senior judge in Britain. Each witness had to decide whether to appear before the tribunal or not. The people in the local community were hopelessly divided, with most people hostile to the tribunal. They did not believe that a British judge could give an objective judgment, where the British army were concerned.[2]

Across Derry, families grieved their loved ones and tried to understand what had happened on the march that Sunday. Some of the wounded remained in hospital, and others continued to recuperate at home, traumatized by their experiences.

As a result of the British army's actions, IRA recruitment numbers grew steadily, particularly in Derry itself, and the group stepped up their retaliation campaign with bombings and shootings intensifying everywhere.

Within bereaved families, life continued yet all was fractured. Few adults discussed what had happened on Bloody Sunday with younger members of the family.

Gerry Duddy: I was fourteen and we thought we had to accept it; we weren't allowed to discuss it at home – the young ones weren't anyway – so I don't know if the big ones discussed it or not. I always had it in the back of my mind that I was going to do something about it, but what was I going to do? If I could do anything, I didn't know what – besides joining the IRA and that. No. Because we didn't talk about what happened, we just tried to get on with life the best we could. It was never forgotten, though.

John Kelly: My mother had a nervous breakdown after Michael's death. She has no memory of the five years after his death. She just existed. My older sisters took over from her looking after all the family. My father found his own way of coping.

Bishop Edward Daly: Jackie's dad came down to see me a few weeks afterwards, and he gave me this photo of Jackie [Duddy] with his boxing gloves on and in front of it is the stole I used on Bloody Sunday. They have been with me since 1972, always sitting on my desk or beside me, and I have left them in my will to the museum, the stole too. They have always been with me since that day.

Sophia Downey: Mammy let herself go. She thought she saw Michael everywhere. I remember once going into a bank with her and she went up to a young man and touched his hair, thinking that he was Michael. She became so ill that I had to move close to her house to look after her.

John Kelly: My mother never left the cemetery afterwards and would take a blanket to cover Michael's grave in wintertime.

She would just disappear sometimes. Especially in the immediate aftermath. Every day she was there in the cemetery after mass, over talking to him. It was worrying. We were worried about her and her state of mind because she definitely wasn't well. I thought she would've died of a broken heart. She was no good to herself, no good to the wains. She wasn't looking after herself, wasn't washing herself, wasn't doing anything. She just wasn't capable. She was heartbroken and in a different world than this planet.

Ita McKinney: For weeks, I lay huddled on my bed, wearing Gerry's coat and tie, holding a picture of him. I didn't fix myself up, I didn't put on nail polish, I was bitter and sore at what had happened. I kept praying for him to come back. Finally, one of my boys came upstairs and asked me, 'Would Dad have liked to see you like this?' After that, I got myself together. The worst thing of all was that the children didn't have a father.[3]

Regina McLaughlin: Although Mammy wasn't bitter, she was afraid of soldiers. When she saw any around the street, kneeling with guns, she panicked because she thought they would kill us too. She had a natural fear of her children being taken away as well. We weren't allowed to go to marches or anything like that. Mammy protected us a lot. But despite everything, she hated the idea of someone else going through what she went through. She never brought us up with any bitter feelings.

Caroline O'Donnell: It was buried afterwards. My father came back a different person. Before that, he was very outgoing and loved going out and bringing his friends back. All that totally stopped – my father became afraid of crowds and we always had to plan family functions at one of our houses.

Mary Donaghey: We didn't get Gerald's belongings back until a while afterwards, and when we did get the belongings back in a big plastic bag, they were all washed. The jumper was washed because it was a new woollen jumper he had on him, and it was shrunk the way you would put a woollen jumper into a wrong wash, you know? I don't know what they were doing when they washed the clothes; normally they don't wash clothes when they give them back to you. It had a hole in it but there was no blood on the jumper whenever we got it. I think they washed them for their own ends.[4]

Maura Young: The army searched our house after John died, when it was only me and my mother and father left in the house. Then they arrested my daddy; they said it was 'Search and Arrest'. My da was a chronic asthmatic. I went into the living room and a soldier was tying his laces on his shoes, and I said, 'Are you for real, arresting him?' They said they had to arrest all men on the premises. They brought a Saracen for him, and I said, 'No way are you putting him in that, because you put my brother in one too.' So, they brought a jeep to take him, and a soldier said, 'Where do you think you're going?' I told them, 'Where he goes, I go. He's sick and if anything happens to him, I'll be there.' I just didn't trust them.

They let me go with him, and I felt so sorry for him sitting beside him in the back of the jeep, trying to get a breath. I just thought this was terrible. We got to Piggery Ridge, the army base behind Creggan, and I got out. Two soldiers were helping my da down off the jeep, and another came out a door with pips [decorations] on his jacket, saying, 'What's this? What's this?' The soldier said, 'You told us to arrest any men who were in that house,' and the big soldier took one look at my daddy and said, 'Send that man home!'

'Send him home?' I asked. 'You'll *take* us home – you brought us up here!' My da said it was okay, we could walk it home, but he couldn't put one foot in front of another. It was awful. They took us home – and they never came back after that.

*

The Widgery Tribunal was to be held in Coleraine, a predominantly unionist town in County Derry.
On 14 February 1972, Lord Widgery held a preliminary hearing in which he described the tribunal to come as 'essentially

a fact-finding exercise'. The first of a total of 17 sessions was held on Monday 21 February 1972. Three more were later held at the Royal Courts of Justice in London. The entire tribunal was over by mid-March.

Olive Bonner: Not many people gave evidence to Widgery, but I just had to go to Coleraine and give mine, and we just presumed he would give us a fair trial. I didn't go for our Hugh because I didn't see what happened to Hugh so I couldn't discuss that, but we lived in the Rossville Flats and I saw some terrible things. I saw Jackie Duddy getting shot, Mickey Bridge getting shot, I saw Paddy Doherty lying on the ground. People were saying that Widgery was a waste of time, but I knew I had to go for Jackie Duddy. I needed to tell them that he had nothing in his hands when they shot him. I actually thought he was hit by a rubber bullet; that's what it looked like.

Bernard Gilmour: I was called to give evidence at the Widgery Tribunal. I spent weeks thinking that Widgery would do great things. I was only actually called for about two seconds. I was asked whether I identified my brother Hugh and I said yes.

Bridie McGuigan: I remember at the time of Widgery I felt it was so important to tell him that Barney did not own the scarf they were trying to say had gun residue on it. So, eventually, I got to give evidence and I was probably the only Derry person he believed. Widgery's report just made everything so much worse.

Leo Young: That was another difficult episode in my life. I remember Widgery's dismissive attitude; they dismissed our evidence as though we were guilty. It was tough seeing all these soldiers in dark glasses being asked nice, easy cosy questions, and their replies – yes, no, I cannot recall. We were naïve, we didn't know anything about tribunals or how they worked, but it was soon blatantly obvious that it had been a total fabrication. Everybody knows that now.

Dr Raymond McClean: I gave a statement to the tribunal but was told that my oral evidence would not be required. This, even though I was a medically qualified person present at the scene of the incident. I had examined and treated the first two casualties shot, had examined four of the dead at the 'scene of the crime', and had been appointed by Cardinal Conway to represent him at the post-mortems. Doctor Kevin Swords, another medically qualified person present, who had treated one casualty at the scene, was called to give evidence, and this was only, according to the *Widgery Report*, to establish whether Gerald Donaghey had anything in his pockets. I began to feel distinctly uneasy about the whole purpose of Widgery and the tribunal.

From the Lord Chief Justice Widgery pertaining to civilian evidence in 1972: The Northern Ireland Civil Rights Association collected a large number of statements from people in Londonderry said to be willing to give evidence. These statements reached me at an advanced stage in the inquiry. In so far as they contained new material, not traversing ground already familiar from evidence given before me, I have made use of them.[5]

Tapes produced by amateur radio ham Jimmy Porter of British army radio communications, before, during and after Bloody Sunday, were also submitted to the Widgery Tribunal.

James Porter: I was requested to attend the Widgery Tribunal on 14 March 1972 in the County Hall in Coleraine. The members of the tribunal had never heard the actual tapes. I was brought into a small room. There were about six people present including Lord Widgery. I informed the group present that I had recorded two tapes. One tape was a recording of the army radio traffic, and the other was of the police radio traffic.

Porter said that, upon hearing a 15-minute extract from the army tape, a murmur had gone around the room and that Lord Widgery had remarked that the reception on the tape was remarkably clear.

James Porter: When the tape demo ended, a Q&A session followed. At the end of this I offered Lord Widgery copies of the two tapes and their transcripts. He declined to accept them. After thanking me, he said, 'I'm tired of hearing of the tapes *ad nauseam*. The inquiry is ended.' He then left the room.

In relation to the comments that I was 'spying on the army and would have been shot for this'; that 'it was a serious matter, and I was facing 20 years on each count'; and that, 'immunity was with the court only, but if I went public, I would be subject to the "rigours of the law"', I am unable to say whether it was Lord Widgery who made them or whether they were made by members of the inquiry team. The general discussion was that I'd done the wrong thing and that I was a villain. I would not say that they were extremely belligerent towards me. I would say though that the atmosphere was antagonistic.

Expecting to be commended by the Widgery Tribunal for having recorded these transmissions, James Porter instead felt belittled and overlooked.

James Porter: The team members referred to their transcript and said that anyone could have made it, as if someone had concocted it. This made me think that they hadn't heard the tapes. I then said jokingly, 'If you heard the General tell you, would you believe it?' Someone said, 'The General's not here.' I said, 'Well, I have him in my pocket.' I then took a hand-held tape machine out of my pocket and played it to them. They were clearly surprised.

The tapes that I offered to Widgery were the army and RUC radio transmissions that are on Tapes 1, 2, 3 and 4. Neither Lord Widgery nor his team accepted my offer, and nor did they want the [paras] graffiti and baton photographs that I also offered them.

*

Damian Donaghy: I was still in hospital when the Widgery Tribunal was held. Mickey Bradley and Danny McGowan were in with me and we were told that our evidence wasn't needed at

Widgery. We did see bits of it on the TV, particularly the paratroopers going into the tribunal in Coleraine. They were wearing [dark] glasses and I remember they were all laughing. It was obvious to us that it was a whitewash. The way they looked at it – they were protecting their own and they were not protecting us.

Raymond Rogan: Widgery was a shambles. Ted Heath set that up and told Widgery what to do. I wasn't going to go to the tribunal, but God rest Bishop Daly, who was the curate at that time on our patch. He persuaded me to go because he went. I was very sceptical. I didn't want to go, but I eventually did – and they just tried to make a fool of me. I remember saying to the Counsel for the army: would you carry somebody into your house with your family with bombs in their pocket?

Joe Friel: After Bloody Sunday I just wanted to get on with my life. I got married within a couple of years and my time was taken up with my family. I felt complete and utter hatred for the soldier who had shot me. I couldn't put the soldier who had framed me out of my mind, either, and I began to hate him, too. Eventually my hatred was replaced by frustration. I never talked about my feelings or what had happened. My son didn't find out until he was ten that I had been injured on Bloody Sunday, and only then after he was told by a school friend.

＊

On 16 February 1972, the IRA killed Private Thomas Callaghan, a part-time member of the Ulster Defence Regiment and a full-time bus driver from Limavady a few miles outside Derry. The next day, the IRA blew up four shops in city-centre bomb attacks, and the OIRA shot and wounded a British soldier elsewhere in the city. In a statement claiming responsibility for the shooting, they claimed it was 'the beginning of the retaliatory action after the massacre of 30 January'.

 A 16-year-old Derry boy and IRA volunteer, Gerard Doherty, died in an accidental shooting on 25 February 1972. A month later, gunfire followed attempted army raids in the Bogside on 14 March, with hundreds of shots exchanged. Two PIRA volunteers were shot and killed by the army: 19-year-old Colm Keenan and 18-year-old Eugene McGillan. Civilian witnesses and the PIRA themselves insist that the men were unarmed when shot. On 20 March, a 19-year-old soldier, Rifleman John Taylor of the Royal Green Jackets, was shot dead by an IRA sniper. Again, the PIRA statement issued afterwards claimed it was in retaliation for the events of Bloody Sunday.

When soldiers from the Parachute Regiment shot dead Joe McCann in Belfast on 16 April, chaos spread across the north. An OIRA leader, McCann was running away from a foot patrol when paras opened fire and shot him in the back. In the riots that followed, two soldiers were shot dead by the OIRA in Derry: 26-year-old Royal Welch Fusilier Gerard Bristow and 21-year-old Martin Robinson of the Worcestershire and Sherwood Foresters.[6]

CHAPTER 34

The Whitewash

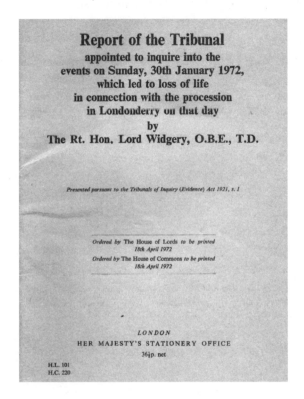

Report of the Tribunal
appointed to inquire into the
events on Sunday, 30th January 1972,
which led to loss of life
in connection with the procession
in Londonderry on that day
by
The Rt. Hon. Lord Widgery, O.B.E., T.D.

Presented pursuant to the Tribunals of Inquiry (Evidence) Act 1921, s. 1

Ordered by The House of Lords to be printed
18th April 1972
Ordered by The House of Commons to be printed
18th April 1972

LONDON
HER MAJESTY'S STATIONERY OFFICE
36½p. net

H.L. 101
H.C. 220

Front cover of the Report of the [Widgery] Tribunal,
April 1972.

When it was published 11 weeks after Bloody Sunday, the
Widgery Report *ran to a mere 36 pages and exonerated the army*
completely.
  Widgery declared that while 'none of the dead or wounded is
proved to have been shot while handling a firearm or bomb ...
there is a strong suspicion that some ... had been firing weapons

or handling bombs ... others had been closely supporting them'.[1]
For those affected, Widgery's report confirmed that the entire
British establishment stood behind those who had opened fire on
Bloody Sunday.

From Lord Chief Justice Widgery on the publication of his *Report*
of the Tribunal, **19 April 1972:** Those accustomed to listening to
witnesses could not fail to be impressed by the demeanour of the
soldiers of 1 PARA. They gave their evidence with confidence,
without hesitation or prevarication. With one or two exceptions,
I accept that they were telling the truth as they remember it.[2]

The Summary of Conclusions from the *Report of the Tribunal,*
published 19 April 1972:

1. There would have been no deaths in
   Londonderry on 30 January if those who
   organised the illegal march had not thereby
   created a highly dangerous situation in
   which a clash between demonstrators and the
   security forces was almost inevitable.

2. The decision to contain the march within
   the Bogside and Creggan had been opposed
   by the Chief Superintendent of Police in
   Londonderry but was fully justified by
   events and was successfully carried out.

3. If the Army had persisted in its 'low key'
   attitude and had not launched a large-scale
   operation to arrest hooligans the day might
   have passed off without serious incident.

4. The intention of the senior Army officers to
   use 1 PARA as an arrest force and not for
   other offensive purposes was sincere.

5. An arrest operation carried out in Battalion
   strength in circumstances in which the

troops were likely to come under fire
involved hazard to civilians in the area
which Commander 8 Brigade may have underestimated.

6. The order to launch the arrest operation was
given by Commander 8 Brigade. The tactical
details were properly left to CO 1 PARA who
did not exceed his orders. In view of the
experience of the unit in operations of this
kind it was not necessary for CO 1 PARA to
give orders in greater detail than he did.

7. When the vehicles and soldiers of Support
Company appeared in Rossville Street they
came under fire. Arrests were made; but in
a very short time the arrest operation took
second place and the soldiers turned to
engage their assailants. There is no reason
to suppose that the soldiers would have
opened fire if they had not been fired upon
first.

8. Soldiers who identified armed gunmen fired
upon them in accordance with the standing
orders in the Yellow Card. Each soldier was
his own judge of whether he had identified a
gunman. Their training made them aggressive
and quick in decision and some showed more
restraint in opening fire than others. At
one end of the scale some soldiers showed
a high degree of responsibility; at the
other, notably in Glenfada Park, firing
bordered on the reckless. These distinctions
reflect differences in the character and
temperament of the soldiers concerned.

9. The standing orders contained in the
Yellow Card are satisfactory. Any further
restrictions on opening fire would inhibit

the soldier from taking proper steps for his own safety and that of his comrades and unduly hamper the engagement of gunmen.

10. None of the deceased or wounded is proved to have been shot while handling a firearm or bomb. Some are wholly acquitted of complicity in such action; but there is a strong suspicion that some others had been firing weapons or handling bombs in the course of the afternoon and that yet others had been closely supporting them.[3]

11. There was no general breakdown in discipline. For the most part the soldiers acted as they did because they thought their orders required it. No order and no training can ensure that a soldier will always act wisely, as well as bravely and with initiative. The individual soldier ought not to have to bear the burden of deciding whether to open fire in confusion such as prevailed on 30 January. In the conditions prevailing in Northern Ireland, however, this is often inescapable.

WIDGERY

10 April 1972

Olive Bonner: When the *Widgery Report* came out I just went ballistic. I can't remember a lot about that period, but I think my mother and father just blanked it out. My mother knew that Hugh wasn't a gunman or bomber and so she just didn't care what anyone thought – she knew the truth and Derry knew the truth. She kept it all locked in; Hugh was her baby: he had that innocence about him.

Mickey McKinney: *Widgery* was rushed. The general feeling among people in Derry was that it was a sham.

Eamonn Baker: If anything, the Widgery Tribunal made everything much worse. It is difficult to imagine how the families of the dead and wounded must have felt to hear Lord Widgery describe their loved ones as terrorists, gunmen and bombers.

Eileen Fox: The tribunal was such a slap in the face. We broke our hearts. We put our faith in it – believing that they would clear Jackie and everybody else's name, but, of course, that didn't happen. My daddy called them a load of cowboys and told us not to worry. He would say, 'They have a conscience – someday they'll be lying in their death beds and they'll need to tell the truth.' Nobody ever did, though.

John Kelly: Widgery completely compounded the grief and devastation felt by my family. Widgery was a whitewash. He did not investigate my brother's murder. He exonerated the paras and condemned the innocent and their families.

*

Across the north, public reaction to the Widgery Report *was predictably divided along sectarian lines. Many in nationalist and republican communities largely rejected its findings, while unionists were pleased that the report cleared the army of any wrongdoing and ended the matter.*

The press were equally as divided, with the Irish press shocked at its findings and the British press very much expressing the military's line of thinking. Only The Times *and the* Telegraph *led with the* Widgery Report's *conclusions on the front page.*

From Britain's *Daily Mail*, 'Widgery blames IRA and clears the army', dated 20 April 1972:

> The first shots that set off the train of death on Bloody Sunday in Londonderry were fired *at* the army – not by them.[4] [Emphasis in original]

From Britain's *Daily Telegraph* editorial, 'Fateful Sunday – Widgery clears paratroops for Bloody Sunday', dated 20 April 1972:

> The Widgery Tribunal has vindicated the action of the 1st Bn the Parachute Regt [...] although individual soldiers are mildly criticised. I understand that the Tribunal concluded that the Provisional IRA had opened fire on the Parachutists and that the troops' response was justified.
>
> ... [Widgery] points out that there would have been no deaths if the Northern Ireland Civil Rights Association had not organised an illegal march.
>
> ... Thirteen deaths is a big and tragic price to pay for the advantages of arresting a handful of hooligans. Yet an even greater toll would result from a different kind of operation which would be more justified and may yet be necessary – one designed to bring the Bogside and the Creggan Estate back under the rule of law.[5]

The following exchange is from the Hansard *Parliamentary Record of the afternoon of 19 April 1972, in which the British prime minister Edward Heath announces the findings of Lord Widgery's Report of the Tribunal to the House of Commons in London.*[6]

> **THE PRIME MINISTER** – With permission, Mr. Speaker, I wish to make a statement. My right hon. Friend the Home Secretary has formally presented to Parliament the report of the Lord Chief Justice into the events of Sunday 30 January 1972, at Londonderry. Copies of the report are now available in the Vote Office.
>
> The Government accept Lord Widgery's findings. All shades of opinion sincerely concerned with the truth must feel indebted to him for his objective and painstaking analysis of events.

<u>The Lord Chief Justice finds that:</u>

There would have been no deaths in Londonderry if those who organised the march had not thereby created a highly dangerous situation in which a clash between demonstrators and the security forces was almost inevitable.

The decision to contain the march was fully justified by events and was successfully carried out.

If the Army had persisted in its 'low key' attitude and had not launched a large-scale operation to arrest hooligans, the day might have passed off without serious incident. The dangers of an arrest operation carried out in the prevalent circumstances might have been underestimated by the Commander 8 Brigade: but he sought to minimise the risks by withholding the order to launch the arrest operation until, as he believed, the rioters and marchers were adequately separated. As Lord Widgery observes, he took his decision in good faith on the information available. Furthermore, Lord Widgery describes the dangerous violence to which the troops were exposed. He observes that the future threat to law and order posed by the hard core of hooligans in Londonderry made the arrest of some of them a legitimate security objective.

The intention of the senior Army officers to use the Parachute Battalion as an arrest force and not for other offensive purposes was sincere. Allegations to the contrary are dismissed as unsupported by any shred of evidence.

Proper orders were given for the arrest operation. The Commanding Officer of the Parachute Battalion did not exceed his orders.

There is no reason to suppose that the soldiers engaged in the arrest operation would have opened fire if they had not been fired upon first.

Soldiers who identified armed gunmen fired upon them in accordance with the standing orders in the Yellow Card. Each soldier had to exercise his own judgment, which reflected differences of individual character and temperament. At one end of the scale some soldiers showed a high degree of responsibility; at the other, notably in Glenfada Park, firing bordered on the reckless. But I should point out that the soldiers' own lives were at risk - as indeed the world must recognise that they have been, and still are, during a great part of their time in Northern Ireland.

Lord Widgery goes on to say that further restrictions on opening fire would inhibit the soldier from taking proper steps for his own safety and that of his comrades and unduly hamper the engagement of gunmen.

None of the dead and wounded is proved to have been shot whilst handling a firearm or bomb. Some are wholly acquitted from complicity in such action; but there is a strong suspicion that some others had been firing weapons or handling bombs in the course of the afternoon and that yet others had been closely supporting them.

Lord Widgery finally concludes that the individual soldier ought not to have to bear the burden of deciding whether to open fire in confusion such as prevailed on 30 January. Unfortunately, he adds, in the circumstances prevailing in Northern Ireland this burden of decision is often inescapable.

The Government deeply regret that there were any casualties, whatever the individual circumstances.

Situations such as that which occurred in Londonderry can only be avoided by ending the law-breaking and violence which are responsible for the continuing loss of life among the security forces and the public in Londonderry and throughout the Province, and by a return to legality, reconciliation and reason. I hope I may have the support of the House in a renewed appeal for a combined effort to prevent any repetition of circumstances such as led to this tragedy.

MR CALLAGHAN, LEADER OF THE OPPOSITION – Lord Widgery also says that the general decision was taken after reference to a higher authority.

THE PRIME MINISTER – Yes, the right hon. Gentleman is right. That is what I meant by saying that the plan was prepared by the Brigade Commander and went to the Commander Land Forces. It also went to the General Officer Commanding, who discussed it with the Chief Constable; and it was known to Ministers. That is what I meant by saying that it was known to higher authority.

*

Leo Young: Widgery knocked me back so much that I thought that was the end of it. I thought that the facts of what happened would be covered up for ever. Bloody Sunday was the catalyst for the Troubles. Had Widgery's report been forthright and honest, we may have been spared the thirty-eight years of hurt and a second inquiry.

Gerry Duddy: My father thought the first inquiry would have been a good thing. He was so naïve that he thought the truth would have come out through Widgery. Well, I know I can only speak for myself, but I thought it would be a complete fucking whitewash, which it was.

Kevin McDaid: To be honest, I never really thought the tables would turn. After the whitewash of the first inquiry, that was it for me. We just had to accept it, even though the Coroner at the time described it as 'sheer unadulterated murder', but that never materialized into anything and there was never any real police investigation into the killings either. Not a soldier has done one second of time for killing my brother or the other thirteen people. We need the equality anyone else would get from the law. It's out of our hands now.

Joe Friel: The Widgery Tribunal was a farce. It added insult to injury. I think the inquiry was called far too quickly at a time when people were still traumatized. There wasn't enough investigation – Lord Widgery should have seen all the wounded, but only Mickey Bridge, Patsy McDaid, Alex Nash, John Johnston and I were called to give evidence, and very few NICRA statements were examined.

Ita McKinney: After I read the report, I felt awful. The Widgery Tribunal has made it more difficult to come to terms with what had happened. It was just another whitewash.[7]

Jed McClelland: Widgery caused real anger and there were riots in the streets because of that report.

Dr Raymond McClean: I do not know how anyone could have thought that the *Widgery Report* would be accepted. Post-mortem evidence was not dealt with in any detail and was not compared with the eyewitness evidence. I felt complete disillusionment.

Joe Friel: To me, the statement in Widgery's report that the firing in Glenfada Park 'bordered on the reckless', means murder. The soldier who shot me should be charged with attempted murder. I was framed on Bloody Sunday and I believe Gerald Donaghey was also framed over the nail bombs. It makes my blood boil.

John Hume speaking to the *Derry Journal* following the publication of the *Widgery Report*, April 1972: It's like blaming a man shot walking down the street, for walking down the street.[8]

Ivan Cooper: It was the greatest recruitment for the IRA in this area, and many of those who became involved in the campaign of violence became involved after that. It was a watershed in terms of the violence. It was a watershed in terms of Irish politics, and it was a watershed in terms of how the whole of Ireland perceived Britain.[9]

Eamonn MacDermott: The day was certainly planned. Of course, it was. All the evidence is there. Basically, I feel the plan was to shoot John Johnston and Bubbles for no reason. Then the word would get back to the IRA and they would come to the Bogside with guns and then the paras could take on the IRA. It doesn't make sense otherwise. There was no reason for their shooting otherwise – they weren't near the riot or anything.

Civil rights activist Eamonn McCann authored a powerful pamphlet in the months after Bloody Sunday, entitled 'What Happened in Derry'. Then, following the publication of the tribunal's report in April 1972, he dissected its findings in another publication, 'The Widgery Whitewash'. He remains an authority on the subject of Bloody Sunday, both locally and internationally.

Eamonn McCann: I just sat with a copy of the *Widgery Report* in London and went through it, picking out things. It was just nonsense. It was all there – all in the body of the *Widgery Report* – and that led me to believe that they all must have known it, the whole cabinet and upper echelons of the law and everyone else. If it was obvious enough for me to work out, then they all must have known it was lies. It meant they knew that Widgery, the Lord

Chief Justice, had deliberately lied about a case of mass killing, so that tells you something about them.

I'd been involved in radical campaigns since the Sixties, but I remember that really shocked me, the blatancy of it. They did know. It wasn't at all subtle. All the upper echelons of politics and military and the judiciary – they all knew that this was lies. That was as much my motivation as anything else; it was outrageous. It wasn't just a terrible thing you had seen: it was their behaviour, and their attitude towards it all was outrageous. That cynicism and dishonesty of them was a big motivating factor for me.[10]

John Kelly: I remember directly after the *Widgery Report*, and people thought that was it – nothing we can do. It's done. People told my family and all the families the same thing. My mother and father were the people who dealt with it and I was on the side-lines with all the girls and so on. I had no real input into it. Naturally, they thought after they were told, they couldn't do anything about Bloody Sunday; that's what they had to live through. Commemorate once a year at the anniversary and that was it.

Alana Burke: At the time of Bloody Sunday, I got hate mail to the house from different people who remained anonymous, some of them from the south but most from England. Then there were articles written and pieces written in papers over the years that stripped away who you were.

I remember one particular piece in the *Sunday Life* that more or less said that we were IRA personnel, and we were protesting that day. I rang Mickey McKinney fuming, and he told me to write to the reporter, but I didn't. I should have done. You just thought to yourself – no, we know the truth.

Billy McVeigh: Although what happened was world news, I always felt that Bloody Sunday was a Derry story, it was very personal to us. Everything about it was just so sad, it cut us to the bone here. People from outside the city felt as though they were intruding if they spoke about it – I think they also saw it as a story personal to us, and so people tended not to talk about it. Everyone in Derry knew someone who was shot or injured; it was a bit like a village in that way.

Eamonn McCann: If the highest judge in the land, the Lord Chief Justice, was involved in the conspiracy to hide the murder of people in Derry – how could you argue with people to not go outside the law? So, in broader terms than Bloody Sunday itself, I think that Widgery really destroyed the credibility of British politics and the British establishment generally over the range of issues that affected Northern Ireland. In that sense, Widgery was an absolute disaster for the British state and their relations with Northern Ireland. I think the *Widgery Report* was at least as important as the Bloody Sunday killings themselves, not in human terms obviously but in political terms.

Michael Mansfield QC: The flawed *Widgery Report* cannot be easily explained away. It was not compiled by someone of inexperience or weak disposition. There was no lack of resources and, importantly, all the necessary evidence was available.

We now know through documentation that came to light subsequently that hundreds of civilian eyewitness statements were ignored or marginalized. Glaring inconsistencies in the accounts of the firers were either not disclosed or barely challenged. It was alleged there were fifteen engagements, of which nine targets were either nail or petrol bombers, the rest were gunmen. The shot list was totally unsatisfactory. The grid references did not make sense. Is nobody bothered that Widgery got it so wrong?[11]

Bishop Edward Daly: What really made Bloody Sunday so obscene was the fact that people afterwards, at the highest level of British justice, justified it.

*

John Starrs, a 19-year-old Provisional IRA volunteer, was shot dead on 13 May 1972 by the British army while on active service in the Bogside. Starrs had been a serving Irish soldier up until the events of Bloody Sunday, whereupon he returned home to Derry and instead joined the PIRA.

On Friday 19 May 1972, a local schoolboy was shot dead by British soldiers near his Bogside home. Fifteen-year-old Manus Deery had been sharing a bag of chips with friends when he was shot dead. The teenager and his friends were gathered near the Bogside Inn when a soldier fired from the city's walls, the shot ricocheting off a wall and hitting Manus in the head. The British army claimed the soldier had been firing at a gunman, a claim refuted by eyewitnesses, the wider community and the Deery family. The teenager had just started his first job, and on the night of his death he had got his first pay packet.[12]

*

The next day, 19-year-old Creggan man and a serving British soldier, William Best, arrived home unannounced, having received a telegram informing him his mother in Derry had taken ill. He travelled back from where he was stationed in Germany, but the telegram was a fraud. Best was serving with the British army's Royal Irish Rangers, and despite being a local boy, he was therefore considered a legitimate target. He was abducted by the Official IRA, beaten and shot dead. His body was found the next morning, 21 May, on the waste ground in William Street.

Ranger Best's death caused an uproar. The next day, 300 women marched to the IRA's official headquarters in Meenan Square. Newspapers ran with front pages, 'Women call on IRA to get out'.

From Eamonn McCann's *War and an Irish Town* on the reported circumstances surrounding the death of Ranger Best: As he wandered about the area renewing contacts with old friends, he was twice warned by Official units to get out 'for your own good'. But he did not. He was picked up by an Official Patrol and taken 'for questioning' to the shops in Meenan Park. Once there, he was doomed. The man who presided over the 'trial' of Ranger Best explained afterwards, 'Once we had him, there was nothing we could do but execute him. Our military orders after Bloody Sunday were to kill every British soldier we could. They didn't say anything about local soldiers. He was a British soldier and that is all there was to it.'[13]

Rosemary Best: My father had been out searching, and apparently it had been on the radio news that morning that a body was found on waste ground in William Street. My father had to go to Altnagelvin Hospital and identify him. He was found hooded and with his hands tied, apparently.

My mother was dealt the worst blow imaginable, to lose your first-born. It's bad enough to lose a child to illness, but to lose your first-born through a deliberate act is terrible. My daddy wouldn't let her go to the inquest. The inquest said Willie was kicked, punched, burned with cigarettes, shot in the back of the head twice through a hood. The Coroner said he never thought an Irishman would do that to another Irishman.[14]

Father Hugh O'Neill, administrator of St Eugene's Cathedral, to the *Derry Journal*, dated 23 May 1972:

> They are finished – it's the end of the road for the IRA. Those officials are not the IRA at all. They are communists pretending to be the IRA. The people have rejected them.[15]

CHAPTER 35

Summer 1972

John Johnston pictured with his wife, Margaret. John died in
June 1972, becoming the 14th victim of Bloody Sunday.

*On Friday 16 June 1972, 59-year-old John Johnson, who had
been shot twice on Bloody Sunday, died in Derry. His family
was convinced that he died prematurely and that his death was
a result of the injuries and trauma he experienced. Johnston's
death brought the number of those killed to 14.*

Jimmy Duddy: Johnny's health declined badly – like a very
quick onset. He went for tests to Belfast. He was always a big
healthy man, but he went downhill rapidly after being shot.
Even when he seemed to be on the mend, he just wasn't the

same. If it wasn't for Bloody Sunday who knows how long he would have lived?

Mary Donaghey: I'd go to bed falling asleep thinking about it; I wake up in the morning. It never really leaves you and some people say, 'Why don't you forget about that? Do you not think you should forget about that? It's in the past.' I know it may be in the past, but justice has to be done before you would think of forgiving. Until their names are cleared, I can't forgive anybody. When their names are cleared you can get on with your life. You can start to live then.[1]

Joe Mahon: My whole personality changed, and I became more withdrawn. After Widgery's report, I never thought there would be another inquiry, so I blanked everything out and never talked about it. My children never knew I was shot until their mother told them.

Bridie Gallagher: My mother used to sing and hum all the time. She'd sing away to herself all over the house. But after Mickey died, we never heard her sing again. She carried on with a heavy heart. We all did. The stress and trauma really affected my brother James in particular. I believe it led to his early death, too, at the age of forty-four. He had taken it all on board and was never the same afterwards. Another sister had a miscarriage after Mickey was killed. The magnitude of what happened was almost too much for people to bear.

Geraldine McBride: I didn't really talk to Hugo about it. He suffered the consequences of it though because we got married that year, what should have been a joyous time for me, and I know now that I had PTSD. I didn't know it then. Back then there was no such thing as mental health, but I was seeing things that weren't there and if there was a loud noise, I was back at Bloody Sunday and terrified. You have no idea. This is when I was only eighteen. The Derry mentality is to just get on with it, keep your feelings to yourself. People were dead, so what right had we to feel bad?

Damian Donaghy: The bullet had fractured my right femur and even to this day I can only bend my leg thirty per cent. I have a seven-inch scar up the side of my leg, and I had one of those big bolts put in to strengthen the leg. When they took that out, I ended up in a calliper. I was only a teenager, but the injury has never healed properly. Now they are talking about reconstructing my knee because it is so bad, but I'm not sure if I want another operation. At times the pain is still terrible, particularly these past few months, but I won't agree unless it gets any worse. I was in the hospital for seven months afterwards. Me and Peggy Deery were the last people to leave hospital.

Hugh McMonagle: I'm not an aggressive person, but after that, the civil rights movement went out the window for me. I wasn't interested in it. I really struggled. What I saw, the innocent young fellas that the British army and the British government killed – they killed our children and our people. It was to teach us a lesson.

Eamonn McCann: Bloody Sunday was unique in that it was done by the state on its own citizens and in broad daylight. There is no other atrocity which had the political resonance and the political impact that Bloody Sunday did. The Stormont government fell weeks after Bloody Sunday – its ramifications were far-reaching and critical for the political development of Northern Ireland. The issue of Bloody Sunday runs right through the historical narrative of the Troubles in Northern Ireland in a way that no other issue did. That in itself tells you about its political significance.

Brendan Duddy: There was a gradual deterioration in the city afterwards. My feeling is that the Bloody Sunday killings legitimized a more open fighting situation. Up until that point, the community exercised reasonable control, but that control was lost as a result, and we headed into thirty years of conflict.

Maura Young: A few months after John died, my mother got a cheque – John was awarded Salesperson of the Year in the menswear shop and they sent her £200. John wasn't for staying in

Derry anyway; he was planning to go to England because there was nothing here for him. He had bright ideas.

In 1973, my mother and father sent me away to my sister, Eilish, in America just to get me out of Derry. I didn't know where my mind was, literally, but America didn't help. I remember thinking when I was coming back on the plane, 'I wonder if our John will come to meet me.'

Mickey McKinney: I was going steady with Greta at the time, and it was only around her that I ever cried. It was as if she got it, you know. We were concerned about how it affected my mother and father and so there was almost an avoidance of the subject, it wasn't talked about very often. It was the parents who were dealing with it. They were suffering terribly and had been pushed into an inquiry within a matter of weeks.

Geraldine McBride: A few months after we got married, I took a severe panic attack, and I was taken to hospital, and they thought it was a heart attack. The young doctor who saw to me asked me if I had seen any trauma and I told her. I was sent down to a psychiatrist or some doctor like that and he listened to what I had to say. Then he said, 'There *was* an inquiry – you had the Widgery Inquiry – and that's the truth about what happened that day.' And I just thought to myself, well, I'm just not going to say anything ever again. I know myself; the girl that came back after Bloody Sunday wasn't the girl who Hugo fell in love with. I was so easy-going, I loved my music and going out, but I became so anxious and so nervous, it was a terrible time for me in my head. I think Hugo must have thought he made the biggest mistake of his life after that first year with me. He persevered, but it wasn't easy for him because I was pushing him away.

Diane Greer: 'We shot one. We shot two. We shot thirteen more than you.' A chant from the past – my past – recited over and over again, celebrating the British army's victory in the Bogside when they shot thirteen Catholic protestors dead. Bloody Sunday happened when I was fourteen and I believed the 'truths' peddled in my own community – the Protestant/Unionist community. I firmly believed that the people who were shot were all linked to the IRA and therefore they deserved to die. After all, the British army – our army – were well trained and would never shoot innocent people.[2]

Maura Young: My daddy never spoke about it. My mammy never spoke about it. We just went through the motions really. I remember we were tortured with press coming to the door and my da would say to them, 'No, the Youngs don't live here any more,' even though we had a big plaque at the front door that said 'Youngs' on it. Nobody talked about what happened. I wasn't offered any help. If you were broken, they couldn't fix you. I never knew until my father died that he had a drawer upstairs full of newspapers about Bloody Sunday. He kept them all. I never knew. He didn't want to talk about it.

Diane Greer: Conversations overheard reinforced the 'facts' – churning out various combinations of words, all of which placed the blame nowhere near the feet of the British and their army. I cannot remember anyone questioning what happened – it was so clear … Civil rights = Protestors = IRA = Exterminate! It was a score on a wall – 13–0 – and we won; it was the stuff of ballads and football chants. The analysis was fed to us, and we gobbled it up, eager to believe it. It was most definitely a victory, sold to us as something to be proud of! Did I buy it? Of course I did. After all, it was the 'truth'.

Media coverage only served to compound the opinion that the dead had deserved it; our eyes drawn to the youths throwing stones and away from any brutality on the part of the army. It didn't occur to me either that there was any other way to see it, or to challenge the information imparted to me. It just simply never occurred … and apart from anything I was a woman and therefore well down the ladder of importance. To question would have been to risk the ducking stool. To dare to step over the party line was (and to a large degree still is) tantamount to treason. Political free thinking is still a dodgy business here and had been known to be punishable by death. Hardly surprising then that 'thems' stick with other 'thems' and the 'us' do the same.

OPERATION MOTORMAN

Across the north, tensions grew worse, and many lives were lost as a result of both paramilitary and military actions. The year 1972 would become the worst of the Troubles, with over five hundred people killed.

In the area where Bloody Sunday happened on 26 June 1972, Rifleman James Meredith of the Royal Green Jackets was shot by the IRA while on duty.

On Friday 21 July 1972, 22 IRA bombs exploded across the city of Belfast, killing nine people and injuring around a hundred and thirty more. The bombings have since become known as 'Bloody Friday'. In the days to follow, the British government prepared to roll out a huge crackdown operation aimed at regaining control of nationalist no-go areas and quelling dissent. In Derry, a former British soldier, 57-year-old James Casey, was shot dead while travelling as a car passenger in Creggan.

On 31 July 1972, the British army launched their Operation Motorman – the single biggest military operation in Ireland since its War of Independence, and the biggest British operation since 1956's Suez Crisis. In the early hours of that Monday, over twenty-one thousand troops were deployed to smash Free Derry and other no-go communities across the north.

Aware of the operation, the IRA offered no resistance and left the no-go areas. Despite this, British soldiers shot dead two teenagers during the Derry operation. The first was a 15-year-old boy named Daniel Hegarty, who was out watching the Centurion tanks roll into the Bogside when he was shot twice in the head at point-blank range. His cousin was also wounded. Following this an unarmed IRA volunteer, 19-year-old Seamus Bradley, was shot five times by the army and left without medical treatment to die of his injuries. The army claimed Hegarty was a gunman and Bradley a petrol bomber. Neither is true. After Motorman and for the next two decades, the Bogside would be one of the most militarized areas in western Europe.

The same night, 31 July, nine people were fatally injured in what's known as the Claudy Bombings after the IRA detonated three huge car-bombs on the main street of the Co. Derry village. The youngest person killed was an eight-year-old girl, Kathryn Eakin, who had been cleaning the windows of her parents' shop on Main Street. More than thirty other people were injured.[3]

Jimmy Toye: After Bloody Sunday everything ramped up until Operation Motorman in July 1972. The Provisionals went from strength to strength, which was almost certainly the effect of Bloody Sunday. The barricades were bigger, stronger. Daily bombings and shootings happened.

After Motorman, the war changed. Instead of attacking military installations, barricades, vehicles, etc., it seemed the Provisionals were hitting foot patrols up close, in our street. In these and later months and years, soldiers would be killed in gun battles around our street, or wounded, or there would be hijackings. I was hijacked three separate times: they used my car for a bombing, a bank robbery and to transport weapons. There were also British army searches of our shop too.

Denis Bradley: The civil rights movement was dead. There was no talking to be done. The young had a flag to carry. The army shot the local people dead. There had been dormant republicanism, but Bloody Sunday blew the civil rights movement off the streets and forced a good many people into the road of republican terrorism. In my view, Bloody Sunday was a horrific political mistake. It was a massacre. There were no political institutions to solve the problem. The *Widgery Report* rubbed salt into the wounds.

*

After Bloody Sunday, widowed mother-of-fourteen Peggy Derry remained in a wheelchair for two years with devastating leg injuries. Six months after Bloody Sunday, one of Peggy's young sons

– fourteen-year-old Patrick – lost an eye when he was hit by a rubber bullet. Like all of those affected by Bloody Sunday, the Deery family suffered intimidation and harassment for months and years afterwards. In an interview dated 1982, Peggy Deery said that her house had been raided by the British army almost a hundred and thirty times in the ten years since Bloody Sunday.

At Westminster on Tuesday 1 August, Britain's Attorney-General, Sir Peter Rawlinson, responded to a parliamentary question about prosecuting the soldiers involved in the Bloody Sunday killings. In his response, the Attorney-General also announced that charges of riotous behaviour against some civilians were also to be dropped.[4]

From Parliamentary Questions in Westminster's *Hansard* Record, dated 1 August 1972:

MR STRATTON MILLS - I ask the Attorney-General whether he proposes to institute criminal proceedings against any members of Her Majesty's forces, or against any civilians, who took part in the events in Londonderry on Sunday 30 January.

THE ATTORNEY-GENERAL - After consideration of the evidence, the Director of Public Prosecutions for Northern Ireland and I have decided that there is no evidence sufficient to warrant the prosecution of any member of the Security Forces who took part in those events. I have also decided that it would not be in the public interest to proceed further with charges of riotous behaviour which have been brought against certain civilians in respect of their participation in the events of that day; and accordingly, directions will be given that no evidence be offered in support of charges already preferred and that the necessary steps

be taken to apply to the court to withdraw such
summonses as have been issued.

*On Tuesday 21 August 1973, the jury in the inquest into the
Derry shootings recorded an open verdict, but Major Hubert
O'Neill, then Coroner of the inquest into the deaths on Bloody
Sunday, issued a statement describing the killings as 'sheer,
unadulterated murder'.*[5]

**From the report of Major Hubert O'Neill, Bloody Sunday
Inquest Coroner, dated 21 August 1973:**

This Sunday became known as Bloody Sunday
and bloody it was. It was quite unnecessary.
It strikes me that the army ran amok that
day and shot without thinking what they were
doing. They were shooting innocent people.
These people may have been taking part in
a march that was banned but that does not
justify the troops coming in and firing live
rounds indiscriminately. I would say without
hesitation that it was sheer, unadulterated
murder. It was murder.

*Despite the Coroner's report, what happened in Derry was buried
by the British army and successive governments. Its importance
and relevance were dictated by the findings of the deeply flawed
and hurried Widgery Tribunal earlier that year. However, those
present could never forget.*

Dr Raymond McClean: The major reaction to Bloody Sunday was
first shock and then anger. Families split, with parents supporting
the approach of the SDLP and their children supporting a more
aggressive attitude [towards British occupation]. Before Bloody
Sunday we were working at grass-roots level to try and get people
in Shantallow and the Creggan to respect the law.

Following Bloody Sunday there was complete disillusionment with law and order, even among older people, and it was impossible to discuss the issue with younger people. The year after Bloody Sunday was dreadful. The violence was extreme. We had army raids all over the city. Following an army raid I would usually receive five calls for sedatives, or even for heart attacks. I was out every night.

Eamonn McCann: They didn't go out of existence, but I do think Bloody Sunday killed the Northern Ireland Civil Rights Association. It was a NICRA march, organized by them, and all the very moderate people on the platform, like Ivan Cooper, Bridget Bond and Presbyterian Reverend Terence McCaughey and Bernadette Devlin. Of them, Bernadette was the only one who could be described as from left-field, outside the mainstream, and she was an MP, so she wasn't totally outside the mainstream.

Mickey McKinney: Very deliberately, my mother kept it private. She was afraid that if any of us saw her in a state, that we'd have joined up. She was very sensitive. My father was bereft. A relative of one of the other victims met him one day in a lift at Du Pont where they worked. My father was crying, and when the man asked him why, he said, 'I just want to see my son.' That was twelve years after Bloody Sunday. All the relatives have similar stories. The effect of Bloody Sunday was devastating. In Creggan, the pain was felt by the whole community. There was always the feeling that the victims could have been anybody. The community gave us immense support and still does, even yet.

Eamonn Deane: The events of that day had a profound effect on me. I became disillusioned with my job as a schoolteacher and wanted to do something that would give members of my community more control over their lives and destinies. I became engaged full time in community work and didn't return to teaching. This feeling was reinforced by the findings of the Widgery Tribunal, and I was very angry that the establishment had failed to reach the truth of what happened that day. That we had to endure the lies told.

Eamonn McCann: There was nobody on the Bloody Sunday platform that day who represented an armed threat to the state. In fact, NICRA represented the alternative strategy to armed struggle. But the NICRA leadership was literally shot off the platform on Bloody Sunday; they had to throw themselves to the ground and jump off the platform. It was very difficult for them [NICRA] to argue afterwards that 'this is the way' and 'join us' in marching in peaceful array, as the view was that you'd get shot at anyway.

Eamonn Baker: Bloody Sunday had an enormous effect on attitudes in Northern Ireland. In particular, many people's attitude to violence changed. I would have signed up to join the IRA immediately after Bloody Sunday, as would the vast majority of people in Creggan at the time.

I was angry, yes, and in some ways traumatized, yet I was privileged too as the first one from my whole family to ever attend university and so I returned to Queen's to finish what I had started: a degree in English literature. I sequestered myself in a corner with poems and novels and pints of Guinness, half-knowing that political violence, in response to the horrors inflicted by the paras, could lead to an endless spiral of killing and bombing.

CHAPTER 36

Decades

A petrol bombing youth in the Bogside, 1980s.

For the next two decades, those affected by Bloody Sunday had little choice but to accept the situation as it was. Widgery's report in 1972 had extinguished all hopes of justice for those lost or injured on 30 January 1972.

After Bloody Sunday, the relatives of the victims were targeted by the security forces, who labelled them 'terrorist families'. This led to army house raids for many families – including my own – and years of harassment and intimidation. To be associated with Bloody Sunday was to be viewed with suspicion and a wide-spread false perception of guilt by association.

Eamonn McCann: I was born and grew up in Rossville Street where the killing took place and so it was deeply personal to me … I knew some of those murdered too, and when you know people personally, and know also that they were not involved with arms, it gives you a certain strength to fight.

Paul Doherty: It wasn't until I was in my teens and started to learn about history that I really took in the full importance of what had happened. At school, sometimes people would point to me and say, 'His father was shot dead,' and things like that. There was one teacher who would get me to stand up and talk of me as an example of a person who'd been hit by the Troubles. I think at times the teachers didn't know how to treat me, but maybe they were just embarrassed.

Gleann Doherty, son of Patrick Doherty: I'm thirty-eight now, and I was seven months old when my father was killed on Bloody Sunday. It's always there. I can't remember a time when it wasn't there; it was nothing out of the ordinary. I have no memories of it being discussed but it was always there. We always went to the annual Bloody Sunday commemoration marches, but that was about all we did.[1]

Martin McGuinness: The murder of fourteen people on the streets of Derry must be recorded as one of the most shocking incidents that ever occurred in this city. From the very beginning, it was obvious to us that many of the families were traumatized by what happened to them and by the reaction of the state.

James Porter: In the following five years my family and I were harassed continually by the army. For fifty years my home was in the mainly loyalist Waterside area of the city. A typical occurrence and one of the most bizarre incidents happened on 10 October 1972. A group of soldiers came to my house on Dungiven Road and asked permission to search my car. No reason was given. There was nothing found. In spite of this, I was arrested and marched through the streets of the Waterside at gunpoint, flanked by six soldiers. This procession attracted a great deal of public attention in the area.

On Christmas Day 1972 my house was searched by the army at 6am. Again, there was nothing found. Rumours began, and members of my family were attacked by loyalists. In 1973, I was forced to leave the Waterside area and my family moved to Culmore on the west bank of the city. The harassment did not abate. On the first day after my move to Culmore, I approached the permanent army checkpoint between Culmore and the city, and my car was stopped by the army. My daughters, who were going to school, were also in the car. We were all arrested and brought to the army base at Fort George.

Army searches proved fruitless, however, in finding Porter's original army recordings from Bloody Sunday. Having been rejected as illegally obtained by Lord Widgery's tribunal, he was advised to destroy them. Porter instead took them to a trusted friend over the border in Donegal for safekeeping. The box of tapes remained hidden, buried in the ground, until the Bloody Sunday Justice Campaign began in the 1990s, whereupon they were retrieved from their hiding place and transcribed. 'I consider my friend to be most reliable. I told him what the box contained,' Jimmy Porter recalled.

Transcriptions of the army radio recordings were submitted to the subsequent Bloody Sunday Inquiry when it was established in 1998. Porter also revealed that he had photographic evidence of a message that 1 PARA had left on the shutters of a shop window in William Street:

'Paras were here and they fucking hammered fuck out of you.'

The graffiti was signed below by a later-identified member of 1 PARA. According to the Derry Journal, *Porter said the shutter itself 'had a crude drawing of six coffins and six crosses, and was later confiscated by the soldiers, but not before he had photographed it in the presence of two witnesses'.*

*

A memorial to Bloody Sunday was unveiled by Derry Civil Rights Association leader Bridget Bond in January 1974 upon the site of the killings in the Bogside.

At the same commemoration event, Jim Wray Senior spoke, calling for action on those still affected by army intimidation and harassment and asking the public to 'unite and intensify their struggle in a courageous and dignified effort'.

From the *Derry Journal* on the second anniversary of Bloody Sunday, Jim Wray Senior, dated January 1974:

> We should all be concerned about the thousands of people who are still suffering the terrible brutalities of harassment, raiding of homes, interrogation and internment carried out by the security forces in this land of ours. We must intensify our struggle to end these acts. They must banish apathy. They must assert to the world that they were a responsible people still denied basic civil rights.[2]

Liam Wray: My father would have been one of the few people to voice their feelings on Bloody Sunday in local papers after 1972. He wasn't intimidated by speaking publicly and was interviewed coming up to every anniversary, seizing every opportunity to get his own word out. After Bloody Sunday, the civil rights movement dwindled, and people became more militant. We were there at every march and every opportunity to remember those who lost their lives and the ripple effect that caused.

John Kelly: We marched every year. It was important to show presence – to keep the memory of it alive as well. It wasn't hard to do because it didn't just affect the families; it affected the whole of the city and all those who witnessed it. People wanted to remember. Sinn Féin then took over the march from NICRA in the Seventies and kept it alive all those years. They may have used it for their own purposes, but that's fine because it became a platform for other issues over the years. My family gave it full support at all times; we attended everything.

Jean Hegarty, sister of 17-year-old Kevin McElhinney: Bloody Sunday was a subject that we didn't talk about. We sometimes talked about Kevin, of course, but not about the Bloody Sunday side of it. We were always quite a non-political family and kept to ourselves. Our involvement came later, towards the end of the campaign.[3]

Diane Greer: When did I have a sense that my 'truth' was not the only 'truth'? I believe that it happened in my very first job after leaving school. I had just turned seventeen and was feeling very superior as the office junior in Huntwright Shirt & Collar Co. Ltd. I have wonderful memories of working there with a workforce drawn from the Bogside and Creggan. These people were from the areas where the Bloody Sunday dead were from. Conversations overheard led me to question how 'wicked' these people really were.

On occasions I would see small groups of women huddled together, clearly supporting someone, and overhear tales of night raids and missing menfolk. I would hear soft sobbing and have a sense of sisterhood at its loveliest. These women would have been subjected to horrific abuse from the army, and whether or not any of them birthed terrorists – and I am sure a small number of them did – I knew them to be good and kind.

I now think of them as brave and courageous, too. I spoke with women who had attended the march on 30 January 1972 and listened while they reminisced with each other about their memories of those who were killed. Strange as it may be to understand, the dead of Bloody Sunday were no longer a football score on the wall – for me, they were people. They had faces and characters, they came from families and they once had futures. From that time on I found it impossible to believe they were all guilty and deserving of what happened, but – for several years – I continued to think that there must have been some IRA gunmen among them.

Kay Duddy: During one army raid when we still lived with my father, I remember following one of the soldiers up the stairs, as you had to do in those days just to make sure there was nothing amiss. When I got to the top of the stairs, I could see this young soldier in the bathroom, shaking his leg, and I could see a gun coming out of the bottom of his trouser leg. I squealed at the top of my voice, 'He's trying to plant a gun up here!' People ran up, but the soldier lifted it and ran on downstairs and out the door. That just shows you what they were willing to do to make us look bad.

Diane Greer: I was working with women who came into the factory at 8 o'clock in the morning and talked about their houses being raided the night before and people being taken away. It never ceased to amaze me how women showed up for their work in the morning after having had horrendous nights at home. By quietly listening to people, I began to hear the real human stories and I think that very much influenced my views after that. On the one side, I was hearing that these arrested men were real bastards: that's why they had been taken away; no smoke without fire; they don't lift them for nothing, etc., and getting the message that everybody who was lifted was guilty of something. I suppose in many ways, looking back, they were only guilty of living in a nationalist area, or being a Catholic, or being a suspected republican.

Susie Campbell: One of the things I remember most is the army raiding our house. It must have happened half a dozen times or more over the years after Bloody Sunday, and just because I was Jackie Duddy's sister. Never with any explanation or reason, and it wasn't just us either – they were raiding families all over the city. My eldest children were just infants the first time it happened, and the army woke up the whole house banging at 6 o'clock in the morning, upsetting the wains and upsetting everyone and leaving the house a mess after them – what right had they? We weren't involved in anything. Once, they arrested my husband and took him away to the barracks. But he was let home again that night. It was just nuisance calls, really, and they got away with it because they were the army. That really bugged me. None of us were political in any way whatsoever, but it didn't matter.

Regina McLaughlin: We never thought about a campaign, we would have been too young. We didn't know anything about it. We were all kids when Daddy was killed. It was never forgotten but it was within our walls and wasn't public and we never really talked about it.

Diane Greer: Over the years I continued to meet people who were there on the day. I bought books on Bloody Sunday and developed a quiet obsession about the rights and wrongs of what happened. Quiet was the operative word because it would have been too dangerous for my health to have aired my thoughts out loud. When I did, I was reminded that I had worked too long with 'Them' on the west bank [of Derry] and it was affecting my judgement. Very quickly, treasonable thoughts were suppressed and as Bloody Sunday anniversaries came and went, so my frustration grew. Frustration at the thought that I could not attend a commemorative march for two reasons: (1) to attend would have been tantamount to associating with Sinn Féin (another equation; Sinn Féin = IRA), (2) I would have needed to carry a banner over my head explaining why I would even want to remember the dead – and another ten people to help me carry it – big enough for me to state clearly why I was there and leaving no room for ambiguity. Who was I kidding?

Susie Campbell: I couldn't sleep if my children weren't home, no matter what age they were. I was always too scared to let them go on marches or to anything with big crowds. Jackie only went on a march for a bit of craic, and he never came home. That was always in the back of my mind. I always told them that I wasn't worried about what *they* would do, but what others could do. I think it was the fear of the unknown, and that fear was passed down to our own children. Maybe it's only natural that we'd end up overprotective, worrying about what could happen, what *might* happen.

*

In 1990, the new Bloody Sunday Initiative set about taking responsibility for the annual march, organizing a broader-based human rights-focused march showing support for wider justice cases. However, an IRA bomb detonated high on the city walls as marchers congregated below. Falling debris showered the crowd and killed one marcher, sixteen-year-old Charles Love, who had travelled in from Strabane for the march.

Anne-Marie Love, sister of 16-year-old Charles Love, killed by bomb debris in 1990: Charles was into Bon Jovi, Def Leppard, Whitesnake, anything. He loved it. He had all the T-shirts ... His two friends told me he went down straight away, and he wasn't aware of anything, which we're grateful for. It [the bomb] wasn't meant for him. It was just unfortunate the debris hit him.[4]

Robin Percival, former Chair of the Bloody Sunday Trust: It was unbelievable. People came to us afterwards, saying, 'We came on this march in good faith and look what happened.' I do believe that was one of the seminal events that led to the first IRA ceasefire.[5]

*

In March 1991, many affected by Bloody Sunday took heart in witnessing the Birmingham Six – who included Derry man Johnny Walker – walk free after 16 years in prison. The six Irishmen had been accused of and charged with two 1974 bombings in Birmingham, England, in which 21 people died.

    Their release came after the high-profile quashing of the Maguire Seven and Guildford Four cases two years earlier. The Maguire Seven had included an entire family, including 14-year-old Patrick Maguire, who were accused of being bomb makers and given sentences ranging from four to twelve years. The Guildford Four were accused of the bombing in Guildford itself and the death of five people, and all four served 15 years in prison, including Carole Richardson, a young English girl

*who was accused and sentenced to life in jail alongside Irish
people she hardly knew. These cases are now widely recognized
as three of the biggest miscarriages of justice in British legal
history.*

*All three cases implicated innocent civilians, the majority
of whom were Irish Catholics, in the IRA's deadly bombing
campaign in Britain in the 1970s. Seeing these latest scenes from
the Old Bailey, many who sought justice for events in Derry
began to feel hope, and a gradual realization that maybe, just
maybe, they could try too.*

Mickey McKinney: As time passed, and I watched the Birmingham
Six being released on the news, I got angry. I thought that's fine,
but what about Bloody Sunday? I felt very strongly about it and
that made me realize we needed to do something.

Gerry Duddy: If the British government got it so wrong with the
Birmingham Six and the Guildford Four, I thought they might
admit that they had got it wrong in Derry, too. Even when the
real bombers came forward, the Brits let the Guildford Four stay
in jail for years until they were forced to admit they were wrong.
It showed you that it wasn't just us whose reputation had been
ruined, and it showed you that the British didn't care about the
truth – even when it was obvious. They just needed Irish people
to blame to satiate those looking for justice, even if there was no
evidence of guilt. It meant, ultimately, that we had a chance to
change things about Bloody Sunday.

Diane Greer: In 1991, I began to meet other Protestants who held
similar views to me, and it was a relief not to feel so isolated. These
people marked the [Bloody Sunday] anniversary in a number of
ways – observing moments of silence, lighting candles, offering
prayers. Each person believed themselves alone in their empathy,
each one angry at a situation that led to their feeling limited in any
support they could offer to the victims' families. Support for the
families could still be translated as support for Sinn Féin/IRA …
enough to silence all of us.

Geraldine McBride: I didn't even tell my children about what happened on Bloody Sunday. Then I helped with a TV documentary called *Secret History*. When I did explain about Bloody Sunday to my children, they said they understood the mother I was. I'd always been overprotective, but that was because I saw how quickly life could be taken. Especially when they were teenagers, I'd have stayed awake until they came back in home. I always needed to know where they were. I couldn't even take them up to the Guildhall Square to see Santa arriving at Christmas because of the crowds there, so Hugo took them up every year. When I did eventually go, I'd stay at the back against the Derry walls and make sure I had an escape route. You have no idea what it does to you.

CHAPTER 37

Igniting Embers

Launch of the Bloody Sunday Justice Campaign in April 1992.
From left, Johnny Walker from the Birmingham Six and campaigners
Eamonn McCann and John Kelly.

*Discussions about campaigning around Bloody Sunday came to
fruition by the twentieth anniversary in 1992. At first novices and
strangers, campaigners had no idea where to start in unravelling
a twenty-year mystery and holding the British government
to account.*

Robin Percival: The twentieth anniversary followed the theme
of 'One World, One Struggle' and included representatives from
the African National Congress (ANC), and a concert by Christy
Moore. At a meeting, the families talked about demands that the
campaign would make, and I was asked to go away and write up
the three demands, which I did. That was my little contribution

to it all. I went away and wrote up a leaflet explaining the Bloody Sunday Justice Campaign.

Mickey McKinney: Tony [Doherty] and Eamonn [McCann] called the meeting in Pilot's Row to discuss the case and that's when I became involved. I remember there were about forty people there, and only seven or eight of the families were represented, so I suggested that we should try to get the rest of the families involved.

John Kelly and I went around and spoke to all the families to get them onboard. This all took time, months maybe. I was aware of party-political problems that existed within the families at the time and still do today, but we assured them that what we were planning to do was non-political. I felt that the only way we were going to succeed was if we were all united.

Olive Bonner: I never really thought about Bloody Sunday much and it was only when my brother Floyd, God have mercy on him, got involved in the campaign that I really considered the possibility. I thought, at first, they were wasting their time, but as time went on and Floyd and the group visited Downing Street and all sorts, I thought to myself there might be a chance. When Floyd died, I had already retired and that's when I decided to take over where he left off in the campaign. The world needed to know it was murder.

Maura Young: I was right there when the campaign started. Jesus, many a cold night we spent sat in Westend Terrace, freezing with the old windows rattling. But we thought, this is it now, our one and only chance to do something about it. We fought for this and fought for that, and we fought hard. We stood out in the rain. We knocked on doors. Some people were so cruel. I remember me and Alice McGuigan getting abuse when standing outside the Richmond Centre asking people to sign the petition. People telling us to get over it, or that the soldiers were fighting for their country and giving up their lives.

John McKinney, brother of 27-year-old William McKinney: I had to do something. I had to try. It was eating me up when I saw how the families were left after Bloody Sunday. I was the youngest of the family and I saw what it did to my mother and father. I was only eight and it still left me bitter about Bloody Sunday. I wanted to get answers for my mother. She never got over it and took it to the grave ... She never saw the end of it.

I think it took one person to decide to start a campaign and get it going. Nobody had really talked about it before then. Nobody had asked, 'Right, what are we going to do about Bloody Sunday?' When Tony held the meeting, I thought it was one of the best things I'd ever heard of. Nothing had ever been done about Bloody Sunday and so you felt good actually trying to do something. I threw myself into it completely. Nobody had any experience, but we made it up as we went along.[1]

Mickey McKinney: In 1992, we officially launched the campaign in Pilot's Row, and news crews from the BBC and ITV were there as well as the local press. At one of the first few campaign meetings, we sat around trying to find ourselves a name. I remember that it was Robin Percival who suggested we call ourselves the Bloody Sunday Justice Campaign, and that was carried. Within the campaign, we tried to organize ourselves as a proper group. John became Chair, I was Vice-Chair, Gerry was Treasurer and Geraldine was the minute taker. Those of us in the campaign felt very passionate about what we were trying to do.

The Bloody Sunday Justice Campaign had three clear demands, which were the repudiation of the Widgery Report *and institution of a new inquiry; a formal acknowledgement of the innocence of all the victims; and the prosecution of those responsible. The press published a statement from the newly formed campaign calling for the public's support. 'We welcome into membership anyone who supports our objectives irrespective of religion or political persuasion', it read.*

Kay Duddy: Why wait twenty years? Personally, I imagined someone would've come clean or done something about Bloody

Sunday long before that. The subsequent governments who put out the lie. I always thought someone somewhere would say, 'Hang on – this is wrong.' But they didn't. So, me and Gerry got involved with the family's blessing. Everyone had waited long enough. I felt personally that Jackie's and all their names were being slandered all over the world. They were buried in the name of being nail bombers and gunmen, and someone had to try to clear their names.

Geraldine Doherty: Every Tuesday night without fail, Mickey McKinney would collect me, my mother and Kay Duddy to go to the meetings, and we would all be huddled around a wee heater in Westend Park. At the beginning, I was minute taker.

Kay Duddy: To begin with, it was hard to talk about, but we were encouraged to talk and put ideas out there and get a discussion going. It was a huge learning process. What do we do? How do we do it? We shared ideas, no matter how ridiculous they seemed. At that stage, we hadn't even a pen or pencil or a writing pad to take notes on, so all that basic stuff was needed. Looking back, because we were with extended family members, it was almost like a support group because we suddenly had a chance to talk about it all. It was very emotional, very highly strung at times.

Paul Doherty: My hope is that someday one of the paras will speak out and tell the truth about what really happened. It's very similar to the Birmingham Six and Guildford Four cases. If people hadn't kept chipping away at the lies and the injustice, they would still be in jail. They got justice eventually, after seventeen years of struggle, but nothing can bring our relatives back.

Spanning only six short years from 1992 to 1998, the Bloody Sunday Justice Campaign achieved international recognition for its ground-breaking work in reigniting the issue of Bloody Sunday.

Gerry Duddy: We had a rule from the first meeting to the last, that no matter what your personal politics were, when it came

346

to Bloody Sunday meetings, you left your politics at the door. I believe it did work. Alright, there were different opinions, but we all had one thing in common: we were all for the one goal – it was all about Bloody Sunday. But it was hard to change the public's perception.

Eamonn McCann: The campaign in the early days was a moral campaign. It was right and proper and certainly necessary for the peace of mind of the relatives that *Widgery* be overturned, and these demands be met.

John McKinney: People used to tell us we didn't have a hope in hell – even relatives used to tell us that – but it never put us off. We were writing to councils, councils in America, to London, anywhere we could think of. Having no politics involved was one of the best decisions we ever made – the campaign was too important to involve politics.

Gerry Duddy: We took the petition around Derry and other areas as well, but like with anything, people can't give you all their time and so we did certain areas at separate times and took breaks in between. But we got bodies around the town, and I remember getting doors slammed in my face in the Bog and Creggan and places, saying, 'Get away from my door, I want nothing to do with you.' You get both sides of the coin: some people are nice to you, others are just ignorant. But we persevered, and we got forty thousand signatures just by working at it. It's like anything, you have to work at it. Some people will tell you that it more or less took up our whole lives.

James Porter: The next time that I listened to the original tapes was in 1992 when I got them back from my friend at around the time of the twentieth anniversary of Bloody Sunday. I wrote the transcripts and provided copies to others before that time using the copies of the original tapes that I had made. When I finally did listen to the original tapes again, which I have done on several occasions since 1992, they were exactly the same as the copies I had made.

Mickey McKinney: One of the ideas that came up at meetings was that we needed a solicitor. Martin Finucane suggested that we ask Peter Madden, and so some of the families went to Belfast to meet with him. A young lawyer for Madden & Finucane, Patricia Coyle, came to talk to us a number of times and spoke of ideas on how to highlight Bloody Sunday.

Patricia Coyle, apprentice solicitor with Madden & Finucane in the 1990s: I was with the firm a few months when Kevin asked if I was interested in dealing with the clients and their case. No hesitation. As a native of Derry and a child of the 1970s, I grew up well aware of the impact of Bloody Sunday on the city, and the stench and notoriety of the Widgery Inquiry. My parents and members of the extended family were on the NICRA march in 1972. The fact that the *Widgery Report* remained as the official record of what happened that day was reprehensible. Reviewing the slim blue file I was given, it was clear that the first step necessary was to locate, copy and collate all the information we could get from all possible sources.[2]

In 1992, Eamonn McCann published the book What Happened in Derry, *once again highlighting the facts behind Bloody Sunday and the importance of addressing the case. Despite the publisher's organizing a launch mere yards from the Irish government in the south of Ireland, just one elected representative came.*

Eamonn McCann:. Now, that tells you something of how people were thinking at the time. They presumed this was some kind of Provo campaign and they would be associated with something dangerous. The same thing happened with the Birmingham Six, but of course in the end they all rushed in to help once the case was near completion.

Mickey McKinney: Patricia would have been our main contact and was working off her own bat; she was brilliant. At one stage, John Hume got a group of MPs together at Westminster and they listened to us, which was all you could expect at that stage.

We were determined to stay non-political, and, at the same time, we were seeking the support of Derry City Council, Sinn Féin and the SDLP in Derry.

John McKinney: About a dozen of us slept outside Mansion House the night before Prince Charles, Colonel in Chief of the Parachute Regiment, came to Dublin in May 1995. We took a busload down. When we went to a protest demo outside the Irish president's residence in 1995, the Gardaí stopped us in Monaghan that morning, and later, when they were hassling us outside Phoenix Park, a guard actually asked us, 'What were you lot doing in Monaghan this morning?' They were letting us know that they were watching us all day – more than we realized. They told us the quicker we got back up north the better. It was actually really bitter – scary too. It was the first time I had ever heard a guard saying, 'Get back up to the black north.' The Gardaí followed us everywhere that day.

Teresa McGowan: My son Danny came to meetings with me. His father was far too emotional for those meetings – he wanted no talk about it. He even got emotional looking at things on TV. Even watching stuff about World War Two would upset him. I felt it was important to go to those meetings. Everything was going for the better; you could see a change and people had lighter hearts.

Jean Hegarty: I came back from Canada in 1995, and when I came back, I started going to campaign meetings with my sister Roslyn and got more involved. I think my mammy and daddy would have always attended commemoration events, but it was fairly late on when my daddy went on his first march. It was probably when commemorations became more family-led that my family really came on board.

Kay Duddy: I think the whole of Derry was in shock after Bloody Sunday, and people didn't realize the immediate aftermath or how many joined the IRA or were deeply affected by it. There must be scores of people in this town who have suffered from post-traumatic stress and were never diagnosed. People who couldn't cope with it and became alcoholics.

I had an experience one night at 6.30pm mass. A man came into the chapel drunk and went up to the altar and was crying up to God about Bloody Sunday – in front of the whole chapel. Fair play to the priest; he came down and was very gentle with him. The priest told me afterwards, 'There but for the grace of God go you and I.' He had just seen too much.

CHAPTER 38

Enough New Evidence

The Heath–Widgery memo discovered during the 1990s.

Crucial to the reopening of the Bloody Sunday issue was finding new evidence to prove that the British army came in firing, and that all those targeted were innocent, unarmed and fleeing. The search for fresh evidence after so many years would be a difficult one, but cumulatively, it changed everything.

Eamonn McCann: It was the discovery of new evidence and the way that unfolded that alerted people to the fact that the story was advancing. It wasn't just the contents of this new evidence; it was the realization that the campaign had reached new ground. People felt that new evidence meant there should be a new trial.

Mickey McKinney: We got a list of names from Don [Mullan] and each of us tracked down people to ask for permission to use their statements in the book. I went to the door of one person, who witnessed the killings in Glenfada Park, and his wife answered. She wouldn't even mention the old statement to him because he had never gotten over what he'd seen on Bloody Sunday. We got permission to use a hundred or more statements, which Don then published in *Eyewitness Bloody Sunday*. I didn't know where the book was going to take us, but we all knew it would help raise the profile of the campaign and remind everyone about Bloody Sunday.

John McKinney: The various campaigns against state violence were invited to meet the Irish president Mary Robinson at her residence in Dublin – she had already refused to meet us twice. So I went down myself, along with the other campaigns.

She shook hands with members of the various campaigns, and when she came to me, I introduced myself and said I had a brother killed on Bloody Sunday. 'I want you to lay a wreath at the Bloody Sunday monument in Derry.' I still remember the language she used, saying she couldn't be seen to be political and that her *constitutional position* wouldn't permit her to get involved in campaigns. I said, 'But you laid a wreath in Enniskillen where there was an IRA bombing. We are not a political group – we are a human rights group – [representing] innocent people who died just like all those in Enniskillen.' She dismissed it.

A campaign ally and then-director of British Irish Rights Watch, Jane Winter, authored and submitted a report on Bloody Sunday to the United Nations in 1994. It was sent to the United Nations Special Rapporteur on Summary or Arbitrary Executions, which dealt with non-sanctioned state killings, but the UN then ruled that they wouldn't investigate anything over two years old.

Jane Winter, former Director of British Irish Rights Watch, London: I worked on the report in my spare time for about six months. Up until then, there had been no reports from the point of view of the victims and what happened to them. So that's what I tried to research and encapsulate: the human rights angle, the fact that these people had been wilfully deprived of their lives.[1]

In August 1995, Jane Winter unearthed a document in the Public Records Office in London that offered disturbing detail to Lord Widgery's appointment to the initial tribunal. This document, since known as the Heath–Widgery memo, records a meeting between British prime minister Edward Heath, the Lord Chief Justice Widgery and Lord Chancellor Hailsham in Downing Street on Monday 31 January 1972, the day after Bloody Sunday.

The memo was a key piece of evidence, as it showed that Widgery was influenced to produce a favourable report. In one section, the prime minister suggests that recommendations on best procedure for inquiries made by Lord Salmon in the 1921 Act 'might not necessarily be relevant in this case'. The Lord Chancellor also noted that the Treasury Solicitor would need to 'brief counsel for the army'. In another section, as we noted earlier, Heath himself famously advised Widgery to bear in mind that, 'We are in Northern Ireland fighting not only a military war but a propaganda war.'

Jane Winter: I thought, well, this changes everything. This was meant to be an independent inquiry by the Lord Chief Justice – who chose to sit on his own with no other judges – and here is the prime minister trying to influence him! That cannot be right. He was also giving Widgery a very political message – that this was not just a military war but a propaganda war.

Families hailed the memo as 'absolute dynamite'. The front-page headline of that week's Derry Journal *read, 'Widgery memo damns British', and the article reported that the newly discovered evidence would 'send shockwaves through the British establishment'.*[2]

*

Patricia Coyle, the young solicitor working on the case, also unearthed a wealth of new evidence during the 1990s that altered the course of the campaign. Among the previously unseen documents were:

- *Original statements of evidence, given by the soldiers who had fired, made to the Military Police on the night of Bloody Sunday.*

- *Further statements, made by some of the same soldiers, weeks after their first statements to the Military Police.*

- *Further formal statements by the same soldiers to the Treasury Solicitor's Office acting as the legal team for the Widgery Inquiry.*

- *A schedule confirming the disclosure of documents at the time of the 1972 inquiry.*

- *Memos from the Tribunal Secretary to Lord Widgery commenting on issues and arguments that had arisen during the inquiry hearings.*

- *Strategic documents relating to evidence before the inquiry and potential witnesses.*

- *Early drafts of sections of the tribunal's report with handwritten notations.*

- *Summaries of Widgery's responses to some of these comments and notations.*[3]

Patricia Coyle: That first reading of those documents will remain with me for ever. It was clear that the soldiers' statements taken by the Military Police on the evening of Bloody Sunday, the first statements of evidence provided by the shooters, had never seen the light of day. There were two other sets of statements from the same soldiers taken a few weeks after Bloody Sunday, essentially a second version, followed by the third version given to the tribunal's legal team. The evidence differed with each version. The final version, ultimately given to the Widgery Inquiry, was, without doubt in my opinion, the result of a tailoring process.

Patricia was convinced – and correct – that these various tailored versions of soldiers' statements had not been disclosed to lawyers for the families and wounded back in 1972. Another piece of primary evidence was especially damning, as it turned out to be an untidy note of direction on one of the original drafts of the Widgery Report.

Patricia Coyle: I was stunned when I saw a black handwritten scribble on the right-hand side of a page. It read: 'The LCJ will pile up the forensic evidence against the deceased.' LCJ is short for Lord Chief Justice – Widgery. I will never forget that moment. From a legal perspective, that one handwritten scrawl was enough to undermine the Widgery Tribunal and Report. In campaign terms, what we now had was a newly discovered body of evidence that had been wilfully withheld from lawyers for the families and wounded in 1972. It was shocking.

Gerry Duddy: That was a big high, and it was a couple of years of constant big highs, a snowball effect. It was like being giving a million pounds when Patricia came back and told us what she had found out, because we knew there was stuff to be dug up. People criticize the legal teams for getting big wages, but for years, Madden & Finucane and Patricia Coyle worked for nothing – and I think a lot of people forget that.

Eamonn McCann: It began to snowball; it injected momentum into the campaign and gave people a confidence – not an inner confidence but a confidence based on material things that were actually happening. The new evidence also began to get wider coverage and the campaign badly needed all the publicity it could get. One lucky stroke in the campaign was Don Mullan's book *Eyewitness Bloody Sunday* about the eyewitness documents they found. It turned out a massive help to the campaign and got so much publicity; there were three or four different reports on Channel 4 News based around Don's theories and that heightened the profile of the campaign beyond measure.

It was around Bloody Sunday's twenty-fifth anniversary in 1997 that it began to gain some traction in the mainstream

British media. Several special reports broadcast by Channel Four News that January highlighted the case further, including an interview with an anonymous paratrooper who admitted that unarmed civilians were shot. Don Mullan's book launch attracted hundreds. At Westminster, over a dozen Conservative and Labour MPs lodged Early Day Motions calling for a new independent, international inquiry into Bloody Sunday. The Bloody Sunday Trust also launched their commissioned analysis of new evidence in 1997, Professor Dermot Walsh's 'The Bloody Sunday Tribunal of Inquiry: A Resounding Defeat for Truth, Justice and the Rule of Law'. Walsh's paper would end up influencing both the British and Irish governments.

Mickey McKinney: When a submission went to the European Court of Human Rights in 1997, John Hume got the families into Number 10 and the Houses of Parliament. That was great PR for us. When we walked into Downing Street with John Hume, I saw this as our first PR stunt. We wrote off to some MPs and Lords looking for support for the campaign. Some got back to us, some positive and some negative. We wrote to Cardinal Cahal Daly and he was a bit sticky on it. He didn't want to be involved, which really surprised me – I was expecting more of a Cardinal of all Ireland.

Martin McGuinness: I think many people outside of the families thought the prospect of getting action from a British government was even less than remote, but all credit to the families: they never gave up. They campaigned all over the world and got the support of everybody that regarded what happened on that day as one of the most blatant acts of murder by state forces on a community.

Mickey McKinney: I have a vision of watching my mother, sometime around the twenty-fifth anniversary before I was due to give a speech, and she was just standing in the kitchen crying, looking out the window. I asked her if she was alright, and all she could say was, 'It never gets any easier.' I never forgot that.

During the 1998 Bloody Sunday commemorations, Irish Taoiseach Bertie Ahern visited Derry and laid a wreath at the memorial on Rossville Street. It was a hugely symbolic gesture.

John McKinney: That was the first time someone from the Irish government ever did so. It was around then that they started recognizing the campaign and replying to our letters too.

Bernard Gilmour: We went everywhere. Meetings were steady, every Tuesday, and contacts with the Irish government, etc., were regular. That went on for seven years until Tony Blair agreed to a new inquiry. I don't think I thought about it much in political terms until the hearings started. My feelings were more basic. Everybody knew that sooner or later something would have to be done about Bloody Sunday.[4]

CHAPTER 39

The Second Inquiry

Lord Saville and his team during their first visit to the Bogside
in April 1998.

In January 1998, those affected by Bloody Sunday came together at the community-enterprise Ráth Mór Centre in Derry for a special news briefing – British prime minister Tony Blair announced a new inquiry into the events of 30 January 1972. The news was welcomed nationally and internationally.

Mickey McKinney: We knew about the announcement of an inquiry beforehand because Mo Mowlam, the Secretary of State at the time, had told us beforehand in the Northern Ireland Office at Millbank. She told us we weren't getting what we wanted – an international independent inquiry – but something close, with a British judge and two Commonwealth judges. Then they got us together up in the Ráth Mór for the announcement and we were all gathered around the TV when Blair said it.

Jean Hegarty: I couldn't really believe it. I was really quite amazed. I suppose I was quite sceptical that the British government would give us a second inquiry.

Bridie McGuigan: I remember thinking that, after everything that had happened, the truth would never be revealed. I mean, we knew Barney was totally innocent, but I just wanted someone to tell the truth to the world.

James Porter: In January 1998 I saw an advertisement placed in the *Derry Journal* by Madden & Finucane Solicitors calling for witnesses of Bloody Sunday. As I had made a statement, I approached them.

By the time Jimmy Porter gave evidence to the Bloody Sunday Inquiry in January 2002, he was 81 years old. His army radio recordings were by now considered valuable evidence, despite having been rejected decades earlier. Later played to the inquiry, the recordings included soldiers reporting incoming fire, discharging fire and claiming 'hits' on the ground. Crucially, the tapes did not contain the order for 1 Para to advance into the Bogside – adding weight to theories that there was no such order given.

Ciaran Shiels, solicitor for a number of Bloody Sunday families: I became involved in the case in March 1998 shortly after Tony Blair announced the new inquiry. In a way the inquiry was like a cast of thousands of people affected in one way or other by the Troubles and what happened that day. What we were dealing with was mass murder perpetrated before the world's media, over really a period of about ten to twelve minutes, within a geographical area not much bigger that the size of two football pitches, with the

British army's Commander of Land Forces and an Assistant Chief Constable of the RUC in close attendance.[1]

Joe Mahon: It was never spoken about until I gave evidence to the Saville Inquiry. The man who was taking my evidence took me right back to the day, and I broke. I never cried until that moment, and it has been in the front of my mind since. I was seeing a psychologist after it, that's how bad it was. It definitely affected my life and left my emotions all mixed up. I still find it difficult to speak out and, to this day, I avoid confrontations, and it all stems from Bloody Sunday.

After almost four decades of failed ceasefires and intermittent peace talks, the Good Friday Agreement was signed on 10 April 1998 as a working agreement between eight of the north's interested parties and groups, the British government and the Irish government. The only major political party to oppose the deal was the Democratic Unionist Party (DUP), the main unionist party in Northern Ireland, with its leader, Revd Ian Paisley, publicly denouncing the agreement as 'the mother of all treacheries'.[2]

Among the commitments made in the Good Friday Agreement were a new, devolved government in which unionists and nationalists would share power, and decommissioning of British troops and military installations. Decommissioning of paramilitary weapons was also made a priority, alongside a commission to examine widespread reforms in policing in the north. It was also agreed that there would be no change in the constitutional status of Northern Ireland for now without the 'principle of consent' of a majority, which could be put to a future referendum when warranted.

Tony Blair, British prime minister 1997–2007: The principle of consent is absolute and is throughout the agreement. The breakthrough is that this is now accepted by all – north and south. Also, those who believe in a united Ireland can make that case now through persuasion, not violence or threats.

Bertie Ahern, Irish Taoiseach 1997–2008: My ultimate political aspiration remains the coming together of all the people of Ireland, achieved peacefully and by consent. I value deeply the close relationship between the Irish government and the British government, and I look forward equally to a new era of friendship and reconciliation between unionists and nationalists in which each tradition can learn truly the value of the other.

Bill Clinton, president of the USA, welcoming the Good Friday Agreement, April 1998: The path of peace is never easy. But the parties have made brave decisions. They have chosen hope over hate; the promise of the future over the poison of the past. And in so doing, already they have written a new chapter in the rich history of their island, a chapter of resolute courage that inspires us all.[3]

Diane Greer: An event that will dwell long in my memory is that of a chance meeting with a sister of one of those killed on Bloody Sunday. We had occasion to be involved in a short television interview together at the time of the Good Friday Agreement.

As we stood there in the freezing cold on the hillside overlooking the Bogside, we passed the time chatting about everything and nothing. I was aware of her story and, from somewhere deep within me, I felt that I had so much to say to her. This may sound so dramatic but, as I stood overwhelmed in her presence, I struggled to find the right words. How could I convey to this woman that I – in some small way – grieved her brother too? Would she understand – or even be interested in – the dilemmas people like me faced?

Although I was shackled by doubt and fear and was afraid my words and tears were years too late, I was compelled to reach out. As fate would have it, I was able to offer her a lift home and we sat outside her house and talked. I found the words I needed; she listened and empathized with my position as a Protestant.

We talked for a long time and, as we cried, I believe that we made a very important connection. Like the women in the shirt factory, here was someone like me, a woman open to others, who cares and is respectful of difference. She is a woman who had the grace and integrity to allow me – almost twenty-four years too late – to tell her how I felt about what had happened that day.

*

Raymond Rogan: I was really encouraged with Saville and his inquiry. The Labour government really wanted to put this issue to bed, and people were much more relaxed and prepared for Saville than for Widgery. I know obviously I was anyway – a lot of time had passed. It was a different situation. I was looking forward to going and giving testimony. Again, I was bitterly disappointed afterwards, because that was the second time that they tried to paint me a liar about young Donaghey not having any nail bombs when we tended him.

Maura Young: The trauma of going through Saville did take its toll on people. So many had put Bloody Sunday in a wee box in the back of their head. Me and our Helen helped out a few days when people were coming in to give their statements before Saville. It took its toll on witnesses who had to relive that nightmare. Fair play to them for coming out and bringing it to the fore, and some said they were so glad to get it off their chest. I'm sure the people at Eversheds taking the statements were amazed at what they heard.

Geraldine Doherty: The people of Derry were brilliant coming forward to give evidence. They put themselves through so much. My mother and I attended the inquiry as much as we could. My mother was going through chemotherapy at the time, so we would have gone for the first chemo appointment early on a Wednesday morning so we could make it back to the Guildhall for hearings. Even going through that, she wouldn't have missed the inquiry.

Patsy McDaid: It wasn't difficult to give evidence. I have nothing to hide, I can only tell the story of what happened to me and that it was a peaceful march and that I was shot in the back by the army as I was running away, unarmed. The British had told the world a bunch of lies. They had blackened the names of the dead and the wounded to justify the murder of peaceful marchers. I'm always amazed at how hypocritical they are, reporting on massacres like Tiananmen Square and the murder of protestors in the Middle East, but they won't show you what they did in Derry. Democracy? They showed their democracy on Bloody Sunday to ordinary people on a peaceful march for civil rights. Our people were literally shot out of the streets, but they don't show you that on TV or highlight the anniversary like they do everything else.

Anne Grant: We heard evidence that soldiers tried to shoot at my father as he crawled out to help Paddy Doherty. The shots came so close he had an actual bullet hole through his shirt collar. It's scary. A soldier said during his evidence that he had aimed at my daddy but didn't get him and shot a fence. My grandparents lived upstairs where that happened, and they were probably worrying knowing he was out there. What it leaves for us is something to be really proud of. What he did for his community, what he did on Bloody Sunday and what he did for us as a family, rearing us to be the people we are.

Olive Bonner: Before I gave evidence to Saville, they gave me the statement I did for Widgery to read. I didn't even look at it. I just went in and told the same story – I remembered it all so vividly I didn't need to read it. I remember everything about that day. The inquiry was so much bigger, and you knew the whole world was watching. But I wasn't afraid of giving evidence. When I was questioned by Widgery and later by Saville, it didn't intimidate me at all because I told the truth. Not one minute did I ever flinch. I didn't care about getting questioned and cross examined. I saw how they were with some people, but I didn't let them worry me.

Caroline O'Donnell: My mother said when the inquiry started and they called my daddy as a witness, 'Bloody Sunday didn't kill him then, but it will kill him now.' He just didn't ever want to talk about it. My daddy's evidence was over two days, and he was so nervous, especially because there were crowds involved.

Jackie O'Reilly: Sometimes I wished Bloody Sunday would just go away. It caused a lot of arguments, there's no point denying it; our house was a nightmare for that whole time during the inquiry. We had doctors here at times because my stepfather really relived every minute of it. He had anxiety attacks and would wake up in the night screaming. As the tribunal went on, his depression and mood swings actually got worse instead of better; it was terrible.

MILITARY EVIDENCE IN LONDON

One of the most traumatic periods of the Bloody Sunday Inquiry was its relocation to London's Methodist Central Hall in late 2002 to hear military evidence. Many were crushed to know that no paratrooper would set foot back in Derry to account for his actions.

The hearings in London opened on 24 September 2002 and would last a year. Inquiry proceedings were broadcast back to the Guildhall in Derry, and to the designated family room in the Bloody Sunday Centre, where relatives and the wounded would gather daily to watch.

Retired General Sir Frank Kitson was the first military witness to give evidence. Later that month, Brigadier Maurice Tugwell apologized for telling the BBC on the evening of the killings that four of those shot dead were on a wanted list. He told the tribunal it had been a 'mistake'.[4] Over coming months, the inquiry heard evidence from hundreds of military witnesses, chiefs and even the former British prime minister, Edward Heath.

Those affected by Bloody Sunday were glad to access support from Cúnamh, a Derry-based group that counselled and supported families throughout the inquiry and has done so in the years since.

Mickey McKinney: I rarely missed a hearing. It could be a very isolating experience. Cúnamh were of great help and were a listening ear for anybody there who needed someone to talk to. They had at least a couple of counsellors in the Guildhall with us every day, and they travelled to London with us too. Of course, there were times you did get emotional, but I didn't let the hearings get me down completely. The worst had already happened in 1972, so it couldn't get any worse.

Olive Bonner: There were very few days at the inquiry I would have missed, including in London. My wains are grown up and I was retired, and so my children and husband were quite happy for me going to London from Monday to Thursday every week. They just let me get on with it and knew I had to do it. I was doing it as much for Floyd as for anybody, and for Bernard's wife, Kathleen. She didn't live to see it either.

Kevin McDaid: I tried to go to the inquiry at least once a week when it was in Derry. None of my family went to England. I didn't think it was right that we had to go to England for military evidence; it was ridiculous. They made a mockery of their own inquiry. London cost them big-time and that's all they cried about, money this and money that. I can see no justice in moving it there for any reasons. It wasn't for security reasons as they were under guarantee from everyone that nothing would happen. The army said nothing at the inquiry anyway.

Among the notable events at the inquiry was one on 15 October 2003, when General Sir Michael Jackson, by now Britain's most senior soldier and Chief of General Staff, was recalled to the tribunal by Lord Saville – the only witness to be recalled in its duration.

He was summoned a second time to account for claims that he was in fact the author of several key documents drafted by the army after Bloody Sunday when captain and adjutant of 1 PARA in 1972. The most notable document in his handwriting was the 'shot list', falsely indicating where each target was when identified, with each labelled as either a gunman or a bomber.

In the years since, every detail on the list had been shown to be wrong. Jackson insisted that he had simply noted down what his senior soldiers had told him and explained away any inaccuracies as due to his being rather tired when writing it.

Counsel for several Derry families, Michael Mansfield QC, told the general that there was a 'serious question mark' over the list of shootings he had compiled.[5]

Michael Mansfield: The big question mark, General, in everybody's mind, and it may not have occurred to you, is that this list does not begin to explain any of the thirteen civilian dead. Did you know that?

General Sir Michael Jackson: I am sorry, I simply do not understand the statement you are making. This list refers to people being hit, and people being killed. It makes no attempt here to say civilian or whatever.

Michael Mansfield: The whole point of the list was to justify publicly why people had been shot. That was why they were described as 'nail bombers', 'pistol firers', and 'carrying rifles' ... None of the thirteen were carrying nail bombs, none of the thirteen were carrying pistols, none of the thirteen were carrying rifles; do you follow that?

General Sir Michael Jackson: I hear what you are telling me, but this is surely a matter for the tribunal.

*

More evidence that the army's actions on Bloody Sunday were premeditated came in September 2000 with the discovery of a leaked recording between two security force personnel.

The tape, covertly recorded by the IRA in 1972 and inexplicably only released to the Derry Journal *newspaper 28 years later, captured a conversation between two unnamed men after the British army had opened fire on civilian marchers.*

In the tape and transcript, one person claimed that the army doctor at the hospital spoke of 'pulling the stiffs out there as fast as they can get them out', and that General Ford was 'lapping it up' in the Bogside. The Derry Journal *said it was convinced the tape was authentic.*[6]

From a leaked security force recording, released to the *Derry Journal* by sources within the IRA in September 2000:

Voice 1: Bombardier [redacted] is here, what does he want?

Voice 2: I don't know, what does he want?

Voice 1: Look there's obviously been a hell of a sort out ... The whole thing's in chaos ...

Voice 2: Yeah, obviously.

Voice 1: I think it's gone badly wrong in the Rossville ... the doctor's just been up the hospital and they're pulling the stiffs out there as fast as they can get them out.

Voice 2: There's nothing wrong with that, Alan.

Voice 1: Well, there is because they're the wrong people ... There's about nine and fifteen killed by the Parachute Regiment in the Rossville area ... they're all women, children, fuck knows what, and they're still going up there ... I mean their Pigs [armoured cars] are just full of bodies ... There's a three-tonner up there with bodies in.

Voice 2: The padre's a bit upset. He's going off to see the commander about all the ill-treatment.

Voice 1: General Ford?

Voice 2: Yeah.

Voice 1: He was lapping it up.

Voice 2: Who was?

Voice 1: Ford.

Voice 2: Was he?

Voice 1: Yeah ... he said it was the best thing he'd seen for a long time.

Voice 2: Interesting, isn't it?

Voice 1: 'Well done, 1 PARA,' he said. 'Look at them 24 million dollar.'

Voice 2: Good, excellent.

Voice 1: And he said, you know, this is what should happen.

Voice 2: Yeah.

Voice 1: He said we're far too passive and I'll tell you later.

Voice 2: Yes, okay. Bye-bye.

Voice 1: Ciao.

In another exchange, one man refers to the troops deployed in Derry, saying, 'They've been here over the weekend. We've had a pretty good bloodbath here this evening … which you'll probably hear on the late news.' Another conversation features the voice of a BBC reporter.

The recording also included dark humour, references to the 'beautiful picture' of a priest leaning over a dead man, and claims that Bogside rioters had brought out the body of an already-dead girl to boost their casualty rates. The original tape and its 25-page long transcript was submitted to Lord Saville.

*

Jackie O'Reilly: Mickey lived through every single day of the inquiry. It was a lifeline to him; he held on to that lifeline believing that maybe, just maybe, this time they would be proven innocent.

Geraldine McBride: The more I found out, I realized that a lot of the soldiers were pawns. I couldn't believe that it was the government who had created the situation. I gave everybody the benefit of the doubt, but when I found out there was preparation behind it all, I realized we were like fish in a barrel. It affected me, and only for Hugo, I don't know how I would have coped. I don't think I ever went back to the person I was.

John Kelly: My mother died six months before the inquiry ended – she didn't live to see the end of it. I told her before she died that we had won the case and Michael's name was cleared. She had become very ill and had taken a few strokes and was deteriorating all the time. I would update her, and she needed that peace of mind. She always had the photograph of Michael beside her on the bedside. I told her that his name was cleared, and everybody else's name was cleared, and she said, 'That's grand, son, that's grand.' So, she was happy, and she passed away happy.

Siblings Kay and Gerry Duddy attended the inquiry when Bishop Daly gave evidence in February 2001 to show support. As a young priest, Daly had tried to save their brother Jackie. Kay brought with her a relic the bishop hadn't seen since 1972 – the white handkerchief he had waved aloft on Bloody Sunday.

Bishop Edward Daly: I had left the handkerchief inside Jackie's shirt to try and staunch the blood. It had been with the Duddy family all that time since. It had come back with Jackie's belongings from the hospital, but I wasn't aware of that. I just knew that it was out there somewhere. Then I found out that Kay Duddy had it because she brought it with her when I gave evidence to the Saville Inquiry. She was standing at the bottom of the Guildhall stairs with the handkerchief; that totally broke me up that day. Giving evidence was bad enough, but that just cracked me up. It was so emotional. I'm aware it has since become a very powerful symbol, but I never thought of that at the time.

Frances Gillespie: It did affect Daniel terrible. The children were never told about it. When the Saville Inquiry started, he just relived it all.

Anne Grant: When he [Paddy Walsh] had to go to the Saville Tribunal to talk about it, he had just come out of a major operation, but nothing was stopping him from going. He had to do it. He was so sick, you can tell my father was just off the operating bed, but he wanted to make sure he gave his evidence. I was living in Glasgow at the time, and I'd phone my daddy at night and talk about what had happened that day.

Regina McLaughlin: I didn't go to a lot of the inquiry. We all went to see the soldier who shot Daddy. I told the family when he was going to be on, and they all wanted to be at that one. Most of us went, and it was quite hard, especially watching Mammy; that was hard. I got more understanding of Bloody Sunday by going to the inquiry than I did at home, because we never actually spoke about it at home.

Mark Durkan: People were generally appreciative of your presence at the inquiry. They would share some of their feelings on particular evidence that week, and you got to see how much it affected those who lost people or who were wounded themselves. I learned a lot about them in that sense. The resilience that they showed through all of this was remarkable.

Kevin McDaid: The people who needed justice most are all dead and buried, with only one parent left by the time the report came through. I saw what my mother and father went through; it was soul-destroying to see what they went through over the years. They never had a life after that, they just survived from day to day. You never saw her enjoying herself. They weren't there for the inquiry; it just wasn't fair. Never in a million years did I think it would take this long to get answers.

Mickey McKinney: I was waking very early in the mornings, and it was constantly part of your life.

Gleann Doherty: Bloody Sunday completely changed my life without me even realizing it. It was there all the time, but I never really sat down and thought about it – my da was shot on Bloody Sunday and that was it. It was a matter of fact and I have lived with it all my life. It's like being born with one arm – you have no choice but to just get on with it. You could see other people around you and their fathers were there, out playing football with them, but because I was so used to never having a father, I can't even say I missed him because I never had him to miss. My sister had the privilege of seeing him for seven years, and me and Colleen had nothing, no memories, nothing.

Geraldine Doherty: It was bad enough hearing all the evidence here in your own town, but in London you felt like strangers, isolated and out in the cold. My mother was sick but she was a very strong, powerful woman and didn't let it beat her. I often think to myself, could I do that?

Eamonn McCann: Until the subject became mainstream, I don't think there ever was a single programme devoted to Bloody Sunday on any of the Irish television stations. In my experience, many campaigns begin to falter because there is simply nothing for people to do and no new initiatives to take. In the Bloody Sunday campaign there was always something to do every day, always a flurry of activity. You had no option but to keep at it.

Ciaran Shiels: There hasn't been another case like it. Ever. It was an epic. In terms of clients or witnesses who we represented over the period of years it took to get concluded, I don't think we will ever see the likes of it again.

The Bloody Sunday Inquiry ran from 1998 until early 2005 and was originally scheduled to report back by 2007. It became the longest legal proceedings in British or Irish history. In the years between the inquiry and its report, the Bloody Sunday Trust set up its award-winning Museum of Free Derry in the city's Bogside in 2006, at the heart of where the killings took place.

In 2010, with the report imminent and rumours of government censorship rife, families campaigned again. This time to see Lord Saville's report in its entirety and without redactions.

CHAPTER 40

'Innocent!'

Derry Journal's front page declares its citizens 'Innocent',
15 June 2010.

Almost forty years after events in Derry, a date was announced for the publication of the Report of the Bloody Sunday Inquiry – *15 June 2010. It was a day long awaited. As the date approached it was agreed that Mark Durkan, then MP for the city's Foyle constituency, would travel to London and make himself available in Westminster for the report's publication.*

Mark Durkan MP: There was a lot of suspicion around the report, how it was going to be handled and the plans for its publication. When we discussed what should happen on the day, it was clear that it was going to be published by way of a statement in the House of Commons and would then be open to questions, so it was decided early on in my conversations with the relatives that I should be in Westminster. I was to attend a controlled reading of the report and to later speak in parliament. I was also to be allowed the only phone call into the Guildhall that day through a secure line to gauge families' reactions back in Derry. That was it, I needed to be in London, but I hated the idea of not being in Derry. It was terrible leaving Derry the day before the report. You felt this sense of trepidation; you hoped for a good report, but had all those natural suspicions and doubts.

Kevin McDaid: For a few days before it, I didn't sleep much and I didn't eat a lot; my nerves were wrecked. That day I got up really early and, before 7am, I wondered: did we need milk? We didn't need milk, but I went out looking for it anyway. I didn't come back for an hour, but I couldn't tell you where I went. I met the rest of the family at the monument, and everything seemed unreal, it didn't seem like it was happening. We were there, but my mind was all over the place.

Regina McLaughlin: I've always said I felt Daddy's presence as soon as I got to the point that their march stopped in William Street. I didn't connect with 30 January because we didn't go on marches, but on 15 June I felt as though we were finishing the steps that he took. I felt Daddy there. To finish what he started was the greatest honour for me. I didn't like all the cameras and the media. Our family would be quite quiet and shy, and the spectacle of it all was difficult for us. But it was amazing to walk through those streets and see the people. I think the Derry people were just amazing.

John McKinney: Looking at the pictures of us walking into the Guildhall that morning, you can really see the pressure we were under. This was it – and it was an incredible amount of pressure. I was the first person in the door of the Guildhall beside Paul Doherty. Everyone was taking their time, but I needed to get in. We were searched and had to go through an electronic scanner and hand in our phones.

Martin McGuinness: The publication of the Saville Report was done in highly secretive conditions in terms of how the families would view it. We were invited on the same terms; in fact I was in a lockdown situation also in the City Hotel, just myself and Connor Murphy. The media were there too and others, but it was just us two in the room with the government officials and we were given our copies the same time as the families.

Olive Bonner: Me and Bernard were inside the Guildhall for the pre-read, but I don't actually remember going up the stairs inside. I was just suddenly upstairs in the main hall. I was shaking. My heart was thumping. There were tables everywhere and the lawyers and solicitor were all standing around. Everyone was allocated a table and the minute we got the report, I just went straight over to Hugh's section. I think, truth be told, everybody flicked straight to their own part looking for their relative; that's only natural. I said to Bernard, thank God. And we started crying. And I looked around us and almost everybody was crying. It felt like a whole weight was lifted. My mother and father didn't live to see it, Floyd didn't live to see it, but we got there. They are declared innocent.

Kevin McDaid: I kept wondering what Michael would think.

Jimmy Duddy: My daddy [campaigner John Duddy] died on 3 May, six weeks before Saville. It was very hard for the family and for me because, after all those years, suddenly he wasn't there any more, and I had to take his place. My son Sean went in with me for the report pre-read. I had terrible mixed feelings that day. Not excitement, but apprehension. What were we going to hear? The legal people had the important bits ready for us, so we didn't have to go through everything, and the nerves were allayed.

*

From the Principal Conclusions and Overall Assessment of the Bloody Sunday Inquiry, published 15 June 2010; Section 5.4:

> Our overall conclusion is that there was a serious and widespread loss of fire discipline among the soldiers of Support Company.[1]

*

Bridie McGuigan: I remember asking Michael Mansfield and Des Doherty what was in the report, and they told me it said quite clearly Barney was innocent. I just cried. Later, I went through the report and just cried as I read it. I think I was in shock that day and am only coming round now.

Frances Gillespie: You had a knot in your stomach about what they were going to say. You knew in your heart they were innocent, but you were waiting. My own son was upstairs at the pre-read with my son-in-law Charlie – they went in because I couldn't do it – and when I walked up the stairs my son burst out crying. It was a good thing in a way, because they were innocent, and you heard their names getting read out. It was brilliant.

Kevin McDaid: Within about ten minutes it was all over. We got what we wanted, maybe more. You just read through your own wee bit, selfishly, and then read it again and again.

*

From the Principal Conclusions and Overall Assessment of the Bloody Sunday Inquiry, published 15 June 2010; Section 5.5:

> The firing by soldiers of 1 PARA on Bloody Sunday caused the deaths of 13 people and injury to a similar number, none of whom was

posing a threat of causing death or serious
injury. What happened on Bloody Sunday
strengthened the Provisional IRA, increased
nationalist resentment and hostility towards
the Army and exacerbated the violent conflict
of the years that followed. Bloody Sunday was
a tragedy for the bereaved and the wounded,
and a catastrophe for the people of Northern
Ireland.[2]

*

Mark Durkan: As I understand it, only one soldier took
their pre-read in the Ministry of Defence, and it was General
Mike Jackson. I assume there were legal people present too, but
I was told that Jackson was the only one to have availed of the
pre-read.

*

*Mary Donaghey, sister of Gerald Donaghey, was seriously ill
by the time of the report's publication. Her daughter and fellow
campaigner Geraldine, and Gerald's boyhood best friend,
Donnacha McFeely, attended the pre-read on her behalf.*

Geraldine Doherty: We were the only family who were disappointed on 15 June. My mother wasn't well – just the week
before we had been told that her chemo didn't work, and they
weren't going to give her any more treatment. She put on a brave
face, but she was scared.

I saw Patricia Coyle coming towards me and I knew by the
look on her face that it was going to be bad news. I asked, 'What
about the nail bombs?' and she shook her head. 'No, Geraldine.'
I just broke down, knowing this was my mother's worst fear,
thinking, 'How am I going to tell my mammy this?'

From the Principal Conclusions and Overall Assessment of the Bloody Sunday Inquiry, published 15 June 2010; Section 3.111:

Gerald Donaghey was taken by car to the Regimental Aid Post of 1st Battalion, The Royal Anglian Regiment, which was at the western end of Craigavon Bridge, which spans the River Foyle. There four nail bombs were found in his pockets. The question arose as to whether the nail bombs were in his pockets when he was shot or had been planted on him later by the security forces. We have considered the substantial amount of evidence relating to this question and have concluded, for reasons that we give, that the nail bombs were probably on Gerald Donaghey when he was shot. However, we are sure that Gerald Donaghey was not preparing or attempting to throw a nail bomb when he was shot; and we are equally sure that he was not shot because of his possession of nail bombs. He was shot while trying to escape from the soldiers.[3]

The main report gave credence to military witnesses over civilian evidence in relation to the planting of nail bombs. Particularly that of a Corporal 150, who 'stated in his written evidence for the Widgery Inquiry that he did not "put a nail bomb or any similar object in his [Gerald Donaghey's] pocket, and no one else had an opportunity to do so". He gave similar oral evidence to the Widgery Inquiry. He told this Inquiry that he had "no idea" how the nail bombs got into Gerald Donaghey's pockets.' The Inquiry's conclusions on this aspect shocked many.[4]

From the Report of the Bloody Sunday Inquiry on the question of planting nail bombs:

> We are convinced that nail bombs could not
> have been planted on Gerald Donaghey when
> he was at Barrier 20. We do not see how, at
> this temporary location, any soldier could
> have been in possession of nail bombs, or how
> any of them could have had the opportunity
> to place four of them in Gerald Donaghey's
> pockets without others, including the civilians
> still in the area and close to the cars,
> being likely to observe what was happening.
> Furthermore, any soldier or soldiers planting
> nail bombs on Gerald Donaghey would have to
> have been content to see a colleague then
> drive the car with these devices on board.
> We accordingly reject the submission made
> on behalf of a number of former and serving
> police officers that the planting of nail
> bombs by soldiers at Barrack Street was 'a
> credible possibility that cannot be dismissed'.
> … In view of Corporal 150's evidence, and the
> fact that at best they had only a very short
> time close to the car as it was driven from
> Barrier 20, there can be no question of the
> police at the junction of Bishop Street and
> Barrack Street having planted the nail bombs.[5]

The report also noted that the officers present at the junction of Bishop Street and Barrack Street were from County Fermanagh so the suggestion that one or the other could have brought bombs to the city with them or sourced them locally, was 'highly implausible, and to our minds, unacceptable'.[6]

The report placed little credence on evidence to the contrary. This included forensics that the fatal bullet in fact went through one of Gerard's pockets before killing him – a pocket supposedly containing one of the nail bombs. Of this, Saville said, 'the fact that the bomb in the left jacket pocket was not damaged by the bullet passing through that pocket does not assist us in determining whether or not the bomb was there when Gerald Donaghey was shot.'[7]

Conal McFeely: I remember going up the stairs in the midst of all the joy; Geraldine was there. Mary Donaghey had come up in the lift and was quite ill, and I just knew without speaking how they both felt; their eyes told the story.

Raymond Rogan: I was interested in trying to guess what they would do about young Donaghey because, on the face of it, it was really the only case where they had said someone was carrying bombs. Just how were they going to get out of that? What kind of answer could Saville come up with? The answer was 'probability'. How can you 'probably' be carrying bombs? The soldier who drove my car went on record as saying he wouldn't have got into my car if he had seen any bombs. That was my feeling: that in this one area – young Donaghey – they were going to try and make a case for some justification, no matter how slight. And they did.

Jackie O'Reilly: I just burst out crying. Everyone was scared to begin with, but once we saw the lawyers' faces we knew it was positive news. Except for Geraldine and Mary; they were devastated. Everybody was so joyful and then you looked at them and realized that one person (Gerald Donaghey) didn't get their full declaration of innocence. That was so unfair.

Bridie McGuigan: I always only ever wanted someone to tell me the truth and finally it was done on 15 June, and, just like at his death, I wanted to be the one to tell our children the results and I did. The heavens wept the day Barney was buried and the sun shone the day he was cleared.

Kay Duddy: All I wanted to do was run downstairs and tell the rest of the families, but we had to wait for literally hours before we could see anybody. Everything was tinged with sadness that day, but the adrenaline carried you on. There was such a calm in the air, an elation that you couldn't put into words.

Martin McGuinness: We went through the summary and were delighted before we had even seen the reactions of the families. We knew it was good and that the families would be pleased with this. We then charged over to the Guildhall.

At around 2pm, the hundreds of other relatives who had gathered downstairs in the Guildhall were finally allowed to join their siblings upstairs and find out Saville's verdict.

Kevin McDaid: I'd been off the cigarettes for a year, but I don't know how many I smoked that day. The whole day felt like a lifetime waiting for the brother and sister coming upstairs in the afternoon; it was like a swarm of bees coming up to find out the news. Bridie was crying.

Susie Campbell: We'd been waiting downstairs for hours, hoping it would be good news. Thank God, when we finally got up to see Kay and Gerry, we knew we'd done it, we'd proved Jackie innocent at last.

Freya McClements, a BBC reporter covering the report's publication: I remember, as a reporter does, stopping these two women outside the Guildhall and asking them why they had come, and they said they had been on the march on the day of Bloody Sunday and they just had to come to hear Lord Saville's verdict; that this was a wrong that had been done to Derry and its people, and those people had to be there to hear it put right. It was as though all the streets running down into the Bogside had been turned into rivers of people, and wherever I looked there were just more and more of them, person after person after person, thousands of them, all making their way towards the Guildhall Square.[8]

Having earlier relinquished his phone to security, former Derry MP and Deputy First Minister Mark Durkan was permitted one phone call from the House of Commons – to the families in Derry.

Mark Durkan: After seeing the report, we had our one phone call just before 2pm. It was Mickey McKinney who answered the phone. He asked me what I thought, but I wanted to know his reaction firstly. It was actually very emotional. Then I spoke to John Kelly and Mickey Bridge about certain aspects. I couldn't speak after the phone call, in light of the report and the full flood of emotion. I just didn't know what to expect in the chamber.

Those inside the Guildhall for the pre-read were to remain under lockdown until the British prime minister officially announced the findings of the report to the British parliament at 3.30pm. Determined to get the word out first, some relatives inside the Guildhall climbed to its windows to give the 'thumbs-up' of a good report to the thousands waiting outside. This gesture eclipsed Cameron's address by mere minutes, amid cheers of relief.

Conal McFeely: The people who stole the show were those who put their thumbs out the window! The Northern Ireland Office had lost at that stage and the families had won. Despite all the protocol and security, it was upstaged by two Derry thumbs. That to me was the story of the day.

Freya McClements: I was in the press area up on the walls directly facing the Guildhall and we were all watching the Guildhall clock tick towards half past three. Then there was this magical moment, when a window opened in the Guildhall and the families inside gave the thumbs-up to the waiting crowd, and the square just exploded with clapping and cheering, with a mixture of joy and tears, because people knew now that it was going to be okay, that the report was going to deliver what they wanted. I knew that would be the start of my piece, and I remember writing later that afternoon: 'It was the sign everybody had been looking for, but it came in a manner nobody had expected.'

John McKinney: Me and Paul Doherty and a few others got our own way when we put our thumbs out the window – imagine, a thumbs-up beat all of their security!

At 3.30pm, an outdoor big screen in Derry's Guildhall Square began live-broadcasting an historic address from the British prime minister in the House of Commons.[9]

From British prime minister David Cameron's address to Parliament on 15 June 2010:

I am deeply patriotic; I never want to believe anything bad about our country; I never want to call into question the behaviour of our soldiers and our Army, which I believe to be the finest in the world. And I have seen for myself the very difficult and dangerous circumstances in which we ask our soldiers to serve. But the conclusions of this report are absolutely clear: there is no doubt; there is nothing equivocal; there are no ambiguities. What happened on Bloody Sunday was both unjustified and unjustifiable. It was wrong.

Lord Saville concludes that the soldiers of Support Company who went into the Bogside 'did so as a result of an order … which should have not been given' by their commander. He finds that 'on balance the first shot in the vicinity of the march was fired by the British Army' and that 'none of the casualties shot by soldiers of Support Company was armed with a firearm'.

He also finds that 'there was some firing by republican paramilitaries … but … none of this firing provided any justification for the shooting of civilian casualties', and that 'in no case was any warning given before soldiers opened fire'.

Lord Saville also finds that Support Company 'reacted by losing their self-control … forgetting or ignoring their instructions and training' and acted with 'a serious and widespread loss of fire discipline'.

He finds that 'despite the contrary evidence given by the soldiers … none of them fired in response to attacks or threatened attacks by nail or petrol bombers' and that many of the soldiers 'knowingly put forward false accounts in order to seek to justify their firing'.

What is more, Lord Saville says that some of those killed or injured were clearly fleeing or going to the assistance of others who were dying. The report refers to one person who was shot while 'crawling … away from the soldiers' and mentions another who was shot, in all probability, 'when he was lying mortally wounded on the ground'. And the report refers to a father who was 'hit and injured by Army gunfire after he had gone to … tend his son'.

For those looking for statements of innocence, Saville says: 'The immediate responsibility for the deaths and injuries on Bloody Sunday lies with those members of Support Company whose unjustifiable firing was the cause of those deaths and injuries', and, crucially, that 'none of the casualties was posing a threat of causing death or serious injury, or indeed was doing anything else that could on any view justify their shooting'. What happened should never, ever have happened. The families of those who died should not have had to live with the pain and hurt of that day, and with a lifetime of loss. Some members of our armed forces acted wrongly. The Government are ultimately responsible for the conduct of the armed forces, and for that, on behalf of the Government – indeed, on behalf of our country – I am deeply sorry.

Kay Duddy: My jaw just dropped when I heard Cameron's speech. I couldn't believe that someone had the guts to stand up and say what really happened – and in the House of Commons of all places. It was incredible.

Mickey McKinney: When Cameron apologized on behalf of the government, that was fantastic. But when he apologized on behalf of the country, I thought Jesus, he's really doing it. That went further – it went the distance. Someone tapped me on the shoulder and said, 'Do you hear that outside?' You could hear the cheers of everyone watching it in the square; it was brilliant.

Jimmy Duddy: There was excitement and tears inside when we watched Cameron's speech on the big screen. I remember Michael Mansfield QC wasn't happy because the report didn't go high enough.

Freya McClements: When David Cameron began speaking, people around me were muttering; they were saying, 'He's a Conservative prime minister, he's not going to apologize', and then there was this moment when the mood changed. It was as if the realization swept over the crowd, and people somehow knew he was going to apologize just before he said it. That people were able to stand in Guildhall Square and watch the British, Conservative prime minister in the House of Commons, apologizing directly to them – that was so significant.

Kevin McDaid: Cameron done well. I was surprised by what he said, but he should have used the word *murder*. It was worth waiting for, but it should have happened years and years ago. I'll never forget it.

Following the prime minister's historic apology, Derry MP Mark Durkan delivered what history will deem the most powerful address of the day. Durkan became visibly emotional as he recited aloud within the House the names of each of those killed on Bloody Sunday, thus fulfilling his promise to families.

From Mark Durkan's address to Parliament following the publication of the *Report of the Bloody Sunday Inquiry* on 15 June 2010:

This is a day of huge moment and deep emotion in Derry. The people of my city did not just live through Bloody Sunday; they have lived with it since.

… Will the Prime Minister confirm that each and every one of the victims Bernard McGuigan, 41; Gerald Donaghey, 17; Hugh Gilmour, 17; Jackie Duddy, 17; Gerard McKinney, 34; James Wray, 22; John Young, 17; Kevin McElhinney, 17; Michael Kelly, 17; Michael McDaid, 20; Patrick Doherty, 31; William McKinney, 27; William Nash, 19; and John Johnston, 59 – are all absolutely and totally exonerated by today's report, as are all the wounded?

… Sadly, only one parent of the victims has survived to see this day and hear the Prime Minister's open and full apology on the back of this important report. Lawrence McElhinney epitomises the dignity and determination of all the families who have struggled and strived to exonerate their loved ones and have the truth proclaimed.

The Prime Minister's welcome statement and the statement that will be made by the families on the steps of the Guildhall will be the most significant records of this day on the back of the report that has been published. However, perhaps the most important and poignant words from today will not be heard here or on the airwaves. Relatives will stand at the graves of victims and their parents to tell of a travesty finally arrested, of innocence vindicated and of promises kept, and as they do so, they can invoke the civil rights anthem when they say, 'We have overcome. We have overcome this day.'[10]

Jimmy Duddy: We had hoped that Saville would go higher. He said there was no evidence, but the evidence was phenomenal. The fact that they had just agreed a policy to shoot selected ringleaders at riots – that's a shoot-to-kill policy. What about all the doctored soldiers' statements? All those versions they altered. What about the helicopter footage that went missing, or all the army photographs? The British military hold on to a lot of stuff; I have a feeling it's all there somewhere. I lost my faith in Saville because of the way he protected the soldiers in England.

Joe Mahon: Will the army learn? They'll learn, yes, but they'll learn the wrong lessons. They'll learn to cover things up better. They'll learn no moral lessons from Bloody Sunday.

Before 4pm, the hundreds of relatives, wounded and their families emerged from the Guildhall to face the estimated crowd of ten thousand that awaited them outside. Several would speak publicly to the square, and details of every one of the dead and injured were read aloud by relatives as they were declared innocent.

Conal McFeely: The families and wounded were tense and wholly unprepared for the media circus awaiting them. In the midst of all the emotion, Dave Duggan, a highly respected Derry writer, had the foresight to go and talk to the family members who were going to go outside and speak to the world. He told them not to be afraid of expressing things in their own words and to relax. That hall was a pressure chamber and here was Dave and Maoliosa Boyle sitting in a corner calmly preparing families to go outside.

Mickey McKinney: I was the first person to come out of the Guildhall and I couldn't believe it when I saw the crowds. They all seemed so close, and I remember thinking, 'Look at the emotion on their faces.' I realized how much this all meant to them.

Eamonn McCann: It's the feeling I remember, not the scenes as such. It was emotions I had never felt before. An emotional buzz spread across the families and the crowd and enveloped everybody. It was a great day for the families, but also a triumph for the campaign, in which the families had played a major and central role.

Jimmy Duddy: I was in tears – I didn't know how I was going to go out there. I couldn't get over the fact my father wasn't there to see it. Just six weeks. If the report had come out in March, like it was supposed to, then he would have been alive to see it.

Regina McLaughlin: I was so aware of Mammy, that she was going to hear me say that Daddy was 'deliberately targeted' – that's the words I used, because they are the words that struck me and that broke my heart that morning. It needed to be said, and I was quite aware of that. My mother was in the house watching and she was very proud, but heartbroken. She didn't know that he was deliberately targeted either.

The other thing was finding out that the bullet that killed Gerald Donaghey came through my daddy and hit him. I just thought, Oh my God, that bullet came through our daddy and killed him. All the accusations they made about Gerald, but in actual fact, he wasn't shot because he had anything on him. He was shot by accident.

Olive Bonner: I never thought so many people would turn up – the crowd was spilling onto the Strand Road. I couldn't believe it. I didn't realize it would be such big news. A friend of mine in Spain phoned me to tell me she was watching everything in Spain; my cousin from America phoned too. It made the news all over the world. The truth was out – now everybody knows they were innocent. Everybody.

Teresa McGowan: I wrote about it in my diary, describing it as one of the greatest days of my life. I'll never forget it. When you're a child, you think your best day is going to be your First

Communion, but I think the publication of that report was my best day. Thank God we got good news. I just remember looking out and seeing my family all standing there. I'll never forget it. It's sad that Danny wasn't there for the end of it all.

Eamonn McCann: My thought in the Guildhall was just, 'Jesus, we've done it, it's amazing.' It had taken so long, and then to finally have the day arrive and the families happy, it just was tremendous. It was the campaign's vindication, but I did feel a great personal joy. This was one of the things in my life that seemed so impossible, but we did it, we actually did it. I was literally jumping with excitement – I couldn't contain myself. I felt a great sense of vindication and joy and of relief that it was over.

Martin McGuinness: Being there in the Guildhall Square and seeing it being thronged with citizens clearly showed how much all of this meant to the people of Derry and people all over Ireland. They were very interested in the Saville Tribunal. We were very interested in it because we wanted the families to get what they demanded.

We also had other motivations. I was very interested to see what Saville would say about the testimony of people like me and others in the IRA. This isn't much talked about, but Saville vindicated everything that we said during the course of the tribunal. He said the IRA held absolutely no responsibility for what happened that day. That was something I never expected, especially from a British law lord, and I suppose that it's to his credit, too, that he was prepared to step across that line.

Joe Mahon: It was great to see so many people; emotions were high. But for them to say sorry means nothing to me; they could have said that at Widgery. They put the families through so much over the years, plus how many young fellas died after joining the IRA after Bloody Sunday or done time in jail. Fellas who would never have considered joining the IRA if it wasn't for Bloody Sunday.

John McKinney: Personally, I think 15 June done me a lot of good, especially because it showed the world what the Brits had done on Bloody Sunday. We got messages from America, from Russia, from China; the whole world was told what really happened, so it was all worth it. It was unbelievable. I think Derry has never seen a day like it, at least not since Dana came home from winning the Eurovision! But seriously, there was just a good feeling in the air; everyone was smiling and crying. It was unreal.

Mark Durkan: It was a great day and a great day in Derry. I felt very detached and disconnected, especially when I saw a few clips of what was happening in Derry. A number of MPs spoke of seeing the pictures from Derry and talking about Derry, as opposed to Parliament, and that said a lot to me about the importance of the images and messages coming from Guildhall Square.

Ciaran Shiels: I think that we have come as close as we will ever do to uncovering the truth as to what happened that day and leading up to it, and exposing the Widgery Tribunal as being procedurally unfair towards the families, wounded and the people of Derry, as well as being substantively corrupt.

Ivan Cooper: I was impressed with Saville's report, and I have never had a doubt about the innocence of those killed on Bloody Sunday. Not a single shred of doubt.

In the decades since Bloody Sunday, Captain Michael Jackson was appointed Chief of the General Staff (CGS) of the British army ahead of the Iraq war in 2003, becoming Britain's top soldier. He was knighted in 1998, becoming General Sir Michael Jackson.

On 3 November 2010, just months after the Report of the Bloody Sunday Inquiry, *campaigner Mary Donaghey died in Derry. She remained determined until the end.*

Geraldine Doherty: My mother died on the day there was a debate about the Bloody Sunday report in Parliament. A week before my mother died, she said to me, 'Geraldine, will you fight on?' And I said, 'Of course I will – I'll do everything I can.' She was there from the beginning and fought it until the end. All I can do is keep highlighting his name.

Conal McFeely: Gerald's good name has never been fully exonerated, and it still beggars belief how Lord Saville, despite a welter of evidence and witnesses, failed to address the issue that soldiers planted nail bombs on his body to justify their actions. Yet Saville concluded all those killed on Bloody Sunday were innocent and that Gerald didn't pose a threat at the time he was shot. The people of Derry know the truth and there is no stain on Gerald's name – he was just seventeen, innocent and unarmed.

*

Caroline O'Donnell: The campaign was worth it – to get some kind of justice. My father would have been in disbelief at what was achieved. To walk around and not be seen as an IRA terrorist or someone who had a gun that day, that would have been brilliant. He had to live with that all those years.

Paul Doherty: The way I think about it is that we buried our fathers and sons and brothers, but they buried the truth. We resurrected that truth when we took on the might of the British establishment, and despite everything, we made them listen to us. We set the truth free.

Frances Gillespie: You have to fight for justice, regardless of who you are or what your religion is. You have to. You can't just sit back and talk about it. It's just a pity Daniel wasn't here to see it. If he had been, I think he'd turn around and say to them, 'I *told you* we were innocent,' with a few four-letter words! It's hard to talk about because he's not here. It's hard because he had a very hard death. He is still here, though. I still talk to him. I still put him out his cup of tea every morning.

John Kelly: Fifty years is a long time in anyone's life. Most of the family members alive today were just children or teenagers, and many others were just starting out in married life when Bloody Sunday happened. Many are now senior citizens, and a lot more have passed away over, but the need for truth has never diminished. That day our lives changed for ever, it dictated how things went. We've dedicated most of our lives to the campaign for truth, justice and accountability. Truth is on our side, so I know we'll fight on now for justice, no matter how long it takes. We shall overcome.

Olive Bonner: I don't care who you are: Catholic, Protestant, Falls Road, Shankill Road – if you think your loved one was murdered, they have a right to go and fight for justice for them. If they see that we got it, they might say, 'The Bloody Sunday crowd did it, and that was after forty years,' and they would try themselves.

Diane Greer: Like so many others, I make no apology for working hard to try to create the circumstances where it will be acceptable to deal honestly and freely with your neighbour; to fight injustice together without fear of being labelled as a traitor, and to work for a society that embraces the principles of justice, equality and independence.

My children won't ever be given one side of the story – they will be encouraged to think for themselves ... form their own opinions and give voice to them, hopefully couched in an appreciation, not a fear, of diversity.[11]

Bridie Gallagher: It's horrifying that we had to wait so long to know what really happened. All those years gone. I would tell anyone that it was worth it. Never give up. I know it must be so hard at times, but keep going. There is no other nation like the British, but that is exactly why we needed to expose the truth. We half expected disappointment, but still tried. You live in hope and die in despair.

Leo Young: The killing of our John and all those who died will remain with me for ever. It's like an unrelenting pain that will never ease. If they had told the truth all those years ago it might have helped a lot, but we had to fight for everything we got. Imagine how people would react if this happened in London or Birmingham or Manchester – if British troops opened fire and shot civilians in the streets and then told lies about it afterwards. They would never forget, either. Nobody could. But we've had to live with it all these years.

John Kelly: In my house I still have a Mars Bar that my mother bought Michael the day he died. She used to buy him a Mars Bar as a treat every week, but that one was left uneaten. My mother wanted it to be buried with her, but we forgot to put it in her coffin along with the rest of Michael's belongings. Since then, I've always kept it. How could I throw it out now?

Kay Duddy: I wonder what our Jackie would make of it all. He never got to grow up, never had the chance to get married, or have babies or a life of his own – all the things people take for granted. We tried our best for him, and that's what matters. Wherever he is now, I hope he's smiling down.[12]

Afterword

John Kelly, brother of Michael Kelly, comforts Alana Burke, one of the wounded, after news that just one British soldier would be charged over the events of Bloody Sunday.

Fifty years on from Bloody Sunday in Ireland, the case remains unresolved.

The families' long campaign for truth and justice had achieved its first campaign aim of overturning the now-disgraced 1972 Widgery Report.

As a result of the subsequent second inquiry and its 2010 Report of the Bloody Sunday Inquiry, *campaigners achieved their second aim: the formal acknowledgement of the innocence of the victims. Clearing the names of all the killed or injured also vindicated the people of Derry. At last, the world knew that its people had, in fact, been telling the truth all along. The third campaign aim – justice against the perpetrators – proves elusive.*

In July 2012, the Police Service of Northern Ireland (PSNI) announced they were initiating a murder investigation into the events of Bloody Sunday. Unbelievably, it was the first ever police investigation into the shootings – 40 years after events had taken place.[1]

The probe, involving up to thirty detectives, concluded in December 2016 with the police submitting their files to the Public Prosecution Service of Northern Ireland, who would consider whether or not to press charges over Bloody Sunday.

In May 2017, news came that prosecutors were considering charges against eighteen soldiers over their involvement in Bloody Sunday as well as two alleged Official IRA members. Correspondence from the PPS also confirmed it was looking into charges of perjury against soldiers who testified.[2]

Finally, news came of a prosecution decision and the date was set for 14 March 2019. Representatives from every family affected by Bloody Sunday gathered in Derry's City Hotel, this author included.

After 47 years, the importance of this moment could not be understated. Saville's damning findings had finally laid the blame with the British army. They had fired first. Derry's dead had been shot in the back while running away, or while going to help others, or while waving redundant white handkerchiefs of truce. The truth was out.

As families waited, they thought of those lost that Sunday afternoon – or in the decades since. Few spoke as we waited for the PPS to address those gathered in the vast Corinthian Ballroom. Hopes were high. Anxieties were higher.

The decision came. Despite examining evidence in nineteen cases, only one former soldier would be charged for Bloody Sunday. Known under his cipher, Soldier F, this soldier faced prosecution for two murders and four attempted murders in Glenfada Park on 30 January 1972.[3]

The Director of the PPS summed up the decision to visibly devastated families.

Stephen Herron, Director of the Public Prosecution Service of Northern Ireland in 2019:

> It has been concluded that there is sufficient available evidence to prosecute one former soldier, Soldier F, for the murder of James Wray and William McKinney, and for the attempted murders of Joseph Friel, Michael Quinn, Joe Mahon and Patrick O'Donnell.
>
> In respect of the other eighteen suspects, including sixteen former soldiers and two alleged Official IRA members, it has been concluded that the available evidence is insufficient to provide a reasonable prospect of conviction.[4]

Emotions ran over. One or two families stormed out of the ballroom. Others sat quietly weeping in disbelief. Our table was silent at first, then just broken. I remember the feeling of watching my elder relatives, who had waited most of their lives for this.

At a press conference in the city's Guildhall afterwards, John Kelly, former chair of the Bloody Sunday Justice Campaign, expressed disappointment on behalf of all those left wanting by the day's decision, but welcomed news that six families would see a soldier in court. 'Their victory is our victory.'

Liam Wray: I'm very saddened for the other families. Their hearts must be broken. There are a lot of sad and heartbroken people today.[5]

John Kelly: It's been a long road, nearly fifty years, we're all getting old, a lot of people are dying, but as long as we're able to walk, we'll go after them and we certainly will not stop until we see justice for our loved ones.[6]

On 18 September 2019, the case of Soldier F began at Derry Magistrates Court, attended by some of the families and wounded.

However, their hopes of justice were halted abruptly on Friday 2 July 2021, when families and wounded were summoned to a meeting with the PPS. Also asked to attend this meeting was the family of fifteen-year-old Daniel Hegarty, who had been shot twice in the head in July 1972, alongside his cousin, who was shot and wounded.

Many other families and supporters, including this author, congregated downstairs and waited for news. The PPS told the families it intended to discontinue the prosecutions of both Soldier F for Bloody Sunday, and Soldier B for the separate killing of Hegarty.

The decision followed the collapse of an earlier case involving two soldiers, A and C, charged with the murder of Official IRA leader Joe McCann in Belfast in 1971– the court ruled that initial statements gathered by the Royal Military Police (RMP) in 1972 were inadmissible.

Following this decision the PPS reviewed the 'related evidential features' in both cases and concluded that there was 'no longer a reasonable prospect' of key evidence in proceedings against Soldier F and Soldier B being ruled admissible at their trials.[9]

Reacting to the news, Mickey McKinney, brother of William, said the decision represented 'another damning indictment of the British justice system', and warned it could undermine all other historical legacy investigation into civilian British army deaths in the early 1970s.[10]

Mickey McKinney: While Soldier F was being prosecuted for two counts of murder on Bloody Sunday, he in fact murdered five people that day. There is no dispute that his actions on Bloody Sunday resulted in two women being robbed of their husbands, twelve children being orphaned of their father, and dozens of young men and women deprived of a brother. Six parents also lost a son. These are the clear findings of the Bloody Sunday Inquiry and the responsibility that it attaches directly and unequivocally to the actions of Soldier F. This issue is far from concluded. We will fight on.

Liam Wray: The reaction wasn't of surprise; it was with some disappointment. It's not that Jim was less innocent today than he was yesterday. It's just that because of that set of circumstances we cannot pursue the case against Soldier F. Nonetheless, what we have done is highlight the injustice; we have pointed fingers at people, and from today on, going forward, others should hold the state to account to make sure such things are never again perpetrated against innocent people.[11]

John McKinney: It's days like this I think of my mother and father.[12]

The following day, a Saturday, around a thousand people came together at Guildhall Square in Derry for an impromptu rally in support of both the Bloody Sunday and Hegarty families.

Joe McKinney, brother of Willie McKinney: The truth about Bloody Sunday was set free on these steps in June 2010. We will keep going and will continue to pursue justice for our brothers and fathers who were murdered on our streets. We will meet head on any British attempts to subvert justice and the rule of law.[13]

As this book ends, families in Derry continue to legally challenge the prosecution decisions on Bloody Sunday.

In summer 2021, thousands of others left injured or bereaved were appalled at news of British government plans to scrap all legacy investigations into the Troubles. Effectively an amnesty, this would include all active investigations as well as future criminal or civil cases – or inquests – into Troubles-era crimes. In so doing, they brought together victims groups in the north, the main political parties north and south, the Irish government and prominent Irish-Americans, all united for the first time in opposition to the proposals, and in anger at what the British government is trying to do.

In September 2021, a report by academics at Queen's University, Belfast and the human rights NGO the Committee on the Administration of Justice concluded that the proposals represented 'one of the most sweeping amnesties introduced in any jurisdiction since 1945'; they were not only 'in clear breach of binding human rights standards' but were 'significantly more expansive' than those brought in by brutal Chilean dictator, Augusto Pinochet.[14]

Martin McGavigan, brother of Annette McGavigan, a 14-year-old girl shot dead by a British soldier in 1971: The soldier who shot Annette may never be questioned. The British government has decided that the rule of law does not apply to Irish people, not even children. If a 14-year-old child was shot in England, it is inconceivable that the investigation would be dropped, but this is exactly what the British government wants to happen in Ireland. [15]

Gerry Duddy: It's a travesty. So many people still need answers. Britain is still playing games with people's lives, still holding back, still keeping its secrets.[16]

*

Fifty years on, the real lesson of Bloody Sunday is the determination of its people. When innocents die or soldiers kill their own civilians, people should always rise and demand that the rule of law should apply. True democracy – and humanity – demands no less.

Acknowledgements

When approached to write this book ahead of the 50th anniversary of Bloody Sunday, I knew that the timing was right. Long overdue perhaps, as the voices of those most affected have so often been lost in the din of 'official' accounts. Despite the passage of time, almost everyone I spoke to wanted to be a part of this project.

Sadly, some died before this came to fruition, including Hugh McMonagle, who was among the men who tried to save my uncle Jackie on Bloody Sunday. When I confided in him about the book, Hugh was the first to put his name forward. Thank you, sir. Another whose encouragement really mattered was my friend Arlene Wege, who died in January 2021. I got there, Arlene. You were right – and I couldn't be prouder.

As the book neared completion in summer 2021, Derry lost yet more of its Bloody Sunday family with the passing of Ita McKinney, wife of Gerry McKinney and the last widow of Bloody Sunday. Of the generation remaining, we also lost Kathleen Brotherton, a sister of Willie McKinney. In September 2021, news came of the death of Fionnbarra Ó Dochartaigh, a Derry co-founder of NICRA featured in this book, and of Pat Hume, a titan of Derry and wife of the late John Hume. My love and respect to all their families.

I realize now that the events of Bloody Sunday have influenced much in my recent career – a path I had not expected but one that changed my perception for ever. For that, I thank the then-Chair of the Bloody Sunday Trust, Eamonn McCann, and a random phone call in 2008 inviting me to join its board of Trustees. Working alongside this group of people over the years since opened my eyes to so many important issues of Derry history and ways in which we could help the families, wounded and community affected by not just Bloody Sunday, but so many other events and incidents throughout our recent history. I wanted to be useful somehow. By helping document and highlight these experiences, I hope I have.

On Bloody Sunday would not be possible without the consent, goodwill, and often, the friendship, of those I've interviewed over the years or anew for this book, and, in some cases, their family and descendants.

This book belongs to the families and the wounded, to eyewitnesses and all the people affected by events 50 years ago – and those who support them. Too numerous to name again here, I'm immensely grateful to everyone involved in this book for their kindness and generosity in contributing new accounts, offering existing material or allowing me to include witness statements or previous work I have published. Many pointed me to other important sources too – thank you.

Others tell the civil rights story preceding Bloody Sunday from various sources – my thanks to them, and to the projects archiving them, like the Museum of Free Derry's *Free Derry Lives* exhibition and film. Collectively, these voices enrich this narrative with vivid memory and emotion. Thank you all for entrusting me to tell your story.

Also, appreciation to the people I wish I had interviewed for this project, but for one reason or another, didn't get the chance to ask, including Charlie Glenn, Scone Deery, Susan North and the family of James Porter. Naturally, this book also belongs to the many voices not mentioned within its pages, be they eyewitnesses, relatives, campaigners and activists. I only wish I could have said more and included more, but no book is long enough.

To my much-missed friends and colleagues at the Museum of Free Derry and the Bloody Sunday Trust, including John Kelly, Jean Hegarty, Rossa O'Dochartaigh, Naomi Petropolis, Jimmy Toye, Robin Percival, Leo Young, John McKinney, Eugene Coyle, Paul Doherty and museum curator, Adrian Kerr. This book follows a narrative of events in and around the Bogside of Derry researched meticulously by the museum, the Trust, and by Adrian Kerr in his book, *Free Derry: Protest and Resistance* (Guildhall Press, 2013), and I'm indebted to them for the guidance. I must also mention the wider Free Derry community who made such an impact during my years working there, and whose collective stories also inspire this 50th anniversary retelling.

Thanks also to newspapers and reporters who helped me when

Covid-19 restrictions kept me from their physical archives, most notably my brilliant former colleagues and friends at the *Derry Journal*, among them Sean McLaughlin, Theresa Casey and editor Brendan McDaid. Also, to the many newspapers from which I have quoted a wealth of highly relevant archive material, including the *Derry News*, the *Guardian*, *Irish News*, BBC News, *Belfast Telegraph*, *Irish Independent*, *New York Times*, *Birmingham Mail*, *Daily Mirror*, *Daily Telegraph*, *Daily Express*, *The Times*, ITN, and AP Archive for transcribed footage, and also to Channel 4 and Peter Taylor for their documentary work. To my friend and colleague Freya McClements, who provided rich source material on civil rights from her *Irish Times* work covering 50th anniversary events. Likewise, thanks to Jimmy McGovern and Charles McDougall for research during the Channel 4 drama documentary, *Sunday*, from which several Mary Donaghey quotes are taken.

To National Archives, UK, which now houses the *Bloody Sunday Inquiry* archive and related evidence and witness statements so integral to compiling this book. To Carol Cunningham and the women involved in our 2016 collection, *Beyond the Silence – Women's Unheard Voices from the Troubles* (Guildhall Press), several of whom appear throughout this book. To the Pat Finucane Centre, Creggan Enterprises, Sara Duddy, Anne Crilly, Diane Greer, Colum Eastwood and Ulster University's *CAIN* (Conflict Archive on the Internet) archive. Thanks also to John Teggart and the Ballymurphy families in Belfast whose own harrowing experience of the British Parachute Regiment in 1971 gives context to Bloody Sunday.

Thank you to Paul Hippsley at Derry's Guildhall Press for his faith, friendship and advice. To Sean O'Keefe at Liberties Press, Dublin, who originally published some of this material in my 2012 book on the Bloody Sunday Justice Campaign. To Four Courts Press in Dublin for allowing me to quote from Bishop Daly's autobiography, *Mister, Are You a Priest?* (2000), and Hachette Ireland, for allowing the inclusion of some details from their 2019 book, *Children of the Troubles: The Untold Story of the Children Killed in the Northern Ireland Conflict*, by Freya McClements and Joe Duffy. To other publishers I have quoted from, including Blackstaff Press in Belfast, Brandon Books in Kerry, Pluto Press in London and *Force 10: An Irish Journal* in Sligo.

I'm very grateful to Fearghal Shiels and Ciaran Shiels from Madden and Finucane Solicitors for advice, support and encouragement on this project, and for supporting my elder family in pursuit of justice. To my supervisors, Brandon Hamber and Adrian Grant, and, also, Rory O'Connell at Ulster University for supporting the first year of my PhD journey at the time of writing of this book. Also, to Carole Adams and Cúnamh in Derry for their support over the past few years.

To Ryan O'Doherty, Eamonn MacDermott and Paul O'Connor for their consistent advice and support and for lending me numerous books from their libraries during research. To Paula Gillespie for her wonderful professional author photographs.

To screenwriter Jimmy McGovern, Michael Mansfield QC, musician Christy Moore, authors Eamonn McCann, Anne Cadwallader, Susan McKay, Freya McClements and Don Mullan, and authors and broadcasters Peter Taylor and Joe Duffy for supporting this book. It means a lot.

I'm hugely thankful to Jake Lingwood, Sybella Stephens, and the team at Octopus Books in London, for recognising Bloody Sunday's importance beyond headlines and hype, and for inviting me to write this account. I'm very proud to be among the authors of Monoray. Thanks to Octopus's vision and initiative, the story of what happened in Derry will reach new audiences and hopefully educate many.

I am also indebted to the photographers whose work is included in this book, bringing these stories to life. My thanks to Bobby White, Eamon Melaugh, Michael McLoughlin, the late Clive Limpkin, Fionnbarra Ó Dochartaigh, Jim Davies, Gilles Peress, Fulvio Grimaldi, Derek Tucker, Stanley Matchett, Colman Doyle and William Rukeyser. Thanks again here to Sean McLaughlin, an authority on the *Derry Journal*'s historic photo archive, to families for allowing use of their personal photos.

On a personal note, I need to thank my immediate neighbours in the Seven Streets of Rosemount who are wonderful and who have had the good grace never to mention my late-night loud music when writing. Especially Jed McClelland, and Noel Duddy next door. To David and everyone in Park Avenue shop, and to Brooke

Park Café, who, unbeknownst to them, kept us sustained when the tide was against us. Also, my gratitude to both Sandino's Bar and the Grand Central Bar, pubs in which history can often be discussed and debated among regulars and civil rights veterans.

To my wider Duddy relatives, including Gerry and Eileen for sharing their stories, and Auntie Kay, who entrusted me with all ten volumes of her Saville Report for research. I hope I have done their story justice. To an abundance of friends who, during lockdown and afterwards, lent ear or respite. Mama Cass, Paula Gillespie, Brenda Brinkley, Freya McClements, Chris McConaghy, Ryan O'Doherty, Aisling Starrs, Katie Fitzpatrick, Áine Hassan, Sabrena Doherty, Mary McMichael, Dermie McClenaghan, Ian Cullen, Cat Pollock, Keith Farrell, Joe Mahon, Eamon O'Kane and, of course, Lynne Edgar and Felicity McCall. To Clarence, my lockdown buddy. Also, to Garry Leach, Patrick Maguire, Colm Wilde, Hugh Harley, Gary Doherty, Chris McDonagh, Paul Cassidy and Paul Martin. To those I love but have not listed here – thank you. A special thank you to St Paul's Primary School and St Mary's College in Derry for their inspiring past and future roles.

Thanks most of all to my family circle. To my mum, Susie Campbell, brothers Alan, Paul, Peter and David, their families, Leandra, Gemma, Claire and those sent to keep us on our toes: Faolan, Caoilte, Connla, Adam, Shannon and Sonny. To Granda Maurice, who left us just days ago. To all my Campbell family living in Derry and in England, my friends there also, including Emma, Amber, Jo, Matthew, Karl, the late Paul, Tom, Jonny and my best mate from university, Edd Barnes. To Jen and Bess in Canada, and loved ones in Belgium, New York, and elsewhere.

Lastly, to my daughter Saffron, who lives with my late nights and deadlines and loves me regardless.

Julieann Campbell
September 2021

APPENDIX 1

Speakers and Sources

Chris Armstrong As an 18-year-old, Chris Armstrong was in the Bogside in the early hours of 5 January 1969 and held the paint as the original slogan 'You Are Now Entering Free Derry' was painted on a wall. (Extract as given to author for the exhibition *Free Derry Lives* in 2019, courtesy of the Museum of Free Derry.)

Eamonn Baker A Queen's University student in 1972, Eamonn Baker returned home to Derry for the civil rights march on 30 January 1972. (Extracts taken from BSI statements, courtesy of National Archives, UK.)

Danny Begley Taller than most, Danny Begley lifted Liam Hillen up on his shoulders to reach the wall and paint the first slogan on Free Derry Corner – now an international landmark. (Extract as given to author for the exhibition *Free Derry Lives* in 2019, courtesy of the Museum of Free Derry.)

Rosemary Best A sister of Ranger William Best, a 19-year-old Derry man who was also a serving British soldier with the army's Royal Irish Rangers. In 1972, Best was lured home after falsely being told his mother was sick. He was then abducted and murdered by the IRA. Public outrage led to an IRA ceasefire. (Interview as given to author in 2017 as part of the Museum of Free Derry's *National Civil Rights Archive* and never before published.)

Olive Bonner Sister of 17-year-old Hugh Gilmour, who was shot dead just yards from his home in the Rossville Flats. Olive Bonner witnessed other people shot from the window of their family home and gave evidence to both inquiries. (Interview from author's research for 2012 book, *Setting the Truth Free* (Liberties Press).)

Denis Bradley Formerly Father Bradley and curate at Long Tower Parish in 1972 and present during the civil rights march on Bloody Sunday. (Extracts taken from BSI statements, courtesy of National Archives, UK.)

Alana Burke Alana Burke was 18 in 1972 and was crushed by an advancing British army armoured vehicle on Bloody Sunday, sustaining serious and lifelong injuries. (Interview from author's research for 2012 book, *Setting the Truth Free: The Inside Story of the Bloody Sunday Justice Campaign* (Liberties Press).)

David Cameron British prime minister in June 2010 at the time of the publication of the *Report of the Bloody Sunday Inquiry*. David Cameron released the report's findings to Parliament and offered an historic apology. 'On behalf of the government, indeed, on behalf of our country, I am deeply sorry,' he said. (Extract of 15 June 2010 speech, from the *Hansard* Parliamentary Record, UK.)

John Campbell Son of 51-year-old Patrick Campbell who was shot and injured as he sought shelter in Joseph Place on Bloody Sunday. (Interview from author's research for 2012 book, *Setting the Truth Free: The Inside Story of the Bloody Sunday Justice Campaign* (Liberties Press).) Mr Campbell died in 1985.

Susie Campbell Sister of 17-year-old Jackie Duddy, who was fatally wounded in the car park of the Rossville Flats as he and others fled the advancing army on Bloody Sunday. (Mother of the author.)

Ivan Cooper Unionist politician and former MP Ivan Cooper was a prominent civil rights activist – one of the few unionist figures to officially support calls for reform. He also organized the anti-internment march that became Bloody Sunday. (Interview as given to author in 2017 as part of the Museum of Free Derry's *National Civil Rights Archive* and never before published, and also from BSI statements, courtesy of National Archives, UK.) Mr Cooper died in 2019.

Martin Cowley Derry-born reporter Martin Cowley covered the 1968 march for the *Derry Journal* and Bloody Sunday in 1972 for the *Irish Times*. (Extracts taken from BSI statements, courtesy of National Archives, UK.)

Patricia Coyle As a trainee solicitor in the 1990s, Coyle uncovered Bloody Sunday evidence from public records in London – propelling the campaign to new levels. Patricia continues to practise law in Belfast. (Interview from author's research for 2012 book, *Setting the Truth Free: The Inside Story of the Bloody Sunday Justice Campaign* (Liberties Press).)

Betty Curran Betty Curran was a young child in 1972 and recalls seeing her mother too traumatized to eat her dinner that Sunday. (Extract taken from the 2019 film, *Free Derry Lives*, courtesy of the Museum of Free Derry.)

Bishop Edward Daly Parish priest in Derry's Bogside from 1962 to 1973, Father Edward Daly was appointed Bishop of Derry in 1974. On Bloody Sunday he administered the Last Rites to many of the dying. (Extracts taken from BSI statements, courtesy of National Archives, UK, and from an interview with the author as part of the Museum of Free Derry's *National Civil Rights Archive* and never before published – Bishop Daly's last recorded interview before his death in 2016.)

Eamonn Deane A Derry primary school teacher in 1972, Eamonn Deane witnessed the military presence ahead of the march. He works as an educator in cross-community reconciliation and community-led projects. (Extracts taken from BSI statements, courtesy of National Archives, UK.)

Margaret (Peggy) Deery Mother-of-fourteen Peggy Deery was the only woman shot on Bloody Sunday. Peggy's husband had died just a few months beforehand in October 1971. Her gunshot injuries were life changing and she spent the next two years in a wheelchair. (Extracts taken from BSI statement, courtesy of National Archives, UK.) Mrs Deery died in 1988.

Eileen Doherty Widow of 31-year-old Paddy Doherty. The couple had six children, the eldest aged eleven, and the youngest just seven months old when their father was killed. (Extracts taken from *Bloody Sunday: What Really Happened* (Brandon Books, 1992), courtesy of Eamonn McCann.) Mrs Doherty died in 2014.

Geraldine Doherty Niece of 17-year-old Gerald Donaghey, who was shot dead in Abbey Park on Bloody Sunday. His body was later photographed with prominent nail bombs protruding from every pocket, igniting one of the biggest controversies concerning the day: the alleged planting of nail bombs. Geraldine and her late mother, Mary Donaghey, tirelessly campaigned to clear Gerald's name. (Interview from author's research for 2012 book, *Setting the Truth Free: The Inside Story of the Bloody Sunday Justice Campaign* (Liberties Press).)

Gleann Doherty The youngest son of 31-year-old Patrick Doherty, who was shot dead on Bloody Sunday. Gleann was just seven months old when his father was killed. Today, he works within peace tourism in Derry. (Interview from author's research for 2012 book, *Setting the Truth Free: The Inside Story of the Bloody Sunday Justice Campaign* (Liberties Press).)

Larry Doherty Larry Doherty had a fifty-year career as a staff photographer for the *Derry Journal* newspaper, covering much of the civil rights era and decades of conflict that followed. That Sunday, 30 January 1972, was his forty-second birthday. (Extracts taken from BSI statements, courtesy of National Archives, UK.) Mr Doherty died in 2015.

Paul Doherty Son of 31-year-old Patrick Doherty, who was shot dead as he tried to crawl to safety behind the Rossville Flats on Bloody Sunday. A strong supporter of civil rights, Patrick Doherty had also been at Magilligan the week before when soldiers attacked marchers. Today, Paul Doherty works within peace tourism in Derry. (Extract taken from a twentieth-anniversary interview, courtesy of the *Derry Journal*.)

Mary Donaghey Elder sister of Gerald Donaghey, who was shot dead on Bloody Sunday aged 17 and upon whose body were planted four nail bombs by the police or army in an attempt to justify his shooting. (Extract taken from BSI statement, courtesy of National Archives, UK, and from a research interview conducted for the film *Sunday,* courtesy of Jimmy McGovern.) Ms Donaghey died in 2010.

Damian 'Bubbles' Donaghy Damian Donaghy was the first person shot and wounded on Bloody Sunday before the main gunfire began and the youngest casualty of the day at just 15. He is also a cousin of Gerald Donaghey, who was shot and killed. (Interview from author's research for 2012 book, *Setting the Truth Free: The Inside Story of the Bloody Sunday Justice Campaign* (Liberties Press), press reports by author, and from BST statement, courtesy of National Archives, UK.)

Sophia Downey A sister of 17-year-old Michael Kelly, who was shot dead on his first civil rights march on Bloody Sunday, Sophia accompanied her father to the hospital when he went to find his son. (Extract taken from BSI statement, courtesy of National Archives, UK.)

Brendan Duddy Brendan Duddy was a prominent Derry businessman who met with both wings of the IRA ahead of Bloody Sunday to ensure they would stay away from the march. Duddy is best remembered as a key intermediary during negotiations for the Northern Ireland peace process. (Extract from BSI statements, courtesy of National Archives, UK.) Mr Duddy died in 2017.

Gerry Duddy A brother of 17-year-old Jackie Duddy and one of 15 siblings, Gerry campaigned alongside his sister Kay in the 1990s. (Interview from author's research for 2012 book, *Setting the Truth Free: The Inside Story of the Bloody Sunday Justice Campaign* (Liberties Press) and from BSI statements, courtesy of National Archives, UK.)

Jimmy Duddy Nephew of John Johnston, the fourteenth victim of Bloody Sunday who died in June 1972 of injuries sustained. (Interview from author's research for 2012 book, *Setting the Truth Free: The Inside Story of the Bloody Sunday Justice Campaign* (Liberties Press).)

Kay Duddy Sister of 17-year-old Jackie, Kay Duddy identified her brother's body at the morgue – a memory that has never returned. (Interview from author's research for 2012 book, *Setting the Truth Free: The Inside Story of the Bloody Sunday Justice Campaign* (Liberties Press) and press reports.)

Mark Durkan Derry politician Mark Durkan is a former Member of Parliament, of the Northern Ireland Assembly and former Deputy First Minister of Northern Ireland. (Interview from author's research for 2012 book, *Setting the Truth Free: The Inside Story of the Bloody Sunday Justice Campaign* (Liberties Press) and from Mr Durkan's 15 June 2010 speech, from the *Hansard* Parliamentary Record, UK.)

Michael Farrell College lecturer Michael Farrell was among those leading the four-day People's Democracy march from Belfast to Derry that was attacked by loyalist mobs in January 1969, particularly at Burntollet outside Derry. (Extracts courtesy of fiftieth-anniversary piece in the *Irish Times* and its author, Freya McClements.)

Lord Fenner-Brockway British politician and ardent socialist, Archibald Fenner-Brockway was one of the speakers lined up to address anti-internment marchers on Bloody Sunday before gunfire began. A lifelong pacifist, anti-colonialist and lobbyist, he was also a founder member of the Campaign for Nuclear Disarmament, among other things. (Extracts taken from BSI statement, courtesy of National Archives, UK.) Lord Fenner-Brockway died in 1988.

Major General Robert Ford Major General Robert Ford was the British Commander of Land Forces in Northern Ireland in 1971 during the events of Bloody Sunday, and he was also present on the ground in the Bogside. (Extracts from the *Report of the Bloody Sunday Inquiry*, 2010, courtesy of National Archives, UK, and from archive press reports.) General Ford died in 2015.

Eileen Fox One of 14 siblings of 17-year-old Jackie Duddy, the first person killed on Bloody Sunday, Eileen Fox was heavily pregnant in January 1972 as word of gunfire spread. (Interview from author's 2016 collection, *Beyond the Silence: Women's Unheard Voices from the Troubles* (Guildhall Press).)

Joe Friel Joe Friel was 20 and lived in the Rossville Flats at the time of Bloody Sunday. He was shot and injured after venturing out to hear the speeches after the march. (Extracts taken from BSI statement, courtesy of National Archives, UK.)

Bridie Gallagher A sister of 20-year-old Michael McDaid, who was shot dead at the rubble barricade. Bridie was also on the march with her late husband, Hugo, taking shelter in a derelict house. She has rarely spoken of Bloody Sunday since. (Interview given to author in 2021 and never before published.)

Maureen Gallagher As a young woman in 1972, Maureen Gallagher was a Knights of Malta volunteer first-aider on Bloody Sunday. (Extracts taken from BSI statements, courtesy of National Archives, UK.)

Danny Gillespie Danny Gillespie was 32 and lived in the Bogside with his young family at the time of Bloody Sunday. He was shot and wounded in Glenfada Park and lay unconscious as the shooting continued. (Extracts taken from BSI statements, courtesy of National Archives, UK.) Mr Gillespie died in 2008.

Frances Gillespie Wife of Daniel 'Danny' Gillespie, who was shot and wounded on Bloody Sunday. (Interview from author's research for 2012 book, *Setting the Truth Free: The Inside Story of the Bloody Sunday Justice Campaign* (Liberties Press).)

Bernard Gilmour A brother of 17-year-old Hugh Gilmour, shot dead on Bloody Sunday not far from his own front door at the Rossville Flats. Bernard, his brother Floyd, and sister Olive, later campaigned for justice. (Extracts taken from BSI statements, courtesy of National Archives, UK, and Eamonn McCann's *The Bloody Sunday Inquiry: The Families Speak Out* (Pluto Press, 2005).) Mr Gilmour died in 2016.

Anne Grant A daughter of Paddy Walsh, one of the heroes of Bloody Sunday. Paddy risked his life to crawl out to Paddy Doherty. (Extract taken from Free Derry Lives exhibition, Museum of Free Derry, 2019.)

Diane Greer Diane Greer spent many years working with the Workers Educational Association, and is a keen environmentalist, having recently established her first polytunnel. (Extracts taken from the anthology *Perceptions* (Guildhall Press, 1998), courtesy of Adrian Kerr, and from a self-penned essay entitled 'Bloody Sunday: A Loyalist's Perspective', in the publication *Force 10: An Irish Journal* (1999; issue 11: Sligo).)

Alice Harper Daughter of 44-year-old Danny Teggart, shot dead by British paratroopers on 9 August 1971 in Ballymurphy, West Belfast, during the introduction of internment. (Extracts from families' personal statements as submitted to the Ballymurphy inquest.)

Sir Edward Heath Former British prime minister Edward Heath was in office from 1970 to 1974 and during Bloody Sunday. The following day,

Edward Heath advised Lord Widgery, then the Lord Chief Justice, ahead of an investigation into the shootings to bear in mind, 'We are in Northern Ireland fighting not only a military war but a propaganda war.' (Extracts from the *Report of the Bloody Sunday Inquiry*, 2010, courtesy of National Archives, UK.) Sir Edward Heath died in 2005.

Jean Hegarty A sister of 17-year-old Kevin McElhinney, who was shot dead on Rossville Street. Jean Hegarty lived in Canada when her brother was killed but returned home in the 1990s. Today, Jean is an administrator with the Bloody Sunday Trust. (Interview from author's research for 2012 book, *Setting the Truth Free: The Inside Story of the Bloody Sunday Justice Campaign* (Liberties Press).)

Stephen Herron Director of the Public Prosecution Service of Northern Ireland in 2019 during the announcement of charges against British soldiers involved in Bloody Sunday. (Extract taken from PPS announcement on 14 March 2019, courtesy of Public Prosecution Service NI.)

Liam Hillen Identified in recent years as the original artist behind the famous graffiti, Liam Hillen mixed old paints to write 'You Are Now Entering Free Derry'. Today's more familiar bold, black lettering was later added by John 'Caker' Casey. (Extracts taken from *Free Derry Wall* (Guildhall Press, 2009), courtesy of Jim Collins and Adrian Kerr.) Mr Hillen died in 2019.

John Hume Derry politician John Hume is widely regarded as a central figure in Northern Ireland's peace process and was named co-recipient of the 1998 Nobel Prize for Peace alongside unionist leader David Trimble. (Extracts taken from the anthology *Perceptions* (Guildhall Press, 1998), courtesy of Adrian Kerr. Mr Hume died in 2020.

General Sir Michael Jackson General Sir Michael Jackson, the former head of the British army, was a Parachute Regiment captain on Bloody Sunday and the second-in-command of 1 PARA. Jackson was responsible for what is known as the 'shot-list' that falsely identified those shot as gunmen and bombers. By the time he testified to the BSI in April 2003, General Sir Michael Jackson was Chief of the General Staff – Britain's top soldier. (Extracts from the *Report of the Bloody Sunday Inquiry*, 2010, courtesy of National Archives, UK.)

John Johnston Regarded as the fourteenth victim of Bloody Sunday, John Johnston was a 59-year-old draper and the second person shot and injured on the day, succumbing to his injuries some months later. (Extracts taken from BSI statement, courtesy of National Archives, UK.) Mr Johnston died in June 1972.

John Kelly Brother of 17-year-old Michael Kelly, who was shot dead at the rubble barricade on Bloody Sunday. John chaired the 1990s Bloody Sunday Justice Campaign, and today is Education Officer at the Museum of Free Derry. (Interview from author's research for 2012 book, *Setting the Truth Free: The Inside Story of the Bloody Sunday Justice Campaign* (Liberties Press), and also from archive press reports.)

Police Chief Superintendent Frank Lagan At the time of Bloody Sunday in 1972, Frank Lagan was Chief Superintendent of the Royal Ulster Constabulary (RUC) and urged caution and moderation ahead of the planned civil rights march on 30 January 1972. (Extracts from the *Report of the Bloody Sunday Inquiry*, 2010, courtesy of National Archives, UK.) Mr Lagan died in 2005.

Clive Limpkin As a young press photographer for London's *Daily Sketch* newspaper, Clive Limpkin was sent to Derry to cover what became the Battle of the Bogside. (Extract taken from *The Battle of Bogside: Revised 50th Anniversary Edition* (Derry: Guildhall Press), and from conversations with the author.) Mr Limpkin died in 2020.

Anne-Marie Love A sister of 16-year-old Charles Love, from Strabane. Charles was hit by falling debris after the IRA detonated a bomb on the Derry Walls during a Bloody Sunday commemoration in January 1990. The explosion showered marchers below with rubble and detritus, killing the teenager instantly. (Extract taken from *Children of the Troubles: The Untold Story of the Children Killed in the Northern Ireland Conflict*, courtesy of Freya McClements and Joe Duffy, 2019.)

Dr Domhnall MacDermott A local general practitioner, Dr MacDermott attended some of the dying and wounded on Bloody Sunday and attended post-mortems also. (Extract taken from BSI statements, courtesy of National Archives, UK.) Dr MacDermott died in 2003.

Eamonn MacDermott As a 14-year-old schoolboy in 1972, Eamonn accompanied his doctor father to the march, and troops and vehicles from the Parachute Regiment were based in his street that entire day. Today, he is a newspaper reporter and commentator. (Interview as given to author in 2021 and never before published.)

Brigadier Pat MacLellan Major General – then Brigadier – Pat MacLellan was commander of British troops and had the power to launch arrest operations against rioters on Bloody Sunday, aiming to delay this until there was sufficient separation between their targets and the marchers. (Extracts from the *Report of the Bloody Sunday Inquiry*, 2010, courtesy of National Archives, UK.)

Joe Mahon Aged sixteen in 1972, Joe Mahon was shot and wounded in Glenfada Park. He pretended to be dead after witnessing the second shooting of Jim Wray nearby. (Interview from author's research for 2012 book, *Setting the Truth Free: The Inside Story of the Bloody Sunday Justice Campaign* (Liberties Press) and from BSI statement, courtesy of National Archives, UK.)

Reginald Maudling Former Chancellor of the Exchequer and British home secretary in 1972, Reginald Maudling was slapped by firebrand Irish MP Bernadette Devlin after insulting her authority as a witness to Bloody Sunday and besmirching the dead. (Extract of 31 January 1972 discussion, courtesy of *Hansard* Parliamentary Record, UK.) Mr Maudling died in 1979.

Geraldine McBride Geraldine McBride (then Richmond) was a teenage eyewitness traumatized by Bloody Sunday. She comforted Hugh Gilmour as he died before witnessing the death of Barney McGuigan. This book's author played the role of Geraldine in Jimmy McGovern's 2002 Channel 4 documentary-drama, *Sunday*, directed by Charles McDougall. (Extracts taken from BSI, courtesy of National Archives, UK, and also from an interview with the author in 2021 and never before published.)

Eamonn McCann Author, journalist and civil rights activist, Eamonn McCann is one of the finest orators Derry has ever produced and he co-founded both the Bloody Sunday Trust and the Bloody Sunday Campaign. (Interview from author's research for 2012 book, *Setting the Truth Free: The Inside Story of the Bloody Sunday Justice Campaign* (Liberties Press) and from BSI statements, courtesy of National Archives, UK, and from *Creggan: More than a History* (Guildhall Press, 2000).)

Dr Raymond McClean Local doctor Raymond McClean attended to many of the dying and wounded on Bloody Sunday and was present for the majority of post-mortems thereafter. In 1973, he was elected Mayor of Derry, the first Catholic to hold the post since 1922. (Extracts taken from BSI statements, courtesy of National Archives, UK.) Dr McClean died in 2011.

Gerard 'Jed' McClelland As a teenager from Westland Avenue in the Bogside, Jed McClelland recalls the early unrest during the civil rights movement and, later, being present during the events of Bloody Sunday. (Interview given to author in 2021 and never before published.)

Freya McClements As a BBC journalist, Freya McClements was present in the Guildhall Square on 15 June 2010 reporting on the publication of Lord Saville's Report. Today, she is Northern Correspondent with the *Irish Times* and, with Joe Duffy, is co-author of the 2019 book, *Children of the Troubles: The Untold Story of the Children Killed in the Northern Ireland Conflict* (Dublin: Hachette Ireland). (Interview given to author in 2021 and never before published.)

Dermie McClenaghan Bogside activist Dermie McClenaghan actively organized and participated in much of the early protest and civil disobedience. From his home, he helped squat hundreds of desperate nationalist families into vacant properties across the city. (Interview given to author in 2017 as part of the Museum of Free Derry's *National Civil Rights Archive* and never before published.)

Vinny McCormack Co-author of *Burntollet*, Vinny McCormack took part in 1969's People's Democracy march from Belfast to Derry. He sought refuge in a river when attacked and watched as police did nothing to break up the violence. Today, McCormack is a lecturer in psychology at Ulster University. (Extracts courtesy of fiftieth-anniversary piece in the *Irish Times* and its author, Freya McClements, and from a self-penned essay entitled 'Route '68: To Burntollet and Back', online.)

Jon McCourt Jon McCourt was present during much of the early unrest and recalls reactions when British troops first arrived in Derry after the Battle of the Bogside in 1969. Today, Jon is a victims' rights campaigner. (Extracts taken from the 2019 film *Free Derry Lives*, courtesy of the Museum of Free Derry.)

Kevin McDaid Brother of 20-year-old Michael McDaid, who was shot dead alongside three other young men at the rubble barricade on Rossville Street. (Interview from author's research for 2012 book, *Setting the Truth Free: The Inside Story of the Bloody Sunday Justice Campaign* (Liberties Press).)

Patsy McDaid Patsy McDaid was shot and injured, aged 25, the bullet narrowly skimming his spine. (Interview from author's research for 2012 book, *Setting the Truth Free: The Inside Story of the Bloody Sunday Justice Campaign* (Liberties Press), archive press reports by the author and from BSI statements, courtesy of National Archives, UK.)

Cahil McElhinney Eldest brother of 17-year-old Kevin McElhinney, who was shot dead on Bloody Sunday, Cahil married and settled in Birmingham in 1972. He last saw his brother the September before his death. (Extract taken from an interview in 2010, courtesy of the *Birmingham Mail*.)

Conal McFeely A former Chair of the Bloody Sunday Trust, Conal McFeely was on the march on 30 January 1972 with his brother and Gerald Donaghey, later shot dead. (Interview from research for 2012 book, *Setting the Truth Free: The Inside Story of the Bloody Sunday Justice Campaign* (Liberties Press), and as given to author in 2021 and never before published.)

Martin McGavigan Brother of 14-year-old Annette McGavigan, who was shot dead by British soldiers near her home in the Bogside on 6 September 1971. She was still wearing her school uniform. The army claimed they had targeted a gunman. (Extract courtesy of *Children of the Troubles: The Untold Story of the Children Killed in the Northern Ireland Conflict*, courtesy of Freya McClements and Joe Duffy, 2019.)

Teresa McGowan Wife of Daniel McGowan, who was shot and wounded. Interview from author's research for 2012 book, *Setting the Truth Free: The Inside Story of the Bloody Sunday Justice Campaign* (Liberties Press).

Bridie McGuigan Widow of 41-year-old Barney McGuigan, who was shot in the head as he waved a white hankie going to the aid of the fatally wounded Paddy Doherty. Bridie spoke publicly only once. (Extracts from Bridie's 2010 account, 'The heavens wept the day Barney was buried, and the sun shone the day he was cleared', courtesy of the *Derry Journal* and its author, Eamonn McDermott.) Mrs McGuigan died in 2016.

Martin McGuinness Derry politician Martin McGuinness was second-in-command/adjutant of the IRA at the time of Bloody Sunday in 1972 and later testified to the Bloody Sunday Inquiry. In 1999, he was appointed Education Minister and then Deputy First Minister of Northern Ireland. (Interview from author's research for 2012 book, *Setting the Truth Free: The Inside Story of the Bloody Sunday Justice Campaign* (Liberties Press) and from BSI statements, courtesy of National Archives, UK.) Mr McGuinness died in 2017.

Ita McKinney Widow of 35-year-old father-of-seven Gerard McKinney, who was shot dead on Bloody Sunday. Ita McKinney was heavily pregnant at the time of her husband's murder and gave birth eight days later, naming her son Gerard after his daddy. (Extracts taken from BSI transcripts of Peter Taylor's 1992 BBC TV documentary, *Remember Bloody Sunday*, courtesy of Peter Taylor and National Archives, UK, and the 2000 Channel 4 documentary, *Secret History*.) Mrs McKinney died in 2021.

Joe McKinney Brother of 27-year-old William McKinney, who had worked at the *Derry Journal* and was shot dead in Glenfada Park. (Extract taken from public statement of 3 July 2021, courtesy of Madden & Finucane Solicitors, Derry.)

John McKinney Brother of 27-year-old William McKinney, shot dead on Bloody Sunday. The McKinney family are currently advised of the prosecution of the soldier involved. (Interview from author's research for 2012 book, *Setting the Truth Free: The Inside Story of the Bloody Sunday Justice Campaign* (Liberties Press).)

Mickey McKinney Brother of 27-year-old William McKinney. Interview from author's research for 2012 book, *Setting the Truth Free: The Inside Story of the Bloody Sunday Justice Campaign* (Liberties Press), and from *Creggan: More Than a History (*Guildhall Press, 2000).)

Philomena McLaughlin As a 13-year-old schoolgirl in 1972, Philomena listened to a portable radio in the street with friends as news of the shootings emerged. (Interview from author's 2016 collection, *Beyond the Silence: Women's Unheard Voices from the Troubles* (Guildhall Press).)

Regina McLaughlin Daughter of 35-year-old Gerard McKinney, who was shot dead in Abbey Park on Bloody Sunday – the same bullet killing Gerald Donaghey behind him. (Interview from author's research for 2012 book, *Setting the Truth Free: The Inside Story of the Bloody Sunday Justice Campaign* (Liberties Press).)

Hugh McMonagle Chair of Shantallow Civil Rights Association in 1972, Hugh McMonagle was among those who helped carry Jackie Duddy's body away from gunfire on Bloody Sunday. (Interview from author in 2017 as part of the Museum of Free Derry's *National Civil Rights Archive* and never before published.) Mr McMonagle died in 2020.

Ruby McNaught Daughter of local woman Kathleen McLaughlin, who brought a fatally injured soldier into her house in the Bogside in March 1971 and tended him as he lay dying. Eighteen-year-old Lance Corporal William Jolliffe was the first British soldier to die in Derry. (Interview from author's 2016 collection, *Beyond the Silence: Women's Unheard Voices from the Troubles* (Guildhall Press).)

Billy McVeigh Bogside teenager Billy McVeigh was often on the front line of riots defending his area during the early conflict, present in both the Battle of the Bogside and Bloody Sunday. Billy's image is today a Bogside mural. (Interview from author in 2021 and never before published.)

Eamon Melaugh A civil rights activist in Derry during the 1960s and 1970s, Melaugh was one of the organizers of the 5 October 1968 civil rights march from Duke Street in which marchers were beaten by the sectarian police force of the time, the Royal Ulster Constabulary (RUC). (Interview from author in 2017 as part of the Museum of Free Derry's *National Civil Rights Archive* and never before published.)

Don Mullan Author of *Eyewitness Bloody Sunday* (Wolfhound Press, 1997), Don Mullan was present on Bloody Sunday as a fifteen-year-old schoolboy. (Interview from author's research for 2012 book, *Setting the Truth Free: The Inside Story of the Bloody Sunday Justice Campaign* (Liberties Press).)

Alexander Nash Father-of-thirteen Alexander Nash was shot and wounded as he ran out to his dying 19-year-old son, William, at the rubble barricade on Rossville Street. He later had to watch his own son's funeral on television from his hospital bed. (Extracts taken from BSI statements, courtesy of National Archives, UK.) Mr Nash died in 1999.

Mary Nelis Mary Nelis is a Derry mother, a former Member of the Northern Ireland Assembly, and former Mayor of Derry. She was heavily involved in the civil rights movement and is a fierce campaigner for prisoners' rights. (Extracts taken from the 2019 film *Free Derry Lives*, courtesy of the Museum of Free Derry.)

Andy Nolan A childhood friend of 17-year-old Jackie Duddy, Andy Nolan spent much of that final weekend with Jackie. They had gone on the march together but were separated by crowds arriving in William Street. (Extracts from a personal letter to the Duddy family, dated 4 February 2000, and included courtesy of his wife, Jackie Nolan-Clarke.) Mr Nolan died in 2008.

Colette O'Connor A daughter of Sammy Devenny. As a ten-year-old, Colette witnessed RUC officers bursting into their Bogside home in April 1969, savagely beating Sammy and his family. He died that July – regarded by many as the first victim of the Troubles. (Interview from author's 2016 collection, *Beyond the Silence: Women's Unheard Voices from the Troubles* (Guildhall Press).)

Paul O'Connor As a 13-year-old schoolboy in January 1969, Paul O'Connor welcomed the four-day People's Democracy march as it arrived in Derry. Today, Paul is Director of the Pat Finucane Centre for Human Rights. (Extracts courtesy of fiftieth-anniversary piece in the *Irish Times* and its author, Freya McClements.)

Fionnbarra Ó Dochartaigh Historian and founding member of the Northern Ireland Civil Rights Association (NICRA), Fionnbarra Ó Dochartaigh helped organize the march on 5 October 1968. (Early extracts from the Springtown Camp website; otherwise from an interview with the author in 2017 as part of the Museum of Free Derry's *National Civil Rights Archive* and never before published.) Mr Ó Dochartaigh died in 2021.

Deirdre O'Doherty As a young activist and twin of NICRA co-founder Fionnbarra, Deirdre O'Doherty attended the civil rights march on

5 October 1968. Later, she went to the hospital, where, as an off-duty radiographer, she and a colleague x-rayed 44 skulls each. (Extract from self-penned fiftieth-anniversary feature on Duke Street, courtesy of the *Derry News*, 2018.)

Caroline O'Donnell Caroline's father Patsy O'Donnell was shot and wounded aged 41. (Interview from author's research for 2012 book, *Setting the Truth Free: The Inside Story of the Bloody Sunday Justice Campaign* (Liberties Press).)

Patsy O'Donnell Father-of-six Patrick 'Patsy' O'Donnell was on the anti-internment march on 30 January 1972. He was shot and wounded in Glenfada Park. (Extract from BSI statements, courtesy of National Archives, UK.)

Major Hubert O'Neill Appointed Inquest Coroner into the deaths on Bloody Sunday, Major O'Neill delivered his report in August 1973. Major Hubert O'Neill remarked of his findings publicly, 'I would say without hesitation that it was sheer, unadulterated murder. It was murder.' (Extract taken from CAIN (Conflict Archive on the Internet), courtesy of Ulster University.)

May O'Neill May O'Neill was a young mother in 1972 and one of many who travelled to Derry by bus for the big march on Bloody Sunday. She helped Damian Donaghy when he was injured, and later remonstrated with soldiers when they tried to interfere with the group of men carrying the body of Jackie Duddy. (Interviews from press pieces by author in 2017 and 2018.)

Jackie O'Reilly The stepdaughter of Mickey Bradley, who was shot and wounded aged 22 on Bloody Sunday. (Interview from author's research for 2012 book, *Setting the Truth Free: The Inside Story of the Bloody Sunday Justice Campaign* (Liberties Press).)

Robin Percival Originally from Widnes near Liverpool, Robin Percival was a founding member of the Bloody Sunday Trust and its predecessor, the Bloody Sunday Initiative, in the 1990s. He is also the former chair of the Pat Finucane Centre for Human Rights. (Interview from author's research for 2012 book, *Setting the Truth Free: The Inside Story of the Bloody Sunday Justice Campaign* (Liberties Press).)

Kevin Phillips Brother of 19-year-old Noel Phillips, shot dead by British paratroopers on 9 August 1971 in Ballymurphy, West Belfast, during the introduction of internment in August 1971. (Extracts from families' personal statement as submitted to the Ballymurphy inquest.)

James Porter Jimmy Porter was a licensed radio amateur who owned a TV repair shop at the edge of the Bogside. In 1972, he recorded British soldiers and police talking in code – including an army order to shoot dead an unarmed civilian the day before Bloody Sunday. His tapes were rejected in the first inquiry by Lord Chief Justice Widgery. (Extract taken from BSI statements, courtesy of National Archives, UK.) Mr Porter died in 2012.

Michael Quinn As a 17-year-old schoolboy in 1972, Michael Quinn was shot and injured on Bloody Sunday – the bullet exiting his face. Today, Michael lives in Dublin. (Extracts taken from BSI statements, courtesy of National Archives, UK.)

Christine Robson A daughter of Sammy Devenny, Christine was nine years old when RUC officers burst into Sammy's home and attacked him and his family. He died that July – regarded by many as the first victim of the Troubles. (Interview from author's 2016 collection, *Beyond the Silence: Women's Unheard Voices from the Troubles* (Guildhall Press).)

Raymond Rogan Former chairman of the Bogside Residents' Association, Rogan was arrested alongside Leo Young as they tried to take Gerald Donaghey to hospital on Bloody Sunday. (Interview from author in 2017 as part of the Museum of Free Derry's *National Civil Rights Archive* and never before published.)

The Rooney family, Belfast On 14 August, as the fallout from Derry's Battle of the Bogside reverberated throughout the north, a nine-year-old boy called Patrick Rooney was shot dead in Belfast by RUC machine-gun fire through the walls of his own home. He was the first child killed in the conflict. (Extracts from siblings Sharon and Con, and parents Alice and Neely, courtesy of a fiftieth-anniversary piece in the *Irish Times* and its author, Freya McClements.)

Ciaran Shiels Solicitor for many Bloody Sunday families on behalf of Madden and Finucane Solicitors throughout the 1990s campaign and subsequent inquiry. (Interview from author's research for 2012 book, *Setting the Truth Free: The Inside Story of the Bloody Sunday Justice Campaign* (Liberties Press).)

John Teggart Son of 44-year-old Danny Teggart, shot dead by British paratroopers on 9 August 1971 in Ballymurphy, West Belfast, during the introduction of internment. (Extracts from families' personal statements as submitted to the Ballymurphy inquest.)

Minty Thompson A daughter of 47-year-old mother-of-six Kathleen Thompson, who was shot dead by the British army in her own back garden in Creggan, Derry, in November 1971. Minty was 12 years old when she and her father discovered her mother's body. (Extract taken from the 2004 documentary, *Lifting a Dark Cloud: The Kathleen Thompson Case*, courtesy of Anne Crilly.)

Jimmy Toye Jimmy Toye was present during both the Battle of the Bogside in 1969 and Bloody Sunday in 1972. Today, he volunteers at the Museum of Free Derry. (Extracts taken from BSI statements, courtesy of National Archives, UK, and from an interview with the author in 2021 and never before published.)

Briege Voyle Daughter of 44-year-old Joan Connolly, shot dead by British paratroopers on 9 August 1971 in Ballymurphy, West Belfast, during the introduction of internment. (Extracts from families' personal statements as submitted to the Ballymurphy inquest.)

Paddy Walsh Known locally as one of the many heroes of Bloody Sunday, Paddy Walsh braved British army gunfire to crawl out to the mortally wounded Paddy Doherty, one of the last men shot. (Extract taken from BSI statement, courtesy of National Archives, UK.)

Lord Widgery Widgery was the Lord Chief Justice of Britain at the time of Bloody Sunday, appointed by Edward Heath to oversee the 1972 tribunal and its now-disgraced 1972 *Widgery Report*. The report took just six weeks to compile, ran to 36 pages and exonerated the army, reinforcing army claims that those targeted were gunmen and bombers. (Extracts of the 1972 *Report of the Tribunal* accessed at CAIN (Conflict Archive on the Internet), courtesy of Ulster University.) Lord Widgery died in 1981.

Lieutenant Colonel Derek Wilford Lieutenant Colonel Wilford was the Commanding Officer of the 1st Battalion Parachute Regiment (1 PARA) during January 1972 with responsibility for the battalion's conduct on the ground. (Extracts from the *Report of the Bloody Sunday Inquiry*, 2010, courtesy of National Archives, UK.)

Jane Winter As former Director of British Irish Rights Watch based in London, Jane Winter was deeply involved in the search for new evidence and highlighting the case in Europe. (Interview from author's research for 2012 book, *Setting the Truth Free: The Inside Story of the Bloody Sunday Justice Campaign* (Liberties Press).)

Liam Wray Brother of 22-year-old Jim Wray, who was shot in the back twice in Glenfada Park. The second shot was fired as he lay mortally wounded on the ground. (Interview from author's research for 2012 book, *Setting the Truth Free: The Inside Story of the Bloody Sunday Justice Campaign* (Liberties Press).)

Leo Young Brother of 17-year-old John Young, who was shot in the face and died at the rubble barricade on Rossville Street. Leo also tried to get Gerald Donaghey to hospital, alongside Raymond Rogan. (Interview from author's 2012 book, *Setting the Truth Free: The Inside Story of the Bloody Sunday Justice Campaign* (Liberties Press).)

Maura Young A sister of 17-year-old John Young, Maura Young was also on the march that day. She later searched for both her brothers, John and Leo, at Altnagelvin Hospital. Leo had been arrested, and John shot dead. (Interview with author in 2021 and never before published.)

Fatalities and Wounded

Bloody Sunday Fatalities

Patrick Doherty was 31, married to Eileen, and father of six children between 11 years and 7 months. He worked in Du Pont. A strong supporter of the civil rights movement, Paddy was an active member of the association and attended all the protests in the late 1960s and early 1970s. He had also been at Magilligan the week before Bloody Sunday and witnessed the brutality of the Parachute Regiment. He was killed as he tried to crawl to safety in the shadow of Rossville Flats.

Gerald Donaghey was just 17 years old and the youngest of three children when he was killed on Bloody Sunday. Gerald was orphaned at the age of ten when his mother and father died within the space of four weeks. He was sentenced to six months for rioting in the Bogside and was released on Christmas Eve 1971. Gerald Donaghey was killed as he tried to escape the paratroopers in Glenfada Park. After his death, he was acknowledged as a member of Na Fianna Éireann.

Jackie Duddy was 17 years old when he was killed on Bloody Sunday. He was born at Springtown camp into a family of 15; the family later moved to Creggan. Jackie worked as a weaver at French's factory, but his real passion was boxing. He was a member of Long Tower Boxing Club, which had fought throughout Ireland, and represented the club in Liverpool. Jackie had no interest in politics and attended the march just for the 'craic' and against his father's advice. He was the first person killed on Bloody Sunday as he ran through Rossville car park, Fr Daly running at his side.

Hugh Gilmour was just 17 when he was killed on Bloody Sunday. Hugh lived in the Rossville Flats and was the youngest of a family of eight. He had worked as a trainee tyre fitter. Living in Rossville Flats, Hugh found himself at the forefront of the civil unrest that swept the north in 1969, and he contributed to the defence of the Bogside in August 1969. He was also an avid Liverpool supporter, went to the pictures every Friday night with his friends, and had just bought a car and was learning to drive. Hugh Gilmour was killed just yards from the safety of Rossville Flats.

John Johnston was 59 and had worked as a draper all his life. He was well dressed and quiet by nature, and had been a keen supporter of the civil rights movement, attending as many marches as he could. His other passion was golf; he was a member of Lisfannon Golf Club and once won the captain's prize, a cherished possession. John Johnston was hit by the first shots fired in William Street on Bloody Sunday and died five months later from his injuries.

Michael Kelly was 17 and the seventh child in a family of 13. He had been training to be a sewing machine mechanic and spent his weeks in Belfast, returning to Derry at the weekends. A keen pigeon fancier, Michael had no interest in politics and the Bloody Sunday march was the first he had ever attended. He was killed at the rubble barricade in Rossville Street.

Michael McDaid was 20 and lived in Tyrconnell Street, the second youngest of a family of 12. He worked as a barman in the Celtic Bar and was an affectionate young man, very close to his parents and especially close to his young nephews, regularly taking his family on runs to Donegal on Sundays. Michael was killed at the rubble barricade on Rossville Street.

Kevin McElhinney was 17 and the middle child in a family of five. He had a keen interest in athletics and soccer and worked at Lipton's supermarket from the time he left school, never missing a day. He regularly attended dances but didn't smoke or drink and was learning to drive in the hope of getting a car. Kevin's real passion was music, especially T-Rex. He was killed as he crawled away from the firing, along Rossville Street.

Barney McGuigan, a married family man and father of six children, was 41 when he was killed on Bloody Sunday. Barney worked in the BSR factory and as a general handyman at Cedric's factory on Carlisle Road. He had no real interest in politics but attended many of the early civil rights marches in the city. Barney was killed as he went to aid the fatally injured Paddy Doherty.

Gerard McKinney was 35 years old, a devoted husband to his wife Ita and father of eight children, the youngest of which, also called Gerard, was born eight days after his father's murder. Other than his family, Gerry's main interests were soccer and roller skating. He managed a junior soccer team and ran the Ritz roller-skating rink on the Strand Road. Gerard had no particular interest in politics. He was killed in Glenfada Park.

William McKinney was 26 and the oldest in a family of 10. Willie worked as a compositor with the *Derry Journal*. Quiet by nature, he was nicknamed 'the professor' by his family. He was interested in music, particularly Irish music and Jim Reeves, and he also played the accordion. However, his true passion was photography. He supported the civil rights campaign and had been at Magilligan the week before Bloody Sunday. He was killed in Glenfada Park.

William Nash was 19 and the seventh child in a family of 13. He worked with his father on Derry docks and loved Country and Western music. William had just celebrated his brother Charlie's success at the National Boxing Championships in Dublin and the marriage of his brother James. He was killed at the rubble barricade in Rossville Street.

Jim Wray was 22 when he was killed on Bloody Sunday. He was the second oldest in a family of nine and had worked in England for some time, becoming engaged to an Israeli girl he had met there. Outgoing by nature,

Jim went to the Castle Bar on a Friday night and the Embassy dance hall on a Saturday. Jim attended the civil rights marches in Derry and the entire family had gone to the march on 30 January after attending mass together. Jim was shot and wounded in Glenfada Park before being shot again at close range as he lay on the ground, unable to move.

John Young was 17 at the time of Bloody Sunday. He was born at Springtown Camp, the youngest of a family of six, and worked in John Temple's menswear shop. John had a passion for showbands and was a roadie for The Scene showband. In 1971, he witnessed the murder of schoolgirl Annette McGavigan by the British army in Derry. He was killed as he sought safety at the rubble barricade on Rossville Street.

Bloody Sunday Wounded

Michael Bradley (deceased) was 22 when he was shot in the courtyard of the Rossville Flats after seeing the murder of Jackie Duddy.

Mickey Bridge was 25 at the time of Bloody Sunday. He was shot in the courtyard of the Rossville Flats when he confronted soldiers after the murder of Jackie Duddy.

Patrick Brolly was 40 and injured by army gunfire as he sheltered in the Rossville Flats.

Alana Burke was 18 and was one of only two women injured on Bloody Sunday. Alana was crushed by an armoured personnel carrier in the courtyard of the Rossville Flats.

Patrick Campbell (deceased) was 51 and married with a family. He was shot as he sought shelter in Joseph Place.

Peggy Deery (deceased) was the only woman shot on Bloody Sunday. She was 38 years old and the mother of 14 children. Her husband had died just four months before.

Damian Donaghy was the first person shot on Bloody Sunday, aged just 15. He had just left school and started his apprenticeship as a plumber.

Joseph Friel was 20 and at Free Derry Corner when the shooting began on Bloody Sunday. He was trying to make his way home to Rossville Flats when he was shot in Glenfada Park.

Daniel Gillespie (deceased) was 32 and married with a young family. He was wounded in Glenfada Park and lay unconscious as the shooting continued.

Thomas Harkin was 18 years old and hit by the same armoured personnel carrier as Alana Burke.

Joe Mahon had just turned 16 in the weeks before Bloody Sunday. Joe was trapped in Glenfada Park as the shooting began and was subsequently shot. As paratroopers approached, he feigned death after witnessing the second shooting of Jim Wray.

Pius McCarron was 30 and injured by flying debris caused by army rifle fire on Bloody Sunday.

Patsy McDaid was 25 at the time of Bloody Sunday. He helped carry Peggy Deery to safety before being shot himself.

Daniel McGowan (deceased) was 38 and married with six children. He had attended the march and was shot while carrying the wounded Patrick Campbell to safety.

Alexander Nash (deceased) was 51 when he was shot on Rossville Street as he attempted to go to the aid of his son William, who was murdered behind the rubble barricade.

Patrick O'Donnell (deceased) was a 41-year-old family man at the time of Bloody Sunday and was shot and wounded in Glenfada Park. Despite his injuries, he was arrested and ill-treated before being released to seek medical attention.

Michael Quinn was 17 and still at school when he was shot on Bloody Sunday. He had become trapped in Glenfada Park and was shot as he tried to escape the army's advance, the bullet exiting through his face.

APPENDIX 3

Chapter Notes

Introduction

1. Estimated figures of deaths in the NI conflict from Fay, M. T., Morrissey, M. and Smyth, M. (1998), 'Mapping Troubles-Related Deaths in Northern Ireland 1969–1998'. Accessed at https://cain.ulster.ac.uk/issues/violence/cts/fay98.htm.
2. Lord Saville of Newdigate, *Principal Conclusions and Overall Assessment of the Bloody Sunday Inquiry*, published 15 June 2010 (TSO); Section 55, p. 58. Accessed at https://assets.publishing.service.gov.uk/government/uploads/system/uploads/attachment_data/file/279167/0030.pdf.
3. Paramilitary figures from 'The issues facing former paramilitary prisoners in NI', by Mervyn Jess, BBC News Website. Accessed at https://www.bbc.co.uk/news/uk-northern-ireland-13689453, published 7 June 2011.
4. Military personnel and recent prosecution figures from 'Investigation of Former Armed Forces Personnel Who Served in Northern Ireland' Research Briefing, published Monday 22 February 2021. Accessed at https://commonslibrary.parliament.uk/research-briefings/cbp-8352/.

Chapter 1 – Rising for Civil Rights

1. 'Nationalist Derry felt abandoned': quote from the Museum of Free Derry, Glenfada Park.
2. 'A Protestant Parliament and a Protestant State', quote by NI prime minister Sir James Craig in 1934, https://www.encyclopedia.com/international/encyclopedias-almanacs-transcripts-and-maps/protestant-parliament-and-protestant-state.
3. Dr Raymond McClean extract: McClean, Raymond (1983), *The Road to Bloody Sunday*, Dublin: Ward River Press, p. 40.
4. Camp details, courtesy of Deery, Willie (2010), *Springtown Camp from the Inside*, Derry: Guildhall Press.
5. Interview with author in 2021 and never before published.
6. Interview with author, 2021.
7. Eamon Melaugh, Bishop Edward Daly and Dermie McClenaghan interview with author in 2017 for National Civil Rights Archive, with speaker/family permission and courtesy of the Museum of Free Derry.
8. Quote from Springtown Camp mothers' protest and Fionnbarra Ó Dochartaigh extract from *Derry Journal*, November 1959, Springtown Camp website. Available at http://www.springtowncamp.com.
9. Fionnbarra Ó Dochartaigh extract from Springtown Camp website. Available at http://www.springtowncamp.com.

10. Interview with author, 2017, National Civil Rights Archive.
11. Mary Nelis, taken from the Museum of Free Derry's *Free Derry Lives* film marking 50 years since the Battle of the Bogside, August 2019. Available at http://freederrylives.com/.
12. John Hume quote, courtesy of Kerr, Adrian (1996), *Perceptions: Cultures in Conflict*, Derry: Guildhall Press, p. 60.
13. Eileen Fox interview from Campbell, Julieann (2016), *Beyond the Silence: Women's Unheard Voices from the Troubles*, Derry: Guildhall Press, pp. 84–9.
14. Interview with author, 2021.
15. Interview with author, National Civil Rights Archive, 2017.
16. Ian Paisley, 'Through Popery', quote from the *Protestant Telegraph*, 4 January 1967, cited in Coogan, Tim Pat (1996), *The Troubles: Ireland's Ordeal 1966–1996 and the Search for Peace*, London: Arrow Books, p. 53.
17. Ian Paisley, 'Fornication and adultery with the Antichrist', quote accessed at https://www.theguardian.com/politics/2010/mar/02/ian-paisley-in-quotes.
18. Ian Paisley 'Catholic homes caught fire', quote from 1968. Accessed at https://www.irishnews.com/news/2014/09/13/news/in-his-own-words-102040/.
19. Ian Paisley 'Behind all the rhetoric', quote from Padraig O'Malley's interview with Ian Paisley, dated 30 December 1981: O'Malley, P. (1983), *The Uncivil Wars: Ireland Today*, a chapter entitled 'Paisleyism: A Question of Intent', Belfast: Blackstaff Press, p. 179.

Chapter 2 – Police Attack at Duke Street, 1968

1. Ivan Cooper and Fionnbarra Ó Dochartaigh interviews with author in 2017 for National Civil Rights Archive, with speaker/family permission and courtesy of the Museum of Free Derry.
2. Interview with author, National Civil Rights Archive, 2017.
3. Deirdre O'Doherty extracts from self-penned fiftieth-anniversary feature 'After the Duke Street march I x-rayed 44 skulls – so did my colleague', courtesy of its author and *Derry News*, dated Thursday 1 February 2018, pp. 12–13.
4. March of 5 October 1968 extract, courtesy of the *Derry Journal*, dated 8 October 1968.
5. Eamonn McCann extract: McClements, Freya, 5 October 2018, *Irish Times* fiftieth anniversary of Duke Street, 'Things are never going to be the same again'.
6. Jed McClelland and Geraldine McBride from interviews with author in 2021 and never before published.
7. Jon McCourt: Museum of Free Derry's *Free Derry Lives* film marking fifty years since the Battle of the Bogside, August 2019. Available at http://freederrylives.com/.
8. Bishop Daly extract on government reaction to Duke Street from Daly, Edward (2000), *Mister, Are You a Priest?* Dublin: Four Courts Press, p. 130.
9. Fionnbarra Ó Dochartaigh extract about 1968: *Free Derry Lives* film, 2019.

10. Michael Farrell, Vinny McCormack and Paul O'Connor extracts, courtesy of McClements, Freya, published 4 January 2019. 'Attack on Burntollet march in Derry occurred 50 years ago today', *Irish Times* (online). Available at https://www.irishtimes.com/news/ireland/irish-news/attack-on-burntollet-march-in-derry-occurred-50-years-ago-today-1.3746978.

11. 'Attack on Burntollet march in Derry occurred 50 years ago today', *Irish Times*.

12. 'Attack on Burntollet march in Derry occurred 50 years ago today', *Irish Times*.

13. Terence O'Neill 1969 quote from McCormack, Vinny (2008), 'Route '68: To Burntollet and Back', published in *20th-century/Contemporary History*, Features, Issue 5 (Sept./Oct. 2008), Volume 16, 'Troubles in Northern Ireland'. Accessed at https://www.historyireland.com/20th-century-contemporary-history/route-68-to-burntollet-and-back/.

14. Vinny McCormack quote, 'Route '68: To Burntollet and Back', 2008.

15. Extracts from Padraig O'Malley's interview with Ian Paisley, dated 30 December 1981: O'Malley, P. (1983), *The Uncivil Wars: Ireland Today*, a chapter entitled 'Paisleyism: A Question of Intent', Belfast: Blackstaff Press, p. 179.

16. Hugh McMonagle and Raymond Rogan interviews with author in 2017 for National Civil Rights Archive, with speaker/family permission and courtesy of the Museum of Free Derry.

17. Interview with author, 2021.

18. Diane Greer quote, courtesy of Kerr, Adrian (1996), *Perceptions: Cultures in Conflict*, Derry: Guildhall Press, p. 49.

19. Interview with author, National Civil Rights Archive, 2017.

Chapter 3 – 'You Are Now Entering Free Derry'

1. Chris Armstrong and Danny Begley accounts by author and from the Museum of Free Derry's *Free Derry Lives* multimedia exhibition, Guildhall, Derry, August 2019.

2. Liam Hillen quote on Free Derry painting, courtesy of Kerr, Adrian, and Collins, Jim (2009), *Free Derry Wall*, Derry: Guildhall Press, p. 56.

3. Report on Derry clashes from the *Derry Journal*, 22 April 1969.

4. Bishop Daly quotes on Sammy Devenny from Daly, Edward (2000), *Mister, Are You a Priest?* Dublin: Four Courts Press, p. 143.

5. Colette O'Connor and Christine Robson interviews about their father, Sammy Devenny, from Campbell, Julieann (ed.) (2016), *Beyond the Silence: Women's Unheard Voices from the Troubles*, Derry: Guildhall Press, pp. 54–69.

6. Fionnbarra Ó Dochartaigh and Raymond Rogan interviews with author in 2017 for National Civil Rights Archive, with speaker permission and courtesy of the Museum of Free Derry.

7. Geraldine McBride from interview with author in 2021 and never before published.

8. June 1969 NICRA demands from Aldous, R. and Puirséil, N. (2008), *We Declare: Landmark Documents in Ireland's History*, London: Quercus Publishing, p. 176.

Chapter 4 – The Battle of the Bogside

1. Bishop Daly quotes about August 1969 from Daly, Edward (2000), *Mister, Are You a Priest?* Dublin: Four Courts Press, p. 151.
2. Clive Limpkin 'best-dressed rioters' quote from conversation with author.
3. Clive Limpkin 1969 quotes from Limpkin, Clive (2019), *The Battle of Bogside: Revised 50th Anniversary Edition*, Derry: Guildhall Press, p. 10.
4. Jimmy Toye from interview with author in 2021 and never before published.
5. Extract of Irish Taoiseach Jack Lynch's televised address during the Battle of the Bogside, aired on 13 August 1969. Available at https://www.youtube.com/watch?v=SRqvus8k1z8.
6. Rooney family, courtesy of McClements, Freya, 11 August 2019, '"He slid down the wall, blood coming from his head": The first child killed in the Troubles', *Irish Times* (online). Available at https://www.irishtimes.com/news/ireland/irish-news/attack-on-burntollet-march-in-derry-occurred-50-years-ago-today-1.3746978.
7. Neely Rooney quote, courtesy of McClements, Freya and Duffy, Joe (2019), *Children of the Troubles: The Untold Story of the Children Killed in the Northern Ireland Conflict*, Dublin: Hachette Books Ireland.
8. Extract from Derry Labour Party, Barricade Bulletin, 14 August 1969.
9. Ruby McNaught interview from Campbell, Julieann (ed.) (2016), *Beyond the Silence: Women's Unheard Voices from the Troubles*, Derry: Guildhall Press, pp. 14–16.
10. Dates and detail on fatalities in the Bogside and Free Derry area from Kerr, Adrian (2013), *Free Derry: Protest and Resistance*, Derry: Guildhall Press.
11. First Communion shoes detail, courtesy of McClements, Freya and Duffy, Joe (2019), *Children of the Troubles: The Untold Story of the Children Killed in the Northern Ireland Conflict*, Dublin: Hachette Books Ireland.

Chapter 5 – Ordinary Lives

1. John Kelly, Liam Wray, Leo Young, Frances Gillespie, Olive Bonner, Kevin McDaid, Jimmy Duddy interviews from source research for Campbell, Julieann (ed.) (2012), *Setting the Truth Free: The Inside Story of the Bloody Sunday Justice Campaign*, Dublin: Liberties Press.
2. Bridie McGuigan interview courtesy of the *Derry Journal*, 'I accept David Cameron's apology: "Sunday" widow breaks long silence', dated 2 July 2010, authored by Eamonn MacDermott, p. 1.
3. Interview with author, *Setting the Truth Free*, 2012.
4. Interview with author, *Setting the Truth Free*, 2012.
5. Interview with author, *Setting the Truth Free*, 2012.
6. Interview with author, *Setting the Truth Free*, 2012.
7. Geraldine Doherty quote from Bloody Sunday Trust/Pat Finucane Centre/Creggan Enterprises publication, *Gerald Donaghey: The Truth about the Planting of Nail Bombs on Bloody Sunday*, Derry; Guildhall Press.

8. Paul Doherty interview courtesy of the *Derry Journal*, special twentieth-anniversary Bloody Sunday supplement published in 1992, p. 15.
9. Interview with author, *Setting the Truth Free*, 2012.
10. Interview with author, *Setting the Truth Free*, 2012.
11. Andy Nolan extracts from a personal letter to the Duddy family, dated 4 February 2000, courtesy of Mrs Jackie Nolan-Clarke.
12. Susie Campbell from interview with author in 2021 and never before published.

Chapter 6 – Imprisonment without trial

1. Definition of internment, from www.dictionary.com.
2. Reference to 1972 Ministry of Defence documents related to arrest policies and internment uncovered by Pat Finucane Centre researchers at National Archives, UK, and entitled, 'Arrest Policy for Protestants'. Available at https://www.patfinucanecentre.org/sites/default/files/2016-11/defe_2.pdf and also at https://www.patfinucanecentre.org/declassified-documents/policy-internment-loyalists-0.
3. Timeline reference, courtesy of Kerr, Adrian (2013), *Free Derry: Protest and Resistance*, Derry: Guildhall Press.
4. Reference to Amnesty International Report on the Hooded Men case, see 'Amnesty International Report on Allegations of Ill-Treatment Made by Persons Arrested Under The Special Powers Act After 8 August, 1971'. Available at https://cain.ulster.ac.uk/events/intern/docs/amnesty71.htm.

Chapter 7 – Murder in Ballymurphy

1. Kevin Philips, Briege Voyle, Alice Harper and John Teggart: Ballymurphy Campaign 2019 inquest witness statements. Available at https://www.relativesforjustice.com/ballymurphy-inquest-day-1/2/3/.
2. Ballymurphy Campaign 2019 inquest witness statement.
3. Ballymurphy Campaign 2019 inquest witness statement.
4. Ballymurphy Campaign 2019 inquest witness statement.
5. Carmel Quinn and Mary Kate Quinn quotes from *Irish Times*, 11 May 2021.
6. Kerr, *Free Derry: Protest and Resistance*, 2013.
7. Martin McGavigan quote, courtesy of McClements, Freya and Duffy, Joe (2019), *Children of the Troubles: The Untold Story of the Children Killed in the Northern Ireland Conflict*, Dublin, Hachette Books Ireland.
8. Kerr, *Free Derry: Protest and Resistance*, 2013.
9. Cahil McElhinney quote, from the article, 'Birmingham brother of Bloody Sunday victim speaks as report is set to be published', from the *Birmingham Mail* and its author, Maureen Messent, published 24 March 2010. Available at https://www.birminghammail.co.uk/news/local-news/birmingham-brother-of-bloody-sunday-victim-121752.
10. Extract from 4 October 1971 British army paper entitled, 'Northern Ireland – An Appreciation of the Security Situation', by General Sir Michael Carver, Chief of General Staff, quoted in the *Report of the Bloody Sunday Inquiry* (BSI) (TSO 2010), Volume 1, 8.80.
11. Kerr, *Free Derry: Protest and Resistance*, 2013.

12. Minty Thompson, from the 2004 film, *Lifting a Dark Cloud: The Kathleen Thompson Case*, Director: Anne Crilly, Derry.
13. Kerr, *Free Derry: Protest and Resistance*, 2013.
14. Mary Donaghey extract, courtesy of Jimmy McGovern from research interview for 2002 Channel 4 drama-documentary *Sunday*.
15. Geraldine Doherty quote from, *The Truth about the Planting of Nail Bombs on Bloody Sunday*.

Chapter 8 – 'Measures to Control Marches'

1. Material from the *Report of the Bloody Sunday Inquiry* (2010) is included courtesy of National Archives, UK. Each extract, its volume and section, are detailed separately. Available at https://webarchive. nationalarchives.gov.uk/20101015151735/http://www.bloody-sunday-inquiry.org/.
2. Minutes of Official NI Committee of 5 January 1972, quoted in the *Report of the Bloody Sunday Inquiry* (BSI) (TSO 2010), Volume 1, 9.92.
3. 'Measures to Control Marches' document of 5 January 1972, quoted in the *Report of the Bloody Sunday Inquiry* (BSI) (TSO 2010), Volume 1, 9.93.
4. Joint Security Council meeting of 6 January 1972, quoted in the *Report of the Bloody Sunday Inquiry* (BSI) (TSO 2010), Volume 1, 9.94.
5. British PM Heath's private secretary, Gregson, to Angel in the Home Office of 7 January 1972, quoted in the *Report of the Bloody Sunday Inquiry* (BSI) (TSO 2010), Volume 1, 9.100.
6. General Ford's memo to General Officer Commanding Harry Tuzo, dated 10 January 1972, quoted in the *Report of the Bloody Sunday Inquiry* (BSI) (TSO 2010), Volume 1, 9.103.
7. Minutes of GEN 47 Cabinet Committee meeting of 11 January 1972, quoted in the *Report of the Bloody Sunday Inquiry* (BSI) (TSO 2010), Volume 1, 9.149.
8. British army HQNI Intelligence Summary of 13 January 1972, quoted in the *Report of the Bloody Sunday Inquiry* (BSI) (TSO 2010), Volume 1, 9.160.
9. 'List of Forthcoming Events', extract of Special Branch assessment of 19 January 1972, quoted in the *Report of the Bloody Sunday Inquiry* (BSI) (TSO 2010), Volume 1, 9.176.
10. British army HQNI Intelligence Summary of 19 January 1972, quoted in the *Report of the Bloody Sunday Inquiry* (BSI) (TSO 2010), Volume 1, 9.17.
11. British army 8th Infantry Brigade's Intelligence Summary distributed 19 January 1972, quoted in the *Report of the Bloody Sunday Inquiry* (BSI) (TSO 2010), Volume 1, 9.178.
12. British army's HQNI Intelligence Summary 'Outlook' of 19 January 1972, quoted in the *Report of the Bloody Sunday Inquiry* (BSI) (TSO 2010), Volume 1, 9.179.
13. From the written statement of Chief Superintendent Frank Lagan to the Bloody Sunday Inquiry.
14. General Robert Ford to the Widgery Tribunal in April 1972, quoted in the *Report of the Bloody Sunday Inquiry* (BSI) (TSO 2010), Volume 1, 9.180.

15. Stormont Cabinet Minutes of 18 January 1972 to approve renewal of march ban, quoted in the *Report of the Bloody Sunday Inquiry* (BSI) (TSO 2010), Volume 1, 9.182.
16. Faulkner announces extension of ban on marches, quoted in the *Report of the Bloody Sunday Inquiry* (BSI) (TSO 2010), Volume 1, 9.183.
17. Revd Ian Paisley, NI prime minister Faulkner and NICRA spokesperson extracts from the *New York Times* of 19 January 1972, and its author, Bernard Weinraub. Available at https://www.nytimes.com/1972/01/19/archives/ulster-parades-banned-for-year-orange-day-march-included.html.

Chapter 9 – Scenes at Magilligan Strand, 1972

1. Dr Raymond McClean and Ivan Cooper extracts: witness statements to the Bloody Sunday Inquiry, courtesy of National Archives, UK. Available at https://webarchive.nationalarchives.gov.uk/20100401174644/http://www.bloody-sunday-inquiry.org.uk/evidence-and-statements/?start=6&search_category=1.
2. Witness statement to the Bloody Sunday Inquiry.
3. Minutes of visit of Chief of the Defence Staff visit by General Sir Harry Tuzo, quoted in the *Report of the Bloody Sunday Inquiry* (BSI) (TSO 2010), Volume 1, 9.237, and by General Ford, 9.238.
4. Chief Superintendent Frank Lagan statement to Widgery Tribunal, 1972, quoted in the *Report of the Bloody Sunday Inquiry* (BSI) (TSO 2010), Volume 1, 9.244.
5. Brigadier MacLellan statement to Bloody Sunday Inquiry, quoted in the *Report of the Bloody Sunday Inquiry* (BSI) (TSO 2010), Volume 1, 9.256.

Chapter 10 – Army Plans and IRA Assurances

1. General Ford's oral evidence to Bloody Sunday Inquiry, quoted in the *Report of the Bloody Sunday Inquiry* (BSI) (TSO 2010), Volume 1, 9.314.
2. From 8th Infantry Brigade Intelligence Summary of 25 January 1972, quoted in the *Report of the Bloody Sunday Inquiry* (BSI) (TSO 2010), Volume 1, 9.269.
3. NICRA statement 25 Jan 1972, 'Reasons for Derry march', quoted in the *Report of the Bloody Sunday Inquiry* (BSI) (TSO 2010), Volume 1, 9.299.
4. General Ford's written evidence to the Bloody Sunday Inquiry (BSI) (TSO 2010).
5. General Ford's oral evidence to Widgery Tribunal, 1972, quoted in the *Report of the Bloody Sunday Inquiry* (BSI) (TSO 2010), Volume 1, 9.292.
6. Minutes of Ministry of Defence meeting on 26 January 1972, quoted in the *Report of the Bloody Sunday Inquiry* (BSI) (TSO 2010), Volume 1, 9.329.
7. Current Situation Report compiled by Head of Defence Secretariat 10, quoted in the *Report of the Bloody Sunday Inquiry* (BSI) (TSO 2010), Volume 1, 9.334.

8. Brigadier MacLellan's oral testimony to Bloody Sunday Inquiry, Volume 1, courtesy of BSI (Day 266/46-B127), p. 348.

9. BSI – Dr Raymond McClean, Ivan Cooper MP, Brendan Duddy and Martin McGuinness extracts: witness statements to the Bloody Sunday Inquiry, courtesy of National Archives, UK. Available at https:// webarchive.nationalarchives.gov.uk/20100401162237/http://www.bloody-sunday-inquiry.org.uk/evidence-and-statements/?search_category=1.

10. Police Chief Superintendent Frank Lagan quoted in the *Report of the Bloody Sunday Inquiry* (BSI) (TSO 2010), Volume 1.

11. Witness statement to the Bloody Sunday Inquiry.

12. From 8th Infantry Brigade Operation Order for civil rights march, dated 27 January 1972, quoted in the *Report of the Bloody Sunday Inquiry* (BSI) (TSO 2010), Volume 1. 9.017.

13. Distribution of Order for Operation Forecast, quoted in the *Report of the Bloody Sunday Inquiry* (BSI) (TSO 2010), Volume 1, 9.439, p. 377.

14. Photographic Coverage Order issued on 27 January 1972, quoted in the *Report of the Bloody Sunday Inquiry* (BSI) (TSO 2010), Volume 1, 9.443–4, p. 340.

15. Minutes of Joint Security Committee at Stormont on 27 January 1972 quoted in the *Report of the Bloody Sunday Inquiry* (BSI) (TSO 2010), Volume 1, 9.489.

16. 'Note for the Record' of meeting between British PM Heath and Northern Ireland PM Faulkner of 27 January 1972, quoted in the *Report of the Bloody Sunday Inquiry* (BSI) (TSO 2010), Volume 1, 9.499, p. 395.

17. NICRA press statement from the *Derry Journal* of 28 January 1972.

18. From the written statement of Chief Superintendent Frank Lagan to the Bloody Sunday Inquiry.

19. From the Confirmatory Notes of Orders Group for 3 Platoon A Company 2 RGJ, taken on Friday 28 January 1972, quoted in the *Report of the Bloody Sunday Inquiry* (BSI) (TSO 2010), Volume 1, 9.669, p. 457.

20. Memo from NI prime minister Brian Faulkner to General Tuzo, dated 28 January 1972, quoted in the *Report of the Bloody Sunday Inquiry* (BSI) (TSO 2010), Volume 1, 9.284, p. 316.

Chapter 11 – The Day Before

1. Joint British army and RUC statement of Saturday 29 January 1972, quoted in the *Report of the Bloody Sunday Inquiry* (BSI) (TSO 2010), Volume 1, 9.662, p. 455.

2. NICRA statement from *Derry Journal* of Saturday 29 January 1972, quoted in the *Report of the Bloody Sunday Inquiry* (BSI) (TSO 2010), Volume 1, 9.732, p. 475.

3. Manuscript notes taken by Colonel Derek Wilford following the Orders Group of 1 PARA on Saturday 29 January 1972, quoted in the *Report of the Bloody Sunday Inquiry* (BSI) (TSO 2010), Volume 1, 9.672, p. 461.

4. General Michael Jackson on 'some sort of violent reaction', quoted in the *Report of the Bloody Sunday Inquiry* (BSI) (TSO 2010), Volume 1, Section 9.679, p. 463.

5. Extract of General Jackson's written statement to the Bloody Sunday

Inquiry, quoted in the *Report of the Bloody Sunday Inquiry* (BSI) (TSO 2010), Volume, 9.679, p. 463.

6. Extract of Major Loden's statement to the Widgery Tribunal in 1972, courtesy of BSI, Volume 1, Section 9.675 (Evidence no. B1012/B2245/B2216), p. 462.

7. Larry Doherty, Mary Donaghey, Sophia Downey and James Porter, extracts: witness statements to the Bloody Sunday Inquiry, courtesy of National Archives, UK. Available at https://webarchive.nationalarchives.gov.uk/20100401162237/http://www.bloody-sunday-inquiry.org.uk/evidence-and-statements/?search_category=1.

8. Witness statement to the Bloody Sunday Inquiry.

9. Witness statement to the Bloody Sunday Inquiry.

10. From a radio operator with Support Company of 1 PARA of the British army, quoted in the *Report of the Bloody Sunday Inquiry* (BSI) (TSO 2010), Volume 1, 9.716, p. 469.

11. Witness statement to the Bloody Sunday Inquiry.

12. Transcript of Porter's tapes of 29 January 1972, courtesy of the Museum of Free Derry.

13. Paratroop graffiti and removal, courtesy of the *Derry Journal*, Friday 17 January 1997, p. 1.

Chapter 12 – Sunday Morning

1. Martin Cowley, Lord Fenner Brockway, Denis Bradley, Eamonn Baker, Bernard Gilmour, James Porter, Eamonn Deane, Dr Domhnall MacDermott and Larry Doherty extracts: witness statements to the Bloody Sunday Inquiry, courtesy of National Archives, UK. Available at https://webarchive.nationalarchives.gov.uk/20100401162237/http://www.bloody-sunday-inquiry.org.uk/evidence-and-statements/?search_category=1.

2. Bridie Gallagher and Eamonn MacDermott from interviews with author in 2021 and never before published.

3. Witness statement to the Bloody Sunday Inquiry.

4. Witness statement to the Bloody Sunday Inquiry.

5. Witness statement to the Bloody Sunday Inquiry.

6. Research interview for Channel 4 drama-documentary, *Sunday*, 2002.

7. Witness statement to the Bloody Sunday Inquiry.

8. Witness statement to the Bloody Sunday Inquiry.

9. Interview with author, 2021.

10. Witness statement to the Bloody Sunday Inquiry.

Chapter 13 – Setting Off from Bishop's Field

1. Ita McKinney interview transcript from the TV documentary, *Remember Bloody Sunday*, courtesy of Peter Taylor.

2. Gerry Duddy, Michael Quinn, Maureen Gallagher, Danny Gillespie, Patsy O'Donnell, Paddy Walsh, Alexander Nash extracts from witness statements to the Bloody Sunday Inquiry, courtesy of National Archives, UK. Available at https://webarchive.nationalarchives.gov.uk/20100401162237/http://www.bloody-sunday-inquiry.org.uk/evidence-and-statements/?search_category=1.

3. Witness statement to the Bloody Sunday Inquiry.
4. Interview with author, *Setting the Truth Free*, 2012.
5. Eileen Doherty extract from McCann, Eamonn, Shiels, Maureen and Hannigan, Bridie (1992), *Bloody Sunday: What Really Happened*, Ireland: Brandon Books.
6. Witness statement to the Bloody Sunday Inquiry.
7. Philomena McLaughlin extract from Campbell, Julieann (ed.) (2016), *Beyond the Silence: Women's Unheard Voices from the Troubles*, Derry: Guildhall Press, pp. 94–100.
8. Interview with author, *Setting the Truth Free*, 2012.
9. Witness statement to the Bloody Sunday Inquiry.
10. Interview with author, *Setting the Truth Free*, 2012.
11. Witness statement to the Bloody Sunday Inquiry.
12. Witness statement to the Bloody Sunday Inquiry.
13. Interview with author, *Setting the Truth Free*, 2012.
14. Witness statement to the Bloody Sunday Inquiry.
15. Interview with author, *Setting the Truth Free*, 2012.
16. Witness statement to the Bloody Sunday Inquiry.
17. Witness statement to the Bloody Sunday Inquiry.

Chapter 14 – Snipers in William Street

1. Alana Burke interview from source research, Campbell, Julieann (ed.) (2012), *Setting the Truth Free: The Inside Story of the Bloody Sunday Justice Campaign*, Dublin: Liberties Press.

Chapter 15 – The Breakaway Riot

1. British army 8th Brigade Log, 30 January 1972; an evidential document used during the Bloody Sunday Inquiry.
2. Interview with author, *Setting the Truth Free*, 2012.
3. Witness statement to the Bloody Sunday Inquiry.

Chapter 16 – Shots Fired at the Waste Ground

1. John Johnston extracts: witness statements to the Bloody Sunday Inquiry, courtesy of National Archives, UK. Available at https://webarchive.nationalarchives.gov.uk/20100401162237/http://www.bloody-sunday-inquiry.org.uk/evidence-and-statements/?search_category=1.
2. May O'Neill interviews from press reports by author.
3. Message from Colonel Welsh to Brigade HQ at 1559 hours, quoted in the *Report of the Bloody Sunday Inquiry* (BSI) (TSO 2010), Volume II, Section 20.189, p. 315.
4. Radio Report of 22 Lt AD Regiment to Brigade, quoted in the *Report of the Bloody Sunday Inquiry* (BSI) (TSO 2010), Volume II, 20.190, p. 316.
5. Museum of Free Derry.

Chapter 17 – 'The Paratroops want to go in'

1. Finding on the decision to deploy, from the *Principal Conclusions and Overall Assessment of the Bloody Sunday Inquiry*, published 15 June 2010 (TSO); Section 3.18, p. 17. Accessed at https://assets.publishing.

service.gov.uk/government/uploads/system/uploads/attachment_data/
file/279167/0030.pdf.

2. British army 8th Brigade Log of 'not to conduct a running battle down
   Rossville Street', quoted in the *Report of the Bloody Sunday Inquiry*
   (BSI) (TSO 2010), Volume II, 20.34, p. 267.
3. From Chief Superintendent Lagan's written statement to the Widgery
   Tribunal, 1972, quoted in the *Report of the Bloody Sunday Inquiry*
   (BSI) (TSO 2010), Volume II, 20.36, p. 268.
4. Jimmy Toye extracts: witness statement to the Bloody Sunday Inquiry,
   courtesy of National Archives, UK. Available at https://webarchive.
   nationalarchives.gov.uk/20100401162237/http://www.bloody-
   sunday-inquiry.org.uk/evidence-and-statements/?search_category=1.
5. General Ford, 'Go Get Them', as quoted from *Irish Independent*,
   'General's battle cry of "Go on the Paras" will forever ring in my
   ears', dated 16 June 2010. Accessed at https://www.independent.ie/
   regionals/herald/news/generals-battle-cry-of-go-on-the-paras-will-
   forever-ring-in-my-ears-27954483.html.

Chapter 18 – Advance into Rossville Street

1. Jimmy Toye from interview with author in 2021 and never before
   published.
2. Peggy Deery extracts: from witness statement to the Widgery
   Tribunal, used at Bloody Sunday Inquiry, courtesy of National
   Archives, UK. Available at https://webarchive.nationalarchives.gov.
   uk/20100401162237/http://www.bloody-sunday-inquiry.org.uk/
   evidence-and-statements/?search_category=1.
3. Bishop Edward Daly interview with author, National Civil Rights
   Archive, 2017.
4. 'Allegations of physical and verbal abuse as the arrests were made', taken
   from the *Report of the Bloody Sunday Inquiry*, Volume 4; 66.30. p. 371.

Chapter 19 – The First Fatality

1. Bishop Edward Daly interview with author, National Civil Rights
   Archive, 2017.
2. Jackie O'Reilly interview with author, *Setting the Truth Free*, 2012.

Chapter 22 – In the Square and Abbey Park

1. Teresa McGowan, Joe Mahon, Caroline O'Donnell, Frances Gillespie
   and Regina McLaughlin interviews with author, *Setting the Truth Free*,
   2012.
2. Interview with author, *Setting the Truth Free*, 2012.
3. Interview with author, *Setting the Truth Free*, 2012.
4. Interview with author, *Setting the Truth Free*, 2012.
5. Susan North Tapes, recorded by journalist Susan North on 30 January
   1972, transcript from Bloody Sunday Inquiry evidence, Museum of Free
   Derry.

Chapter 23 – The Final Shots

1. Army Statement issued by British army's HQ in Lisburn, Northern Ireland, on evening of 30 January 1972.
2. Anne Grant extract from the Museum of Free Derry's *Free Derry Lives* film marking fifty years since the Battle of the Bogside, August 2019.
3. From written statement of General Sir Michael Jackson to the Bloody Sunday Inquiry. Accessed at https://webarchive.nationalarchives.gov.uk/20100401162237/http://www.bloody-sunday-inquiry.org.uk/evidence-and-statements/?search_category=1.
4. From written statement of Chief Superintendent Frank Lagan to the Bloody Sunday Inquiry. Accessed at https://webarchive.nationalarchives.gov.uk/20100401162237/http://www.bloody-sunday-inquiry.org.uk/evidence-and-statements/?search_category=1.

Chapter 24 – Aftermath

1. General Robert Ford BBC Interview transcript 30 January 1972, Evidence in Bloody Sunday Inquiry.

Chapter 25 – Word Spreads

1. Ita McKinney interview from *Derry Journal*, twentieth-anniversary supplement, January 1992, p. 14.
2. From the written statement of Chief Superintendent Frank Lagan to the Bloody Sunday Inquiry.
3. Mark Durkan MP interview with author, *Setting the Truth Free*, 2012.
4. Betty Curran courtesy of the Museum of Free Derry's *Free Derry Lives* film marking fifty years since the Battle of the Bogside, August 2019.

Chapter 26 – The Morgue

1. Telegram from Most Revd Dr Farren, Bishop of Derry, to British prime minister Edward Heath, *Derry Journal*, 1 February 1972.
2. Press statement from Cardinal Conway, Primate of All Ireland and Archbishop of Armagh, *Derry Journal*, 1 February 1972.

Chapter 27 – A Cover-Up Begins

1. Transcript of ITN interview with Colonel Wilford by Gerald Seymour, 30 January 1972, Bloody Sunday Trust, Derry.
2. 'Shot List' written after Bloody Sunday by Captain Michael Jackson, Bloody Sunday Trust, Derry.
3. Extract of press statement issued from British army HQ, Lisburn, on 30 January 1972, *Derry Journal*, 1 February 1972.

Chapter 28 – The Next Morning

1. 'Ulster's Bloody Sunday', *Derry Journal*, 1 February 1972, p. 1.
2. *Daily Express*, 'Gun fury: Paras open fire as violence flares – 13 shot dead in Ulster', Republic of Ireland edition, 31 January 1972.
3. *Daily Telegraph*, '13 killed in Londonderry – troops in battle with IRA', 31 January 1972, p. 1.

4. *Guardian*, '13 killed as paratroops break riot', by Simon Winchester, dated 31 January 1972.
5. Public statement from all teachers across Derry's Catholic schools, *Derry Journal*, 1 February 1972, p. 3.
6. *New York Times*, 'British soldiers kill 13 as rioting erupts in Ulster – deaths come as Catholics defy ban on Londonderry march', 31 January 1972, p. 1.
7. *New York Times*, 'IRA vows vengeance', 31 January 1972, p. 1.
8. 'Go on, the paras. Go and get them' quote, and the quote concerning how the paras appeared to 'relish their work', both from an editorial in *The Times*, 1 February 1972, by Brian Cashinella.
9. *The Times*, 'March ends in shooting', by Brian Cashinella and John Chartres, 31 January 1972.

Chapter 29 – Seven Priests Accuse

1. From a press conference held by seven Derry priests on 31 January 1972, *Derry Journal*, 1 February 1972.
2. Bishop Daly reflecting on a 1972 priests' conference, from 'Bishop Daly "filled with joy"', *Derry Journal*, 18 June 2010.
3. Captain Michael Jackson to the Widgery Tribunal, 1972.
4. *The Times* (London), Quote from Bernadette Devlin MP, 31 January 1972.
5. British home secretary Mr Reginald Maudling's address to House of Commons and Bernadette Devlin's response in the Chamber, dated Monday 31 January 1972 (*Hansard* 1.2.72, column 325).
6. 'Bernadette Devlin and the Slap Heard 'Round the World', (online), Radical Tea Towel, 23 April 2019. Accessed at https://radicalteatowel.co.uk/blog/bernadette-devlin-and-the-slap-heard-round-the-world.
7. Transcript from TV interview with Bernadette Devlin, dated 31 January 1972, AP Archive (Story No. z011569). Accessed at https://www.youtube.com/watch?v=KLlpVQFdjC0.
8. *Guardian*, 'Furious Miss Devlin swoops on Maudling', 1 February 1972.
9. Transcript from ITN interview with Colonel Derek Wilford, broadcast on 31 January 1972.
10. Transcript from Irish Taoiseach Jack Lynch's televised broadcast to the nation, Monday 31 January 1972.

Chapter 30 – The Wakes

1. British army press statement on the events of Bloody Sunday from British Information Services, *The Irish Independent – Derry Supplement*, 'How the British told it to the US', 1 February 1972.
2. *Derry Journal*, statement by Eddie McAteer, leader of the Nationalist Party, dated Tuesday 1 February 1972 (*Derry Journal*, p. 12, twentieth-anniversary supplement of January 1992).
3. *Guardian*, 'Bogsiders insist that soldiers shot first', by Simon Hoggart in Londonderry, dated Tuesday 1 February 1972.
4. *Derry Journal*, 'Reported clash between British soldiers', Tuesday 1 February 1972, p. 15.

Chapter 31 – Nail Bombs and Hate Mail

1. Gerald Donaghey arrest detail from booklet, *Gerald Donaghey: The Truth about the Planting of Nail Bombs on Bloody Sunday* (2012), by Bloody Sunday Trust, Pat Finucane Centre and Creggan Enterprises, Derry: Guildhall Press, p. 34.
2. Letter addressed to James and Sarah Wray, parents of Jim Wray, signed from the Ulster Volunteer Force (UVF), dated 1 February 1972, courtesy of the Wray family and the Museum of Free Derry.

Chapter 32 – The Funerals

1. Ita McKinney interview transcript from the TV documentary, *Remember Bloody Sunday*, courtesy of Peter Taylor.
2. *Derry Journal*, 'The skies wept, too, as Derry laid its dead to rest', dated 4 February 1972, p. 1.
3. Extract from the *Derry Journal*, 'Internees' "Utter Revulsion"', dated 4 February 1972, p. 6.

Chapter 33 – The Widgery Tribunal

1. 'Propaganda war' quote from memo from British prime minister Edward Heath to Lord Chief Justice Widgery, dated 31 January 1972.
2. Bishop Edward Daly quote on Widgery expectations from Daly, Edward (2000), *Mister, Are You a Priest?* Dublin: Four Courts Press.
3. Ita McKinney interview from *Derry Journal*, twentieth-anniversary supplement, January 1992, p. 14.
4. Mary Donaghey extract, courtesy of Jimmy McGovern, Jim Keys and Stephen Gargan's research interview for 2002 Channel 4 drama-documentary *Sunday*.
5. Lord Chief Justice Widgery pertaining to civilian evidence in 1972, from the *Report of the Tribunal*, 19 April 1972.
6. Details on deaths and incidents in the immediate area courtesy of the Museum of Free Derry.

Chapter 34 – The Whitewash

1. Paraphrased conclusions drawn from the *Report of the Tribunal*, 19 April 1972.
2. 'Those accustomed to listening to witnesses could not fail to be impressed by the demeanour of the soldiers of 1 PARA', quote from Lord Chief Justice Widgery on the publication of the *Report of the Tribunal*, 19 April 1972.
3. The Summary of Conclusions (dated 10 April 1972) from the *Report of the Widgery Tribunal*, 19 April 1972.
4. *Daily Mail*, 'Widgery blames IRA and clears the army', 20 April 1972.
5. *Daily Telegraph* editorial, 'Fateful Sunday – Widgery clears paratroops for Bloody Sunday', dated 20 April 1972.
6. Extract from the *Hansard* Parliamentary Record of 19 April 1972, in which the British prime minister Edward Heath announces the findings of Lord Widgery's *Report of the Tribunal* to the House of Commons (*Hansard*, HC Deb 19 April 1972, Vol. 835 cc519-28). Accessed at

https://api.parliament.uk/historic-hansard/commons/1972/apr/19/northern-ireland-widgery-tribunal-report.

7. Ita McKinney interview from *Derry Journal*, twentieth-anniversary supplement, January 1992, p. 14.

8. John Hume speaking after the publication of the *Widgery Report*, April 1972, 'It's like blaming a man shot walking down the street, for walking down the street', *Derry Journal*, twentieth-anniversary supplement of January 1992, p. 12.

9. Ivan Cooper quote on effect of Bloody Sunday: Channel 4 TV documentary, *Secret History*, December 1991.

10. Eamonn McCann interview with author, *Setting the Truth Free*, 2012.

11. Michael Mansfield QC, quoted from his piece, 'Bloody Sunday – Is nobody bothered that Widgery got it so wrong?' *Belfast Telegraph*, 21 June 2010. Accessed at https://www.belfasttelegraph.co.uk/opinion/michael-mansfield-bloody-sunday-is-nobody-bothered-that-widgery-got-it-so-wrong-28542614.html.

12. Details on deaths and incidents in the immediate area courtesy of the Museum of Free Derry.

13. Extract on details that emerged about Ranger William Best's death from McCann, Eamonn (1993), *War and an Irish Town*, London: Pluto Press.

14. Rosemary Best interview with author, National Civil Rights Archive, 2017.

15. Quote from Father Hugh O'Neill, administrator of St Eugene's Cathedral, *Derry Journal*, 23 May 1972.

Chapter 35 – Summer 1972

1. Mary Donaghey extract, Jimmy McGovern's *Sunday*, 2002.

2. Diane Greer extracts from her essay, 'Bloody Sunday: A Loyalist's Perspective', *Force 10: An Irish Journal* (1999, issue 11, Sligo), and Kerr, Adrian (1996), *Perceptions: Cultures in Conflict*, Derry: Guildhall Press, p. 49.

3. Details on Operation Motorman and related deaths and incidents courtesy of the Museum of Free Derry.

4. 'British Attorney-General, Sir Peter Rawlinson, responds to a Parliamentary Question about prosecuting the soldiers', *Hansard* Parliamentary Record (*Hansard*, HC Deb 01 August 1972, Vol. 842 c122w). Accessed at https://api.parliament.uk/historic-hansard/written-answers/1972/aug/01/northern-ireland-londonderry.

5. From the report of Major Hubert O'Neill, Bloody Sunday Inquest Coroner, dated 21 August 1973, from CAIN (Conflict Archive on the Internet), courtesy of Ulster University. Accessed at https://cain.ulster.ac.uk/events/bsunday/sum.htm.

Chapter 36 – Decades

1. Gleann Doherty, Jean Hegarty and Robin Percival interviews with author, *Setting the Truth Free*, 2012.

2. Jim Wray Senior quoted from the *Derry Journal* on the second anniversary of Bloody Sunday, January 1974.

3. Interview with author, *Setting the Truth Free*, 2012.

4. Anne-Marie Love on her brother, Charles Love, courtesy of McClements, Freya and Duffy, Joe (2019), *Children of the Troubles: The Untold Story of the Children Killed in the Northern Ireland Conflict*, Dublin: Hachette Books Ireland.
5. Interview with author, *Setting the Truth Free*, 2012.

Chapter 37 – Igniting Embers

1. Interview with author, *Setting the Truth Free*, 2012.
2. Interview with author, *Setting the Truth Free*, 2012.

Chapter 38 – Enough New Evidence

1. Jane Winter interview with author, *Setting the Truth Free*, 2012.
2. 'Widgery memo damns British', courtesy of the *Derry Journal* in August 1995. Available at https://museumoffreederry.org/bloody-sunday-justice-campaign/widgery-memo-damns-british/.
3. List of newly uncovered evidence from Campbell, Julieann (ed.) (2012), *Setting the Truth Free: The Inside Story of the Bloody Sunday Justice Campaign*, Dublin: Liberties Press, pp. 98–9.
4. Bernard Gilmour extract from McCann, Eamonn (2005), *The Bloody Sunday Inquiry: The Families Speak Out*, London: Pluto Press.

Chapter 39 – The New Inquiry

1. Ciaran Shiels interview with author, *Setting the Truth Free*, 2012.
2. Revd Ian Paisley on the Good Friday Agreement being the 'the mother of all treachery', *Irish Independent*, 16 April 1998. Accessed at https://www.independent.ie/irish-news/peace-deal-treacherous-26190342.html.
3. Extracts from Tony Blair, Bertie Ahern and Bill Clinton statements on the signing of the Good Friday Agreement, 10 April 1998.
4. Brigadier Maurice Tugwell apologizes for claiming that four of those shot dead were on a wanted list. 'Ex-army chief admits Bloody Sunday "mistake"', *Irish Times*, 30 September 2002.
5. Exchange between General Sir Michael Jackson and Michael Mansfield QC, during Jackson's second oral hearing at the Bloody Sunday Inquiry, *Guardian*, 16 October 2003.
6. Leaked IRA recording of security force communications. 'Army tape reveals "joy" over Bloody Sunday', *Guardian*, 29 September 2000. Accessed at https://www.theguardian.com/uk/2000/sep/29/bloodysunday.northernireland.

Chapter 40 – 'Innocent!'

1. Overall Assessment finding from the *Principal Conclusions and Overall Assessment of the Bloody Sunday Inquiry*, published 15 June 2010; Section 5.4.
2. Overall Assessment finding from the *Principal Conclusions and Overall Assessment of the Bloody Sunday Inquiry*, published 15 June 2010; Section 5.5.
3. Finding on Gerald Donaghey, *Principal Conclusions and Overall*

437

Assessment of the Bloody Sunday Inquiry, published 15 June 2010; Section 3.111.

4. *Report of the Bloody Sunday Inquiry* (BSI) (TSO 2010), Volume 7, Ch 130, 130.34. p.565
5. *Report of the Bloody Sunday Inquiry* (BSI) (TSO 2010), Volume 7, Ch 130, 130.35–36. p.565
6. *Report of the Bloody Sunday Inquiry* (BSI) (TSO 2010), Volume 7, Ch 130, 130.37. p.565
7. *Report of the Bloody Sunday Inquiry* (BSI) (TSO 2010), Volume 7, 141.14. p. 644.
8. Kay Duddy (on Jackie smiling) and Freya McClements from interviews with author in 2021 and never before published.
9. Extracts of British prime minister David Cameron's address and Mark Durkan MP's response on the publication of the *Report of the Bloody Sunday Inquiry* on 15 June 2010. Available at https://hansard. parliament.uk/commons/2010-06-15/debates/10061522000002/ SavilleInquiry.
10. *Hansard* Parliamentary Record, 15 June 2010.
11. Diane Greer quote, courtesy of Kerr, Adrian (1996), *Perceptions: Cultures in Conflict*, Derry: Guildhall Press, p. 52.
12. Interview with author, 2021.

Chapter 41 – Afterword

1. BBC News Online, 'Bloody Sunday: Police to investigate Derry deaths', 5 July 2012. Accessed at https://www.bbc.co.uk/news/uk-northern-ireland-18721686.
2. BBC News Online, 'Bloody Sunday: 18 soldiers "considered for prosecution"', 12 May 2017. Accessed at https://www.bbc.co.uk/news/ uk-northern-ireland-foyle-west-39894229.
3. Public Prosecution Service NI announce prosecution decisions, dated 14 March 2019. Accessible at https://www.ppsni.gov.uk/news-centre/ bloody-sunday-decisions-press-release, and also of interest from same date, https://www.ppsni.gov.uk/publications/bloody-sunday-summary-reasons.
4. Stephen Herron, Public Prosecution Service NI, announces PPS decision, 14 March 2019. Available at https://www.theguardian. com/uk-news/2019/mar/14/one-soldier-to-face-charges-over-bloody-sunday-killings.
5. Liam Wray and John Kelly on 14 March 2019. Available at https:// www.theguardian.com/uk-news/2019/mar/14/one-soldier-to-face-charges-over-bloody-sunday-killings.
6. *Guardian*, 14 March 2019.
7. PPS announce Bloody Sunday prosecution decisions upheld, dated 29 September 2020. Accessible at https://www.ppsni.gov.uk/news-centre/ pps-upholds-decision-not-prosecute-15-soldiers-connection-bloody-sunday.
8. High Court grants permission to challenge PPS decision on prosecutions, dated 22 April 2021. Available at https://madden-finucane.com/2021/04/22/high-court-grants-bloody-sunday-families-permission-to-challenge-public-prosecution-service-pps-decision-not-

to-prosecute-former-paratroopers/.

9. Prosecutions of Soldier B and Soldier F to be discontinued after PPS review, 2 July 2021. Accessed at https://www.ppsni.gov.uk/news-centre/prosecutions-soldier-b-and-soldier-f-be-discontinued-after-pps-review.

10. Mickey McKinney on PPS decision to drop charges, 2 July 2021. Accessed at https://madden-finucane.com/2021/07/02/press-statement-from-mckinney-family-and-madden-finucane/.

11. Liam Wray on PPS decision to drop charges, 2 July 2021. Accessed at https://www.derryjournal.com/news/crime/liam-wray-brother-of-bloody-sunday-victim-jim-wray-reacts-to-soldier-f-non-prosecution-decision-3294841.

12. John McKinney's personal response to author on PPS decision, 2 July 2021.

13. Joe McKinney statement from public solidarity rally, 3 July 2021. Accessed at https://madden-finucane.com/2021/07/03/todays-speech-by-joe-mckinney-brother-of-willie-to-bloody-sunday-rally-in-derry/.

14. Report from Queen's University, Belfast, addressing the British government's Command Paper on Legacy, 2021. Accessed at https://www.dealingwiththepastni.com/project-outputs/project-reports/model-bill-team-response-to-the-uk-government-command-paper-on-legacy-in-ni

15. *Irish Times*, 'Family of girl killed in Troubles calls on British to scrap legacy proposals', 6 September 2021. Accessed at https://www.irishtimes.com/news/ireland/irish-news/family-of-girl-killed-in-troubles-calls-on-british-to-scrap-legacy-proposals-1.4665587

16. Gerry Duddy's personal response to author on British government's amnesty plans, 8 September 2021.

Picture credits

Alamy Stock Photo/PA Images: 60, 393.

Bloody Sunday Inquiry: 253.

Bloody Sunday Justice Campaign: 351.

Jim Davies: 26.

Derry Journal: 1, 90, 137, 268, 276, 289, 297, 333, 343, 358, 372.

Duddy family: 322.

Courtesy of Fulvio Grimaldi: 151, 179, 191, 226.

McKinney family: 46.

Sean McLaughlin: 307.

Michael McLoughlin: 12

Eamon Melaugh: 71, 84, 106.

Mirrorpix: 253.

The National Library of Ireland/Colman Doyle: 242.

News Licensing/The STimes/Derek Tucker: 167.

© Gilles Peress/Magnum: 143, 204, 215.

Shutterstock/Clive Limpkin/ANL: 33, 54.

Unknown: 119.

Bobby White: 127, 159, 182, 186.

Wray family: 284.

Every effort has been made to trace the copyright holders. We apologize in advance for any unintentional omissions and would be pleased to insert the appropriate acknowledgement in any subsequent publication.

Index